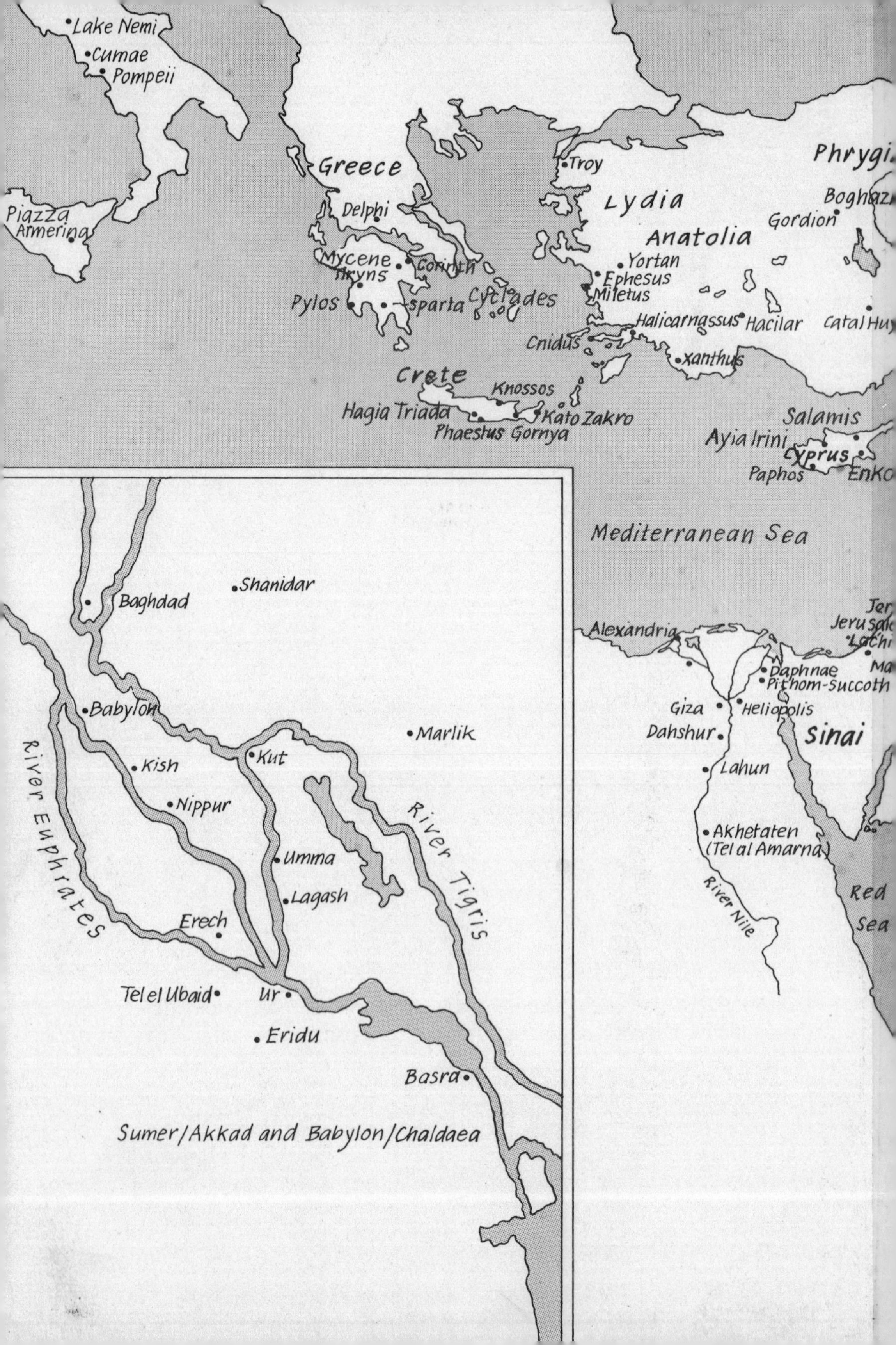

Lake Nemi
Cumae
Pompeii

Piazza
Armerina

Greece

Delphi

Mycene
Tiryns
Pylos
Sparta   Corinth
Cyclades

Troy

Lydia
Anatolia

Phrygi

Boghaz

Gordion

Yortan
Ephesus
Miletus

Halicarnassus   Hacilar
Cnidus
Xanthus

Catal Huy

Crete
Knossos
Hagia Triada   Kato Zakro
Phaestus Gornya

Salamis
Ayia Irini
Cyprus
Paphos   Enko

Mediterranean Sea

Alexandria
Jer
Jerusale
Lachi
Ma

Shanidar

Baghdad

Babylon

Kish

Nippur

River Euphrates

Kut

Marlik

River Tigris

Umma
Lagash

Erech

Tel el Ubaid   Ur
Eridu

Basra

Daphnae
Pithom-Succoth
Giza   Heliopolis
Dahshur   Sinai

Lahun

Akhetaten
(Tel al Amarna)

River Nile

Red
Sea

Sumer/Akkad and Babylon/Chaldaea

Black Sea

Caspian Sea

ultepe

•Toprak Kale

Lake Van
Urartu
Lake Urmia

•Tabriz

Caratepe
•Carchemish

River Tigris
Assyria

•Khorsabad
•Nineveh
•Balawat
•Nimrud
•Assur

•Hasanlu
•Ziwiye

•Amlash

Tureng-Te

•Kalar Dasht •Damgha

•Alalakh

•Hurvin

•Demavend

Hissar

•as Shamra

River Euphrates

•Ecbatana

•Tehran

Syria

•Mari

Mesopotamia

•Behistun
•Nehavend
•Giyan

Persia

•Kashan
•Sialk

Hit •

•Asmar
•Eshnunna

•Isfahan

Surkh •Marlik
Dum

•Susa
•Choga Zambil

87

Elam

•Eridu

•Basra

Naqshi •Pasargade
Rustam •Persepolis
•Shiraz

•Bushire

Persian
Gulf

•Dilmun •

The Bull of Crete. Late Minoan ritual masterpiece found by Sir Arthur Evans at Knossos. *c.*1700–1400 BC.

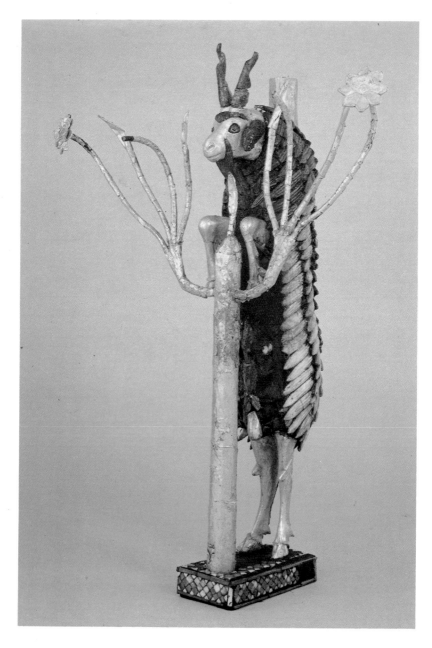

'Ram in Thicket' from Ur. Gold adorned he-goat rears to sniff the flowers of a tree. Found by Sir Leonard Woolley in the great death-pit at Ur. *c*.2500 BC.

H.V.F. WINSTONE

Uncovering
the Ancient World

CONSTABLE · LONDON

First published in Great Britain 1985
by Constable and Company Limited
10 Orange Street London WC2H 7EG
Copyright © 1985 by H.V.F. Winstone
Set in Monophoto Garamond 11pt by
Servis Filmsetting Ltd, Manchester
Printed in Great Britain by
BAS Printers Ltd, Over Wallop

British Library CIP data
Winstone, H.V.F.
Uncovering the ancient world
1. Antiquities
I. Title
930   D80

ISBN 0 09 464720 8

To Christopher, Matthew and Lucy

By the same author

Captain Shakespear
Gertrude Bell
Leachman: 'O.C. Desert'
The Illicit Adventure

Contents

Illustrations

Chronology of the Ancient World

	General	Rome	Greece	Palestine/Syria	Anatolia
4000	LATE NEOLITHIC	LATE NEOLITHIC	LATE NEOLITHIC	LATE NEOLITHIC	LATE NEOLITHIC
3500				Proto-historic CHALCOLITHIC	CHALCOLITHIC
				EARLY BRONZE	
3000			CHALCOLITHIC Early Minoan I Early Minoan II	Proto-urban Proto-Syrian	
2500			EARLY BRONZE Early Minoan III Middle Minoan I	Semitic speech	EARLY BRONZE
2000	EUROPEAN BRONZE AGE		MIDDLE BRONZE Middle Minoan II Proto-Palatial First Greeks Mycenaean shaft graves	MIDDLE BRONZE Disruption	Assyrians in Cappadocia Indo-Europeans MIDDLE BRONZE Old Hittite Kingdom
1500	MID BRONZE EUROPE LATE BRONZE		LATE BRONZE Late Minoan I Late Minoan II Mid Mycenaean Late Minoan III Trojan war Sea Peoples	LATE BRONZE Hyksos Habiru Philistines	Hittite Empire Sea Peoples Phrygians
1000	ATLANTIC BRONZE IRON AGE EUROPE	Rome founded	IRON AGE Lycurgus of Sparta 1st Olympiad Solon at Athens	IRON AGE Israel, Homeric legends Solomon Assyrian invasion Fall of Jerusalem Exile	Cimmerians Urartu Caria Lydia Assyrian Achemenid (Persian)
500	Rome conquers Gaul	Etruscan tombs Gallic invasion Punic wars Conquest of Greece	Marathon Herodotus Alexander to India Roman	Sack of Jerusalem Ptolemaic/Seleucid Roman	Seleucid Roman
0		Triumvirate Empire Hadrian Goths Constantine		Herod Destruction of Jerusalem	
500					

Iran	Assyria	Sumer/Akkad/Babylon	Egypt	
				4000
LATE NEOLITHIC	LATE NEOLITHIC	Ubaid	Amratian/Naqada I	
		LATE PREHISTORIC		
CHALCOLITHIC	CHALCOLITHIC	Uruk	Naqada II / Early Gerzean	3500
		First writing	Late Gerzean / CHALCOLITHIC	
			1st Dynasty (Narmer)	
EARLY BRONZE Susa		EARLY BRONZE		
Proto-Elamite	EARLY BRONZE	Jamdat Nasr	EARLY DYNASTIC	3000
		EARLY DYNASTIC Sumer	Solar calendar	
			OLD KINGDOM	
Sumero-Elamite			3rd Dynasty	
			Memphite Cheops	2500
		Akkad Sargon		
	Old Assyria	3rd Dynasty of Ur	FIRST INTERMEDIATE PERIOD	
	38 kings of unknown date	MIDDLE BRONZE	7th Dynasty Theban	2000
	Shamsi-Adad I	Isin and Larsa	MIDDLE KINGDOM	
MIDDLE BRONZE	26 kings	Old Babylonian	11th Dynasty	
		Hammurabi	SECOND INTERMEDIATE PERIOD	
		Hittites	Hyksos 13th Dynasty	
		Kassite	NEW KINGDOM	
			18th Dynasty	1500
		LATE BRONZE	Amarna period	
LATE BRONZE			Akhenaten	
Choga Zanbil			Sea Peoples	
Middle Elamite	Tiglath-pileser I	2nd Dynasty of Isin	21st Dynasty	
Indo-Europeans		2nd Dynasty of Sealand		
IRON AGE		Elamite		1000
Neo-Elamite				
Median	Sargonid	Assyrian conquest	SAITE PERIOD	
Assyrian		Neo-Babylonian	26th Dynasty	
Cyrus/Pasargade	Destruction of Nineveh			
Darius/Persepolis	Persian rule	Persian rule	Persian rule	
			LATE PERIOD	500
Seleucid	Seleucid	Seleucid	Ptolemaic	
			27-31 Dynasties	
		Macedonian conquest		
Parthian	Parthian	Parthian	Roman	
			Cleopatra	0
Sassanian	Sassanian	Sassanian		
			Coptic ascendancy	
				500

Apologia & Acknowledgements

Many experts held my hand through the thickets of ancient language and custom, guided me to vital sources, and saved me from taking the most hazardous paths. Even with their help I expect that I am often in error, in fact and opinion. If so, I am in distinguished company, as the following pages are intended to demonstrate. In attempting to discharge my debt, it seems invidious to name individuals. All the same, I must make particular my gratitude to Dr Dominique Collon who not only gave me the benefit of her knowledge in the specialist field of the cylinder seal and in the broader aspects of Mesopotamian archaeology, but with the cosmopolitan ease of a lady who is as much at home in one land or language as another, led me into those hidden chambers of the British Museum and other learned institutions where all – or almost all – knowledge resides. As for the British Museum itself, I express the customary thanks of the writer to the Trustees, but in this instance rather more than polite acknowledgement is called for. I leaned heavily on the Museum's resources, particularly the Western Asiatic, Egyptian, and Greek and Roman Departments, and in several months of research I, like the many writers and scholars from all over the world who regularly seek the hospitality of that unique institution, had ample reason to be grateful to it. The Western Asiatic Department especially suffered my persistent questions and requests for documents, books and photographic records with fortitude and good humour. I record my gratitude to Mr T.C. Mitchell the Acting Keeper and to the academic staff, in particular: Dr Julian Reade, Dr Irving Finkel, and Dr John Curtis. The Egyptian and Greek and Roman Departments too, gave of their time and knowledge and I thank their keepers and assistants. The British Library, the India Office Library and Records, the Royal Geographical Society, the Royal Society for Asian Affairs, the Royal Asiatic Society, and my 'home' library of Bromley in Kent, provided books, articles, photographs and documents. My thanks to their directors, archivists and librarians.

Near Eastern archaeology is, of course, an international activity, and no nation nowadays has a greater stake in field work and the academic studies which go

[13]

with it than the United States. I was fortunate in being able to meet several eminent scholars of the American universities, among them Professor John Brinkman of Chicago University and its world-famous Oriental Institute, to whom I am especially grateful for permission to use his 'Mesopotamian Chronology'; Dr Erle Leichty, Curator of Akkadian Language and Literature at the University of Pennsylvania, and Professor Edith Porada of Columbia University. All were most helpful in fields of study which they occupy with great distinction. I am indebted also to Mrs M.S. Drower, biographer of Sir Flinders Petrie, for her invaluable help. Professor Seton Lloyd, whose life's work has embraced excavation at many of the sites of the Near East along with high academic posts, has allowed me to quote extensively from his published books and from unpublished papers. Dr Eva Strommenger-Nagel of the Deutsche Orient-Gesellschaft has helped me over several years in matters concerning my biographical subject, Gertrude Bell, who so admired the archaeological institutions of Berlin; in connection with this book I thank her for advice and photographs relating to the work of her Institute during the past eighty-six years, not least to its present-day activities in Syria and Iraq. My thanks too, to Monsieur P. Amiet, Curator of the Musée du Louvre. Returning to the home front, I am indebted to the Egypt Exploration Society and the Palestine Exploration Fund in London for much help, and I thank their Committees and their respective administrators, Dr Spencer and Dr Chapman. Also, the Petrie Museum (University College, London), the British School of Archaeology in Iraq (Gertrude Bell Memorial), and the British Schools of Archaeology in Athens and Rome, and the Iraq Cultural Centre in London. Those famous saleroom institutions Sotheby's and Christie, Manson and Woods, went to a great deal of trouble to produce photographs of items in the category of 'ancient art'; they like other photographic sources are acknowledged in the table of illustrations, but I would like to express my gratitude to them. Of the many picture libraries used, I thank especially the *Illustrated London News* library (now part of Thomson Publications of London) which, through the foresight of past editors, is a prior port of call for anyone writing about archaeology. The National Portrait Gallery supplied a well-known picture of Layard and an unsuspected one of Gertrude Bell, for which my thanks. I list the many individuals who have helped not in any kind of priority, but as they appear in my haphazard notes: Mr John Guest of New York, Mr Michael Rice, Mr Colin Imray, Mr Will Facey, Mr Clive Rassam, my daughters Ruth Mallas and Gillian Quinn, my wife Joan, Mr Zakki Ahmed, Mr Christopher Gordon, Mr Bruce Norman of the BBC, Mr and Mrs Trevor Sennett. If I have omitted to give credit where it is due, especially with regard to the provision of books, photographs or documents, I hope that amends are made elsewhere. I must add that none of the people or institutions named is in any way responsible for the views or conclusions expressed in this book. Its errors and omissions are entirely my own.

A few words must be said on the vexed matter of transliteration. In quoting from different versions of ancient inscriptions and legends I have generally accepted Professors Kramer and Oppenheim as the final authorities in respect of Sumer, and Akkad/Babylon/Assyria respectively. In transliteration from Egyptian sources I have likewise used Dr T.G.H. James and Dr I.E.S. Edwards of the British Museum as arbiters. In general I have used the Greek versions of Pharaonic names, since they are undisputed; where Egyptian synonyms appear in the text I give the alternative version in parenthesis or in the index. It must be said, however, that there is no expert agreement on such matters; indeed, it is hard to find two writers or scholars who agree about a simple English word like 'civilis(z)ation'. I, with Fowler and Gower, prefer the 's' rather than the OED's 'z', but I have reluctantly gone along with the latter. As for the transliteration of modern Semitic words such as 'Amir' or 'Emir', 'Tell' or 'Tel', 'Abraham' or 'Ibrahim', 'Bedouin' or 'Badawin', I simply bow to the wisdom of anyone who knows better.

HVFW April 1985

A chronology based on carbon-14 dating shows Jericho to be the earliest township so far discovered by archaeologists. Mesolithic hunters began to settle there in about 8000 BC. By 7000 BC the inhabitants surrounded their settlement with massive fortifications. In Late Neolithic and Chalcolithic times, c.7000–3500, descendants of the Mesolithic hunters produced sculpture in the form of portrait heads with artificial features moulded on to the skulls of the dead. This primitive art was probably connected with ancestor worship. Eyes were inlaid with shells and facial features delicately restored in plaster.

Cosmological Incantation

After Anu had created the Heavens,
The Heavens created the Earth,
The Earth Created the Rivers,
The Rivers created the Canals,
The Canals created the Marshes,
The Marshes created the Worm.
Came the Worm and wept before Shamash,
Before Ea came her tears: —
'What wilt thou give me for my food?
What wilt thou give me to devour?'
'I will give thee dried bones,
      And scented ... wood.'
'Nay, what (are) these dried
      bones of thine to me,
And thy scented ... wood?
Let me drink among the teeth,
And set me on the gums;
That I may devour the blood of the teeth,
And of their gums destroy their strength
Then shall I hold the bolt of the door.'

Babylonian text transl. by R. Campbell Thompson

And the doors shall be shut in
the street; when the sound of
the grinding is low, and one
shall rise up at the voice of a
bird, and all the daughters of
music shall be brought low ...
Vanity of vanities, saith the
Preacher; all is vanity.

Ecclesiastes 12:4–8

[17]

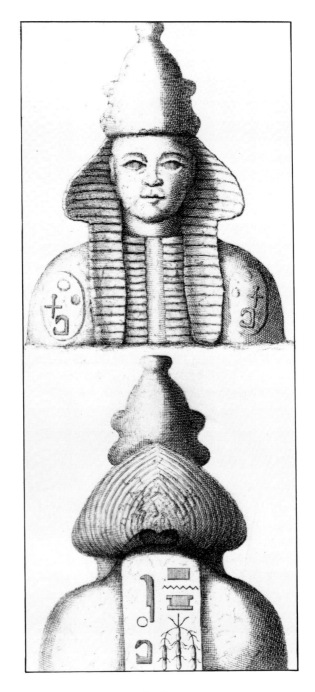

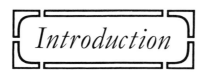

Introduction

Who, a century and a half ago, reading the Old Testament or the history of Herodotus, could have guessed that two thousand years before either came to be written a vast granary stretched like a golden carpet across the lands that biblical tribes and a thousand armies trod? That a labyrinth of canals brought irrigation and abundant food to great cities and thriving townships? That from the Nubian desert at the cataracts of the Nile, across Syria and Anatolia to the confluence of the Tigris and Euphrates, and beyond to the Persian Gulf and the Valley of India, empires had reached their zenith and crumbled to dust? That some of the finest achievements of artists and craftsmen lay derelict in burned and buried palaces? That evidence of the superstitions of the earliest communities, manifest in the remains of millions of jewel-bedecked and scorched and tortured bodies, lay in wait for the tomb robber? The secrets of the ancient world were as remote as the subtleties of space invasion.

Opposite: Ozymandias, from Dr. Richard Pococke's *Description of the East*, London, 1743

I met a traveller from an antique land
Who said: Two vast and trunkless legs of stone
Stand in the desert . . . Near them, on the sand,
Half sunk, a shattered visage lies, whose frown,
And wrinkled lip, and sneer of cold command,
Tell that its sculptor well those passions read
Which yet survive, stamped on these lifeless things,
The hand that mocked them, and the heart that fed:
And on the pedestal these words appear:
'My name is Ozymandias, king of kings:
Look on my works, ye Mighty and despair! . . .

Percy Bysshe Shelley, 1818

Who were the Pharaohs of the Bondage and Exodus of Israel, or the Sea Peoples, will-o'-the-wisp destroyers of the thirteenth century BC? Who the Mycenaeans 'rich in gold', the Achaeans and Trojans? Who, indeed was Homer, and where and when did he live? Whence came Cyrus and Darius, and where the palaces of the Medes and Elamites, Babylonians and Assyrians? And what before them? What, if anything, accounted for the implausibilities of Genesis? Was there, indeed, an Exodus at all, and was Moses perhaps no more or less a figure of imagination or mythology than Priam or Helen of Troy? What were the origins of the occult practices employed by priests and god-kings to ward off the 'evil eye' and a host of enemies, seen and unseen?

At the start of the nineteenth century such questions could be asked in the perfect assurance that nobody knew the answers. Only approximate geographical locations of ancient cities and states were known during the long centuries of ignorance. Myth and fact met at some undefined point and became one.

The Bible Lands, Cradle of Civilization, Fertile Crescent: such were the evocative names given by Europe to those sprawling regions – stretching from the eastern Mediterranean to the Nile and the Persian Gulf – which became the focal points of study and research when the intellectual pursuit of 'truth' took a practical turn and scholarship went, as it were, underground. Much of the excitement of uncovering the past resides in a sense of its remoteness and mystery. Archaeology can never be an exact science, though it has been fashionable in the present century to believe otherwise. If the recorded history of the ancient world as handed down to us by Hebrew and classical scribes had proved demonstrably accurate, there would have been little point in digging up its relics. Fortunately, even after a century and a half of intensive digging and sifting, much remains to be discovered and verified.

This is the story of the ancient world as it was revealed to the men and women who uncovered it in that relatively brief span of time between the Napoleonic campaigns and the present; a time span in which archaeology itself has outgrown the voyeurism and amateur enthusiasms of its infancy to become a skilled, many-sided discipline, capable of remarkable feats of identification and classification. The past is revealed in mosaic as the excavators relinquish one site and proceed to another, or give way to newcomers who can generally be relied upon to weigh in the balance the judgements of those they have supplanted. Archaeology has never lacked personal rivalry, disputed theories or unshakeable misconceptions.

For those who nowadays continue the search for a lost past, there is still the reward of surprise discovery. Many a royal palace, many a hoard of treasure waits to be discovered under the accretions of the years, and doubtless a nearby necropolis conceals reminders of the ravage, torture and sacrifice with which our ancestors sought to impress their fellow men and appease their gods. Some sites, on the other hand, will never be examined. It has always been the habit of urban settlers to build on existing habitations. Such matters are dictated by the lay of the land, by natural and artificial amenities. Many places known to have been inhabited by early communities are today thriving townships which cannot be displaced for archaeological purposes. Whatever the prizes awaiting disclosure, the rewards of the past 150 years have been spectacular, filling some of the world's great museums to overflowing and taxing the resources of scholarship almost to bursting point. It is estimated that the inscribed tablets of Mesopotamia alone, weighing many tons and taking up much valuable space, will occupy the hundreds of scholars engaged in reading and translating them well into the next millennium.

The search for lost and forgotten worlds began as a response to eternal questions about life and death and after-life; about legend and history. The feasibility of the Bible's genealogy, accepted more or less without question since the Middle Ages, was called into question even by the most devout believers by the late eighteenth century. Was it possible to produce material evidence of the existence of the people and places, the conflicts and the miracles which inspired the divine literature inherited by Christian Europe from Judaism?

Classical scholarship also posed questions which had a distinct bearing on archaeological enquiry at the end of the eighteenth century and the beginning of the nineteenth. Had the Homeric legends, the very flesh of European culture, a basis in historical truth, or were they simply inspired inventions, heroic tales of love and war which had come down by word of mouth over many centuries, miraculously retaining their unique poetic force?

How insistently the questions were asked, and how splendidly the names tripped off the nineteenth-century tongue! carried forth on the poet's hot breath, or ranted from the pulpit with the churchman's promise of brimstone and hellfire for the wicked and redemption and everlasting life for the good and the repentant.

> My name is Ozymandias,
> king of kings . . .

Who was this king among kings of whom Diodorus Siculus wrote nearly 2,000 years before Shelley, whose headless torso of stone rose out of the sand of Thebes to greet the traveller? None other than the great Pharaoh Ramesses II of the Nineteenth Dynasty of Egypt, who reigned in the thirteenth century BC, today's archaeologist would reply. The dynastic dates might be disputed by chronologists, moving him on a hundred years or so into the early twelfth century. But until very recently no expert would have believed it possible to argue powerfully,

[21]

if not with widespread approval, that the accepted chronology of the Pharaohs is, in the case of Ramesses II, six centuries too early. That he is, in fact, identifiable with the Pharaoh Necho of the Old Testament, Nebuchadnezzar's foe at Syrian Kadesh. Such an argument has nevertheless been put forward, and it is not lacking in supporters.

Assyria, Babylonia, Chaldaea, Elam. Was it here, or there, that the garden lay where Adam was invested with the knowledge of good and evil? Here or there that Noah, entering upon his seventh century of age, was bidden to the Ark in that miracle of salvation which followed the heavenly warning —

'My spirit shall not strive with man for ever'?

I am the Lord that brought thee out of Ur of the Chaldees, to give thee this land to inherit it.

Was this, the dishevelled mound of Muqayyar beyond a muddy reach of the Euphrates, the place of Haran's nativity and of his father Terah's before him, and his son Lot's? Was this the birthplace of Abraham, lineal descendant of Shem the father of the Semitic races? Was this perhaps the very house from which he went forth into the desert with the nonagenarian Sarai, to rename her Sarah at God's command and find in her the new fertility that gave birth to Isaac the patriarch of the Jews?

Was this the land of Shinar where the children of Noah built a city of brick and slime (for mortar) when the whole earth was of 'one language and one speech'? Or the land of the Kenite, Kenizzite, and Kadmonite, the Hittite, Amorite and all the other peoples over whom God made a covenant with Abraham, 'from the river of Egypt unto the great river, the river Euphrates'?

Some questions have been resolved by archaeology and its sister disciplines; but seldom answered in the positive 'yes or no' sense that the committed wish for.

The search for the ancient world underlines the thesis that history is a fluid and capricious record of events. Kings and their scribes wrote the story of their own times subjectively, according to their whims and vanities, their own predilections. The process is common enough in art and life. The quest for abnegation, *catharsis*, in Greek drama was original; and it has never enjoyed much of a following in the world. One of the most eminent of nineteenth-century biblical scholars, Julius Wellhausen, decided to ignore all the written evidence produced by archaeology up to his time, the 1870s, in the belief that the Hegelian approach based on 'idealistic tradition' was a good deal more reliable than so-called 'evidence', not excluding the patriarchal narratives. His *Prolegomena zur Geschichte Israels* was a standard work for at least two generations, though it must be admitted that in the end *evidence* upset a good many of his judgements.

There is certainly overwhelming evidence that the precocious creativity of ancient man existed side by side with deceit and dishonesty, with pathological pleasure in destruction, conspiracy, conquest and oppression. The ancient and modern worlds have fundamental similarities. In neither are the noble ideals of artists, philosophers and law-makers ever far removed from conspiracy and war, from superstition and obsession with sacrifice and death. Even allowing for a basic ambivalence in human nature, however, the destructive capacity of early mankind was by any standard remarkable. The colossi and royal libraries of Assyria and Babylon, the treasures of the Mycenaean and Minoan palaces, the pyramids and papyri of Egypt and the tombs of the Pharaohs are one side of the story. There is another less apparent side in which cities were burned to the ground as a mere token of conquest, the innocent taken in battle flayed alive, entire nations wiped off the face of the earth; in which the solemn duty of human and animal servant was to follow its master to the death pit, thence to enter the next level of life at the insistence of the knife or, if lucky, the poison chalice.

The first excavators of the ancient civilizations and the pioneer translators of their forgotten languages, combined an appetite for adventure with that spirit of enquiry which took them eastward in the first place. Some were military men with a penchant for classics and the Bible. Some simply had an attachment to the past and found their way to remote and buried civilizations as if by instinct, on the way to engage in trade or political or diplomatic careers. Others were armed with formal training in one or other of the academic disciplines which pointed to a career in digging up the past. Most would have made reputations as explorers had they not been waylaid in the desert lands by the challenge of the past. They were the gladiators of the nineteenth century.

Champollion the prince of Egyptology, Grotefend, Rawlinson, Hincks, Oppert, Smith and others who made the first written records of man available to the world; Layard, with whom the names of Nineveh and Nimrud will ever be associated; Schliemann, whose vacillating reputation rests securely on Homer's Mycenae; the pedantic genius of Egyptology, Flinders Petrie; Evans of Knossos and Woolley of Ur; Carter and Carnarvon, whose Egyptian discovery hardly need be named. This is their story, though other names and places inevitably come into it.

Their successors have become more specialized, dividing their labours into a thousand branches of Greco-Roman study, Assyriology, Sumerology, Egyptology, epigraphy and allied disciplines; men and women who, so says one of them, 'know the mostest about the leastest'. The popular renown of the men who unwrapped Egypt and Mesopotamia and ancient Greece and Rome, cannot easily be repeated in the present. In the age of space invasion, the seeker of lost civilizations on earth is seen in a changed perspective. Television, that obtrusive artificial eye of our time, has taken over some of the functions of journalism in bygone days, reviving at least for the specialist audience an interest in a subject which once rivalled sport and royalty in the popular imagination.

Some of the discoveries of recent years have been just as significant and luminous as the glamorous revelations of fifty and a hundred years ago. But nowadays thousands of experienced, highly skilled archaeologists are at work at any given time all around the world. National and international teams have taken over where until recently the task was left to a few European countries and the United States. New and important discovery has become matter of fact. Unlike the diggers of Troy, Nineveh, Ur of the Chaldees and the Valley of the Kings, present-day archaeologists are unlikely to find their photographs in popular newspapers. Their work is nonetheless a vital part of that most fascinating of jigsaw puzzles whose assembly is never quite complete, nor ever will be.

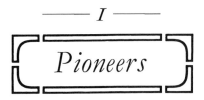

Pioneers

Napoleon's conquest of Egypt in 1798 marked the beginning of a process of investigation and discovery in which the military authorities, scholars and art thieves of Europe would combine in unholy alliance to uncover the evidence of past civilizations. They approached ever more expertly the first tentative urban groupings of mankind, filled the galleries of the West with the treasures of the East, and – most importantly – confirmed a new discipline in the quest for historical fact.

For three hundred years prior to Bonaparte's invasion, Egypt had been isolated from the West; a poor and blighted dominion of the Ottoman Sultan. Even the Crusading armies eight centuries earlier had more or less ignored it, though its Arabic-speaking peoples embraced Islam as enthusiastically as their neighbours. A few curious travellers had passed through in the centuries which followed Europe's medieval awakening. Notable among them was the seventeenth century scholar Dr Pococke, chaplain to the Levant Company's factory at Aleppo, editor of neglected New Testament epistles, and Professor of Arabic at Oxford. His descriptions and drawings of a land rich in antiquities yet stricken with poverty and squalor aroused no more than academic interest when they were first published.

The Napoleonic occupation, though it lasted only three years, brought about a dramatic change in Europe's mood. Indifference quickly gave way to imperial rivalry as Britain followed the lead of France in recognizing Egypt's strategic importance in trade and in its promise of a short route to India. The British occupation which followed was even briefer than the French. The country was left in the hands of the Ottoman Viceroy Muhammad Ali and an army of apostate Circassian slaves who had virtually ruled Egypt until that moment, the Mamluks. Muhammad Ali, an illiterate, wily Albanian, usurped the authority of his master in Constantinople and exterminated the Mamluks. Yet in many ways he showed himself to be an enlightened ruler, not least in the manner of his co-operation with French scholars and political officials in preserving the country's relics.

Britain's interest at the beginning of the nineteenth century was chiefly commercial, a term which embraced both legitimate trade and a considerable traffic in the artefacts which lay strewn along the banks of the Nile, the debris of hundreds of years of tomb robbery and the destruction of ancient buildings. The French consuls and savants who arrived with Napoleon were more concerned with the country's cultural resources than were their British counterparts. They formed themselves into an elite body known as the *Institut d'Egypte*, and set out as their objectives: *The progress and propagation of enlightenment in Egypt; the research, study and publication of natural, industrial and historical facts about the country; and advising the French political administration.* The *Institut* had four sections, devoted to mathematics, physics, political economy, literature and the arts. They made full use of what was perhaps Bonaparte's chief legacy to Egypt, the printing press which was set up in the first place to issue imperial proclamations. The press, *L'Imprimerie Nationale du Caire* as it came to be called, established under private ownership, published the country's first weekly newspaper, *Le Courrier de l'Egypt*, and the Institute's journal *La Décade Egyptienne*.

Archaeology was not officially part of the savants' brief. Yet it soon became the largest and most distinguished of their many endeavours, carried out against the backcloth of a rich national tradition stemming from the work of institutions such as the *Académie des Inscriptions*, established in 1663. The contribution of collectors like the Comte de Caylus, whose eighteenth century *Recueil d'Antiquités Egyptiennes, Etrusques, Grecques, Romaines et Gauloises*, was exemplary.

The work of the French was spectacular and insular. It gave rise to a specialization within the broad boundaries of archaeology – *Egyptology* – and was in marked contrast to the activities of the dilettante English (a British antiquarian body set up in the eighteenth century by gentlemen with a penchant for the ancient world was known as *The Society of the Dilettanti*). They seldom returned from a visit to Egypt without a 'mummy' or some other relic with which to amuse their friends and stimulate a spate of humorous articles in *Punch* magazine, which centred on the eccentricity of antique hunting and the folly of trying to climb the pyramids.

If Napoleon was the unsuspecting father of Egyptology, it was a British diplomat at the Court of Naples during the Napoleonic Wars, Sir William Hamilton, whose discriminating collection of classical works of art was to set the seal on a movement which dominated the taste and critical appreciation of Europe in the last two decades of the eighteenth century. Many of Hamilton's acquisitions were given to the British Museum, the most famous of them the so-

Opposite: Portland or Barberini vase, a classical masterpiece in glass, from Sir William Hamilton's 18th century collection.

called Barberini or Portland vase, a cameo glass piece of which Josiah Wedgwood undertook to make a 'perfect' copy in his jasper pottery body. Wedgwood had already copied an Homeric vase from a Flaxman model of about 1776, which he presented to the British Museum. An assortment of 'jasper ornaments', several of them based on the possessions of the Dilettanti Society, was ordered on behalf of the King of Naples in the last few years of Hamilton's embassy. Such wares became in the public estimation the apotheosis of the heroic age. 'Reason, Truth and Nature', might as well have been made part of the 'backstamp'. As a twentieth century art historian has put it, 'passionate partisans' became 'Olympian voyeurs'.

Winckelmann, the eighteenth century German art historian, had predicted the new mood, inspired by Greek statuary which had found its way to the Dresden palaces of the Elector of Saxony. The Greeks alone had thrown forth 'true beauty' and 'noble simplicity'. Thorvaldsen, at work in Rome by 1797, realized the critic's vision in imitation classical sculpture which gave Homeric proportions to the men and themes of his time. Flaxman and Wedgwood conveyed the same themes to the breakfast tables and mantelshelves of the rich. Courtly frivolity, the masked ball, the frothy petticoat, gave way to earnestness, the military dance, the Grecian bodice; rococo art and its decorative outgrowth, chinoiserie, were thrust aside by pagan deities, classically pure in form and dress, untainted by the subsequent excrescences of Christian civilization.

Archaeology, just emerging from its dilettante status into a professional discipline, was separated into factions, with the contrary aims of tracking the interrelated legends of Judaism and Christianity to their biblical sources, and of rediscovering the former glories of polytheistic Greece and Rome. The Grand Tour was already in full swing. By the beginning of the nineteenth century the treasures of the classical world were competing for space on museum shelves with those of the Pharaohs and Ptolemies. Soon they would be vying for space with the artefacts of other lands.

Oriental studies in England had progressed apace since the establishment of a chair of Hebrew at Cambridge by Henry VIII in 1540. The Reformation gave new impetus to scriptural studies and Hebrew took its place alongside Greek in the study of the original biblical texts. The interest of the Roman Catholic church in the East and in Oriental languages was confined to the missionary orders. Wider academic interest prevailed in the Protestant countries. Holland and England

Opposite: Detail of Amazon from tomb of Mausolus at Halicarnassus, one of the seven wonders of the ancient world, c.350 BC. Acquired by the British Museum in 1859.

[29]

became the main centres of Oriental learning, and the opening of the Levant, of the Muscovy Company territories of central Asia in Elizabethan times, and the Indies in the seventeenth century enabled scholars to follow on the heels of trading compatriots with enormous benefits to the libraries and universities of Europe. Other eastern languages – Arabic, Syriac, Aramaic, Ethiopic, Coptic, Farsi, Turkish – were mastered. The great European collections of Oriental manuscripts were born. And archaeology, in its modern sense, was conceived. The word belongs of course to the Greek language. But to the Greeks it meant simply ancient history, and its professors were specialist actors, skilled at rendering the themes of antiquity. In the seventeenth century a French physician, Dr Jacques Spon, revived it and set it free on a sea of contrasting liberalism and bigotry, where it acquired new meaning: an amalgam of art and scientific enquiry, objective observation and subjective assumption. The conflicting forces which influenced and inspired it from the beginning would bedevil it to the end.

In 1632 Sir Thomas Adams established a professorship of Arabic at Cambridge, and four years later Archbishop Laud installed an Arabic chair at Oxford, with Pococke as its first occupant. Some fifty years earlier the University of Leiden had begun to build up its incomparable collection of Oriental manuscripts. It quickly earned a rich reputation in eastern scholarship which owed much to Thomas Erpenius, whose Arabic grammar was published in 1612. Like its English counterpart, the Dutch Oriental school gained impetus from Protestant antipathy to the spread of Catholic missionary activity. Inevitably, polemical studies of Islam, and opposition to the Deists at home, competed with genuine scholarship and exploratory zeal among the early pedant-travellers who wandered in lands which were at the heart of Christian tradition.

Simon Ockley, Professor of Arabic at Cambridge in the early eighteenth century, wrote of:

> The Importunity of those perverse Times that thought every minute of Study lost that was not employed in their insipid way of Application to Theology, should rob us of so much of the Life of our great Doctor Pococke, who could have unlocked to us the Treasuries of the East! Whilst he, good Man! out of Compliance to a stupid Generation, was reading over and comparing tedious Commentators.

Humphrey Prideau's *The True Nature of Imposture Fully Display'd in the Life of Mahomet*, published at the end of the seventeenth century, had laid down the lines along which Oriental scholarship would travel for much of the next hundred years:

> Mahomet began his Imposture about the same time that the Bishop of Rome

... claimed to himself the Supremacy which he hath been ever since endeavouring to usurp over the Church of Christ. And from this time Both having conspired to found themselves an Empire in Imposture ... the one in the East, and the other in the West.

Among the few dissenting voices, Adrian Reland, Professor of Oriental languages at Utrecht, set out to discover whether civilized people could embrace such an absurd religion perpetrated by 'a mentally sick man', and concluded by refuting the 'false charges' brought against it. Henri, Comte de Baulainvilliers, another deist, glorified Islam and the Prophet. Jean Gagnier, Professor of Oriental Languages at Oxford, found de Baulainvilliers 'audacious', but condemned the blind prejudice of other writers. Sale's translation of the Koran (1734) and his *Discourse* were standard sources of reference for the rest of the eighteenth century among unbiased students of Persia and the Arab-speaking East. Such works were in a minority, but they provided a healthy climate in which the researches of isolated scholars and travellers could become a genuine flowering of Orientalism.

The first European of broad education and keen eye to visit the ancient sites of Mesopotamia, the Land Between Two Rivers, was an Italian nobleman Pietro della Valle. Places and peoples of past millennia in the countries he traversed were dimly outlined in classical literature and biblical legend, which told of Nineveh and Nimrud, Babylon and Ur of the Chaldees, of mighty kings and great empires. The Italian's purpose was not so much to pursue antiquity as to 'escape the pangs of unrequited love'.

He left Venice in June 1614 for Constantinople where he learnt enough Turkish and Arabic to serve his needs, and departed a year later for Syria, where he met and married a young Christian girl, Sitti Maani, who was to die in his arms soon after they reached Baghdad. Della Valle had her body placed in a lead-lined coffin and his vast entourage of servants carried her in procession across the deserts and mountains and along the rivers of Western Asia on a spectacular journey which took him eventually to India. He found comfort in the attentions of Sitti Maani's Georgian servant girl, who subsequently bore him fourteen sons. He described his eventful journey in letters to his friend Mario Shipano, Professor of Medicine at Naples, and was thus able to write an accurate account of his travels on his return, twelve years after he set out.

In 1621 he visited Persepolis in Persia, which had been identified as the city of Darius four years earlier by Don Garcia Silva Figuero, the Spanish Ambassador at the Persian Court, from the description of Diodorus Siculus. There he copied an inscription carved on a rock face in wedge-shaped characters unknown to the western world.

Pietro della Valle, from his own account of his voyages.

He inspected the mound of Babylon on his way to Persia, and became, so far as is known, the first westerner to use pick and spade to investigate the remains of that buried and almost forgotten city. He also collected numerous specimens of bricks and clay tablets inscribed in the same wedge-like script that he found in Persia.

Della Valle's sensitive investigations were to point the way to important advances in the study of that part of the ancient world which lay between and along the banks of the Tigris and Euphrates. Yet he regarded his own knowledge and investigative skills as but poor imitations of those of another traveller he met on his way.

While in Persia he was introduced to an emigré Scot, George Strachan, whom he described as the finest Oriental scholar of his day, not excluding even the distinguished d'Herbelot, the author of the *Bibliothèque orientale*. Strachan, a Catholic escaping from the persecutions rife in his country during the seventeenth century, had been a student at the Scots' College in Rome, a teacher at the College du Mans and tutor to the King of France before departing for Syria and the East. When della Valle met him he was taking refuge with the Discalced Carmelites of Isfahan, after being accused of attempting to poison the entire resident staff of the East India Company. Whatever the truth of such accusations, and they seem to have rested rather more on jealousy than fact, he sent back to Europe in the hands of a Carmelite messenger a remarkable collection of Oriental manuscripts, and if the nobleman of Rome is to be believed he may well have accumulated other treasures and recorded antiquities which he found and

Minoan 'snake' goddess, suggesting the elegance and sophistication of Cretan society in the late bronze age.

Gold statuette from Elamite temple of Inshushinak excavated by the French at Choga-Zanbil in the Susa region, *c.*1200 BC.

observed in Babylon and Persia. But he disappeared from sight. He is believed to have spent his last days in India.

Others came the same way in the seventeenth and eighteenth centuries, such as Jean Chardin and Jean Baptiste Tavernier, both wealthy traders in precious jewels and the Abbé de Beauchamp, the Pope's Vicar-General in Baghdad, who found inscribed bricks among the ruins and, like della Valle, hired workmen to dig at Babylon. There were even earlier clerics such as Vicenzo of Sienna, Procurator-General of the Carmelite Order, and the Dominican Emmanuel de St Albert, and perhaps others who neglected to commit their impressions to paper. As far back as the twelfth century, a hundred years before the Moghul horde, the Rabbis Benjamin of Tudela in Navarre and Pethahiah of Ratisbon had wandered by in search of Jewish communities and geographical information. And in the fourteenth century John of Monte Corvino visited Moghul Persia on his way to China. John Eldred travelled to Baghdad in the reign of Elizabeth I. And a contemporary of Eldred, the Bavarian physician Leonhard Rauwolf, described a visit to Mesopotamia.

It was the anglicized Frenchman Chardin who perhaps more than any other traveller of these early times, foresaw the way of archaeological research in his three-volume account of his travels in Asia Minor.

> I daily perceived that I was finding more truth and beauty in divers passages of the Sacred Books than ever before, since I had before my eyes the natural and moral objects to which these passages referred.

But della Valle took the first practical steps in the rediscovery of lost Mesopotamian civilizations. The inscribed bricks and tablets and the other 'curiosities' with which he returned to Rome eventually enabled others to decipher the most ancient of written languages.

In 1700, Thomas Hyde, Regius Professor of Hebrew at Oxford, wrote significantly of the Persepolis inscription and the language of the della Valle tablets: *dactuli pyramidales seu cuneiformes*: signs of pyramidal or wedge shape. Cuneiform, a word that would become inseparable from one of the most remarkable of all the essays in antiquarian scholarship that were to follow.

Such voyagers would have known no more of Mesopotamia's distant past than was contained in the reminiscences of Xenophon, whose army marched across it 2,000 years before, or in the hearsay of Herodotus and a few other Greek writers. The best informed among them often mistakenly referred to Baghdad as 'Babylon', and confused other mounds with the site of the true Babylon.

To the north also, cities lay somewhere beneath the mounds which Arabs call 'Tal' or 'Tel', perhaps built upon, perhaps crumbled in the dust. Did not Genesis

Persepolis in 18th century AD, from Niebuhr's *Travels*.

speak of 'A mighty hunter before Yahweh like Nimrod' ruler of a great dominion the beginning of whose kingdom 'was Babel, Erech, Accad, and Calneh in the land of Shinar'? And 'Out of that land he went forth into Assyria, and built Nineveh, Reboboth-Ir, Calah and Resen between Nineveh and Calah'? The Rabbi Benjamin had noted when in Mosul that Nineveh 'now lies in ruins', and Rauwolf that it was inhabited by poor people 'like ants in their heap'. Most, like Sir Antony Shirley, the seventeenth-century Parliamentarian, who passed nearby on his way to visit the Shah of Persia, thought that Mosul was Nineveh, degenerate and 'rather to be a witness of the other's mightiness and God's judgement, than of any fashion of magnificence in itself'.

In 1761 Carsten Niebuhr sailed from Copenhagen with four companions and a Swedish servant, bound for the Near East on a voyage of discovery which turned out to be at once tragic and immensely productive. Niebuhr alone, the youngest of the party, returned to his native land. His argumentative, arrogant colleagues all died of disease or in needless combat between Alexandria and India. But Niebuhr returned with notebooks and specimens which were high examples of

[34]

keen observation and careful recording under the most adverse conditions. He copied the Persepolis inscriptions which della Valle had noted 140 years earlier. For seven months during the years 1765–66, he wandered alone through Mesopotamia and Syria, disguised as a humble Arab, making the first expert sketches of the mounds around Mosul which he believed to be the sites of Assyrian cities. For another year he wandered in the Levant and Asia Minor before finally returning to Denmark. His great work, *Beschreibung von Arabien*, was published in 1772. His diaries and notes filled three subsequent volumes. His researches probed both ancient and modern life in the Arab countries and Persia. The mass of information, the clay tablets and other memorabilia with which he returned to Europe provided at last the basis for a true understanding of the region.

Soon after Niebuhr's return to Denmark, the French botanist M. Michaux sold to the Bibliothèque Nationale a boundary stone found near Ctesiphon, the seat of Chosroes, just below Baghdad. It contained another valuable inscription in the cuneiform writing which gave rise to some premature and bizarre attempts at translation.

It was a resourceful beginning. But more information was needed before even the most recent of the nations of Mesopotamian antiquity could be identified and located with certainty. The oldest of such places, the like of Ur and Akkad, spoken of by the Prophets and scribes of the Old Testament, had surely become dust in the interval of 4,000 years or more since their demise.

By the end of the eighteenth century Europe had begun to sense that the frontiers of existing knowledge might be extended back into a dim and distant past if only it could turn the essential keys to the decipherment of ancient language. The East India Company promoted Oriental studies out of self interest. By 1780, Britain had superseded France as the dominant power in India and by Pitt's act of 1784 the Company became the recognized government of Bengal. Warren Hastings, the first Governor-General, understood the importance of a command of eastern tongues, not only of India but of those territories which surrounded it and acted as a buffer to the imperial ambitions of others. The Company's own public school, Hartford (later Haileybury), began to turn out young men with a grounding in the Oriental languages which would facilitate their mastery of the East.

In the new burst of practical Oriental study, Sir William Jones, author of *Dissertation sur la littérature orientale* and of extracts from Latin commentaries on Asiatic poetry, became the standard-bearer of an enlightened approach to Empire. A Fellow of the Royal Society, grammarian of the Persian language, member of Dr Johnson's exclusive club, he exerted more influence than any other man of his century on that sympathetic interplay of cultures which was to be the foundation stone of future exploration.

In 1783 Jones was appointed High Judge of the Bengal bench, and a year later he founded the Asiatic Society of Bengal, 'for inquiring into the history and antiquities, the natural productions, arts, sciences, and literature of Asia'. His Bengal Society was the embryo of organized study in Europe, spurring the foundation of similar bodies such as the Asiatic Society of St Petersburg (1810), the *Société Asiatique* of Paris (1822), the British Asiatic Society (1829), and *Deutsche Morgenländische Gesellschaft* in the 1840s.

The East India Company appointed its first Resident in Baghdad in 1798. Ten years later Claudius James Rich was appointed to the post. Already scholars were at work in France, Germany and Denmark, attempting to decipher the cuneiform inscriptions brought home by della Valle and Niebuhr, and the hieroglyphics of Egypt. Rich was 21 when he took up his appointment. The Napoleonic Wars had galvanized British activity in the Near East and no better incumbent could have been found for office at the heart of the Ottoman power's Asiatic empire. Rich was born in France, at Dijon in Burgundy, but was taken as a child to Bristol in England. He had no formal schooling but was taught Latin and Greek by an uncle. By the age of 16, assisted only by borrowed text books, he had mastered Arabic, Hebrew, Syriac, Farsi and Turkish. He sought a cadetship in the East India Company. 'Let me but get to India, leave the rest to me', he said, and in 1804 he sailed from England to join Sir James Mackintosh, the Recorder of Bombay. Mackintosh was impressed:

He far exceeded our expectations, and we soon considered his wonderful oriental attainments as the least part of his merit. I found him a fair classical scholar, and capable of writing French and Italian like the best educated native. With the strongest recommendation of appearance and manner, he joined every elegant accomplishment and every manly exercise; and combined with them, spirit, pleasantry, and feeling. His talents and attainments delighted me so much, that I resolved to make him a philosopher ...

An even happier outcome was in store. The ambitious young man married Mackintosh's daughter Mary. In January 1808 the couple sailed on the Residency yacht from Basra to the Pashalik of Baghdad, with a colourful flotilla of convoy ships carrying the Sepoy guard and a retinue of servants. Mary was taken ashore on a mule-borne palankeen, and the procession wound its way to the Residency on the bank of the Tigris, through a thousand-strong guard of troops. In the next twelve years he would establish a reputation for strength and honesty among peoples of all races and religions in the territory. By force of example he became

Claudius James Rich.

the most influential man in Baghdad. Between official duties he surveyed the sites of Babylon and Assyria, collected sculptures and inscriptions, and noted the places and antiquities he encountered. In 1820–21 he and Mary left for a tour of Kurdistan, in the course of which he made a close inspection of the mounds which rose in profusion out of the plains and valleys. On 27 October 1820, he wrote:

'I was up by peep of day . . . All around are ruins, or rather heaps of rubbish, like those in the ruins of Old Baghdad'. At Arbil he traced an ancient wall and ditch. 'The town was once very large, probably about the size of modern Baghdad'. From there he went to the Mosul, to the mosque-crowned mound of Jonas, tracing its ancient boundaries, and then to the nearby mound of Kuyunjik, a Turkish name meaning 'little sheep'; the site, he rightly supposed, of Nineveh.

The Mount of Kuyunjik is, except at its west and part of its eastern face, of rather an irregular form. Its sides are very steep, its top nearly flat; its angles are not marked by any lantern or turret. The perpendicular height is forty-three feet; the total circumference 7,691 feet ... Some part of the surface of the mound, probably where the buildings were either less solid or perhaps entirely wanting, is ploughed over ... We now went along the wall in a north-west direction on horseback, till we came to a part of it higher and broader externally than the rest. Here, some years ago, an immense bas-relief, representing men and animals, covering a grey stone of the height of two men, was dug up from a

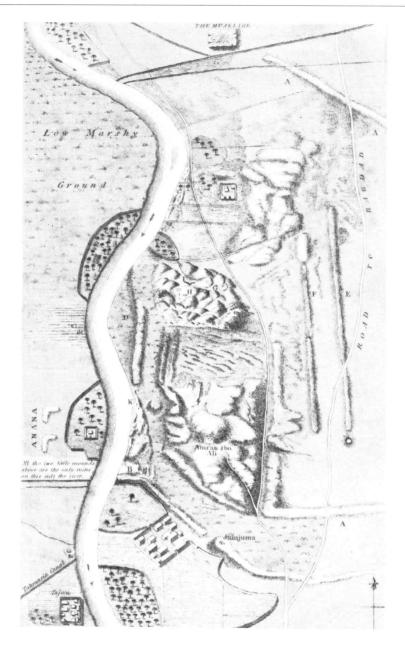

The ruins of Babylon on the east bank of the Euphrates, from Rich's
Memoir, 1818.

Nineveh in distance, the mosque-crowned mound of Nabi Yunis (the Prophet Jonah), in foreground; from Rich's *Narrative of a Residence in Koordistan.*

spot a little above the surface of the ground. All the town of Mosul went out to see it, and in a few days it was cut up or broken to pieces. ...

When he returned to Baghdad in 1821, he intended to write to a German scholar, Georg Friedrich Grotefend, with whom he had already corresponded in connection with the translation of the cuneiform tablets. But a more immediate problem engaged his attention. In his absence, and jealous of his reputation among the peoples of the Pashalik, the Turkish Governor had ordered his troops to attack the Residency. Rich gathered his Indian guard and forced an entry, an action which did not please the Foreign Office in London at a time when Turkey was being placated in the face of Russian incursions in central Asia and eastern Europe. The Company had offered Rich an appointment in Bombay. He decided to accept it and sent Mary on to India while he waited for his successor.

In the meantime he made up his mind to visit Persia and examine the inscriptions at first hand. He arrived at Shiraz in the midst of an outbreak of cholera. Every foreigner except Rich left the area, as did the wealthier Persians. He stayed on to minister to the sick and calm the population, and inevitably contracted the disease. He died on 5 October 1821, and was buried in the royal garden of Shiraz, where Persians erected a monument to his memory, and an epitaph was inscribed: 'Never did the British character attain so high an eminence in Turkish Arabia, as when he presided in Baghdad.' He was 34 years old. His account of his travels, *Narrative of a Residence in Koordistan and on the Site of Ancient Nineveh*, was published posthumously in 1836, edited by his wife. His notes on the inscriptions eventually reached Europe, but not in time to be of much help to Grotefend.

The son of a Hanoverian shoe-maker, Grotefend was admitted to Göttingen University in 1795 at the age of twenty, where he studied theology and philosophy. Classical languages were compulsory in the curriculum, and such was his ability that within two years he was offered a tutorship in Latin and Greek. In one of those asides which are as much the stuff of history as great battles and profound discoveries, he went for a stroll one day with his friend Rafaello Fiorillo, director of the royal library at Göttingen. They discussed one of their favourite topics, code breaking and the conundrums of secret correspondence. Grotefend entered into a wager that he could decipher a message even though it was in an unknown language and he was entirely ignorant of its subject. 'Could you, for example, translate the cuneiform inscriptions in Niebuhr's book'? asked Fiorillo, casually. 'I believe I could', said Grotefend.

He knew that the cuneiform inscriptions copied by della Valle and Niebuhr at Persepolis were in three languages, Old Persian, Elamite and Babylonian, none of which was understood, though the distinguished philologists Professor Tychsen of Rostock University and Friedrich Muenter of Copenhagen convinced him that the Old Persian was most likely to yield to investigation. Grotefend decided to make his attack on that section of the Persepolis inscription. He guessed from known Sassanian references that the first word would be a monarch's name, and that it would be followed by something like 'great king'. He guessed too, from the similarities of some early signs in the text that more than one name was given. The list of Achemenian kings suggested a probable dynasty. Hystaspes, Darius, Xerxes ... The translation seemed to follow easily. 'Darius, great king, king of kings, son of Hystaspes', and then in a succeeding text, 'Xerxes, great king, king of kings, son of Darius ...'. Unfortunately the letters needed for Darius simply did not fit the promulgated translation. No combination of letters, it seemed, would form the name. Perhaps the king was known by a name other than the Latin version which had come down to nineteenth-century Europe, *Darius*, or the Greek *Dareios*? By trial and error he eventually arrived at the values of 'd' for the first letter, 'a' for the second, 'r' for the third, 'ÿ' for the fifth; 'sh' became the last syllable. *Darayavahush* was the name by which the king was known in his time. The rest followed with comparative ease. Grotefend's achievement was the transliteration of the Old Persian, though even in that language severe grammatical problems remained.

Georg Friedrich
Grotefend.

Not until 1847 was his work of compiling a syllabary for the Babylonian language, by comparison with the Persian, sufficiently advanced to merit publication. In the meantime other European orientalists such as Rasmus Christian Rask, Eugene Burnouf, and most importantly the Sanskrit scholar Christian Lassen of Bonn, had completed the Old Persian alphabet and resolved the major problems of grammar. By then the patient scholarship of Grotefend, and the indifference of his senior colleagues, were rewarded by the discovery that an Englishman, Major Rawlinson, had published a first translation of the Babylonian cuneiform, a Semitic language it transpired, cognate with Aramaic, Hebrew and Arabic.

Jean François Champollion was fifteen years younger than Grotefend. Born at Figeac in 1790, he was called 'Le Jeune' to distinguish him from the elder brother,

Jean Francois Champollion.

known as 'Figeac', who educated him at the family home before he was awarded a state-aided place at the newly founded Lyceum. At the age of fourteen he read a learned paper purporting to show that the giants of the Bible and classical mythology were the personifications of natural phenomena, and at sixteen he announced that Coptic was the ancient language of Egypt. In 1809 he was appointed Professor of History at Grenoble. He was sent by Charles X to study Egyptian antiquities in Italian museums and on his return to France was made director of the Egyptian Department of the Louvre. In 1828 he was commissioned to take joint charge, with the Tuscan Rosellini, of a scientific expedition to Egypt.

The decipherment of the Egyptian hieroglyphic language presented problems which were more radical than those of the ancient Mesopotamian tongues. The hieroglyphics presented an entirely foreign challenge. The cuneiform scripts of Asia Minor represented writing with discernible outlines such as the Indo-European languages possessed. Hieroglyphics were pictographic. They bore no relationship to European language. But Egyptian decipherment was provided with a more accessible key than were the cuneiform researches.

The Rosetta stone.

In 1799, one of Napoleon's officers, Lt Bouchard, found a basaltic slab north of the town of Rosetta on the Nile, containing a decree of the priests assembled at Memphis in favour of Ptolemy V. It would eventually fall into British hands and find its way to the British Museum, but its immediate importance lay in the fact that it proclaimed its message in three languages, hieroglyphic, demotic (a cursive version of ancient Egyptian) and Greek. The latter version was a sure guide to Champollion in deciphering the other scripts. His linguistic conclusions were disputed by almost all scholars in his lifetime, but he was vindicated after his untimely death from a stroke in 1832, at the age of 42.

Grotefend and Champollion, working at almost the same time, had placed archaeology on an academic footing. The ancient world could henceforth be revealed in its physical remains and understood by reference to its own records, classified and described by its bricks and mortar, its bones and pottery; and by its words.

The twin incentives of biblical verification and scientific 'truth', would bestride the efforts of the excavators and epigraphists, the argument gaining in intensity and malevolence as time went on. Darwin left England aboard HMS *Beagle* in January 1831. Not until 1859 would he pronounce in *The Origin of Species* that simple beginning from which 'endless forms most beautiful and wonderful, have been and are being evolved'. Words which would sound the death knell of inspirational philosophy, and the notion of the literal truth of the Bible.

2

Layard and Rawlinson

Reconnaissance and the translation of the cuneiform

Major Rawlinson of the Indian Army had seen thirteen years' service in the East when, in the winter of 1840, Austen Henry Layard made his first journey through the Syrian desert and across the river Euphrates. The lands he set out to explore were marked on the maps of the West by, as he put it, 'a vast blank stretching from Aleppo to the banks of the Tigris'. The two men would converge on the buried civilizations which lay between them. For the moment they went the ways of soldier and gentleman traveller.

Layard was twenty-three years old. Born of Huguenot stock in Paris in 1817, much of his childhood was spent in Italy where he grew up on terms of easy familiarity with the masterpieces of classical, renaissance and baroque art which surrounded him, gaining as much knowledge 'as a child could who was constantly in the company of artists and connoisseurs'. At sixteen he was sent to London to study law. He spent six years in the uncongenial embrace of a solicitor's office before deciding to travel to Ceylon where he intended to find employment as a barrister. He left London in July 1839 with a friend, Edward Ledwich Mitford, who suffered from seasickness, and so they decided to go overland. For a young man who carried with him the memory of an often solitary boyhood spent in the exotic company of the *Arabian Nights*, the temptation to remain in the Near East was overwhelming. He never reached Ceylon.

It was a characteristic start in life: a journey destined not to reach its intended end, largely unplanned, and unsuspecting in its discoveries. But here was no innocent abroad. An upper-middle class Englishman with a haphazard education and cosmopolitan upbringing, he was dogged from the outset by a failure to understand the ways of his countrymen. He sought recognition all the same, and

Sir Austen Henry Layard from a painting
by G.F. Watts.

as he set out on his first journey there was an awareness of mysteries which might
yet be unmasked in the lands he travelled through. Armed with a confident
manner and a smattering of Herodotus and other ancients, he parted from
Mitford in Jerusalem after a disagreement about the dangers of traversing the
tribal country of Arabia Petraea beyond the Dead Sea, and set off with a Christian
Arab boy, Antonio, as his guide, leaving Greeks and Latins to fight their
'scandalous battles' in the holy city.

Petra, carved out of the rock of a remote mountain region, bridged the world
he had known from childhood and the world he was entering. Its Nabataean
tombs and caves, its great treasury and labyrinthine passages had been described
by the Frenchman de Laborde who brought it to the notice of Europe in 1836.
The focal point of the blushing city which had remained concealed for a thousand
years, was the open-air Roman theatre built after Trajan had incorporated Petra
into the Empire.

It is astonishing that a people should, with infinite labour, have carved the
living rock into temples, theatres, public and private buildings, and tombs, and
have thus constructed a city on the borders of the desert, in a waterless,
inhospitable region, destitute of all that is necessary for the sustenance of man –

a fit dwelling-place for the wild and savage robber tribes that now seek shelter in its remains.

He retraced his path through Syria. Ammon, Jerash, Baalbek, their original names 'still used, though they are better known as Philadelphia, Gerasa and Heliopolis', names 'given by Rome to whom they owe all their splendour'.

As he made his way through the so-called bible lands, he formed a not very favourable impression of indigenous Arabs and Jews. He was robbed of almost all his possessions on his way to Damascus by deserters from the army of Ibrahim Pasha – who then ruled the Ottoman dominions of Egypt and Syria in lieu of his demented father Muhammad Ali. He arrived dirty and dishevelled, his mind occupied by thoughts of the buried cities of Assyria, Babylon and ancient Persia which lay ahead; thoughts enhanced by an aricle in the *Journal of the Royal Geographical Society* for March 1840 by H.C. Rawlinson, entitled 'Note on march along the Zagros Mountains to Khuzistan (Susiana) and through the Province of Luristan to Kirmanshah in 1836.'

He halted at the mouth of the Nahr al Kalb, Dog River, to examine 'Phoenician, Egyptian, Greek and Roman inscriptions' and some remarkable sculptures which he supposed were Phoenician. In fact, sculptures and inscriptions related to Assyrian kings whose armies had marched that way nearly 3,000 years earlier to wage war in Israel and Egypt. He was reunited with his fellow-traveller Mitford at Aleppo and the pair went on together towards Baghdad. Descending the Tigris from Mosul on a kellak, a native raft kept afloat by inflated goatskins, they visited the ruins of Nimrud, where Xenophon's army had camped. It was the place and time of the most momentous decision of Layard's life. He would 'excavate in Assyria', adding as an afterthought, 'should I ever have the opportunity'.

From Baghdad they followed Rawlinson's route across the Hamrin hills and the Kurdish mountains to Persia, a land of past splendour and present dereliction, and of 'notorious cowards and boasters'. Layard had more or less perfected his Arabic. Now he was able to practise Farsi, surrounded by the antiquities and inscriptions and concealed cities which had become a dominating passion.

There were references to the extinct places on his route in Ctesias's *History of Persia*, preserved in the works of Diodorus Siculus and Photius; and in Eusebius and the Armenian author Moses of Chorene. He had studied those descriptions and he knew of the inscriptions sent to Europe by Niebuhr, Rich and others, as yet imperfectly translated by Grotefend and his colleagues at Gottingen. Layard would gird the wondering impressions of youth with words born of experience:

[47]

A deep mystery hangs over Assyria, Babylonia and Chaldaea. With these names are linked great nations and great cities dimly shadowed forth in history; mighty ruins, in the midst of deserts, defying by their very desolation and lack of definite form, the description of the traveller; the remnants of mighty races still roving over the land; the fulfilling and fulfilment of prophecies; the plains to which the Jew and the Gentile alike look as the cradle of their race.

Henry Creswicke Rawlinson was 17 when he sailed for Bombay in July 1827 as a military cadet in the East India Company's service. As luck would have it he travelled on the same ship as the diplomat-scholar Sir John Malcolm, then Governor of Bombay, and like his famous predecessor Claudius Rich he gained encouragement and stimulation from his clear-sighted superior. His father was a well-known breeder of racehorses and equestrianism was another of his accomplishments. In less than a year he was made an official interpreter in India, and by the age of 19 he was paymaster of the 1st Bombay Grenadiers. In 1833 he was sent with other officers to Persia to reorganize the Shah's army in readiness for an expected Russian incursion in the north. He used his time profitably, learning the dialects of the Persian tribes and becoming acquainted with their leaders; and recording the cuneiform inscriptions which he found on mountains, rocks and ruins throughout the province of Khuzistan.

In 1837 a Russian agent, Captain Vikovich, arrived at Herat, from where he proceeded to the Afghan cities of Kandahar and Kabul to make secret treaties with the Amirs. Rawlinson, who was at Herat with the British military mission, rode the 750 miles to Tehran to warn the ambassador, Sir John McNeill. (Coincidentally, McNeill had met Layard in London and advised him to go East). Rawlinson's was a famous journey, made in 150 hours, in the saddle the entire time except when changing horses. It did not prevent the First Afghan War, but it at least forewarned the British Government. He went on to explore Kurdistan, a journey which won him the gold medal of the Royal Geographical Society in London.

When war came in 1841 Rawlinson was sent to Kandahar as Political Agent. He raised a corps of Persian cavalry and led it into battle against the Afghan forces. He was mentioned in despatches for his bravery in the defence of Kandahar, and went on to serve with distinction at Ghazni and Kabul. He was rewarded for his part in that incompetently led campaign with the Companionship of the Bath and the Persian order of the Lion and Sun. In 1844 he retired from active military service and was offered the post of Political Resident in Baghdad.

He arrived in Baghdad to the welcome of a thirteen-gun salute, and quickly made an impression on his Turkish hosts and on the people of Mesopotamia, or Iraq as it was to become. It is said that his regal bearing and confident manner

Colonel Sir Henry Rawlinson as a young man.

were such that pashas bowed to him, and when he appeared in the city – accompanied as often as not by his favourite pets, a mongoose and a baby leopard – even the most fanatical of Shi'a and Sunni zealots ceased fighting. But the monuments and inscriptions of Persia, recalled from his army days in that neighbouring country, occupied his mind.

On 19 August 1844, he left Baghdad for the plain of Kirmanshah on his way to a secluded rock face which he had noted while on military duty in 1833. His companion, Commander Felix Jones of the Indian Navy, described their journey along the Tigris and Diyala rivers towards their destination, Kirmanshah. In early morning, they rode with their ladders towards the distant mountains, exchanging salaams with pilgrims on their way to Baghdad and the holy Shi'a cities of Kerbala and Najaf.

Over this vast plain is scattered the remnants of antique edifices, whose very names are lost in obscurity. Headless columns and baseless capitals, of an unknown and unique order . . . These serve to attract and excite the attention of the traveller, who is soon rewarded for his past toils by the sight of monuments of a more absorbing interest. I allude to the Taki-Bostan sculptures and the engraved tablets of Darius at Behistun.

Now, through the 'talents and acumen' of his fellow traveller, the inscribed tablets of Behistun would, he believed, excite great interest throughout Europe. His description reads like a naval log. 'From 9.45 to 10.15h, road turned north in a gradual curve as we rounded the termination of the Parrow range, known by the appellation "Rock of Behistun".'

The ladders were attached to ropes, which winched them and Rawlinson up the almost perpendicular cliff, until he was positioned alongside one of the figures or inscriptions which he would first clean and then copy by making paper rubbings. For much of the time he was perched precariously 300 feet above the ground, working on the four main 'tablets', or sculptured slabs, chiselled on the polished surface of the cliff, the largest of which was 30 feet wide and 26 feet high, its legend written in four columns in the Old Persian cuneiform character. There was an extra, much defaced column which seemed to be supplementary to the main inscription. To the left of the Persepolis-style inscription was a projecting slab 21 feet in length with a three-column version of the text in the Elamite or 'Median' language. And above that was another inclined slab bearing an inscription in the Babylonian cuneiform.

The sculptures comprised a group of fourteen figures, one of which clearly represented Darius and his attendants; another, it was thought, must be Ormuzd, the supreme god of the ancient Medes and Persians. The mountainside itself had been covered with figures and inscriptions, crudely carved and obscured by time and water. At the foot of the mountain were the remains of a colossal figure group, executed in the rock in *alto-relievo* but mutilated by time and the graffiti artists of the ages. More importantly for Rawlinson, a Greek inscription nearby retained a few traceable letters.

Commander Jones's description of the Darius figure and the surrounding acolytes suggest close scrutiny and over-sophisticated judgement:

> If we except the central and more elevated figure . . . we may pronounce the rest of the group as deficient in artistic beauty, and, indeed, shows but a hieratic style. Their forms are diminutive, stiff and ill-defined; and their habiliments, though well marked, betray no elegance of drapery whatever . . .

Jones was enjoying the roles of handyman and art-critic to which his friendship with Rawlinson had introduced him. His observations betray the prejudices which would always colour the western attitude to the monumental sculpture and stylized art of the East. Later archaeological revelation would demonstrate that other civilizations adopted like themes in their sculpture and pottery, animal-human images and the vainglory of the battle field, the hunt and the delectable moment of the 'kill'. But Greco-Roman art and neo-classical Europe despised such crudities. Rawlinson and his aide began the search for oriental history and art within two decades of the deaths of Napoleon, Goethe, Beethoven, Byron and Shelley. The art which was firmly fixed in the consciousness of the nineteenth-century European traveller with its idealization of the human form, its emphasis on proportion, purity of line, and rhapsody of movement was altogether inimical to Persian and Assyrian hyperbole.

'Badness of design . . . coarseness . . . appealing to the ignorant and uninitiated . . .'. Commander Jones, like the many sensitive occidentals who came before him, was unmoved by the candour, robustness and sheer magnitude of Elamite, Persian, Babylonian and Assyrian art.

Rawlinson worked for eleven days, from early morning until sunset. Exhausted by his efforts he gave up on a cold September afternoon and returned to Baghdad. But he went back several times to complete the work of copying the Behistun inscriptions, often enlisting the help of a Kurdish boy whose acrobatic skill on the ladders enabled him to reach the most inaccessible corners of the mountain side. The work was completed in 1847, after three years, and Rawlinson gave credit to his young helper: 'fixed upon his seat [the ladder] he took under my direction the paper casts of the Babylonian translation of the records of Darius'.

Rawlinson the Political Resident made a great impression in Baghdad as he worked at the translation of the Behistun inscriptions, observed from a discreet distance by curious locals. He erected a strange contraption on the Tigris, not far away from the Residency steps, a water-splashing machine like a monocycle which he pedalled under the shade of a tree-house overhanging the river, thus protecting himself from the intense heat of the Iraq summer. When he returned to the Residency from his visits to Behistun and his work on the decipherment of its inscriptions, it was to the enthusiastic welcome of his pets, the leopard and mongoose, and a lion cub. The larger animals often extended a friendly paw to visitors and passers by. The gesture was seldom well received.

Text and notes on the 'Persian cuneiform Inscriptions at Behistun' were published in the Journal of the Royal Asiatic Society in 1846, a year before Grotefend was able to announce the completion of a 26-sign transliteration of the Old Persian language derived from the Persepolis inscriptions. By 1851, Rawlinson was able to publish an accurate translation of 112 lines of the Behistun Babylonian text. But still the remaining language of the Darius inscriptions was obdurate. Rawlinson placed the untranslated tongue, along with Babylonian, in the 'Scythian rather than the Japhetic family'. Generally, the terms 'Susian' and 'Elamite', came to be used.

Coincidentally, while Rawlinson laboured through summers in which the temperature sometimes reached 130 degrees in the shade, a remarkable Irish scholar, Dr Edward Hincks of Co. Down, had worked at the cuneiform languages independently and with uncanny success. Of Presbyterian background, he was a first-place entrant at Trinity College, Dublin, at the age of 15. His father was Professor of Oriental Languages at Belfast. While Grotefend and Rawlinson laboured, Hincks made incisive sorties into learned circles with observations on the 'Susian' translations from the Persepolis and Behistun inscriptions, and he had been in correspondence with the mathematician and father of modern photography Fox Talbot, another of the scholars and amateur philologists of the day who were fascinated by the 'cuneiform question'.

They had exchanged ideas and attempted translations of the Persepolis inscriptions based on known Greek references, and on various permutations of recurring signs. Hincks was able to publish his own version, including several proper names, syllables and ideograms, in the *Transactions* of the Royal Irish Academy at almost the same moment as Rawlinson's work was revealed. And Hincks was the first to demonstrate a Babylonian word, other than a proper name, the pronoun 'I'; *a-na-lu*, almost exactly the rendering of its Arabic and Hebrew counterparts.

Such rarefied scholarship could hardly fail to give rise to differences of opinion, and eventually to controversy, especially since Hincks and Fox Talbot depended for the development of their work on the material which Layard had begun to unearth in Assyria, and Rawlinson was beginning to make available. In 1847 Rawlinson returned to Behistun to make fuller paper-squeezes of the Babylonian version of the Darius legend. At considerable risk to himself and his young assistant, he obtained an exact copy of the 112-line inscription. By comparing it with the already translated Old Persian he was able to list some 150 signs and their meanings, and to devise the first modest lexicon of some two hundred words in a language which had the 'Semitic' quality of relying on the stable consonant and on vowel signs of variable weight and value. It became evident that, as the perceptive Hincks had already suggested, the script of the Babylonians was not alphabetic but syllabic and ideographic. Its signs could have several meanings. They could represent whole words or syllables which could be combined in various ways to form words. Within a few years, discoveries in Mesopotamia would give rise to a wealth of new material, enabling scholars to extend their knowledge, and their differences.

In 1850 Hincks read a paper before the British Association for the Advancement of Science in which he suggested that the language of the Babylonians differed in fundamental respects from the known features of surviving languages of the Semitic races, Aramaic, Hebrew and Arabic. It was an involved argument, based on the linguistic distinctions inherent in soft and hard palatals and dentals. Hincks's conclusion contained a perceptive proposition.

Page from Rawlinson's Baghdad notebook, 1843–8.

The cuneiform writing and the languages it expressed were, he believed, the inventions of a non-Semitic peoples who had brought civilization to the distant regions between the Tigris and Euphrates before the Semites inhabited the area.

Two years later, Rawlinson moved north from Baghdad to the sites of Nineveh and Nimrud in ancient Assyria, where he studied tablets which contained bilingual syllabaries in the Semitic tongue of Babylonia and in the unknown language which he called 'Akkadian', a name derived from the frequently mentioned dynasty of Akkad (or Agade) established in about 2330 BC. He called the people of this unknown culture 'Babylonian Scyths or Turanians'. These were, he said in a lecture to the Royal Asiatic Society in 1853, the peoples who 'had built the primitive temples and capitals of Babylonia, worshipping the same gods, and inhabiting the same seats as their semitic successors'. He suggested that the language of the 'Babylonian Scyths' had a close affinity with the word systems of the Mongol and Manchu languages. Rawlinson was confused. The language which he believed to have a Scythic origin was Elamite. Akkadian would prove to be the basic language of Babylonians and Assyrians. The other, essentially pictographic script which he, like Hincks, had been unable to make any sense of, represented a quite distinct non-Semitic culture, *Sumerian*.

Rawlinson was resigned to the need for much more work before he could safely make a pronouncement on the cuneiform inscriptions. 'We do know a little about it', he told the many people who were pressing him, 'but there is a great deal more to find out; and until I have studied all the tablets from Nineveh and Babylonia, I shall say no more'. Matters were brought to a head, however, in March 1857, when Fox Talbot suggested to the Royal Asiatic Society that several cuneiform scholars should each be asked to translate a lengthy Assyrian inscription, sending their efforts in sealed packages to the Society. A committee would compare their translations and report on them publicly. Fox Talbot had himself translated an inscription of the Assyrian king Tiglath-pileser I (1114–1076 BC), contained on three clay prisms found at Kalat Shergat in Mesopotamia. Fox Talbot sent his own translation to the Royal Asiatic Society and lithographed copies of the original text were sent to Rawlinson, Hincks and the distinguished French scholar M. Jules Oppert, who happened to be in London. A mixed committee of orientalists and classicists was set up to compare their submissions. The adjudicators decided that Hincks and Rawlinson were in close agreement, that Fox Talbot's rendering was rather 'vague and inexact', and that Oppert differed in some essentials from his English rivals. All the same, the academic test which took place in 1857 settled once and for all the question of the broad reliability of the 'cuneiformists', and of the lines on which they were working.

The Behistun inscription related the events of the first year of Darius's accession, 522–21 BC, telling of the satrapies of Persia, the extent of the empire, and of its conquests, laws and rebellions. Rawlinson's translation of the inscription, with the additions and modifications which Hincks, Oppert and others were able to contribute, was the cornerstone of a previously unimagined spurt of scholarship. Knowledge of the ancient world henceforth relied on the written records of the ages, rather than the indirect evidence of classical historians. Perversely, history receded into an ever remoter past, and the written word did not always prove as reliable as pottery and other 'material' evidence.

In 1859 Jules Oppert published his *Déchiffrement des inscriptions cunéiformes* which would place the new study on an unassailable academic footing. And he would acknowledge the pre-eminence of Rawlinson's contribution: 'Rawlinson était un homme d'un genie prime-sautier, et ce qui est encore plus rare, il avait le don de tomber juste'.

3

Nineveh Revealed

There had been much in Persia for Layard to note and write home about. The ruined Sassanian city of Shirin-i-Khusrau, built it was said by Chosroes for the beautiful Shirin, heroine of Persian fable, was his first encounter with Iranian antiquity as he approached the cool waters of the Halwan river from the Kurdish mountains. Near the remote village of Ser-puli-Zohab he found more Sassanian remains; sculptures *in situ* and broken on the ground, a rock-cut tomb on the face of a precipice, a relief below the entrance carved in the image of a high-priest of the Zoroastrians, one hand raised in benediction, the other holding a scroll, probably the sacred folios of the Zend-Avesta. The tomb was known locally as *Dukkani Daud*, David's Shop. Layard's guide kissed the ground repeatedly, calling on King David to protect him, lending support to the widespread belief (shared by Afghans) that the heirs to Mosaic tradition in Western Asia derived from one of the lost tribes of Israel. But such traditions were, as they would always be, infused with the bitter sense of injustice and martyrdom of the Shi'a followers of the Imam Ali, whom they believed to be one of the thousand-and-one incarnations of God. Despised as infidels by fellow Moslems, they had become dissolute, providing dancing boys and girls for the 'indecent entertainment' of Persian and Turkish nobles to supplement their meagre incomes.

Layard went on to Kermanshah, to the plain which Rawlinson and Commander Jones would traverse four years hence to copy the legend of Behistun. He noted the inscriptions high up on the cliff face, and the sculptures of Taki-Bostan portraying Sassanian kings and the hunting themes which they, in common with monarchs before and after, favoured as the symbol of their virility. The French artists Flandin and Coste, sent by Paris to the Tehran Legation, were drawing the sculptures of the region when Layard was there, near the camp of the Shah and 13,000 of his troops whom the Englishman described as 'rabble'. There were Greek ruins too, including those of Kangavar, said to be ancient Pacobar, where according to tradition an Assyrian queen erected a temple to Artemis and established an erotic cult in which she was supposed to be the most enthusiastic of worshippers.

The Frenchmen teamed up with Layard, and while Coste was drawing a Sassanian capital, his horse's bridle threaded through his angled arm as he worked, a Bakhtiari tribesman slipped the animal's harness and led it away. Coste went on drawing oblivious of the crime. It was, despite the dangerous presence of lions in the mountains and the insults of Shi'a pilgrims and Persian tribesmen who washed ostentatiously after contact with the 'filthy' Christians, a period of contentment and of Anglo-French cordiality.

Like his companions, Layard seems to have taken an ambivalent view of the monumental pictorial art around him. In a subsequent difference of opinion with Rawlinson, he was to write: 'The marbles I have found are beautiful, full of life and movement'. Later he remarked: 'The objects to be discovered cannot have any intrinsic value for their beauty'. He no more than expressed the limitations of his own 'classical' upbringing, surrounded by the arts of Greece and Rome; or of most fellow westerners. The Persian 'marbles' were, on the whole, more propagandist than was to the taste of the mid-nineteenth-century westerner. To Layard and Rawlinson and their contemporaries they were an invaluable source of data; indicative of skills which were 'brought to the highest perfection in Asia Minor and Greece', as Layard wrote in *Nineveh and Its Remains*.

To the Persian tribesmen of his day, Layard was merely another perverse Englishman obsessed by old stones and buildings which to them were of significance only as building materials of the present. Undeterred by native companions who subscribed to that view, he planned to cross the mountains to Shuster, the region of ancient Susa, and to go on to Afghanistan. But he was artfully detained at Hamadan. It was no great inconvenience. Here was the alleged site of Ecbatana, the ancient capital of the Medes. Greek writers had described it as rivalling Babylon in size and exceeding it in magnificence. Its walls were said to have been lined with plated gold and according to Herodotus its palaces and temples were surrounded by seven concentric walls representing the seven heavenly bodies. It was here that Alexander had rested on his journey home from India, offering up sacrifices to the gods, and lamenting the death of his favourite Hephaestion. Layard found a few marble columns which suggested the existence of palaces; and a few minor mounds which were hardly worthy of investigation. Yet the great city had remained intact during succeeding dynasties of the Parthians and Sassanians, standing astride the highway which led from Babylon across the Zagros mountains into Media. Three miles away in the mountains he found himself at the village of Abbasabad, surrounded by cuneiform inscriptions, tree-lined valleys, orchards and clear streams. The

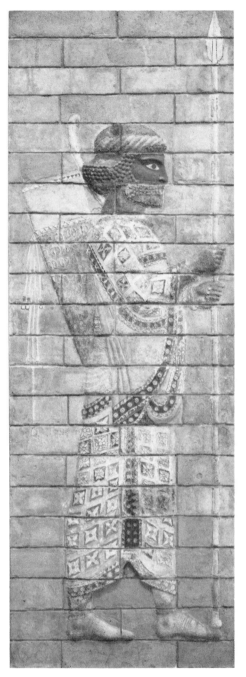

Above: Susian guard holding shield and lance. Detail from relief in palace of Darius I at Persepolis.

Left: Glazed brick panel showing archer from palace of the Persian king Artaxerxes II (404–359 BC), Susa.

contrast with Hamadan, unsalubrious and denying by its very appearance a glorious past, was apparent. Cut in a cliff overlooking a narrow gorge were two trilingual inscriptions, similar to those of Persepolis and Behistun. The work of the cuneiformists in Europe would enable their message to be deciphered in due course: an invocation to the supreme god Ormuzd, and the names of Darius Hystaspes and his son Xerxes. Layard returned to Hamadan to find that it had been pillaged by the Shah's troops before they left for Tehran.

He had brushed shoulders with the later stages of ancient Iranian civilization; with the Median culture which represented the late Iron Age of the region, from about 800 BC until the Achemenid dynasty of Cyrus II was established at Pasargadae in 549 BC, and later at Persepolis, the capital of Darius. The temptation to remain, and perhaps to search for evidence of even earlier urban sites, was countered by the need for money and a growing dislike of Persians. His companion Mitford had gone on to India. Layard calculated that in two years in the East their daily expenses had come to one shilling and sixpence each, including the hire and feeding of horses. Frugality was not enough however. He survived on a modest private income and needed to return home to secure funds if he was to realize his ambition to excavate the buried cities of the East. Anglo-French collaboration in Persia and adjoining Mesopotamia, begun by Layard, Coste and Flandin, was soon to develop into rivalry, spurred by the demands of the national museums of the two countries and the political ambition of the European empires. Competitive, sometimes destructive digging resulted. Coste stressed the enlightenment of his own countrymen when he returned to Paris: 'The French government wished to do for Persia what it had done for Egypt and Greece. It realised that the monumental history of this country was complimentary to those of the other two. . .'.

Layard returned to Mesopotamia by way of the disorderly territories of the Bakhtiari and Bani Lam tribes, in almost constant dread of failing to awaken from a night's sleep. He carried for several days the memory of a last 'orgy' in Isfahan, liberal food and arak consumed to the accompaniment of Hafiz and Sadi in lilting song, and 'beautiful dancing girls, eyes heavily made up, loose silk gowns entirely open at the front', cavorting 'in attitudes of outrageous indecency'. Evenings round the camp fire were enlivened by his young Arab companion Saleh, a philosopher guide who would be immortalized in a drawing of master and servant by the American artist M.K. Kellogg. He held forth confidently, explaining on one occasion to an assembly of tribesmen how indispensable he was to European travellers. 'The kings of Europe', he told them, 'send their subjects to travel in different countries in order that they might inquire into the histories of ancient monarchs, ascertain how they lived, and inform themselves of their good and bad actions'. He, Saleh, was able to explain such matters to them, and

[59]

Paul-Emile Botta, from a painting by Champmartin.

thus their peoples could 'regulate their own conduct, and govern their own countries with justice and wisdom'. Many an archaeologist who followed Layard might have prayed that this servant boy's glib phrases contained a substantive truth.

Susa was on the route to Baghdad. Lion and leopard roamed the hills to add to the dangers of the journey, though emaciated, mangy versions of the proud creatures so mercilessly hunted and recorded by the kings who once dominated the area. The Book of Daniel came to mind as he traced the windings of the Dizful river and observed a great mound in the distance: 'And I saw in a vision; and it came to pass when I saw, that I was at Shushan in the palace, which is in the province of Elam; and I saw in a vision, and I was by the river of Ulai'. Tribal warfare broke out almost as soon as he arrived and he was able to make only a cursory inspection of the mound before moving on, noting that 'The mound itself, which is of enormous size, and the face of the soil to a considerable distance around it, was strewn with bricks, fragments of pottery, glazed tiles, and the various remains which mark the sites of ancient cities in Babylonia'. It would remain for another Englishman, W.K. Loftus, and later for the French explorer Marcel Dieulafoy and his wife to uncover the great palace of the kings of Susa, many years after

William Kennett Loftus

Layard's visit.

The Englishman's path was smoothed in the territories of a suspicious Shah by the ubiquitous first Secretary of the Russian Legation at Tehran, Baron de Bode, who himself wrote numerous articles on the topography of the country and its ancient sites for the journal of the Imperial Geographical Society of St Petersburg. In fact, de Bode spoke very good English, being of half-British and half-German descent. He was well-known for the property claims he made at intervals through the British parliament. He followed on the heels of Layard in 1843 to compose a detailed description of the Shuster region.

Layard completed his journey by Indian Navy steamship from Muhammerah to Basra on the Shatt-al-Arab. A plague epidemic had broken out there and so he went on to Qurna at the junction of the Tigris and Euphrates, the swampy, fly-ridden township which was the reputed Garden of Eden. Arabs and Jews worshipped there in competitive adoration at the Tomb of Ezra. At Baghdad he was welcomed by Lt-Col. Robert Taylor, Rich's successor as Political Resident in 'Turkish Arabia'. Taylor was a quiet man, almost a recluse. In Layard's words, he was 'a man of much learning and an excellent scholar, acquainted with the various Eastern languages'. He placed his library at Layard's disposal, but was not it seems able to offer his visitor the shelter of the Residency. Layard rented a small

Gold model of chariot and drivers. Achaemenid, 5–4 centuries BC, part of Oxus treasure rescued by a British political officer in region of Kabul in 1880.

hut near the official compound, compelled to economize since he had come to the last shillings of the two hundred pounds with which he had left England two years before.

His attention at this time was focussed on Assyria to the north, and the search for Nineveh. The French consul at Mosul, Paul-Emile Botta, had already dug with some success at a mound known as Kuyunjik, which Layard had examined on his way to Mosul two years before. But before he could start digging he needed money. Poverty had driven him to importunity. Wandering in the Baghdad *suq*, still in Persian dress, he met an English merchant, Mr Hector, who was sympathetic, suggesting an approach to the company's English agent, Mr Stirling of Sheffield. Layard wrote straight away, assuring the gentleman that his finds would almost certainly make the investment lucrative. Meanwhile, he gathered his belongings, and the faithful Saleh, and went on to Mosul in search of Botta.

The French consul was in fact Italian by birth, the son of an eminent historian, and had adopted his present nationality. His charm and knowledge won Layard over. But there was a tragic side to the encounter. Layard discovered that his 'delightful companion' was a drug addict, the victim of a habit acquired when he was a consul in China some years earlier, of smoking the opium pipe. His health had been ruined and he was liable to sudden fits of melancholy and distressing seizures. He tried to convince the Englishman that he should take up the habit, 'an unlimited source of comfort and happiness'. Layard declined the invitation. They went together to the mounds of Kuyunjik and Nabi Yunus outside Mosul, where Botta had opened up one or two trenches. Only a few kiln-baked bricks and pieces of alabaster with cuneiform inscriptions had been found. Botta believed that he had discovered a more rewarding site to the north, at Khorsabad, and proposed to continue his researches there. Layard encouraged the idea and departed with Tartar escort across the 'sultry Assyrian plain' for the Black Sea and Constantinople.

Though he carried urgent despatches from Baghdad, connected with a worsening frontier dispute between Persia and Turkey, he was received with indifference by the staff of the embassy at the Ottoman capital. The ambassador, Sir Stratford Canning, was an urbane and high-handed envoy. Nevertheless, when Layard eventually received an invitation to dine with him he took an immediate liking to his young guest. Canning wanted to take Layard on to his staff, and to use his knowledge of men and affairs in Mesopotamia and Persia, but the Foreign Secretary, Lord Aberdeen, would not hear of it. A modest assignment in the Balkans was permitted, followed by an abortive attempt to help the British officers Stoddart and Conolly who were imprisoned in Bokhara, through the agency of an eccentric priest, Dr Wolff, who proposed to go to their aid by donkey. Predictably, Dr Wolff arrived too late in Bokhara, and Layard kicked his heels at Constantinople until Canning proposed, in October 1845, that he should return to Mosul to look for Nineveh at his expense. It was a generous offer. No reply to Layard's letter had been vouchsafed by Mr Stirling, and there had been indifferent responses from the British Government and the British Museum to requests for help. In the meantime Botta had begun to make sensational finds at Khorsabad and the French Government had allocated funds to pay for continued excavations, and for M. Flandin, Layard's Persian companion, to make drawings of the artefacts and crumbling sculptures of the palace unearthed by its consular agent.

Armed with a temporary authorization to dig in the Ottoman vilayet of Mosul, Layard took the Black Sea steamer to Samsun on the Anatolian coast, and made the overland journey to the Tigris valley by post-horse. The journey of about 1,000 miles took twelve days. He took on a work force of Chaldaeans from the Kurdish hills who would be his excavators and Arabs for earth-carrying tasks. In

Relief wall sculpture from Khorsabad, c.710 BC. Sargon II, on left, faces a high official, perhaps the crown prince Sennacherib.

Layard's reconstruction of Neo-Assyrian Nimrud, from his *Monuments of Nineveh*.

Lioness attacking negro slave, one of hoard of ivories found in a deep well at Nimrud. Surround of stylised flowers with gold stems, inlaid with blue frit and red carnelian.

his two years of waiting and honorary diplomatic activity in Turkey he had been instrumental in bringing the world's attention to the work of Botta. Some of the huge stone figures and sculptured slabs of Khorsabad, some weighing more than twenty tons, had been transported to Mosul by primitive carts, hauled by five work gangs of five or six hundred men at a time. From there they were floated on rafts along the 1,000 miles of the Tigris which separated Mosul from Basra, and thence transported by ship to France. The public of Europe was able to glimpse the first of the great monuments of the northern palace built for King Sargon II, around the year 710 BC.

Layard dug first at Nimrud, which Xenophon called 'Larissa'. He arrived there on 19 November 1845. Within days the great mound was giving up its treasures. Walls were revealed with immense stone panels, inscribed in cuneiform. Unpractised in the techniques of excavation – indeed, there were no accepted techniques – Layard simply used rule-of-thumb methods to guide his labourers along the wall traverses of what had been a royal palace many centuries before, uncovering massive sculptured slabs as they went; hoping, often in vain, that the mixed fear and enthusiasm with which they worked would not give rise to too much destruction. The picture which gradually came to light was of a palace built of mud-brick, its walls lined with inscribed and sculpted stone slabs. Layard traced the outlines of the palace by following the stonework, where necessary through doors, in order to delineate rooms and halls and passageways. Within ten days of the start of the excavations, two decorated slabs were discovered and gradually exposed. Battle scenes and richly bedecked horses came into view.

At first sight he was eloquent in his praise: 'I observed with surprise the elegance and richness of the ornaments, the faithful and delicate delineation of the limbs and muscles, both in the men and the horses, and the knowledge of art displayed in the grouping of the figures, and the general composition'. It was a spontaneous response rather than a lasting impression. Layard like others who came after him, tended to regard the great wall panels of the Assyrian and Persian palaces as individual works of craftsmanship and art, and to judge them accordingly, often in classical terms. In fact, they were the parts of some of the most immense historical narratives ever created, recording with unique precision and great skill the events of their time. It was art infused with purpose and the enthusiasms of the moment. To the western connoisseur, such panels were, like Italian altarpieces, easily viewed as separate scenes and, if necessary, dismantled. In a letter Layard used the phrase 'mere duplicates'. He found himself in an architectural dilemma over the question of the column as a feature of the Assyrian palaces. At first he believed that the colonnades so familiar in Egyptian, Greek and Persian buildings were entirely absent from Assyrian design. Yet after committing himself to that thesis, he argued that columns were structurally

Assyrians and Elamites at the battle of Til-Tuba, relief sculpture of Ashurbanipal from
Sennacherib's palace at Nineveh, c.650 BC

almost essential and drew impressively colonnaded reconstructions of the
Assyrian palaces in his later books.

There was a violent rainstorm as Layard examined the panels. Some showed
scorch marks and the damage of time, and perhaps of stone robbing. One panel
represented a battle scene with a beardless central figure, a eunuch in mailed-suit
and helmet, bow at full stretch, enemy wounded trampled under the horses' feet,
and the siege of a castle or walled city. The other panel showed two warriors with
horses surmounting the battlements of a two-storey castle, a woman tearing her

hair in grief and a fisherman by a stream. Scenes and cuneiform inscriptions, though he could not read them, were clearly different from the legends and sculptures of the slabs he had seen at Khorsabad.

There were inevitable problems attached to the employment of a large labour force in lawless tribal territory. The Ottoman Pasha of the Mosul district, Keritli Oglu, was venal and weak. The tribes around the excavation site, particularly the belligerent Abu Salman, were torn between superstitious fear and the anticipation of rich pickings as they observed the progress of the excavations. It was claimed that Layard was digging up a Moslem burial ground. The Pasha, not wishing to be thought guilty of fabrication, decided that they should bury some dead there, thus establishing the claim. Layard was forced to halt work and go to Mosul to negotiate with the Pasha, who was about to be deposed. He found

[67]

Keritli sitting in his serai, the damaged roof of which was penetrated by intense rain. 'Thus it was with God's creatures', said the Pasha. 'Yesterday all these dogs were kissing my feet; today every one and everything falls upon me, even the rain!' Layard went on to Baghdad to seek the help of Rawlinson, who had taken over from Taylor, in arranging the despatch of the Nimrud sculptures to England. Layard went ahead of his finds to await their arrival in London.

He arrived back at Nimrud in January 1846. In his absence the black tents of the Badu had covered the plain and corn grew over the palaces of the Assyrian kings in the land that was biblical Calah. He was accompanied by Hormuzd Rassam, a young man – he was twenty years old at the time – who was to play a vitally important part in the further excavation of Nimrud, and in the mounds closer to Mosul which Layard had yet to investigate. Rassam, a Christian from the Nestorian community and the brother of the British vice-consul at Mosul, became his administrator and pupil. Contrived graves were demolished and digging was resumed. Massive winged bulls and lions, more bas-reliefs, damaged by fire but intact, began to emerge. The most perfect of the reliefs showed a king with a high conical tiara, standing over a prostrate captive, a scene which would become ever more familiar as the story of Assyria unfolded. A eunuch brandished a fly-swatter over the king's head, while the monarch held court with another figure, perhaps the crown prince, wearing a simple, banded headdress. Above that relief was another, almost destroyed by fire, though Layard could just trace horses and horsemen, and captive figures wearing helmets with curved crests resembling the headgear of Greek warriors. Lion hunts, sieges, warriors swimming rivers to attack walled cities, mounted archers on war chariots, formed an astonishingly vigorous and belligerent narrative. As trenches were dug round the expanding site walls, he could just make out the shadowy shapes of gigantic figures. Some of the sculptures had been deliberately defaced with sharp instruments. Many were disfigured by fire.

A picture began to form in Layard's mind of a vastly powerful empire at whose centre were the palaces he was uncovering. Kings, battles, royal hunts, colossal figures and anthropomorphic images, were revealed in an endless array of limestone panels. Sometimes a figure sported the head of an eagle, sometimes the body of a lion or bull. Here was the art of a mighty and boastful empire which had been destroyed by fire and sword. He was at the capital city of Ashurnasirpal II, who ruled Assyria from 883–859 BC. One of the many inscribed stone tablets or stelae found at the site contains in a single powerful representation of that monarch, a précis of that martial, lion-hunting, element-worshipping kingdom of the ninth century BC. In his left hand the King holds a mace, symbol of his authority, while his outstretched right hand suggests that he has just snapped his fingers in supplication to the symbols of five gods at his side. A helmet decorated

Top part of stela of Ashurnasirpal II (883–859 BC), from Nimrud. Mace symbolises authority. King appears to snap fingers in gesture of respect towards the symbols of the gods.

[69]

Phrygia

• Kültepe

Anatolia

Hacilcar•
•Catal Hüyük

Carchemish
•Harran
Tel Halaf
TelAhmar •Tel Brak

Aegean
Sea

•Antioch
• Tel Atchana
• Ras Shamra
(Ugarit)

•Amar
•Tel Mardith
(Ebla)
•Hama
• Qatna

Cyprus

• Palmyra

M.

R.

•Byblos
Phoenicia •Baalbeck

Sidon•
Tyre •

• Tel Ramad

Mediterranean Sea

•Hazor

Syria

Megiddo•
Beisan•

•Gerasa

Palestine

•Samaria
•Jericho
•Jerusalem

Gezer Taanrak•

•Lachish Dead
Sea

•Petra

with horns represents the supreme god Ashur (or Assur); a winged disc which may have had Egyptian origin stands for the sun god, Shamash; a crescent within a circle symbolizes the moon god, Sin; the thunderbolt of the storm god Adad is represented by a fork-like sign; and a star, the planet Venus, signifies Ishtar, the goddess of love and war. The King sports a row of like symbols on his chest, except that a Maltese cross replaces the Egyptian-style disc in honour of the sun.

With only human and animal muscle-power at his disposal, Layard had to use the most primitive methods to bring up the reliefs and colossi from the pits. Ropes were tied to the objects and fed over makeshift pulleys to the surface where hundreds of site workers strained and cursed in a relentless tug-of-war, static building up in the ropes with such intensity that they crackled and flashed as though struck by lightning. The objects themselves caused consternation. When the top half of a colossal winged-lion with human head came up one morning Arab workmen decided that they had found Nimrod himself. Their shaikh, Abdurrahman, was called to the scene by his tribesmen, and the great man announced that they beheld the works of devils. He told his followers: 'This is not the work of men's hands, but of those infidel giants of whom the Prophet – peace be with him! – has said that they were higher than the tallest date tree; this is one of the idols which Noah – peace be with him! – cursed before the flood.' Another widespread theory was that such idols were the work of the Magi, and that they were being taken to England to form the gateway to the palace of the Queen.

Layard worked on at Nimrud during 1846 and the first half of 1847, unearthing the palace of Tiglath-pileser III, its sculptures stacked in a courtyard ready for re-use in a new palace for a later king. They had remained undisturbed for two and a half millennia.

Perhaps the most important of the finds of this period was the Black Obelisk of Shalmaneser III, carved on its four sides and inscribed with legends which provided a vital synchronism with the biblical record, and helped to establish the chronology of Assyria. A relief drawing of richly dressed envoys accompanies the text, 'Tribute of Jaua of Bit-Humri: Silver, gold, a golden bowl, golden goblets, a golden beaker, pitchers of gold, tin, sceptres for the king and balsam-wood I received from him'. Jaua of Bit-Humri would be identified as Jehu, King of Israel, who drove out the dynasty of Omri from the kingdom of Israel in the ninth century BC, and brought on the Israelites the wrath of Hazael of Damascus.

In the summer of 1847, the great reliefs and colossi of Assyria began to arrive at the British Museum. Popular interest had been fostered by newspaper reports of almost limitless finds of ancient art. The appearance of the objects themselves caused a fever of public excitement not to be equalled until the most sensational finds of ancient Egypt such as Tutankhamen, and that other place foreshadowed in the inscriptions of Assyria, Ur of the Chaldees, were revealed three-quarters of

Hormuzd Rassam.

a century into the future. Crowds gathered at the British Museum as they had gathered at the Louvre to see the arrival of the Assyrian masterpieces.

A popular English journal founded in 1842, the *Illustrated London News*, had shown a modest interest in archaeology from its inception. With the arrival of the Assyrian sculptures it became the public's window on the ancient world, and the progress of field work in Mesopotamia and elsewhere would be described in its pages for the next century and more by some of the world's most renowned archaeologists, and illustrated profusely. In France, journals such as *L'Illustration*, and *Gazette des Beaux-Arts* presented their readers with the same fascinating and unfamiliar fare. Such indeed was the popular enthusiasm for archaeological discovery in the wake of the first Assyrian displays in London that, in 1848, leading citizens of the north of England held a celebratory dinner, a Grand Antiquarian Banquet, at Newcastle-upon-Tyne. The fruits of recent excavations in Assyria and classical Greece were toasted along with discoveries of Norman relics in the British Isles. According to the *Illustrated London News* the

Above and opposite: Scenes and inscriptions from the Black Obelisk of Shalmaneser III, from Nimrud c.825 BC.

packed assembly drank the health of her Majesty the Queen, after which a twenty-one gun royal salute was fired from the top of the city's restored Norman castle, 'and the company responded with three times three'. Even that splendid feast, attended by the rich and renowned of England in the heyday of the Industrial Revolution, was diminished by the inscription on a sandstone stela which awaited discovery in the courtyard of Ashurnasirpal II at Nimrud. It told in 154 lines of the building of the palace, of the principal gods, of nations conquered, buildings erected, canals dug, trees planted, temples adorned. Flora and fauna within the boundaries of Nimrud were listed. And the inscription ended with an account of the great feast given to celebrate the completion of the palace, c.879 BC, at which 69,574 people wined, dined and bathed for ten days on end, before 'returning to their homes with joy'.

As the first Assyrian objects arrived in London, Layard returned to Mosul to excavate at Kuyunjik, trenched in vain by Botta four years earlier. The Englishman had dug there briefly during his first expedition when he discovered the palace of Sennacherib (704–681 BC). Within a few days of his return to the site,

it became apparent that this was perhaps the largest, and certainly the most spectacular, of all the royal palaces of Assyria. Soon the sculptures and reliefs of Nineveh were making the precarious journey to London, to join their counterparts from Nimrud, and indeed from Khorsabad, for some of the French-dug antiquities found their way by one route or another to the British Museum. In June 1847, the *Illustrated London News* was reproving rather than enthusiastic.

The accounts which have reached this country from time to time of the recent excavations and discoveries amongst the supposed ruins of Nineveh, have excited the curiosity not only of the antiquarian but also of all scriptural students, from the illustration they afford of passages of Holy Writ, of which all material traces appear to have been lost. We are indebted for such remains as have hitherto come to light to the indefatiguable labours of M.Botta, the French consul at Mossal [sic], and to our own countryman, Mr Layard; and it is no more than justice to the latter to remark that he was the first to indicate the probability of these ruins, though his suggestions were so coldly received by our Government that he was left to pursue his researches unaided, except by the private resources of Sir Stratford Canning. The French government, however, with its accustomed liberal sympathy in the cause of science, stepped in and most nobly assisted M. Botta, who was thus able to precede Mr Layard in discoveries of sculpture etc, etc., at Khorsabad ...

True it was that Botta had found the first artefacts of Nineveh in its northernmost palace. But Layard uncovered its administrative centre, with its collection of records which would make it possible to retrace the path of civilization backwards from the destruction of the Assyrian Empire to its predynastic origins.

Newspapers and magazines were able to carry illustrations of the royal hunting expeditions of the ancient world, of long forgotten wars and sieges, the torture of prisoners, the peaceful pursuits of farmers, priests and tribute bearers; of sacrificial ceremonies and magnificent chariots taking their masters helter-skelter to war. And, most graphic of all, they illustrated the colossi of Nimrud and Nineveh, tributes as much to the logistical skills of their transporters as to the genius of craftsmen who had carved them from solid blocks of stone. There were obelisks or stelae too, in white and black stone, public memorials to the monarchs of the time who are shown in all the usual kingly pursuits. None claimed more rapt attention in Europe than the Black Obelisk of Shalmaneser found by Layard, and the similar black stone of Ashurnasirpal II found by Rassam. Both stood in public places and their messages insisted on the might and stability of Assyria at the height of its influence in the ninth century BC. Representatives of the rich city states of Syria and Phoenicia are seen to bring exotic gifts from far-off trading partners; monkeys, favourite pets of royalty, and horses from Iran, vital to the cavalry of a mighty empire. The Shalmaneser obelisk also contained the earliest known illustration of an Israelite.

Excavation funds were exhausted by the end of 1847. Layard returned to England, leaving Rassam and a few workmen at Nineveh and Nimrud to prevent others from taking over the sites. It seemed that the British authorities were willing to leave the further exploration of Mesopotamian antiquity to France, or any other country willing to face the cost. Canning was able to persuade the British Museum to provide limited backing, however, and Layard returned to the Assyrian sites at the end of 1849, accompanied by an official artist, Frederick Cooper. There quickly followed the most significant of his discoveries, the library of Ashurbanipal, grandson of Sennacherib, who ruled between the years 668–627 BC. Here was the first of the great royal archives of Mesopotamia, which would supplement the records of Egypt and Babylonia, and restore to the world several millennia of lost history.

Booty of Lachish. Detail from relief showing Sennacherib inspecting booty from throne heavily decorated with protective genies.

Layard and Rawlinson were in regular correspondence, the digger constantly urging the translator to publish his findings. But Rawlinson was still reluctant, despite the chance that the Germans and French might beat him to the post. 'I still walk very darkly and doubtfully in the Assyrian light and am often half inclined to chuck the whole of my Babylonian papers into the fire in sheer disgust', he wrote in August 1845.

Hincks came more and more into the picture, offering scholarly and reliable suggestions when there was doubt about a name or a transcription. Other Europeans were involved too, and there is an occasional note of disparagement in Rawlinson's diaries and letters: 'those people like Lassen, Westergaard and Reverend Hincks who rush into print half prepared to prevent anticipation. If I

[77]

do anything at all I must do it fully and deliberately and have no objection whatever if all the savants of Europe should work simultaneously with me'. Rawlinson was not a vain or affected scholar, but he was sensitive to criticism, and Hincks with his sharp Irish tongue and pen did not hesitate to disparage his English rival.

Layard, the source of most of the material on which the translators were working, tried to bring the two men together, and he let it be known that it was through the 'accidental possession' of his, Layard's, papers that Rawlinson had been able to publish an important Assyrian text relating to Hezekiah. Layard was certainly convinced of Hincks's usefulness in what had become a competitive exercise in cuneiform scholarship. He declared some twenty-five years after the event that 'in any country but England, a man of such attainments, and so eminently calculated to confer honour upon the nation to which he belonged, would have received some reward, or would have been placed in a position of independence, to enable him to pursue his studies'. At the time of the dispute, Layard thought it a pity that discoveries 'of such interest and importance should be, as it were, lost in the columns of the *Athenaeum.*' In the end, however, Hincks gave up the challenge and retired to his Irish parsonage. 'The Irishman had indeed attacked me so wantonly and bitterly that I shall certainly retaliate and do all in my power to expose his dogmatism, excessive conceit, and what I call his systematic dishonesty. We shall see who comes off best in the mêlée', Rawlinson had written. Inevitably, the practised diplomat came off best. He was, nevertheless, given to snap judgements, and even his life-long friend General Sir Frederic Goldsmid accused him of 'occasional *brusquerie* of manner'.

Against this background of esoteric argument and occasional abuse, industry and actual achievement were considerable. A first-hand portrait of one of the great empires of the ancient world had begun to take shape, alongside the literary record so familiar to the West in Kings and Chronicles. Decorative art, in the shape of the relief-carved limestone tablets which covered the palace walls of the Assyrian kings, was the vehicle of historical narrative and contemporary record. Inscriptions and graphics on wall slabs and stelae substantiate many a biblical passage, even if differences of emphasis are sometimes marked. One of the Ashurnasirpal reliefs from Nimrud shows two merchants, one in Phoenician dress the other with characteristic Syrian coiffure. The Phoenician snaps his fingers in what seems to be the accepted salutation of the commoner to the mighty. His companion leads two monkeys, offered as tribute to the Assyrian Court. Yet another relief shows a long-prowed galley typical of the ships of Tarshish. These and many other pictorial records taken from the ruins of Nimrud, Nineveh and Khorsabad, and later from Assur, provided a detailed record of a period in which the great warrior kings of Assyria contended with the

Nimrud reliefs from the saleroom. *Right:*
Eagle-headed genie tending the tree of life,
sold at Sotheby's in December 1979 for
£95,000–$200,000; and, *below*, bearded and
winged protecting spirit, sold at same sale
for £240,000–$505,000; acquired by Lord
Sandon in 1853 when he visited site of
Nimrud with the Earl of Carnarvon. Both
items from palace of Ashurnasirpal II
(c.883–859 BC).

majesty of Egypt, and with the illustrious empire of King David and his successor (c.950 BC) Solomon. In their exuberant manner, their confident yet stylized execution and sometimes charmless subject matter, these relief carvings interpret and expand the written record. Here is pictorial, eye-witness confirmation of Old Testament legends which tell of Solomon's alliance with the Phoenicians, an alliance which gave Israel access to the world's best sailors and strongest maritime power, so that a dockyard was built at Elath close to the Hebrew king's copper-smelting plant on the Gulf of Aqaba. Thus, the combined powers could gain access to the Red Sea and the rich markets of India and perhaps the Persian Gulf.

And Hiram sent him by the hands of his servants ships and servants that had

Opposite and above: The 'Lion Hunt' reliefs from Ashurbanipal's palace at Nineveh, c.645 BC. Said to have been found by W.K. Loftus in 1854. This royal pastime was not as intrepid as the detail above suggests. Captive animals were set free for the chase.

knowledge of the sea; and they came with the servants of Solomon to Ophir, and fetched from thence four hundred and fifty talents of gold, and brought them to King Solomon.

Once every three years, we are told in Kings and Chronicles, 'came the ships of Tarshish, bringing gold, silver, ivory, apes and peacocks', and many things besides.

While Israel was united under David and Solomon, Phoenicia was happy with a loose and profitable alliance. Assyria kept a respectful distance. But following the death of Solomon and the rise of the dissolute House of Omri, the Assyrian kings rattled their sabres. With the marriage of Ahab to the Phoenician Princess Jezebel (c.850 BC), the Hebrew scribes seem almost to have despaired: 'Now the rest of the acts of Ahab and all that he did and the ivory house which he built, and all the cities which he built, are they not written in the book of the Chronicles of the kings of Israel?'. By the eighth century, the divided kingdom of Judah and Israel was at the mercy of the Assyrians. Tiglath-pileser III (744–27 BC) brought ceaseless pressure to bear on the Phoenician and Palestinian kingdoms. His son, Shalmaneser V (727–22 BC), continued the same policy and in 725–23 BC campaigned against the Israelite capital of Samaria, where Hoshea reigned who had done 'that which is evil in the sight of the lord'. But it was Shalmaneser's successor, Sargon II (721–705 BC), who delivered the final blow. The capture of Samaria took its place in a long list of bloody and decisive conquests.

> *Year 1. The deportation of the Israelites; a minor raid into Babylonia* ... At the beginning of my rule, in my first year of reign, the people of Samaria ... (of Shamash) who caused me to attain victory ... (27,000 people who lived therein) I carried away ... The city I rebuilt, I made it greater than it was before; people of the lands my hand had conquered, I settled therein. My official I placed over them as governor. Tribute tax I imposed upon them, as upon the Assyrians ... On the Tu'munu tribe I imposed Assur's yoke. ... Merodachbaladan, King of Chaldea, who exercised the kingship over Babylon against the will of the gods ... x + 7 people, together with their possessions, I snatched away ... In the land of Hatti I settled them.

The inscriptions of the Assyrian kings contained in wall reliefs, on stelae and obelisks, and cut into cliffs and rocks in the time-honoured manner of military graffiti artists, are seldom guilty of understatement. But the kings themselves are usually represented as dignified rulers, set apart from the events which they order and direct. One portrait of Ashurnasirpal, in a unique hatless pose, from the shrine of Ishtar at Nimrud, is positively benign. But it was erected in the confident anticipation of divine favour.

The annals which Sargon II had caused to be engraved on the walls of his palace at Dur-Sharrukin (Khorsabad), revealed the prowess of the empire in its final centuries of dominance. Other inscriptions, from the hand of that king and his forefathers and successors, revealed contemporary accounts of some of the most dramatic episodes of ancient history.

Tiglath-pileser III had recorded victories over Hanno of Gaza and Sib'e the Pharaoh's military chief in Palestine, the subjugation of Carchemish, the receipt of tribute of gold dust, horses and camels from Shamsi the 'Queen of Arabia' and It'amar the Sabaean, after inflicting grievous defeat on the kingdom of Saba (biblical Sheba). Even Urartu (Armenia) and distant Meluhha (Ethiopia) were said to have fallen victims to the Assyrian army. Within a few years (721–705 BC),

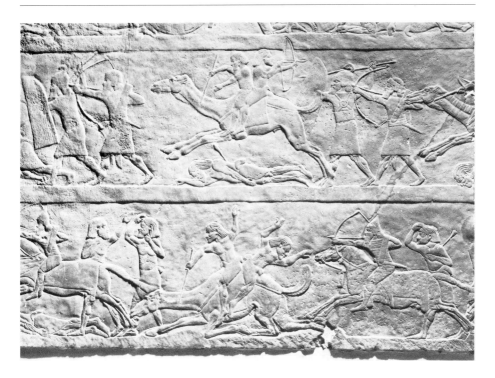

Assyrians attack an Arab force, c.645 BC, from Ashurbanipal's palace, Nineveh.

Sargon's scribes were recording campaigns against much the same foes; and yet more victories. And they told of the rape of a Syrian city: 'Hanno I seized with my own hand, and took him to my city, Assur, in chains. The city of Rapihu I destroyed, I devastated, I burned with fire; 9,033 people, together with their many possessions, I carried off.' In far away Cyprus, midst the Western Sea, the hearts of kings 'began to pound' as they heard of Sargon's victories over Samarians, Chaldaeans and Hittites. 'Ia'ubidi from Hamath, a commoner without claim to the throne, a cursed Hittite, schemed to become king of Hamath, induced the cities Arvad, Simirra, Damascus and Samaria to desert me . . . I conquered and burnt. Himself I flayed; the rebels I killed in their cities . . .'

Sargon's son, Sennacherib, recorded the capture of Lakisu, biblical Lachish, in 701 BC, and the submission of Hezekiah following the siege of Jerusalem. His battle victories were illustrated in the wall panels of Nineveh, and Layard made

[83]

meticulous copies of the magnificently detailed originals as they were revealed.

> As to Hezekiah, the Jew, who did not submit to my yoke, I laid siege to 46 of his strong cities, walled forts and to the countless small villages in their vicinity, and conquered them by means of well-stamped ramps and battering-rams brought near to the walls (combined with) the attack by foot soldiers, (using) mines, breeches as well as sapper work. I drove out 200,150 people, young and old, male and female, horses, mules, donkeys, camels, big and small cattle beyond counting . . . Himself I made a prisoner in Jerusalem, his royal residence, like a bird in a cage. I surrounded him with earthworks in order to molest those who were leaving his city's gate. His towns which I had plundered, I took away from his country and gave them over to Mitinti, king of Ashdod, Padi, king of Ekron, and Sillibel, king of Gaza . . . Hezekiah himself, whom the terror-inspiring splendour of my lordship had overwhelmed . . . did send me, later, to Nineveh, my lordly city, together with 30 talents of gold, 800 talents of silver, precious stones, antimony, large cuts of red stone, couches, inlaid with ivory . . . daughters, concubines, male and female musicians. In order to deliver the tribute and to do obeisance as a slave he sent his messenger.

Layard left the Sennacherib wall reliefs intact, making do with copies. Some had been damaged by fire and he was reluctant to risk further damage. But art which gave contemporary witness to biblical history roused the acquisitive instinct of Christian Europe. In 1853, the British Museum told Rassam to send the Lachish panels to London. They represent, all in all, one of the finest examples of military narrative art.

Among the finds at Khorsabad, Nimrud, and Nineveh were several large clay cylinders. One of them, found by Rassam in Layard's absence and translated by Rawlinson, contained a passage from Ashurbanipal (668–627 BC), the grandson of Sennacherib, telling of a mystery surrounding the old King's death; and relating the details of a gory palace feud in which iconoclasm was carried to an extraordinary extreme:

> I tore out the tongues of those whose slanderous tongues had uttered blasphemies against my god, Assur, and had plotted against me, his god-fearing prince; I defeated them. The others, I smashed to insensibility with the very same statues of protective deities with which they had smashed my own grandfather Sennacherib – now . . . as a burial sacrifice for his soul – I fed their corpses, cut into small pieces, to dogs, pigs, zibu-birds, vultures, the birds of the sky (also) to the fishes of the ocean . . .

Protective genie carrying deer. From Ashurnasirpal's throne room, Nimrud, c.865 BC.

Triumphal journey of Tiglath-pileser III, Nimrud c.730 BC.

Esarhaddon (680–669 BC), son of Sennacherib and father of Ashurbanipal, kept up the ostentatious chronicle which went hand in hand with the decline of the empire. 'I am Esarhaddon, the conqueror of Sidon, which lies amidst the sea, who has levelled all its buildings – I even tore up and cast into the sea its wall and its foundation ...'. The Syro-Palestinian campaign of the king who ruled between 680 and 669 BC was preceded by a fratricidal debauch.

'I am Esarhaddon, great king, legitimate king, king of the world, king of Assyria, regent of Babylon, king of Sumer and Akkad, king of the four rims (of the earth), the true shepherd ...'. He boasted falsely of the extent of his empire. The son of Sennacherib said:

In a propitious month I happily entered ... the palace of the crown prince, this highly venerable place ... the real meaning dawned upon my brothers, they abandoned godliness, put their trust in bold actions, planning an evil plot ... my brothers went out of their senses, doing everything that is wicked in the eyes of the gods and mankind ... and butted each other – like kids – to take over the kingship. Assur, Sin, Shamash, Bel, Nebo, the Ishtar of Nineveh and the Ishtar of Arbela looked with displeasure upon these doings of the usurpers ... But I, Esarhaddon, who never turns around in a battle, trusting in the great gods, his lords ... cried out 'Woe! rent my princely robe ... I became as mad as a lion, my soul was aflame ... I did not wait even for the next day, nor for my army ... I followed that road to Nineveh which is difficult for travelling but short. In front of me, in the territory of Hanigalbat, all my brothers' best soldiers blocked the advance of my expeditionary corps. But the terror of the great gods, my lords, overwhelmed them and they turned into madmen when they saw the attack of my strong battle array. Ishtar, the Lady of Battle, who likes me her high priest ... stood at my side breaking their bows ... And then they spoke among themselves. 'This is our king!'

Esarhaddon entered Nineveh on the eighth day of the month of Addar, 'a favourable month', the day of the Nebo festival, and sat 'happily upon the throne of my father'. For his brothers he reserved grievous punishment. 'I even exterminated their male descendants.'

Layard went on to examine other possible sites. At Kalat Shargat further south along the Tigris there was a mound believed to be the site of the Assyrian capital, Assur, but he could find nothing worthy of investigation. At Nabi Yunus, next to the mound of Kuyunjik, he discovered a few sculptures, but he was unable to dig there because of the presence of the shrine of Jonah, apocryphal but nonetheless

Chaldaeans hiding from Assyrians in reeds, from Sennacherib's palace, Nineveh, c.630 BC.

sacred to Moslem inhabitants, at the summit of the mound. Arbela (modern Arbil), referred to in the Assyrian inscriptions as an important city, was covered with habitations, and would probably never be investigated. He exposed nearly two miles of sculptured walls at the palace of Sennacherib, before his resources ran dry. He returned home at the end of 1849. It was the year in which his first book, one of the literary successes of the age, *Nineveh and its Remains*, was published. It was followed by his *Discoveries in Nineveh and Babylon*, an account of his second expedition, 1849–51. The two books revived flagging public interest in Mesopotamian antiquity and stimulated the setting up, in 1853, of the Assyrian Excavation Fund.

He began to receive the recognition of government and institutions: honorary doctorates of the universities, the freedom of the City of London (with a silver-gilt casket decorated with Assyrian scenes), gold medal of the Royal Geographical Society, and the offer of diplomatic posts. The *Illustrated London News* had

Phoenician tribute bearer bringing monkeys, Nimrud c.865 BC.

become the keeper of the national conscience in the race to acquire 'Scriptural Antiquities', lamenting the lack of official support for Layard's expedition, and finally, as hundreds of tons of lion- and bull-figures began to arrive to the delight of Press and public, raising the standard of St George jingoistically:

It is gratifying that England has not only rendered herself the first of the nations by those sterling qualities which so strongly characterise her natives – that she is not only distinguished by her arms and commerce, but that she used these means to extend and disseminate the wealth, and comfort, and advantages produced by the arts of civilisation, at the same time that she administers happiness and contentment by inculcating the tenets of pure religion ...

Layard left Mesopotamia for good in 1851 after returning to examine possible excavation sites at Babylon and Nuffar (Nippur) in the south. They would become focal points of some of the largest and most important finds in the history of archaeology, but Layard found nothing to detain him. He returned to England to take up politics and became Under-Secretary at the Foreign Office. In the satirical press, especially *Punch* magazine, the 'Lion of Nineveh' temporarily succeeded to the place of John Bull. He occupied much the same niche in the hearts and minds of the educated public. But British politicians and academics, as much as British businessmen, are uncomfortable in too close proximity to actual achievement. At a time when all respectable attention was focused on the rediscovery of classical Greece and Europe's 'incomparable' heritage, Layard had inundated Europe with the artefacts of an alien Semitic culture, with the massive, some would say gross, statues of people who understood the disciplines neither of art nor life. He was ridiculed at every opportunity in the House. In the Crimean War he went with Delane, the editor of *The Times*, and Kinglake to Sevastopol. Richard Ford, in his *Spanish Handbook*, noted that 'Eothen and Nineveh' had 'exchanged the pen for the sword', adding elegiacally that he hoped they would return with 'thoughts that breathe to words that burn'. In later life he became estranged from the British Museum through the hostility of its assistant Oriental Keeper E.A. Wallis Budge. He eventually took up a diplomatic career, serving as ambassador in Spain and Constantinople. He retired to Venice, where he renewed his early love of classical art.

The Assyrian Excavation Fund appointed as its field supervisor W. Kennett Loftus, a surveyor who had been engaged in Sir Fenwick Williams's commission for the delimitation of the Turco-Persian frontier in the 1840s, and had been the first to excavate at Susa. The Quai d'Orsay had appointed Victor Place, another scholar-diplomat, to succeed the ailing Botta at Mosul. In 1853, Rassam had uncovered the finest of all the palaces of Assyria, that of Ashurbanipal. But that part of the great mound under which the palace was concealed had been offered to the French excavators by Rawlinson, who administered the affairs of the Assyrian Fund from the Residency at Baghdad. Although Place's attitude was not possessive, Rassam decided to play safe and work by moonlight. On the third night of digging there was a sudden fall of earth and Layard's assistant found that his trench was in the middle of a sculptured passage. Among its treasures were the large-scale reliefs of the lion-hunt, perhaps the most celebrated of all Assyrian sculptures. Rassam had to leave the site early in 1854, and Rawlinson awarded part of the concession to Loftus. Victor Place worked at Khorsabad. Agreement was reached between the Louvre and the British Museum for the apportionment of finds, but one of Place's largest consignments was vandalized by tribesmen as it approached Basra in May 1855. The British consignment arrived safely.

4

The Riddle of Greece

Schliemann at Troy and Mycenae

'But to resume, – should there
be (what may not
Be in these days?) some
infidels, who don't,
Because they can't, find out
the very spot
Of that same Babel, or because
they won't
(Though Claudius Rich,
Esquire, some bricks has
got,
And written lately two memoirs
upon't)
Believe the Jews, those
unbelievers, who
Must be believed, though they
Believe not you ...
Don Juan, Canto V

Byron took the turnpike road of fantasy with Don Juan as his companion in 1818. Venice was his lookout. But it was Hellespont and the Isles of Greece across the Adriatic that beckoned England's poet and all the artists and writers of note in Europe. The classical revival which rumbled through the second half of the eighteenth century had reached its zenith. In 1816 the British nation had purchased Lord Elgin's marbles, the magnificent sculptures of the Parthenon removed by His Britannic Majesty's Ambassador with the connivance of the occupying Turks who had made the Acropolis their Athenian citadel. Since then there had been a steady stream of classical sculpture from Greece and Rome to the European museums. Among the acquisitions of the British Museum alone were the marbles decorated in bas-relief from the tombs of Xanthus, collected by the traveller Charles Fellowes in ancient Lydia; the finely decorated vases from the necropolis of Cumae in Syracuse; friezes representing the legendary battle of Amazons and Greeks from the Mausoleum of Halicarnassus, the royal metropolis of ancient Caria and birthplace of Herodotus; the colossus of a pawless lion from Cnidus. These and many other priceless works of Greco-Roman art resulted in the British Museum having to announce in 1857 that it could no longer find space in its public galleries for all the exhibits which had arrived by the ship-load in the past three or four decades. Rich's examination of the mounds of Babylon and Nineveh may have excited the interest of theologians and antiquarians; to the poet and sculptor the sun-baked bricks of Babylonia with their weird unreadable inscriptions were worth little more than a homily. The glory of the past lay in classical Greece and Rome. Above all, in Homeric legend.

Brave men, wrote Byron, were living before Agamemnon, and after, but they 'shone not on the poet's page' and were thus forgotten. No one could offer more than an informed guess as to when Homer lived, or indeed if he lived at all. Were the epic stories attributed to Homer simply legends, inspired myths, or did they contain, as surely they must, some elements of historical fact? Troy, Mycenae, Tiryns. Surely these places of the creative imagination existed in reality. The poet would almost certainly have chosen actual places for his dramatic settings, as other writers had done over the centuries. Where then were the scenes of the epics of chivalry, of love and war, described in the *Iliad* and the *Odyssey*, the scenes of Paris's seduction of the lovely Helen, of the long and bitter war between the Achaeans and their allies, and the Trojans gathered at King Priam's city? Who, indeed, *were* the Achaeans and the Trojans; what and where Hermione, Asine, Troezen and vine-clad Epidaurus, Aegina and Mases, Arcadians of the land where Mount Cyllene lifted its peak? Herodotus believed that Homer lived some 400 years before his own time, about the ninth century BC, and he spoke of all the early settlers, the non-Greek peoples as Pelasgians, 'barbarians'. Grote, in modern times, was indifferent. 'If any man is inclined to call the unknown ante-Hellenic period of Greece by the name Pelasgic, it is open to him to do so. But this is a name ... no way enlarging our insight into real history.'

Europe's cultural inheritance, its religion, art and science, owed a vast debt to Greece, yet it knew nothing for certain of Greece's own distant past, at any rate of the time before the first Olympiad of 776 BC, the point at which most histories of Greece began. Ironically, Greece knew less of its own ancient history than of its Asiatic and African neighbours in centuries which preceded the classical age.

Almost all that the world knew of the early civilizations of Asia Minor and Egypt was from Greek sources, chiefly Herodotus who, though widely travelled, inevitably relied on second-hand evidence. His contemporary, Thucydides, was harshly critical. In comparing his own history with the great man's Athenian recitations, he remarked contemptuously that Herodotus's words were perhaps lacking in charm 'due to the absence of mythical elements'.

Darius's inscription at Behistun was only forty or so years older than Herodotus, relating as it did the events of the first year after the King's accession, 522–21 BC. Yet the Greek historian depended for his description of the Persian monument on Hecataeus of Miletus, who constructed his *Periodos* or map of the earth on a bronze tablet which contained the royal road from Sardis to Susa and a list of all the satrapies of the Persian Empire. In fact, Herodotus had not seen the inscription of Darius, though he had travelled close by, and his list of the satraps of Achaemenid Persia was unreliable, even omitting Hyrcania altogether.

'The Greeks all alone fought 46 nations at Marathon', wrote the historian. The Bible speaks of 127 nations, and the original Persian list probably contained something like that number within the count of its satrapies. The Greek historian was lacking, too, in his account of the religions of Persia, making no mention of the essential dualism – the contrasting elements of light and dark, good and evil – at the heart of the religion variously described as Mazdeism (Magism) or Zoroastrianism (Fire Worship). Generally, the Greeks and their historians ignored those parts of the Magian ritual which they found not to their taste, and preserved those which were congenial to their own form of mysticism. But hindsight should be tempered with humility. In seven of the standard works of reference on Persian religion published in the present century, most with the imprints of major universities, dates for Zoroaster based on readings of the Old Persian texts are given variously as c.1400–1000, c.1700–1500, 630–541, 628–551, and c.1000–600 BC! We owe to Herodotus more than to any other source our knowledge of the Median power from the eighth to the sixth centuries BC, its alliance with the Babylonians in the final destruction of Assyria, and the merging of Media and Persia in the Achaemenian dynasty from 549 BC.

Herodotus was almost entirely ignorant, however, of the true history and the might of Assyria, a nation whose influence on the great land mass flanking Greece's Asiatic boundary was decisive. It may be argued in his defence that after its destruction and the fall of Nineveh in 606 BC, the very name 'Assyria' was despised and was quickly blotted from the memories of all who had suffered under its yoke. Xenophon's army retreating from the Persians marched past the

Contemporary drawing of the Grave Circle at Mycenae, with Schliemann and wife at centre of composition, 1875.

ruins of Nineveh without even knowing what they were. Of Babylon and Egypt the Greek historians had first-hand knowledge, though they lacked the detailed information that the bricks of Claudius Rich might have provided. In any event, Greek history as it had come down to the western world would only be checked when the great libraries of the ancient lands disgorged their contents – the tens of thousands of inscribed tablets and cylinders which Layard and Botta, and their successors, had begun to unearth from the depredations caused by Scyths, Medes, Lydians and, finally, Babylonians and Persians. Greeks seldom spoke the language of Egypt, the country they came to dominate in the last stages of its antiquity. Their history, useful though it was, found its substance in the tittle-tattle of the market place and the traditions handed on by priest and courtesan. Herodotus was jumbled and inaccurate in his account of the pyramids and the chronology of the kingly pyramid-builders of Giza. Diodorus, writing at the time of Roman ascendancy, merely repeated his errors. Herodotus was, on the other hand, astonishingly reliable in his description of ancient Media, which may have been the legacy of the Median satraps who once ruled the western seaboard of

Asia Minor where his birthplace, Halicarnassus, lay and where tradition was rich in the history of the Medes. For the Father of History there were, generally speaking, few written sources. He was almost entirely reliant on observation and hearsay. The wonder is that he knew so much and was right about so many things.

As the excavations in Assyria gathered pace and the excavators moved southward along the converging Tigris and Euphrates rivers to the more ancient sites of Babylonia, increasing evidence of Greek familiarity with the empires and royal households of Mesopotamia began to come to light. Clay tablets from the royal libraries would demonstrate a literary connection, even dictionaries of Babylonian words translated into Greek. Many questions would be answered. Even more would be left unresolved. The historian has always been hostage to the wishful memories and vanities of kings and the pretences of priests; to say nothing of the imperfections of the official record. The task of archaeology was not to make material evidence comply with preconceived notions but to put history to the test by building up a picture of everyday life in the communities it unearthed; humble dwellings as well as royal palaces, simple articles of folk art as well as the mighty monuments and precious adornments of the powerful and rich. Thus they could construct a model of society as it was. Such a discipline was doubly important in the case of Greece, for the ancient history of its peoples, so important a part of the intellectual tradition of Europe, derived wholly from legend and mythology.

Grote's *History of Greece* was written between the years 1843 and 1856. From the first volume, which dealt with the 'Legendary Period', to the twelfth and last which embraced the Hellenistic world of Alexander, it was praised so widely and unstintingly that his wife was compelled to write: 'Thus I became, for once, witness of a state of feeling on his part approaching to gratified self-love, which at times would pierce through that imperturbable veil of modesty . . .'. Fifty years later, with a call for an abridged and edited version of the work, Grote's editors, Mitchell and Caspari, were able to dispense with the whole of the first part, the first ten chapters of the second part, and over fifty subsequent chapters with the apology:

> . . . we are now in possession of a mass of evidence which fifty years ago was lacking. This new evidence is of every kind – literary, epigraphic, numismatic, artistic. The very word 'archaeology' has acquired a wholly new connotation. Half a century ago archaeology was, to most people, merely the search for ancient objects of beauty, regarded as curios and collected by uncritical enthusiasts without reference to their relative age or their historical meaning. It is scarcely an exaggeration to say that archaeology was then merely a hobby; it is no exaggeration to say that it is now perhaps the most important part of the science of ancient history.

Detail of birds from an Egyptian tomb, from drawing by Mrs N. de G. Davies.

Bronze of Anubis, the Egyptian god of death from early dynastic times.

Grote's *History* had enjoyed little more than twenty years' recognition as the standard English work on Greece when the Homeric legends were put to the test. The English historian had said, '... if we are asked whether there was not really some such historical Trojan war as this, our answer must be, that as the possibility of it cannot be denied, so neither can the reality of it be affirmed ...'

In 1868 the wealthy German businessman Heinrich Schliemann, obsessed since childhood by the Homeric epics, examined the Turkish coastal stretch which had long been known to the world as the Plain of Troy. He looked for the 'two lovely springs' of the *Iliad*, the sources of Scamander's eddying stream, one hot and the other cold. He found many such water spouts, and so he settled instinctively for the site of Hissarlik, close to the Hellenic and Roman town of 'New Troy', Novum Ilium. Schliemann was the passionate amateur. Unlike the French and British excavators of Assyria, he enjoyed neither political nor academic patronage. He was a self-made man, the son of a Protestant Pastor of Mecklenburg, who spoke no Greek but knew Latin and encouraged his son to read the classics. He was a merchant prince who had risen from errand-boy to millionaire, learning dozens of languages on the way, and always keeping at the front of his mind the childhood ambition to rediscover Troy.

'Thanks to God', he wrote, 'my firm belief in the existence of that Troy has never forsaken me amid all the vicissitudes of my eventful career; but it was not destined for me to realize till in the autumn of my life, and then without Minna – nay, far from her – our sweet dreams of fifty years ago'. Schliemann was in his fiftieth year when his eighty hired workmen began to dig the first trench at Hissarlik in September 1871. He had achieved the first of his ambitions, financial self-sufficiency, early in life. His first fortune was made in Hamburg, Amsterdam and St Petersburg, chiefly from the dye of the indigo plant, his plant, his command of languages, especially Russian, helping him on the way. He visited America during the gold rush and in 1851 he sought citizenship in the New World and made another fortune, almost accidentally, out of gold-dust and banking. His boyhood romance with the farmer's daughter Minna, the only companion of his youth who failed to scoff at his devotion to Homer, came to nothing and he married a plain but 'sensible and clever' Russian girl, Ekaterina Petrovna Lyshin. She turned out to be cold and indifferent, but the sensuous, infatuated Schliemann tried for fifteen years with entreaty and bribe to win her loyalty. In the end she returned to Russia and he sought refuge in the Aegean islands, following his hero Agamemnon from place to place along that route which led inexorably to Hades.

He returned to America in 1869, taking up residence in Indianapolis in order to qualify for citizenship, and obtained a divorce in the same year. He had decided that his next wife must be Greek, his own Helen perhaps, and through the

Heinrich Schliemann, about 1877.

intervention of his one-time teacher Archbishop Theokletos Vimpos, he was introduced to Sophia Engastromenos, a draper's daughter who turned out to be in every respect the 'ideal' companion; intelligent, beautiful, and above all 'enthusiastic about Homer and about a rebirth of my beloved Greece'.

Sophia was to be at his side from the first days of his excavation of Troy. 'My dear wife, an Athenian lady, who is an enthusiastic admirer of Homer, and knows almost the whole of the *Iliad* by heart, is present at the excavations from morning to night. I will not say anything about our mode of life in this solitude, where everything is wanting, and where we have to take four grains of quinine every morning as a precaution against the pestilential malaria', he wrote in October 1871.

Work went on with what he called 'utmost energy'. Energetic it was. It was also indiscriminate. Allowance must be made for the fact that he had no good precedent to guide him. The pioneer excavators of Mesopotamia had shown little regard for stratification, for the preservation of later levels of habitation through which they sliced and hacked their way to reach the palaces which contained the most desirable treasures. In Egypt, excavation had not yet superseded the ordinary devices of tomb robbery. But Schliemann's depredations were of a different order. He was devil-driven by an impetuous, almost crazed determination to reach Troy. The Assyrian diggers had tried within the confines of their crude technology to work their way round rather than through buildings and stone hurdles. Schliemann paid no heed to anything resembling an obstacle. Though he had visited the Syrian provinces of the Ottoman Sultan, who ruled over Greece also, he cared little for the achievements of the Assyriologists on the other side of the Euphrates. In trying to reach Troy with such singlemindedness, he destroyed much that might have been of the greatest value to historians at the intervening levels.

From Hissarlik he wrote at the end of 1871:

> I made an immense cutting on the face of the steep northern slope, about 66 feet from my last year's work. This cutting was made in direction due south, and extended across the highest plateau, and was so broad that it embraced the whole building, the foundations of which, consisting of large hewn stones, I had already laid open last year to a depth of from only 1 to 3 feet below the surface. According to an exact measurement, this building, which appears to belong to the first century after Christ, is about 59 feet in length, and 43 feet in breadth. I have of course had all these foundations removed as, being within my excavations, they are of no use and would only have been in the way.

By April 1872, according to the calculation of his site engineer, M. Laurent, he had removed in seventeen days of that month alone some 8,500 cubic metres (about 11,000 cubic yards) of debris from the mound of Hissarlik. That amounted to nearly 700 cubic yards each day, a figure which would not disgrace the most highly mechanized contractor of the twentieth century engaged in nothing more sensitive than road building. By now he was beginning to scent success. 'We have already advanced the platform 49 feet into the hill, but to my extreme surprise we have not yet reached the primary soil.' At depths all the way down from ten feet onward he had found fine marble figures with owl's faces and female girdles. '... upon one there are in addition two female breasts ...'. There were vases too with the same themes, with moulded covers shaped as owls' heads. He was convinced that they represented a goddess; one and the same goddess: '*What* goddess is it who is here found so repeatedly, and is, moreover, the only one to be found, upon the idols, drinking-cups and vases? The answer is: – she must be the Ilian Athena, and this indeed agrees perfectly with the statement of Homer'. Here was the 'goddess Athena with the owl's face' of Homer. He was nowhere near the level of Troy yet. Later Greeks and Romans had built over the remains of whatever ancient city lay beneath. Alexander the Great had made sacrificial offerings at the temple which stood on the site before he departed for the East in the fourth century BC. To Heinrich Schliemann nothing must stand in the way of discovering Troy and its remains.

An Englishman, Frank Calvert, who acted as American Consul in the Dardanelles region, owned half the area of the Hissarlik site. By June 1872 Schliemann had extended the area of his dig with the agreement of Calvert, who had himself excavated there – if somewhat half-heartedly – and who had probably drawn it to the German's attention in the first place. A Scottish explorer, Charles Maclaren, had also noted the place as the likely site of Troy as early as 1822 in a *Dissertation on the Topography of the Plain of Troy* and Grote had opted for it. The condition was that Schliemann shared with Calvert any objects he found.

He worked through the hot summer and freezing winter of 1872, his young wife always at his side helping to sort the pottery and marble idols, paying his large workforce above-average wages to ensure that they applied themselves to his almost maniacal excavation programme. As the 'finds' grew in volume so the destruction increased in magnitude.

> As it was my object to excavate Troy, which I expected to find in one of the lower cities, I was forced to demolish many interesting ruins in the upper strata; as for example, at a depth of twenty feet below the surface, the ruins of a prehistoric building ten feet high, the walls of which consisted of hewn blocks of limestone perfectly smooth and cemented with clay.

He found a 'pretty bastion' near the surface, composed of large blocks of limestone, which he thought must date from the time of Lysimachus, Alexander's general and titular king of Thrace in 303 BC. But though the bastion was of 'Homeric proportions' it was too late and was consigned to the rubbish heap.

The frantic search went on into 1873. The previous year had drawn to a close with an outbreak of marsh fever which affected his workmen and Sophia. Schliemann had begun to lose his early drive and enthusiasm. His considerable financial resources had been drained by the scale and extravagance of the work at Hissarlik. He began to look for official support, especially from the newly established German Empire of Wilhelm I. No offers were forthcoming, however, though Dr Ernst Curtius, who was to lead the Olympia excavations a year or two hence and who became a pioneer of the scientific archaeology that followed Schliemann's work at Troy, expressed some interest. To Schliemann's financial worries was added the problem of an abrupt change of mood on the part of the Ottoman Governor, who suddenly withdrew the *firman* or royal warrant issued in the name of the Sultan of the Turkish Empire.

Schliemann had asked for trouble. Towards the end of the previous season he had found a remarkable two-handled goblet, 'the *amphikypellon* of Homer', and

Above: Old woman in terracotta, Athens, c.420 BC.

Right: Terracotta lute player, no provenance, c.300 BC.

even more to his liking a beautiful relief sculpture which had perhaps adorned a temple. It was probably Hellenistic but even the German's Homeric prejudice gave way before the sight of the Apollo triglyph as it came to be called. He decided to cut off parts of the sculpture to enable him to smuggle it more easily out of Turkey into the now independent kingdom of Greece where he had bought a home. Calvert talked him out of that act of desecration, but he nevertheless exported the object illegally to his home, and then proceeded to have plaster casts made for the classical departments of various universities, including

Berlin, and the British Museum. The Ottoman authorities must have heard of his activities. It was hardly surprising that they withdrew his authority to dig. Still, they gave him verbal permission without renewing his *firman*. As with the British and French removal of the gems of the Athenian Acropolis fifty years earlier, 'export' was a thinly disguised solecism for theft when it came to complying with Ottoman regulations regarding archaeological finds.

The third season began in chaos. Schliemann's own account of the excavation of Troy was published in German as *Trojanische Altertuemer*. Its English title was *Troy and its Remains*. There were significant differences in the two versions. In both there are references to north-west corner, northern slope, platforms and trenches; the kind of terminology used by Layard in his book *Nineveh and Its Remains*. But there is no evidence of a genuine plan or organization. Schliemann jumps from place to place, claiming discoveries which could only have been made at different levels and in different parts of the site: Hellenic, classical, Homeric and then, suddenly, Christian. As he went further down the great trench his men had dug he was convinced that every building was Priam's Palace, every paved road the route to the city gate – to Homer's Scaean Gate. At one stage he was so sure that he had struck Priam's Palace that he decided to keep local sightseers away by spreading the story that Christ had passed that way on a visit to the Trojan King. It would have been a naive Christian who swallowed the story, but since most of the local inhabitants were Moslems its point is obscure indeed. The story, given in his German account, is omitted from the English version.

In March 1873 he began to excavate a pile of masonry which constituted two walls, each about twenty feet high, described by him as 'the Great Tower'. Eventually he came to a well-paved street, seventy feet wide, which ran in a south-westerly direction. A hundred workmen were promptly set to work to dig through the ground in the same direction and thus follow the road to what must surely be a great building. The roadway was covered with a thick layer of yellow, red and black ash mixed with partly vitrified fragments of brick and stone. The ruins of a large building gradually emerged. To the north-east two gateways were revealed, twenty feet apart, almost hidden by piles of impacted rubbish. Without producing the slightest evidence, he announced that he had found the Scaean Gate and the Palace of Priam. The world waited impatiently for a sight of the treasures he had unearthed. Scholars who had learnt of his almost ruthless methods of digging were sceptical. If his methods were those of an impatient amateur, his claims and conclusions were almost certainly suspect. The overwhelming view of the academic world remained unchanged: there was not a jot of real evidence that Priam ever existed outside the poetic imagination of Homer.

In May he wrote: 'Now, however, we are weary, and since we have attained our goal and realised the great ideal of our life, we shall finally cease our efforts in Troy on June 15th'. He kept a diary but its content was not known at the time. All that the world then knew was contained in his letters to friends and relatives, and to museum curators, subsequently brought together in his book, which he began to discuss with the publisher Brockhaus of Leipzig in 1873. He spoke of the 'Treasure', or 'golden objects' found in the Palace of Priam. There was no evidence as to where this treasure had been found or when. But treasure there was. Schliemann gave various accounts, most of which were subsequently revised or abandoned. In May, Sophia had been called to Athens where her father was dying. She was called back by her husband who had momentous news. He was able to show her the 'golden riches' of which Homer had written. Within two days of his announcement of closing the site of Hissarlik he and Sophia were on their way back to Greece. The 'Treasure of Priam' had gone before them, smuggled out of Asiatic Turkey with the help of the Calverts. 'I, therefore, take the liberty to deposit with you six baskets and a bag, begging you will kindly lock them up, and not allow by any means the Turk to touch them', he wrote to Frank Calvert's brother Frederick.

The finds, carried conspiratorially to their hut at the top of the Hissarlik mound, according to Schliemann's written account, were breathtaking, but not as unusual as their discoverer imagined. They consisted of innumerable items but by far the most eye-catching were two gold diadems, the largest of which contained ninety pendant chains made up of tiny heart-shaped plates of gold, attached with other fringe-chains to a gold head-band of the finest workmanship. Each of the hanging chains terminated in a small 'Trojan idol' at shoulder level. Altogether the piece contained 16,353 separate gold pieces. In addition, there were thousands of gold rings, sixty gold earrings and bracelets, as well as bottles, goblets and other items of the same precious metal. And there were bronze weapons and silver and copper vases. The vision of Helen was not hard to conjure. It is no wonder that Schliemann went to great pains to hide the treasure that he insisted was 'his personal property'.

Schliemann's fame was immediate. But it was founded not on evidence of the discovery of Homer's Troy and the treasures of its king but simply on the German's announcement of his discoveries. They were taken at face value. He claimed to have solved 'the greatest and most important of all the historical riddles'. Scholars may have doubted his word, the public at large was only too willing to believe him, especially when photographs of his wife appeared – looking for all the world like a stage version of the incomparable Helen of Troy – wearing the jewels from Priam's treasure chest which, with her help, he had removed, reckless and unthinking of danger, from behind a large copper object embedded beneath a fortification wall. Where was this wall, and when did the

Sophia Schliemann wearing the jewels from 'Priam's Troy'.

discovery occur? Not for a hundred years would plausible answers be forthcoming.

Schliemann's own reservations were obvious from his letters in the days following the supposed closure of the site. On 17 June he admitted that he had probably cut through the layer of Homer's Troy in his implacable belief that the Trojans were the earliest occupants of the place and therefore to be traced at its lowest level. 'In consequence of my former mistaken idea, that Troy was to be found on the primary soil or close above it, I unfortunately, in 1871 and 1872, destroyed a large portion of the city, for I at that time broke down all the house-walls in the higher strata which obstructed my way ...' And then: 'I formerly believed that the most ancient people who inhabited this site were the Trojans ... but I now perceive that Priam's people were the succeeding nation'. Finally, 'I am extremely disappointed at being obliged to give so small a plan of Troy; nay, I had wished to make it a thousand times larger, but I value truth above everything ...'. The claims, sanguine yet tending to face both ways, aroused great excitement in the world at large, though most scholars remained doubtful that he had even found the site of Troy. Most continued to insist that the Palace of Priam and the Scaean Gate, the scenes of mighty battles fought by Achilles and Hector, by Achaean and Trojan on the Troad, the Plain of Troy, remained the figments of poetic imagination. In particular, Germany's formidable band of classical scholars ridiculed his alleged discoveries. With the passing of time, the claims and the verdict would still be equivocal, but Schliemann was not a man to wait on posterity. While his workmen sifted through the great piles of earth deposited near the mound in the hope of finding items of gold that had been cast aside in the rush for Troy (some of them were arrested by the Turks for the theft of just such articles), Schliemann went to Athens to propose a new venture to the authorities. He found the Greeks as sceptical as the Turks. For the next two years he worked on his book about the discovery of Troy, fought several law suits in Turkey, and pestered the Greek authorities for permission to dig at Homer's Mycenae, the city of Agamemnon. He was haunted by the thought that the treasures of Priam he had so carefully concealed might be stolen, and he seldom left his Athens home. But by 1875 even Troy was cast aside by the vibrant contemplation of Mycenae, golden Mycenae, for which there was more recent testimony than was the case with Troy.

He had applied in 1873 for permission to dig at Mycenae and Olympia when he finished at Troy. To his annoyance, the Olympia concession was given to the Imperial Government of Germany whose Institute of Archaeology, founded in Prussia in 1829, was unlikely to nominate the amateur Schliemann, a voluntary exile and, if he was to be believed, a citizen of the United States, to undertake the work. Unabashed, Schliemann decided to dig at Mycenae. But the Greeks were adamant. Early in 1874, having spread the story that he was preparing for a journey abroad, he covertly hired twenty men and began to dig secretly at the acropolis or citadel of Mycenae. He found a few terracotta figures, some ancient pottery sherds, and an undecorated stela. The pottery figures were of a female with large eyes. Schliemann, true to his Trojan form, decided without further ado that they represented the goddess Hera, Homer's *bo-opis*, analogous to the owl-eyed Athene of Troy. Here, within two or three days of hurried exploration, was proof that he was at Agamemnon's city. Experts had long known that the region of Morea which lay between Corinth and Argos, was the site of Mycenae. But there were differences of opinion as to where the tombs of the royal house of Atreus might lie. Most took the words of Pausanius's *Itinerary* to imply that they were within the walls of the lower city. Schliemann interpreted the Roman geographer as meaning that they were within the ramparts of the citadel itself. Nothing less than the tomb of King Agamemnon would satisfy him. For the moment the matter was academic; after five days the authorities caught up with

Wilhelm Doerpfeld as professor at Heidelberg. Schliemann's assistant at Troy, excavator of Mycenae and Olympia.

him and the local prefect issued instructions that digging should cease.

Schliemann sent a letter of complaint about his 'shabby treatment' to King George of the Hellenes before embarking on a European tour. At last the world would learn at first hand of the discovery of Troy. Not until 1876, when he returned to Greece glowing in the admiration and flattery of all Europe, save his native Germany, was he finally given permission to continue digging at Mycenae.

Mycenae, August 19, 1876
I arrived here by the same road which Pausanius describes. The distance from Argos is only 50 *stadia*, or 5.8 English miles ... The situation at Mycenae is beautifully described by Homer, 'In the depth of the horse-feeding Argos'.

Sixty-three workmen divided into three parties constituted his workforce. 'I put twelve men at the Lion's Gate, to open the passage into the acropolis; I set forty-three to dig at a distance of 40 feet from that gate, a trench 113 feet long and 113 feet broad; and the remaining eight I ordered to dig a trench on the south side of the Treasury in the lower city, near the Lion's Gate, in search of the entrance.'

He had fixed his eye on the circular terrace south-east of the Lion Gate when he dug his illegal trenches in 1874. Knowing their man, the Greeks had stipulated that all finds belonged to the nation. Overseers of the Greek Archaeological Society would have absolute discretion. Schliemann's only privilege was the right of 'first publication'. The principal overseer was Panagiotes Stamatakes, a man who would subsequently earn a high reputation as an archaeologist and student of Mycenaean history. The haughty Schliemann treated him as a 'mere government clerk', brushing him aside as an interfering fool. Sophia was sent to Athens on several occasions to plead for the removal of Stamatakes. The guns of the overseer and the Greek authorities were spiked by Schliemann's almost incredible good fortune.

By the second week of September a catalogue of rich finds had been compiled, though as at Troy the journals gave no real indication of where or exactly when the discoveries were made. There were diadems, drinking cups, belts, seal rings, breast plates, face masks and dozens of other objects of solid gold. In five grave shafts within the area discribed as the *tholos* or 'treasury' where Sophia had been in charge, he also found ceramics, bronzes, copper articles, gems, weapons and, last but by no means least, the 'remains of at least fifteen bodies'. Here, surely, were the ruins that Thucydides had seen long after the event, the sights that Pausanius had recorded in the second century AD: the Lion Gate, the 'treasures' of Atreus and his sons, the tombs of Agamemnon and his companions, murdered by Aegisthus the seducer of Clytemnestra after they had returned from the victory over Troy with Priam's daughter Cassandra as their prize. But the tragic poets make Clytemnestra alone the killer of her husband, and Orestes the avenger. Schliemann was sure that everything obeyed Homeric tradition. In the last grave that he emptied the face of the mummified man was reasonably well-preserved. He lifted the golden face mask reverently and kissed it. Then he sent a telegram to Athens, announcing that he had found a warrior resembling Agamemnon as it 'had previously appeared to him'. Others who visited the site said that there were eighteen bodies, including two infants, thus evoking suggestions of Cassandra's two children murdered in the avenging wrath of Orestes. Scholars were soon to doubt some of Schliemann's latest discoveries. Charles T. Newton, Keeper of the British Museum, quickly drew attention to the fact that vases from Rhodes of the same style as those found at Mycenae could be dated with reasonable accuracy to 1400 BC, some two hundred years earlier than the date now generally accepted for the Trojan war, c. 1200 BC, according to the evidence of Schliemann's own finds at Hissarlik.

The dazzling finds from Mycenae continued to surface.

The five bodies of this fourth tomb were literally smothered in Jewels . . . all

Excavation in the Troad, 1877–8.

Opposite: 'Treasury of Atreus' at Mycenae, from contemporary drawing.

of which ... show unequivocal marks of the funeral fires.

We find copper vessels ... continually referred to in the *Iliad*, together with tripods, as prizes in the games or as presents.

Close to the copper vessel with the gold buttons, I found a cow's head of silver, with two long golden horns ...

In the Cyclopean houses by the Lion Gate, he found fragments of a vase – the famous Warrior Vase, showing bronze-age soldiers on their way to war. The sense of the pictorial legend was obvious. The vase would eventually be housed in a building of its own in Athens, a magnificent tribute to the bronze age of Greece. The National Museum at Athens would be made the richest in the world by the Mycenaean finds of Schliemann which could only be described as breathtaking in their splendour. Characteristically, the claims were as sensational as the discoveries themselves.

Mycenae, 6 December, 1876
For the first time since its capture by the Argives in 468 BC, and so for the first time in 2,344 years the acropolis of Mycenae has a garrison, whose watchfires seen by night throughout the whole Plain of Argos carry back the mind to the watch kept for Agamemnon's return ... and the signal which warned Clytemnestra and her paramour of his approach ...

There were many more finds of magnificence and great interest before work at Mycenae was brought to a close in the spring of 1877. Schliemann had kept the world informed of his spectacular progress through despatches to *The Times* in London, contributing six long articles which were published in eight issues by an 'exclusive' arrangement. They formed the basis of his book *Mycenae*, published a year later in German and English editions, and soon after in French.

In March 1877, within days of the closing of the site, Schliemann arrived in England to deliver a lecture to the Society of Antiquaries. The welcome was ecstatic. The *Illustrated London News* had published brief accounts of his work at

Mycenae during February, with drawings of objects which he had shown privately to Lord and Lady Salisbury in Athens. Since then the Royal Bank of Greece had taken the articles into its custody. The illustrations were barely adequate and the reports suggested a healthy scepticism on the part of the writer.

> The object marked No. 1 in our illustration is one of the thin gold masks which had covered the faces of the skeletons in Agamemnon's tomb. These are extremely curious, but, alas! extremely ugly, the features being very coarsely fashioned, with sharp lines and angles, like the face a child might make out of wood with his pocket-knife. If Agamemnon is to be judged by the portrait of him, thus disinterred, he cannot certainly have represented the Greek traditional beauty; and if his brother was like him, it is little to be wondered at that Helen should have preferred Paris.

That report was dated 24 February 1877.

In March, the much vaunted lecture was delivered at Burlington House in London. The audience included Mr Gladstone, Lord Aberdeen, the Master of Trinity, the Poet Laureate (Alfred Lord Tennyson), Lord Acton, MPs, and academic luminaries of every kind. Little more than twelve months earlier he had lectured to a similar audience in London on the discoveries at Troy. He was unequivocal in his references to the Mycenaean excavations. The ruins, he said, could hardly have deteriorated since Pausanius visited them in AD 170. He described the great wall and its Lion Gate, the work of the Cyclopes who built the wall for Paetus in Tiryns. Then he quoted Pausanius:

> There is a sepulchre of Atreus, with the tombs of Agamemnon's companions, who on their return from Ilium were killed at dinner by Aegisthus ... There is a tomb of Agamemnon and that of his charioteer, Eurymedon. Telemados and Pelops were deposited in the same sepulchre, for it is said that Cassandra bore these twins, and that, when still little babies, they were slaughtered by Aegisthus, together with their parents ... Clytemnestra and Aegisthus were buried at a little distance from the wall, because they were thought unworthy to have their tombs inside of it ... .

Thus, Schliemann arrived at the nub of his thesis. Other scholars, the most noted of his own and past times, had misunderstood Pausanius's references to the 'walls'. They thought he meant the walls of the city. He, Schliemann, on the other hand, had always understood the words to refer to the great wall of the citadel. Three years earlier (while working illegally), he had sunk 34 shafts in different parts of the acropolis to search for the tombs. In 28 of them he found nothing, but

'Agamemnon's mask' from Mycenae.

the other 6, in the west and south-west terraces, had produced encouraging results. There followed a discussion of the finds in that amalgam of scholarship and boyish enthusiasm for heroics so characteristic of Schliemann. In an aside, he told how impossible it was for his wife and himself to pass by Tiryns on their way from the village of Nauplia to the site at Mycenae – 'the Royal city of Proteus and the birthplace of Hercules ... its huge Cyclopean walls, deemed by the Greeks themselves the work of the demons, and more stupendous than the pyramids of Egypt'. They had been spellbound, the more so since 'the pickaxe of no explorer had ever touched its virgin soil'.

When *Mycenae* was published by Mr John Murray it contained a preface by Britain's classicist Prime Minister, William Ewart Gladstone, an essay which combined much knowledge with seemly caution. In a passage which would cause some surprise if it came from the hand of a prime minister or president of modern times, he wrote:

[111]

The buildings improperly called Cyclopean, and still more improperly endowed with the alternative name of Pelasgian, have long been known, more or less, to exist in Argolis; but Dr Schliemann had thrown some light on what I may perhaps be allowed to call their diversity of style. He admits three forms found in this kind of building. I have objected to the current names, the first because it does not inform; the second because it misleads, for these buildings have no connection with the Pelasgian tribes. What they indicate is the handiwork of the great constructing race or races, made up of several elements, who migrated into Greece, and elsewhere on the Mediterranean, from the south and east, and who exhibit as usual, though perhaps not an invariable connection with the Poseidon-worship, a worship with which the Cyclopean name is, through the Odyssey, perceptibly associated, and which is one of the main keys, as I have long been persuaded, wherewith in time to unlock . . . the secrets of antiquity.

In the beehive-like building 'which is rather loosely called the Treasury of Atreus', Gladstone noted the enormous slabs found over the doorway, one of them supposedly weighing over 130 tons. 'I only refer to them for the sake of reminding the reader that, as I think, we must be prepared, in this and other matters, freely to recognise the hand of the foreigner at work; who brought with him into Greece attainments, not to be despised, of material civilisation'. The 'Grand Old Man' obviously shared some of the reservations of Mr Newton of the British Museum, quoting that authority liberally. But on the whole he was in sympathy with 'the famous explorer', as in 'the rude figures of cows, and cow-heads, pointing to the traditional worship of Hera, which Schliemann asks us to connect with the use of *Boopis* (cow-eyed) as a staple epithet of this goddess in the Poems'. This appeared to Gladstone to be 'a reasonable demand'. He went further: 'We know that upon some of the Egyptian monuments the goddess Isis, mated with Osiris, is represented in human figure with a cow's head. This was a mode of exhibiting deity congenial to the spirit of Egyptian immigration'. In a footnote he added, 'Since this Preface was put in type, the fragments of an ostrich egg, originally mistaken for an alabaster vase, have been tested and verified. This object seems to afford new indication of prehistoric relations between Mycenae and Egypt'.

Schliemann would return to Mycenae and to Troy, and would go on to Tiryns, still giving free rein to his Homeric obsession, seldom stopping to think of the wider implications of his finds. His discoveries were more or less incidental to his single-minded dedication to Homer. Nevertheless, they were considerable in quantity and they would contribute significantly to an understanding of ancient Greece.

Schliemann could not see that Pausanius had been unable to observe the tombs he described in Homeric terms, since in Antonine times they were concealed by accumulated earth and rubbish. Neither could he see that Pausanius was wrong in calling the *tholos* of Mycenae 'treasuries' rather than tombs, which they patently were. He insisted that the shaft graves he had revealed were all of the same period, hastily dug. It was a view designed to confirm his thesis that they were associated with the death of Agamemnon. Stamatakes, the despised overseer, found a sixth grave a year after Schliemann left the site and realized that the shaft graves were of different ages, many of them earlier than the Homeric scenes they were made to depict. Homeric legend also demanded cremation at the funeral pyre, and so to Schliemann signs of burning were proof of cremation. In fact, indications of fire and ashes may just as well have pointed to animal or even human sacrifice at the burial ceremonies.

It was the less spectacular finds at Mycenae which would contribute most to the building up of a picture of prehistoric Greece. Glassware, pottery and bronzes, the ostrich egg and alabaster vessels, ivories; pointing to Egyptian and other foreign influences from the still enigmatic regions of Tuscany, Syria, the Aegean islands, Cyprus and Rhodes. Already wares similar to those of Mycenae had been found at Ephesus in Asia Minor, at Thera and Cyprus. The ruins of prehistoric Greece had not so far produced documentation such as came from the great library of Nineveh to confirm or deny Schliemann's essentially literary view of the ancient world. In 1882, he took on a brilliant young assistant, the German Wilhelm Döerpfeld, who would conduct much more scientific investigations of the sites of ancient Greece and re-examine his master's testimony. And he would tell Schliemann magisterially, 'Scientific questions cannot be decided by abuse, but only by objective proof'. In 1886 the two men went to Crete and dug there briefly. But Schliemann, against Döerpfeld's advice, insisted on a significant share of any finds, and arguments with the authorities led him to abandon the project and to go to Egypt instead. An Englishman would come in his place to provide the most profound evidence of Greece's prehistoric past. Others would cast such a shadow of doubt on some of Schliemann's claims as to make him out a liar and a fraud. For the moment it was enough that he returned to the world a civilization which flourished from about 1600 BC to 1150 BC.

5

Egypt and the Pharaohs

Mariette and Petrie in the Nile Valley

Champollion supplied the key to the decipherment of the Egyptian hieroglyphic script on 27 September 1822, in the form of a famous letter to M. Dacier, *Secrétaire perpétuel de l'Académie royale des Inscriptions et Belles-Lettres, relative a l'alphabet des hiéroglyphes phonétiques.*

His was the supreme contribution to Egyptology, but there were other pioneers whose work was scarcely less important in the long drawn-out process of unravelling the history of civilization in the Nile Valley.

The gifted artist Vivant Denon, who accompanied the Napoleonic General Desaix on his river journey to Aswan and the discovery of the islands of Philae and Elephantine, had taken advantage of his official duties as illustrator to the French Institute by bringing out his own book, *Voyages dans la basse et la haute Egypte,* in 1801. That work alone was sufficient to whet the world's appetite. When the sumptuous *Description de l'Egypte* was published between the years 1809 and 1813, recording in beautiful engravings based on Denon's original drawings the work of the French Scientific and Artistic Commission, Europe and America began to share Napoleon's own vision of a world much larger and more fascinating than anything that had been imagined hitherto. 'This Europe of ours is tiny', the Emperor had told the learned men of the *Institut*, 'only in the East, where 600 million human beings live, can we found great empires and carry through great revolutions'.

Within three years of Bonaparte's invasion, the French were expelled from Egypt. Two years later their British successors made a somewhat ignominious withdrawal. Muhammad Ali and his family despatched the Beys and Mamluks who had been the covert power behind the viceregal rule of the Ottoman Turks, and entered upon a 'perpetual' reign. In an episode as deplorable as it was brief, the work of the French artists and academics who had followed on the heels of Napoleon was a glittering exception. The *Description* contained a great many hieroglyphics but was silent as to their meaning. The French scholar de Sacy, thought the problem of translation was 'scientifically insoluble'.

The Rosetta stone, of which the French took copies from a wax cast before it fell into British hands, contained a Greek inscription of fifty-four lines, a demotic text of thirty-two lines, and fourteen lines of the pictographic or hieroglyphic signs. Clearly the same thing was being said in three languages. The Greek was easy enough. It recorded divine honours bestowed on Ptolemy Epiphanes by the high priests. In 1815 a dual inscription, in Greek and hieroglyphic, came to light on an obelisk found at Philae. The eccentric British consul Henry Salt had acquired the stone through his 'field agent', the intractable Italian giant Giovanni Belzoni, who had already used his massive bulk (he stood six foot eight inches in his socks) to remove the colossal head of Ramesses II from the Ramesseum at Thebes to the Nile and thence to Alexandria. Some idea of the man's strength may be gained from the fact that he dragged the seven-ton granite head on rollers over a three-mile stretch of swampy ground. The Ramesses head was presented to the British Museum in 1817 by Salt and J.L. Burckhardt, the scholar-traveller of the Arab lands. The obelisk was given by Salt to another noted scholar among Egyptian wayfarers, William J. Bankes MP, who installed it in his west-country garden in the presence of the Duke of Wellington, in 1839, after a hazardous journey in the course of which the pier at Philae collapsed under its weight (it was twenty-two feet long and weighed six tons). Meanwhile, Bankes had been able to identify the name of Cleopatra within one of the stone's cartouches, with the aid of the Greek inscription on the obelisk pedestal. That was in 1816, six years before Champollion's decipherment and his announcement of a working hypothesis.

Salt and the Italian-born consul of France, Bernardino Drovetti, became the great rival collectors of antiquities of this early nineteenth-century period. Ironically, a large part of Salt's collection, made with Belzoni's mighty contribution of muscle and impudence, was purchased by the Louvre; while Drovetti's equally valuable acquisitions went to Turin and Berlin. A British physician and antiquarian, Thomas Young, had also used the Philae obelisk, along with papyrus texts which were then available, to isolate the hieroglyphic groups which stood for 'Ptolemy' and 'Cleopatra'; and he was able to show most importantly that the demotic texts were essentially cursive forms of the hieroglyphic texts. The earlier assumption that the hieroglyphs were simply symbolic picture words was disproved. Young's philological work was published in his article on the language of Egypt in the 1819 edition of *Encyclopaedia Britannica*. It remained for the painstaking Champollion to provide, three years later, a phonetic syllabary of the hieroglyphs, with transcriptions of cartouches representing some seventy rulers from Alexander to Antoninus Pius. He was also able to show that Coptic had superseded the old spoken Egyptian, of which the demotic and hieroglyphic scripts were the written forms.

Despite the interest aroused by these etymological excursions, and by the increasing familiarity of the world with the pyramids, the sphinxes and colossi of the Nile Valley, there was a gap of thirty years between the revelations of the French scholars and the onset of systematic field research and excavation. Admittedly, Champollion himself led a joint French and Tuscan expedition which resulted in the publication, between the years 1836 and 1844, of a dictionary and grammar of the hieroglyphic language, an elaboration of his *Précis du Système hiéroglyphique* of 1824. In four years from 1837, Sir John Gardner Wilkinson, one of the foremost Egyptologists of his day, published a six-volume account of the *Manners and Customs of the Ancient Egyptians* and in 1850 John Kenrick's *Ancient Egypt under the Pharaohs* came out. But such works, massively conceived and perceptive as they were, relied mainly on observation of surface artefacts and on the historians of Greece and Rome.

The expedition led by the distinguished Lepsius and financed by King Frederik Wilhelm of Prussia in 1843–5, was of enormous value in its survey of the Nile from the Delta to Khartoum and on to Ethiopia, its catalogue of the antiquities found near Memphis and Thebes, and its exploratory work beneath ground. Yet however well-intentioned and academically respectable, such expeditions merely added to the depredations of the tomb robbers and wealthy looters in the first half of the nineteenth century. The Lepsius survey resulted in the publication of *Monuments of Egypt and Ethiopia* (in twelve volumes), with its marvellous illustrations in folio, which remains to the present day the corner-stone of modern Egyptology. It also removed thousands of valuable items from their historical settings and placed them, magnificently, in the Egypt galleries of the Prussian Imperial Museum. The vast quantities of stonework, wall paintings, papyri and other antique works removed by the rival consuls Salt and Drovetti, and by academic expeditions, was as nothing compared to the destructive activities of the Egyptian villagers. Over the centuries they had hacked indiscriminately at any accessible objects in order to build and furnish their own dwellings. Unlike the Mesopotamian antiquities which were mostly concealed by subsequent layers of habitation and great mounds of brick and clay, those of Egypt (and Greece for that matter) often rose out of the landscape to beckon the local mason or the passing antique hunter. There was cause for alarm when, in September 1850, Auguste Edouard Mariette was sent to Egypt by his employers, the Musée du Louvre, on a modest mission to collect rare Coptic books.

Giovanni Belzoni.

'Beneath my eyes I had Giza, Abusir, Saqqara, Mitrahina. My lifelong dream took shape. There, almost within reach, was a world of tombs, stelae, inscriptions, statues ...'. By October he was working at the necropolis of Memphis at Saqqara. The head of a sphinx rising out of the sand recalled Strabo's 'Serapaeum at Memphis', where the winds piled up the sands 'beneath which we saw the sphinxes buried up to their heads'. Strabo the factual, unpretentious geographer for whom Mariette shared with other explorers an unqualified admiration, recorded seeing a bull-god being led from the sanctuary of the divine Apis at Memphis. Mariette was standing in the avenue of the sphinxes which led to the tombs of the bull-gods. 'I forgot my mission, I forgot the Patriarch, the monasteries, the Coptic manuscripts ...', he wrote. By 1 November 1850 he was digging close to the sphinx, aided by thirty hired workmen, 'at one of the most beautiful sunrises I ever saw in Egypt'.

Mariette was born at Boulogne-sur-mer in 1821, within a year of Champollion's transcription of the hieroglyphs. He crossed the Channel at the age of eighteen to teach French at the Shakespeare House Academy, Stratford-upon-Avon, returning to Boulogne after a year to become part-time editor of a local newspaper. By coincidence, a customs officer named l'Hôte, a distant relative of the

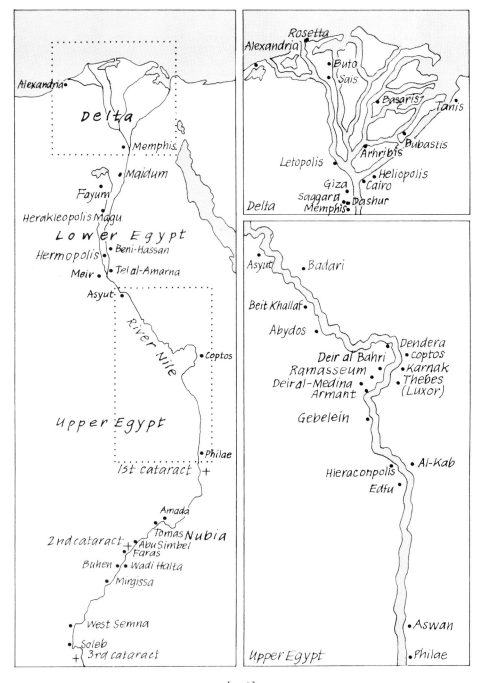

Auguste Edouard Mariette.

Mariettes, moved to Boulogne-sur-mer at the time of Auguste's new-found literary bent, and he was the father of a temperamental artist, Nestor l'Hôte, who had been chosen by Champollion to accompany the 1828 expedition to Egypt. Nestor had made countless drawings and notes on the Valley of the Kings, where he and his companions resided in the tomb of one of the Ramesses. The death of Champollion in 1832, following a terrible fit of apoplexy, caused Nestor to make a nostalgic pilgrimage in the path of his master in 1838. He found that the Valley which invoked so many precious memories seemed 'forsaken'. He placed his bed where Champollion had slept, in his fancy making the great man live again. And he wrote that in his opinion there remained many important, unopened tombs in the Valley. 'But who will undertake such immense works, which would rival that of the monarchs who caused the tombs to be hewn?', he asked. Just beneath the tomb of Ramesses, the temporary home of the Frenchman, lay a young king by the name of Tutankhamen! But how could he or anyone know or guess the extent of the riches that lay a few feet lower down?

Nestor died on the Red Sea coast in 1842, at the age of 38, exhausted by his work, robbed and deserted by his own servants, bemoaning to the last the never-

Ka figure of Meryrehashtes, one of several likenesses from tomb at Sedment; 6th dynasty,
C.2250 BC.

ending stupidity of his fellow countrymen and all the other 'idiots' who were destroying at an almost unimaginable pace the irreplaceable works that he and his fellow artists had recorded. His father asked Mariette to edit his surviving notes and papers. Mariette undertook the task reluctantly at first. Some years later he was to tell his own successor of the seductiveness of the Egyptian decoy-duck: 'One peck and he injects his venom, and there you are, an Egyptologist for the rest of your life.'

Mariette carried to Saqqara and the Serapaeum of Memphis an unqualified admiration for at least some of the Frenchmen who had preceded him, and for Strabo his unfaltering guide. He had no good opinion, however, of that earlier visitor from Greece, Herodotus. He called him a 'criminal' who could have told so much and who yet conveyed 'only stupidities'.

> I detest this traveller who came to Egypt at a time when the Egyptian language was spoken, who with his eyes saw all the temples still standing; who only had to ask the first comer the name of the reigning king, the name of the king who preceded him, who only had to refer to the first temple for the history, religion – for everything of interest concerning the most fascinating country in the world. And who, instead of all that, tells us gravely that Cheops built a pyramid with the fruit of prostitution.

The stricture was not entirely fair. In a sense, Herodotus's crime, if crime it was, consisted of exaggerated enthusiasm for the land he described more colourfully than any other he visited. Professor Spiegelberg, one of the leading Egyptologists of the twentieth century, compares the Greek historian's account of Egypt with the *Germania* of Tacitus, 'overpowered by the suggestion of (its) high antiquity', as was Tacitus by the 'virtues of the youthful Germans'. Herodotus saw Egypt as the birth-place of Greek religion, thus giving prominence to stories of fabulous happenings related to him by ordinary folk. It was Mariette's successor, Gaston Maspéro, who put the matter in perspective, saying 'He gave us stories of the days of yore, told by the populace'. Of the few kings mentioned by Herodotus, he makes much play of the mythical escape of Sesostris from a burning chamber over a bridge formed by the bodies of two of his sons. There is an Homeric quality to the story. Spiegelberg calls it 'a dragoman's tale', explaining accounts of 'the triumphant Pharaoh' with his feet on the heads of enemies.

In fact, Herodotus was captivated by Egypt. The Pharaohs depicted in wall drawings and on monuments were altogether more benign a race of monarchs than the boastful, blood-lusting kings of Assyria and Babylon, Elam and Persia, of which he, like the Old Testament scribes, had an all too vivid picture. The fact that he largely ignored the king lists, which would indeed have been helpful to Mariette and his successors, was not as great a crime as would have been a distortion of the true nature of the land of the Pharaohs. It has been said that his was 'a veiled picture'. It was not deceptive.

The excavations at Memphis were productive from the start. Mariette and his workmen – who lived with their families, pets and worldly goods in the tombs surrounding them – collected legions of sphinxes and statues of every size. Tomb after tomb was opened up to reveal an astonishing array of treasures. One of the first was a sandstone statue of a scribe sitting cross-legged in the act of writing, a figure which would become for many Europeans the archetypal specimen of realistic Egyptian sculpture. He worked his way along the avenue towards what he hoped would turn out to be Strabo's Serapaeum, occasionally losing his way and having to dig warily at angles to find his way back to the ancient processional route of Memphis. On the eve of Christmas 1850, he found another sitting figure, which he recognized as Pindarus; further digging revealed the lyric poet's companions, a row of poorly sculpted Greeks, among whom Plato and Pythagoras were recognizable. Others were too badly damaged and worn to be identified. Mariette had not come in search of the Greeks who knew Egypt in its dying years, but the kings and priests of its most distant antiquity. He had spent very nearly all of the 7,000 francs which the Louvre had given him to buy Coptic books. By February, after two months of relatively easy digging, he came to a chapel-like structure built by Nectanebo I, whose name was inscribed on one of the sphinxes he had found in the avenue. The building was guarded by two magnificent lions of sandstone. It was dedicated to the bull-god Apis. He knew from these superficial finds that he was at the Serapaeum. But how long would it take to penetrate to its lowest level? How many men, and how much money would be needed? He carried on with money loaned by the French consul, M. Le Moyne. He sent a report of his progress to Charles Lenormant, Professor of Egyptology at the Collège de France, who had found him his original employment at the Louvre.

The French Government, on Lenormant's recommendation, advanced 30,000 francs for work in clearing the Serapaeum. It was a good investment, but it might have been even better had not the Khedival Prince Abbas Pasha, successor to Muhammad Ali within the 'perpetual' viceroyalty of his family, realized the value of Mariette's discoveries to Egypt. In November 1851 he ordered the cessation of digging until France renounced any future claim to objects found by the expedition. Muhammed Ali had issued an ordinance in 1835 forbidding the export of antiquities and commanding the setting up of a museum in Cairo, constructed 'in the manner of those in Europe'. The museum was established in the Ezbekia gardens, but it did not stop foreigners from removing their discoveries to Europe and America, often at the insistence of the Khedival authorities who regarded them as a nuisance. Some of the museum's most valuable pieces were given by Egyptian princes to visiting nobilities, and after a few years of the museum's existence the remaining collection was given in entirety to the Archduke Maximilian of Austria.

The Frenchman saw no point in sharing his finds with so cavalier a host, but he agreed to the Pasha's demand, and in return for donating future finds to Egypt he was given permission to remove his existing haul, 513 items, to France. Gallic subterfuge was not exhausted by that arrangement. Among the pieces he was allowed to keep were hundreds of small bronze statues found beneath a pavement, representing the gods of Memphis, including many representations of Apis, Osiris, Ptah, Isis and Horus. With these he would secrete the most valuable new discoveries, working in the isolation of a packing shop which he and his foreman, Bonnefoy, devised at the bottom of a forty-foot pit. Already the Memphis finds had begun to add significantly to existing knowledge of the Egyptian cults and of the European divinities which stemmed from them. Apis, whom the Egyptians called Hap, was the incarnation of Osiris and the reincarnation of Ptah. Seker the god of the underworld, entered into a union with Osiris to create Serapis (Asar-Hap), and thus the divine bull became Ptah-seker-asar, the three-part god of resurrection. The Greeks identified Serapis with Hades, and his worship only ceased when the great temple dedicated to him at Alexandria was destroyed following the edicts of Constantine and Theodosius. Herodotus had described Apis, saying that it had a white, four-sided blaze on the forehead. The figures found by Mariette had triangular blazes. The historian was mistaken in a matter of detail, but the error hardly justifies some of the critical assertions made in our own era with regard to his faulty powers of observation.

Mariette 'slipped through' into the tomb of Apis on 12 November 1851. He found himself in a vast complex of underground galleries, the massive stone coffins of the sacred bulls standing in recesses. Many of the tombs had been plundered. The coffin lids had mostly been removed; inscribed stones and stelae had been torn from the walls and lay scattered – and often smashed – on the floor. When the great sandstone door of the tomb was opened, after several months in which Mariette worked secretly within while the Pasha's supervisors were absent, there was an expulsion of blue vapour which poured forth for several hours: gases which had built up in the vast subterranean chambers over many centuries.

Mariette could follow the footprints of workmen who had laid their Apis god to rest 3,700 years before, in an unopened tomb. In March 1852 he found a wood sarcophagus, and inside it a mummy, its face covered by a gold mask, wearing an amulet suspended from a chain necklace, a golden hawk with outstretched wings resting on its chest; all in tribute to Khamwase, the favourite son of Ramesses II, who in Egyptian legend, searched among the tombs of Saqqara thirty-seven centuries earlier for the magic book of Toth. The devotion of the early Egyptians to magic and fetish, and the meaning of their cults, began to emerge from the shadows of the tombs and temples. Perhaps the solemn, red-bearded Frenchman's most important contribution to the immediate understanding of Egypt, and to the impact of ancient Egypt on the world at large, was his revelation of its arts and crafts – especially its sculpture – at once sacerdotal, stylized, historiographic and mightily accomplished.

In eight years he excavated over thirty sites at the centre of the Old Kingdom, Memphis in Lower Egypt, and Abydos, site of the earliest royal necropolis, containing the tombs of the First and Second Dynasty kings. The Pharaohs of Abydos would rest for a while longer, however. The Frenchman failed to find the tombs and they awaited discovery by the Englishman who came next on the scene at Abydos.

When Mariette's Arab workmen opened a tomb chamber close to the pyramid at Maydum, some fifty miles along the Nile from Saqqara, they met the luminous gaze of two life-size, limestone statues. They were representations of the Princess Nefert and her husband Ra-Hotep, a general in the army of Sneferu, the first ruler of the Fourth Dynasty. The workmen drew back in terror, believing the figures to be demons. And no wonder for the inserted eyes of the couple, made from quartz and crystal, gleaming in the dark sepulchre, seemed to follow the observer wherever he went. These painted statues, utterly naturalistic, were sure guides to the racial characteristics of the citizens of the Old Kingdom; heavy, strongly-built people, with full sensuous lips, prominent noses and high cheeks. They and their like, subjects of the 'pyramid kings' at Giza, Saqqara and Maydum, the centres of Memphite empire, dated back to within 400 years of the earliest Egyptian civilization. Beyond them, to the surprise of generations of archaeologists, there appeared to be an almost inexplicable void; no substantial flint-evidence of a Neolithic past, little evidence of pastoral communities settling down to an urban existence; simply the sudden emergence of a strong, inventive people, ruled by mighty kings, each with his own pyramid. And then darkness.

The tomb figures of the princess and the general represented a unique feature of the pyramid cities, which came to light with startling regularity as Mariette moved from one chamber to another. Within the tomb walls were hidden recesses, the resting places of these painted figures of wood and stone, their colours as fresh as if they had just been touched by the artist's brush. They were the *Ka* statues, manifestations of the personality cult; each an exact likeness of its owner, an artistically contrived twin, expressing an abstract notion of life in its eternal cloak. The mummies and funerary attachments of the dead had mostly been removed by vandals and thieves over the centuries, but the *Ka* figures had remained intact in their secluded hiding places. What made these people create works of art in order merely to hide them away for all eternity? The answer must be that they were not commemorative, but actual companions of the dead, left close to their host to subsist harmoniously alongside them in the earthly grave, feeding on offerings of bread, milk, honey, wine and beer in enclosures which sometimes bore the legend 'House of *Ka*' on painted false-doors with hinges and appropriate signs. *Ka* had a special hieroglyphic sign, representing uplifted arms as if registering adoration. It was Dr Heinrich Brugsch of Berlin, who visited Mariette in 1853 for a few days and stayed for eight months, who described the figure as meaning 'The person, the individuality, the being'. Later study suggested the *alter ego*, the duality of the owner, or simply *life* itself. After all, most Egyptian tombs were built in the lifetimes of their occupants. They wrote their own epitaphs. All their successors had to do was keep them supplied with food and drink. *Ka* would presumably find a way of sharing in the feast from its recess within the chamber wall.

Whatever the religious or social significance of the *Ka* figure, it was an artistic revelation. Its inspiration was truth. If the subject was ugly or deformed, whether of royal or common blood, then the statue must be a true likeness. There was no need of flattery in what was essentially a secret compact of deceased and other-self within the privacy of the burial chamber. Until Mariette brought these life-like statues from their hiding places within the tomb walls, Egyptian portraiture as exemplified by its sculpture was regarded in the West as stylized and unnatural; slave to a convention which had remained virtually static over thousands of years. These masterpieces of early Memphite portraiture anticipated the realism of early Italian art: realism combined with that indefinable quality of personality and charisma which distinguishes three-dimensional art from mere representation. If they lacked the grace and formal perfection of the masterpieces of classical Greece, it was not for want of skill; rather that the mentalities of the two peoples were diametrically opposed. From the Old Kingdom onward, the Egyptians showed themselves to be industrious, creative and insular. They were neither imaginative nor imitative. Subsequent finds in Egypt and Mesopotamia would show close links of trade and political compact between the kingdoms of the Nile and the Tigris-Euphrates valleys; but in the visual arts and literary tradition, there seems to have been an almost complete absence of interchange.

Critical appraisal of the arts and crafts of the ancient world, especially by comparative method, is notoriously dangerous. The French poet Paul Valéry puts it thus:

Works of the mind exist only in action. Beyond this action what remains is only an object that has no particular relation to the mind. Transport the statue you admire among people sufficiently different from your own, and it becomes an insignificant stone. The Parthenon is only a small quarry of marble. And when the text of a poet is used as a collection of grammatical difficulties or examples, it ceases at once to be a work of the mind, since the use to which it is put is entirely foreign to the conditions of its creation.

The West consciously adopted the culture of classical Greece. Even out of context, the Parthenon friezes are intelligible. They invite a conditioned response. Eastern art attracted much attention in the nineteenth century, even plagiarism, but its influence on western thought was transitory (with the exception of decorative themes which have had a permanent impact in the form of conventions such as chinoiserie and the arabesque). Assyrian and Egyptian sculptures, removed from preconceived and often elaborate settings, and placed *en masse* in a museum gallery, may be admired for their scale or even for their brutal directness; artistically they are alien. To the Greek as to the modern viewer, an inherent failing of Egyptian sculpture in particular was its domination by political considerations. With the exception of the tomb figures, size and scale were usually determined by the importance of the subject, as in the colossal statue of Ramesses II at Karnak, in which the diminutive figure of the pharaoh's wife rises only to knee height. Equally, the king rests inconspicuously between the head and legs of his god in the statue of the Ram of Aman and Taharqa. The Greeks learnt willingly from the mathematics and science of Egypt, but they were disdainful of its art. Yet Egyptian art and science were alike the opposites of everything Hellenistic. Both were preoccupied with specific problems. The pyramid builders understood geometry, but they never attempted to prove theorems or to pose abstract questions. They thought in terms of unit fractions, but could not conceive of, for example, three-quarters; only an adding-up of three one-quarters. True multiplication and division, the imaginative short cuts to calculation, were unknown. They obtained an exact figure for the essential division of circumference by diameter: 3.16. As art was devoted to the particular demands of immortality, so science was there to solve down-to-earth problems. It was left to Euclid and his fellow Greeks to show that mathematics is capable of beautiful constructions and abstract propositions; that *pi* is an irrational recurrent: to Praxiteles, more than 2,000 years after the carving of the *Ka* figures at Saqqara, to seek perfect harmony of form and movement.

Brugsch was but one of many visitors shown round the cleared Serapaeum of Saqqara. Another was the Vicomte de Vogüé, who was with Mariette when Charles de Rougé died, leaving vacant the chair of Egyptology at the Collège de France. Mariette was offered it. But as de Vogüé remarked rhetorically, 'You

Scale in Egyptian sculpture. The Ram of Aman with King Taharqa, 25th dynasty.

Sir Flinders Petrie.

would never desert your children of Bulac'. Mariette was by now the victim of diabetes, his eyes raw from years of exposure to the sun and dust of the desert, poverty stricken in consequence of a natural improvidence. He saw the prospect of security. But he nominated his brilliant young assistant Gaston Maspéro who was the obvious choice for the job. Mariette stayed to the last with the museum he had created. In 1873, the Khedive authorized the building of a new museum at Giza to house Mariette's collection, and the *Académie des Inscriptions* awarded him 20,000 francs for his contribution to Egyptian scholarship. The death of his eldest daughter in the same year almost destroyed him. Political problems had brought excavation and most other activities to a halt in Egypt. He concentrated on the publication of one of his later finds, the 600 place names in the list of Thutmosis III which he had found at Karnak, along with a description of the Serapaeum. He returned to Cairo in the year of the Nile flood, 1878, when the Bulac museum was drenched and books, papers and papyri were destroyed. In 1879 he was made a Pasha of Ottoman Egypt. A few weeks later the Khedive, who invested him, Ismail, was deposed by Britain and France, and Tewfiq became Viceroy. Sick and frail, Mariette worked on as best he could, still digging at Saqqara and labouring to restore the old museum.

Mariette had always insisted that there were no inscriptions within the vaults of the pyramids, but Maspéro believed there were. As the chief lay on his death bed at Bulac, his friend Brugsch brought evidence that Maspéro was right. They had found inscriptions at Saqqara. It was his last, if somewhat negative contribution to the study of antiquity. He died on 18 January 1881, after a week of death pangs during which friends and enemies alike came to pay homage. The Egyptian Government in its last months of independence gave him an almost royal funeral. He had wished to be buried alongside his wife and daughter in Cairo, but the authorities decreed that he should be laid to rest by the door of his museum at Bulac. If the museum should be moved, his body must go with it. A tomb was erected in granite and white marble, surmounted by a bronze statue, bearing on its pedestal the words:

A MARIETTE PACHA L'EGYPTE RECONNAISSANTE

Within a year of Mariette's death, Britain invaded Egypt. France had been invited to take part in the occupation when Ahmad Arabi Pasha was thought to threaten the Khedival authority. But France refused the invitation, and so Britain – determined to protect the Suez Canal from the ambitions of competing imperial powers – became the *de facto* ruler of the country, under the consulship (from 1883) of Sir Evelyn Baring, or Lord Cromer as he became, who was known far and wide as 'The Lord'. From then on the first and last words on virtually all matters rested with Britain, though France insisted on priority in antiquarian research.   It was an opportune moment for the most prodigal of British archaeologists to make his appearance. William Matthew Flinders Petrie was heir to a kind of stubborn independence which could be known only to a man who was declared stillborn by the midwife who delivered him, dropped on his head within a short time of being slapped into life so that his temple was permanently dented, and prevented from enjoying a formal education through a combination of chronic asthma and nervous breakdown in youth attributed to a family determination to engulf him in half a dozen languages at a time.

His devotion to the subject which was to be the *alpha* and *omega* of his life began not with languages or any of the formal paths of scholarship; rather with the delight of a lonely boy in rummaging through the marine store shops around his home territory of Woolwich and Greenwich on the Thames, collecting coins, minerals and fossils to add to the collections he inherited from his mother.

He was born on 3 June 1853, the year in which Mariette had excavated the Serapaeum at Saqqara and revealed to the world the treasures of Memphis. By the age of 13, Petrie had read Piazzi Smyth's *Our Inheritance in the Great Pyramid* and was rapidly catching up with advances in Egyptian studies. His own inclination was towards mathematics and surveying techniques. Early on he made his own sextant out of cardboard and a looking-glass and began to survey earthworks in and around his native heath. From the age of 15 he spent every spare moment in the British Museum, where all the Egyptian collections were housed in a single room upstairs – the giant sculptures and other objects from Mesopotamia occupying by far the largest areas (often makeshift galleries with leaking roofs as Dr Birch, the Keeper of the Oriental Department, never ceased to remind the Trustees). The Medal Room too attracted him, and he was given five pounds for his collection of copper coins, mostly Roman and Byzantine. An interest in late Greek coinage followed, with its reflections of the fringe civilizations of Mesopotamia, Bactria, 'and that gorgeous name of Attambelos, King of Characene'.

At 22 he began to traverse the counties of southern England, constructing more than 150 plans of ancient sites and producing a 'Mathematical report of *Stonehenge*'. At 24 he published his first book, *Inductive Metrology*, setting out a method of comparative measurement. He made his first visit to Egypt at the end of 1880, two years before the British occupation and a few months before the death of Mariette. His purpose was to demonstrate the truth of Smyth's wide-ranging theories on the building and functions of the pyramids. In the event, the mentor was found wanting. Petrie was permitted to do surface work at the Giza pyramids, measuring the sites by triangulation and making notes on interior features. Though new to Egyptology, his single-minded devotion to his chosen tasks and belief in his own powers and methods was soon in evidence. He had little time for the French, and none at all for Mariette. He roundly accused them of incompetence, wanton destruction, and capricious methods.

> I hear that Mariette most rascally blasted to pieces all the fallen parts of the granite temple by a large gang of soldiers, to clear it out instead of lifting the stones and replacing them by means of tackle. The savage indifference of the Arabs, who have even stripped the alabaster off the granite temple since Mariette uncovered it, and who are not at all watched here, is partly superseded by a most barbaric sort of regard for the monuments by those in power.

The criticism was largely deserved, though there is no recognition that Mariette was a sick and dying man who had lost his grip on things. And there is a suggestion in this early remonstrance of attitudes which would bedevil Petrie's life as an archaeologist, brilliant and incomparably productive though it was to be. There were hints of an inability to work within a team discipline – unless he was at the helm – in youthful correspondence with his lifelong friend Flaxman

Spurrell, physician and anthropologist, who encouraged and developed his archaeological interests.

Petrie had become involved in the field work of the local archaeological society in his native county of Kent when his family moved to the suburb of Bromley. There was also a project for drawing a 'true map' of England and Wales according to Ptolemy, and the survey of a 'splendid Roman camp' at Barking in Essex. A dignitary of the Church had undertaken the publication of his papers on these subjects. Correspondence with Spurrell describes his 'brangle with the Canon' and the 'unholy mess' to which his uneasy relationship with that prelate gave rise. The year before his first journey to Egypt was marked by an admission to Spurrell which might well have served as an epitaph at the end of his long life. It followed an invitation to a social event: ' . . . that sort of thing is not in my line at all. To tell the truth I abhor all ceremonies and festivities, and all concourses of people; I want to be *doing*, instead of *being and suffering*. I would rather do a week's hard work than assist in a day's "pleasure".'

The great pyramids of Egypt, rather like Stonehenge, had excited not only wonderment at the sheer magnitude of technical achievement to which they bore witness, but also a good deal of eschatological and crackpot theorizing. Two winter seasons of single-handed work at Giza enabled him to make the first serious pronouncements of his professional life, though they did nothing to deter the 'pyramid theorists'.

Supposed proportional variations, the relationship of one ground point to another, of base to height, hypotenuse to vertical and horizontal, angles of slope, directions of chamber openings, orientation; all had been adopted by pleaders of outlandish theories for a hundred years or more as pointers to ancient cults and systems of measurement. Petrie demonstrated that the real wonder of the pyramids was the technical skill involved in their construction, the use of bronze saws set with corundum or diamond to cut massive blocks of hard stone, granite, diorite and basalt. Even more astonishingly, he found evidence of the use of tubular drills with 'bits' almost identical to those of modern diamond rock-drills, some 3,000 years before the Christian era, to hollow out the rocks to receive the sarcophagi, funerary figures and other accoutrements of the burial chamber. Petrie had found the construction work so sound as to insist that had it not been 'for the spite of enemies and the greed of later builders it is probable that every pyramid would be standing in good order at this day'. He observed a gradual development of building techniques up to the period of the Fourth Dynasty when the great pyramids were built. An almost perfectly square base and an angle of slope of 50 degrees were the common features. Familiarization with the great pyramids was a gradual process. Some twenty years later he discovered that the First Dynasty kings had been buried in wood-lined chambers within simple pits, roofed over with poles and brushwood, and covered in with sand. Then came a wooden chamber, free-standing within the pit, with beam roof and eventually a staircase at the side, with a 'dwarf' wall holding aloft the pile of earth over the tomb. By the Third Dynasty the wall had become a solid mass of brickwork measuring nearly ten million cubic feet. These were the *mastaba* tombs, each with a long, sloping underground passage to the chamber far below. At Saqqara some of the tombs of this period had replaced the brickwork with stone. The solid, upper part of the tomb was gradually heightened by the addition of slabs of masonry. Then a smooth outer casing was added, made of massive stone blocks, and the first true pyramids arose in the Fourth Dynasty (2613–2494 BC). There was a gradual decline from the Sixth Dynasty to the Twelfth, the dominant mass of masonry becoming increasingly haphazard and finally a pile of mud-brick. But to the end of the great age of pyramid building, whatever the hidden core, the visible parts were of finely cut and polished stone, joined with skill and care, as were the inner chambers. The sepulchral chamber was always near the base and usually below ground, and was always approached by a passage leading from the north. The entrance was sometimes in the pyramid face, sometimes sunk into the foundation rock on the north side.

Petrie did not concern himself greatly with the purpose of the pyramid, being more entranced by its structure and changing form from the early dynastic mud-brick *mastaba* or, from the Arabic meaning of the word, 'bench', to the stepped buildings inaugurated by Zoser's architect Imhotep at Saqqara in the Third Dynasty, and the geometrically true pyramids of the Fourth to Sixth Dynasties at Maydum, Dahshur and Giza. European speculation from the Middle Ages onward ranged from the idea that they were Joseph's granaries to the notion that they were the divinely inspired work of a non-Egyptian chosen race. The astronomer Piazzi Smyth's calculations based on the 'pyramid inch' (1.001 inches) were summarily dismissed by Petrie. Even at the present day Smyth's theories find support, however. Breasted regarded the pyramidal form of the king's tomb as of 'the most sacred significance'. In 1912, he wrote: . . . when in mountainous proportions the pyramid rose above the king's sepulchre, dominating the royal city below and the valley beyond for many miles, it was the loftiest object which greeted the Sun-god in all the land . . .'. A present-day Egyptologist, comments: 'Although it now seems probable that the stone symbol of The Sun-god at Heliopolis, the *benben*, was conical and not pyramidal in shape, Breasted was undoubtedly right in associating it with the true pyramid'. The same authority states that the *benben* and its architectural derivative, the pyramid, necessarily represented 'the rays of the sun shining down on earth'.

As for suppositions about the fantastic dimensions of some pyramids, particularly those that had been destroyed (or never found), and time-theories

Limestone statue of Inebny with hieroglyphic inscription, infilled in blue and white stone. Black wig and eyes.

[133]

based on pyramidal multiplication and division, Petrie was contemptuous. In 1880, he had examined the great pyramid of Khufu (Cheops) at Giza in detail, as well as the lesser structures around it. He corrected the base measurement of the former from 9,140 inches to 9,069 inches. Examination of the Giza and Maydum pyramids showed that the recurrence of 7 and 11 as multiples of dimension was simply a convenient system for dealing with large numbers of cubits. 'Hence all theorizing about the days of the year being represented was entirely erroneous. ... The theories as to the size of the pyramid are thus proved entirely impossible. ... It was seen that there is seldom a tenth of an inch of uncertainty in the final results'. Occultists, lucky-number merchants, flat-earthers, fortune tellers and the rest were condemned but not easily persuaded.

> The fantastic theories, however, are still poured out, and the theorists still assert that the facts correspond to their requirements. It is useless to state the real truth of the matter, as it has no effect on those who are subject to this type of hallucination. They can but be left with the flat earth believers and other such people to whom theory is dearer than fact.

His first technical work on Egypt's ancient past was vindicated by the Royal Society. That august body invited Francis Galton to report on it and he found it worthy of a hundred-pound grant to assist publication. A lasting friendship between the famous scientist and the apprentice archaeologist ensued.

Petrie had heard of the work of the Swiss archaeologist Edouard Naville while working at Giza. He also heard a good deal of the lady novelist Amelia Edwards and of her devotion to Egypt. Miss Edwards had travelled up and down the Nile for some years and had become familiar to many of the archaeologists at work along the banks of the river; indeed, she had tried her hand at excavating a small temple. She wrote an account of her journeys, *A Thousand Miles up the Nile*, which produced the funds necessary for the launching of an excavation project which was to be the culmination of a long and intense passion for the land of the Pharaohs. Based largely on the work of Mariette and Maspéro she had written many articles which had contributed to the popularization of ancient Egypt, especially of its arts and crafts. In 1882, with the support of several department heads of the British Museum, she set up the Egypt Exploration Fund, with herself and R.S. Poole as joint honorary secretaries. Naville, a linguist whose chief interest was in epigraphy and who saw archaeology largely as a means of illuminating the biblical record, was appointed to lead the Fund's site work. In 1883 Petrie asked if there was an opening for him with the Fund. Erasmus Wilson, the Society's president, had read his pyramid work and insisted that he be given a chance. In November of the same year he was on his way to Tanis in the

Nile Delta to begin excavating there.

By the end of 1881 news had come through to the Fund of Maspéro's remarkable finds at Thebes, the royal capital of the dynasties of Upper Egypt. Maspéro had handed over part of the great necropolis, which others had found unpromising, to Emil Brugsch who was now Keeper of the Bulac Museum. In February 1882, Amelia Edwards was able to describe for readers of the *Illustrated London News* the astonishing finds along several miles of burial ground on the west bank of the Nile. Hidden behind a great limestone cliff, concealed by a huge fallen rock, the entrance to a perpendicular shaft led to the sepulchral vault with thirty-six mummies, including twenty or more kings and queens, from the Seventeenth Dynasty, beginning in about 1750 BC (later dated to c.1650) to the Twenty-First Dynasty beginning in about 1100. Names and dates would change as the king lists and the burial chambers were uncovered. Here, it was claimed, were the mummy-cases, if not always the actual mummies, of Ramesses I and II, and Seti, Queen Hathor Hont-Taui, and a host of other Theban royals and priests. Miss Edwards explained: 'The mummy of Ramesses II (to whose memory, as the supposed Pharaoh of the oppression of the Hebrews, so strong an interest attaches) appears to have been removed more frequently, and to have suffered more vicissitudes of fortune than any of the others. That his sepulchre in the Valley of the Tombs of the Kings had been violated by robbers can scarcely be doubted, for his original mummy cases were either destroyed or damaged beyond repair. The very beautiful coffin of carved sycamore wood in which the mummy now reposes, is a new one, made probably during the first years of the reign of Her-Hor [Herihor of the Twenty-First Dynasty of Thebes] . . .' Dr Birch of the British Museum had estimated that some 420 million embalmed corpses had been buried in ancient Egypt. There was some way to go yet.

Petrie had explained his own attitude to field work before leaving England. He spoke of 'the true line', which for him was 'the careful noting and comparison of small details'. Dramatic, hurried clearances, designed to fill the museums with eye-catching and rewarding relics, were not for him. Contemptuous of 'theorists', his own devotion to fact and detail was liable to lead, and eventually did lead in a spectacular manner, to an assumption that his own 'facts' were necessarily superior to other people's. Perhaps his credo was best expressed in the two quotations with which he introduced his autobiography, in 1931, seventy years after his first tentative essays in surveying and digging. The first, addressed 'To the mundane' by Sallustius the Splendid, began 'It behoves all Men that labour to excel all other Creatures, to make it their chief Endeavour not to waste their lives in silence like the Brute Beasts . . .'. The other, from Epictetus the Slave, bade all men to 'Dare to look up to God' and say, 'I am content that I have used thy gifts so long. Take them again, and set them in what place thou wilt, for thine were all

Mummy and coffin from Thebes, late 18th dynasty.

Alabaster head of Hathor as cow. Probably adorned with feathered headdress and horns, and gilded and inlaid eyes originally.

things, and thou gavest them me'.

Petrie was pre-eminently a man with a scientific mission, and he disapproved of Naville's 'literary' method. His concern for minutiae, apparent since boyhood, was reflected in his field work. So was his sense of preserving the antiquities he found. In his autobiography he wrote: 'I weaved history out of scattered evidence ... approaching excavation in a completely professional spirit. Assiduous in preventing diggers from selling objects secretly to dealers and in order to secure good relations with them paid the workmen myself.' Ironically, it was in the conclusions he would draw from his most devoted and expert labours, that he was to prove hopelessly mistaken. He was the father of scientific chronology, of dating by the most careful examination and measurement of objects, and by inductive method. It was that very specialization which led him eventually to dispute the chronology of dynastic Egypt with almost every other authority. He was not inclined to listen to contrary opinion once he had made up his mind.

While examining the pyramids of Lower Egypt, Petrie had been fascinated by a wealth of pottery finds. Until he arrived on the scene, archaeologists had virtually ignored such trifles. The discovery of fragments of eating and drinking vessels and the remains of items such as vases and ceramic figurines, hardly ever caused them to consider that such remnants showed marked and significant changes of style, decoration and manufacture from level to level. At Nineveh, Nimrud and Khorsabad, Troy and Mycenae, and in Egypt itself, pottery sherds had been scooped up with the rubbish of the great trenches created by hundreds of workmen wielding picks and shovels in a frantic search for palaces and colossi, sarcophagi and the gold-encased dead of the royal tombs. Petrie, even before he reached Egypt, had 'begun to suspect that the varieties of glazes and fashions of Egyptian work changed rapidly and clearly'. He made a prediction which would alter the entire course of archaeological investigation, bringing in scientific method where the *ad hoc* procedures of the gentleman diggers had prevailed, already, for the best part of a century. By finding sufficient examples of these small and hitherto despised samples, he said, 'we may be able to pin down the changes, so that the mere look of a thing may fix its age within a few reigns'. It was indicative of Petrie's consummate approach to archaeological field work that he made his first task the sifting of the rubbish heaps left behind by others. Mariette, Maspéro and even the excavators of fifty years before like Howard Vyse (whose basket-boy in 1837, Ali Gabri, became Petrie's foreman in 1881) had all been guilty of neglecting these valuable fragments of dating evidence.

There was not a great deal to excite his interest at Tanis in the Delta, scene of his first prospecting for the Fund. The Frenchmen had exhausted the temple site, but some distance away from it Petrie found part of a stela of Ptolemy II, and two monuments exposed by Mariette's team but apparently neglected by the great man and his successors. The former discovery proved to be the upper part of a stela of Taharqa, the Kushite king of the Twenty-Fifth Dynasty, and it led him to the inscribed lower half. He searched out the place where he believed a small archaic Greek figure, purchased in Cairo, originated, in the direction of Sais, the town which gave its name to the Saite Dynasty of the sixth century BC.

'The whole ground was thick with early Greek pottery, and it seemed almost a sacrilege to walk over the heaps with the fine lustrous black ware crunching beneath one's boots.' He picked up pieces with fretted and honeysuckle patterns, limbs broken off from figurines of people and horses. 'It seemed as if I were wandering in the smashings of the Museum vase-rooms'.

He had found Naucratis, the place which Herodotus described in detail in the age of its independent King, Amasis, friend of Solon, Polycrates and Pythagoras. There were contradictions in the Greek account of its origin. Amasis had gained the throne as a reaction to Greek rule, yet he was a 'philhellene'. Had the Greeks settled at Naucratis before the time of Amasis, who occupied the throne in 570 BC, twenty years before Solon promulgated the Athenian legislation? Did the Athenian idea of punishing idleness, or as Solon preferred it, of insisting that every son should acquire a trade, arise from the work ethic, the social conscience, of Saite Egypt? If so, where were the Greek settlements? Petrie returned in 1884 to answer at least some of the questions which had tantalized classical scholars and

Egyptian explorers alike. He did not have to look far. Two stone slabs on the side of the Pasha's dwelling, where Petrie was a temporary guest, contained Greek inscriptions, one of them a decree of the people of Naucratis, not unlike that which the Athenians had adopted in deference to the crafts and the desirability of useful employment. The location of the Greek colony and its philosophical connection with Athens had been established. Naucratis was one of 18,000 towns and villages which according to Diodorus existed in the region in the 'golden age' of the Saite Dynasty.

The earliest remains found in the flat Nile mud of the district were Greek potsherds, and the date of the first Hellenic occupation was shown to have predated Amasis. In 1884 Petrie uncovered a fortress at Defeneh, Daphnae of old, south-east of Tanis. The origins of the Greek presence became clearer from the strategic layout of the area and from inscriptions on stelae and statues from the period of the rule of the Kushite kings, the dark-skinned traditionalists who came from Ethiopia via Napata, near the Fourth Cararact in Nubia, and established the Twenty-Fifth Dynasty. The first of these kings, Piankhi, was enthroned in about 750 BC. The fourth of the line of Kushite rulers was Taharqa, and after his death Lower Egypt was ruled by local princes, the Dodecarchy of the Greeks. In 665 BC Psammetichus I wrested the throne from these upstarts, basing his own power on the 'brazen men of the sea', mercenaries from the Greek islands chiefly, establishing fortresses at Naucratis in the west, facing the Libyan foe who constantly threatened, and Daphnae looking towards Asia Minor in the east. The Saite ruler had very recent recollection of the power of Egypt's chief opponents, the Assyrians, who had reached as far as Memphis in 671 BC, and almost to Thebes under Ashurbanipal in 667 BC, causing the last of the Kushites to return to Nubia with their beloved horses, rather than face further conflict with that ruthless foe. The dominant influence in Upper Egypt at this time was the Divine Adoratrice and her high priest at Thebes. The Adoratrice was persuaded by Psammetichus's followers to adopt his daughter, Nitocris, as her successor. Thus the country was reunited under the first of the Saite kings.

Psamtik (Psammetichus I) figures in the tablets of Assyria, in the annals of Ashurbanipal, as the prince of Memphis and Sais, and Herodotus tells the romantic tale of his accession. How an oracle had foretold that whichever of the twelve princes of Sais should pour a libation out of a bronze cup would become king over them all; and how one day, when the princes were sacrificing to the god Ptah, the priest forgot to bring out the twelfth cup of gold. When it came to Psamtik's turn he unthinkingly snatched off his bronze helmet and used it for his libation. The oracle thus fulfilled, the brother princes decided to drive him into the marshes of the Delta where, brooding over his fate, he heard the oracle again, telling him that vengeance would come from the sea, 'on the day that men of

Scarabs from New Kingdom period, 1567–1080 BC.

bronze should come out thence'. And the bronze-clad warriors of Caria and Ionia duly came from across the sea to vindicate Psamtik and make him a powerful monarch.

Necho, the son of Psamtik, carried on his father's ambitious schemes, conquering all Syria, and overthrowing Josiah and placing his puppet Jehoiakim on the throne of Judaea. In gratitude for the valiant service of the Greeks, Necho dedicated the garment he had worn in battle at the Temple of Apollo at Miletos. Doubtless it was of these same Greeks that Jeremiah spoke: 'Lydians that handle and bend the bow'. Necho died in 595 BC. The Saite kings 'the broken reed' of Egypt, would combine with Phoenicia and Judaea against the might of Assyria and in that alliance against Babylon which led to the Captivity.

> Declare ye among the nations and publish, and set up a standard; publish and conceal not: say, Babylon is taken, Bel is put to shame, Merodach is dismayed; her images are put to shame, her idols are dismayed.

When Herodotus arrived, Egypt was under Persian rule, and Daphnae was in ruins, though the port was held by a detachment of Persian troops. The history of Naucratis and Daphnae ended with the deportation of the Greeks under the last but one of the Saite rulers, Amasis (Amosis I).

Petrie with his assistants Griffith and Gardner uncovered several temples of

[140]

the Greeks, some of them mentioned in Herodotus, dedicated to Apollo, Aphrodite, and Hera. The buildings were carefully recorded, every artefact labelled for place and time (one of Petrie's many important contributions to the techniques of archaeology which were so haphazard until his appearance). The 'necking' and other details of the Greek columns were noted. But such refinements were by the way. Inevitably, it was fragments rather than buildings and sarcophagi which occupied Petrie's mind.

'Very precious was this rubbish to me, layer under layer of broken vases, from the innumerable small bowls to the great craters of noble size and design; and most precious of all were the hundreds of dedications inscribed on the pottery, some of them probably the oldest examples of Greek writing known, and altogether far outnumbering all our past material for the archaic alphabets.' Here were discoveries of the utmost significance. These pottery inscriptions in the archaic language of the Greek islands suggested an infusion of words containing Phoenician-Semitic vowels. Ionic invaders of the Aegean had absorbed into their consonant-alphabet regular vowel signs which almost certainly made their way westward with the restless movement of Asiatic tribes and seafaring peoples. Resultant studies would highlight the interaction of the Semitic and Indo-European languages, and the development of European alphabets. Such language and grammatical studies would also help with the difficult – some would say insoluble – problems connected with the period of 'Great Migrations' in the first two centuries of the second millennium BC; the movements of peoples on an unprecedented scale which led to the supplanting of entire nations, to disruption in Egypt, the passage of the Hebrews to Palestine, and the appearance of the Ionians in the Aegean.

Flinders Petrie pursued his single-minded course for another sixty years in Egypt and the adjacent lands of Sinai and Palestine. But not in conjunction with the Egypt Exploration Fund. After just two years' work for that organization he was complaining of its 'inefficiency and incompetence'. His chief supporter, Sir Erasmus Wilson, died two years after his own appointment, in 1884. Amelia Edwards, another ally, was being bypassed by the 'stubborn' joint secretary Stuart Poole. Petrie arrived in London in June 1886 with boxes filled with his precious pottery fragments from the delta, to announce that he could no longer endure 'the constant mismanagement of affairs', or continue to deal with a committee which now 'lacked the advantages of autocracy in promptitude and foresight'. Poole subsequently explained to the committee that Petrie's health had suffered in Egypt. Galton, hearing of the break with the Fund immediately arranged for him to receive a small grant from the Royal Society for making portraits of the foreign races represented in Egypt under the Persian kings. Petrie was otherwise forced back on his private means, seventy pounds a year after paying his living expenses in England, in order to finance further exploration in Egypt. Determined all the same to continue his work, he went back in November of the same year, 1886, to journey up the Nile with his assistant Frank Llewellyn Griffith.

At Aswan, where he devoted much time to copying rock inscriptions on squeeze-paper, often suspended from a rope ladder, like Rawlinson at Behistun, he wrote of the inscriptions, 'Their main interest is in the great number of personal names which they preserve'. Most were, in fact, funerary lists, recording kings, queens and priests of the Eleventh to Thirteenth Dynasties, though some went back to the Fifth, and others forward to the Twenty-Sixth. He had embarked on his invaluable regnal lists, and on an idiosyncratic chronology of the dynasties.

The academic luminaries of the Fund found Naville an altogether more congenial representative. Petrie despised his obsession with epigraphy and his 'primitive' digging methods, not to mention his single-minded pursuit of Egyptian and Judaeo-Christian theological themes.

Much of Naville's time was spent in searching out the path of the Exodus, and in 1883 his first excavation for the Fund bore fruit with the announcement that he had uncovered Pithom-Succoth, the 'store' or treasure city built by the Jews for the anonymous Pharaoh. Lepsius was one of several leading scholars who believed the site to be that of Ramesses. Naville the epigraphist was able to identify without difficulty the dedication of the temple to Pithom, the 'Abode of Tum'. Pithom was its sacred name, Thukut, 'Succoth' of the bible, its civil designation – founded by Ramesses II in the Nineteenth Dynasty, restored by Sheshonq (Shishak) in the Twenty-Second. The Greeks called it Heropolis, the 'store house' and the Romans destroyed it. 'It is now certain that the Israelites passed along the valley of the Freshwater (Ismailiya) Canal ... The first definite geographical fact in connection with the sojourn in the Land of Egypt has been established by the excavations at Pithom', said the *Illustrated London News* excitedly. Naville also claimed to have identified Ramesses II as the Pharaoh of the Oppression.

The journeys of the Hebrews into and out of Egypt and on to the Promised Land was one of the great dramatic episodes of the Bible but the Old Testament scribes had neglected to tell the world who were the Pharaohs of the Oppression and the Exodus. In 1889 Amelia Edwards had declared herself a reluctant sceptic of Old Testament history.

I still think Ramesses II was the Pharaoh of the Oppression, and I accept M. Naville's discovery of Pithom and his recent discoveries ... with all their consequences. And I still think that Mernepthah or Seti II, or perhaps

Ani and Wife, from Book of the Dead, Thebes, New Kingdom.

[143]

Sethnekht, must have been the Pharaoh of the Exodus ... but never was a history so imperfectly – so ignorantly – written. What a poor opinion it gives one of the Hebrew intellect that they never gave the name of any of the Pharaohs – neither the Pharaoh of Abraham, of Imhotep of the Oppression, or the Exodus! ... All chronology starting with Abraham or Joseph is mere moonshine ... I no longer believe in Joseph ... la donna è mobile!'

It is easy enough to see why some of those who dispensed the money and authority for excavation work preferred the tangible rewards of Naville's biblical scholarship to the pottery sherds which were Petrie's stock in trade, or to the irritating doubts of the literati. Egyptology came to its most prodigious period of fulfilment thirty years after the intellectual furore which followed the publication of the *Origin of Species*. In that time the climate of thought in the western world had undergone a complete transformation. The doctrine of verbal inspiration still had its supporters, of whom Naville was one. But in a world inflamed by evolutionary theory, in which the sciences of anthropology and geology had, like archaeology, attained to academic respectability, the Bible had come under renewed attack. Claims to racial precedence, whether Semitic or Aryan, had as much validity as the burning bush and the miracle of water to sceptics who would admit rather to kinship with the apes than with the implausible ancestry of the generations of Noah. It was characteristic of Petrie that while such matters were debated feverishly by his colleagues and his arch rival Naville, that 'armchair archaeologist', he went on quietly sorting and systematizing his sherds and flints, unmoved.

For Petrie, generality and theory were always subordinate to the bedrock of hard evidence. He built up an edifice based partly on common evidence such as the king lists, monuments and inscriptions, but decisively on his own remarkable system of pottery classification. From these sources, and with his considerable mathematical skill, he deduced his chronology. Essential to that corpus, of course, was the dating of the kingships. A calendar had been in use from pre-pharaonic times, but it did not count the years. It employed a standard 365 days for the year without taking account of leap years, so that a day was lost every four years. Thus, after 120 years the calendar began a month too soon. In thousands of years the discrepancy became considerable. This was compounded by attempts, particularly in Ptolemaic times, to compensate for this known error. A method of noting absolute months became necessary. This demanded an observation of the relationship between the sun and the stars. In practice they used Sothis (Sirius), the 'dog-star'. Ingeniously, they noted the first night of the year on which Sirius could be seen emerging from the glow of the sun at dawn. This they called the heliacal rising. From this starting point a period was projected on the basis of the months rotating within the seasons. They called it the Sothic Period and it lasted 1460 years. He calculated the cycles of Egyptian time back to 4242 BC, 'or thereabouts'. He had added a full Sothic period to his time scale, and then dated the earliest reigns to fit into his chronology, giving some of the Pharaohs inordinate lengths of life so that later dynasties fitted into demonstrable date brackets. Later on, enthused by the ingenuity of his system, he added even more years to the time scale, taking it into the sixth millennium BC.

Fellow Egyptologists soon began to question his method. He had taken the First Dynasty of Egypt some 1500 years beyond any generally accepted limit. His conclusions were published in 1894. By then he had become the first occupant of the chair of Egyptology at University College London, that secular institution founded in 1827 by Bentham, Brougham, Grote, the poet Thomas Campbell and other freethinking men who rejected the Oxbridge tradition.

Petrie's appointment in 1893 was due to the foresight of Amelia Edwards, who died in 1892 leaving a bequest for the establishment of a professorship for the study of Egypt 'through the medium of objects rather than language and traditional historical method'. She even laid down age limits. After early disagreements, she had come to admire Petrie in the ten years of their connection through the Fund (later renamed 'Society'). He met all the requirements set out in her last will and testament. He was, in effect, the only candidate. The objects he brought back from Egypt and Sinai, along with Amelia Edwards' own collection of artefacts and books, formed the core of the Petrie Museum and the Edward Library at University College, London. For the next sixty years, Petrie's chronology was the subject of controversy. From his position of authority as Edwards Professor of Egyptology he defended it through thick and thin, insisting upon it, despite all contrary evidence, in his contributions to learned journals and to the world's most important encyclopedias and reference works.

——— 6 ———

The Promised Land

Palestine Under Egypt and Israel

A stela found by Petrie in one of the temples of Thebes contains a hymn of praise to the Pharaoh Merenptah, who sat on the throne from 1234 BC. It celebrates a number of victories, particularly over the Libyan tribes who were a constant thorn in the side of Egypt. And it concludes:

> Canaan is despoiled and all its evil with it. Askelon is taken captive, Gezer is conquered, Yanoam is blotted out. The people of Israel is desolate, it has no offspring. Palestine has become a widow for Egypt.

Here, for the first time in historical record, mention is made of Israel. Despite Naville's excavation of the store cities of the Delta region, there was still no material evidence to support the Old Testament account of the Israelites in Egypt. The Oppression, the Exodus, the years in the wilderness, the routes of the Metalworkers and the Spies, and the arrival at the Promised Land, were affirmed by the Bible alone. Nothing in Egypt or along the route that Moses and the tribes are supposed to have followed corroborated the story. But the victory hymn of Merenptah, which was written in 1229 BC, shows conclusively that the Israelites were in the land of Canaan in the thirteenth century BC.

Here was a matter of consuming interest to the Christian world. Palestine with its shabby, emotive townships became the meeting place of cleric and biblical scholar, pilgrim and tourist, *the Book* in one hand, camera in the other, treading the routes of the Disciples and of Christ himself, seeking out the temples and shrines of the Israelites and early Christians.

The view of the majority of Victorian visitors to the Holy Land is expressed

Iron Age pillar figurine of woman holding breasts, found near Bethlehem, 8–6 centuries BC, period of the Divided Monarchy.

with charming directness by one of their number who travelled back and forth in the first years of the twentieth century, the Revd. James Kean:

> Thus the topography of at least the Jerusalem of our Lord's days – the most interesting to us – becomes sure and simple: any man standing on the spot, and letting the historic scenes flow through his mind, will not be long in coming to conclusions and forming convictions from which no amount of argument will ever again move him.

Victorian England had something of the mind of Imperial Egypt – the Egypt of the Eighteenth and Nineteenth Dynasties – in its make up. Its conquests were designed to confer the inestimable advantages of purity of religion, efficiency of administration and refinement of culture on the less fortunate, its aims and manners firmly rooted in monarchic and priestly traditions. And most surely it was suspicious at the highest levels of government and political service of those unorthodox ideas which were liable to rock the boat of state yet were the inevitable consequence of the vibrant achievements of the age.

Egypt of the Pharaohs, like Homeric Greece, was a source of endless fascination to the Victorians. If France and Prussia produced, on the whole, the finest biblical and antiquarian scholars, it was Britain in the heyday of empire which sensed an identity with the ancients in their more glorious moments. If prime ministers, ministers of state and senior diplomats were able to devote much of their time to digging and searching for antiques, and to taking part in controversies and academic disputes which arose from the pursuit of antiquity, the fact was not in the least resented by the general public which, in the main, shared their enthusiasms, admired their knowledge and paid readily to see their acquisitions. They flocked in their tens of thousands to see Lord Elgin's marbles. Gladstone could attract vast audiences to listen to passionate homilies on such subjects as the *Odyssey* or the potter's art as easily as he could draw the multitude to speeches on vital political issues of the day. The establishment view and popular enthusiasm in such matters came together with conspicuous force at the Great Exhibition of 1851, where the most popular display by far was the Egyptian room.

But even Egypt and the Isles of Greece lacked the universal appeal of the Holy Land. Christian and Jew throughout Europe looked to Jerusalem and the lands of the Israelites, of Christ and the disciples, as the mainspring of their very different but contiguous cultural inheritances.

Not unnaturally, the Palestine Exploration Fund was the first of the national societies to be formed with the objective of investigating the buried civilizations of the past. It was set up in 1865 with the purpose of pursuing 'accurate, systematic and scientific investigations of the archaeology, topography, geology and physical geography, and manners and customs, of the Holy Land, for biblical illustration'. The final clause was all important. The Queen willingly became Patron of the Society and had a good deal to say in the formulation of its aims. The first field work on behalf of the Society in Palestine was conducted by Lieutenant Charles Warren, a young officer of the Royal Engineers who became – if he was not already – one of his regiment's many recruits to the War Office 'intelligence' staff. As General Sir Charles Warren he was appointed, in 1886, Commissioner of London's Metropolitan Police force, in which post he showed a certain eccentricity, issuing his orders in rhyming couplets to the amusement of subordinates and the consternation of the Home Secretary. As a field commander in the Boer War he added to his reputation for odd behaviour by insisting on bathing in front of his troops and leading his men into one tactical trap after

The Merenptah or 'Israel' stela.

another. In his younger days, at the time of his secondment by the army to the Palestine Fund, a Turco-Egyptian army was squaring for a fight with the Druses in the mountains of Syria. It was merely the latest phase in a history of wars and shifts of authority which had proceeded in much the same way for several millennia. His first despatch unconsciously bridged the thirty centuries which separated the inscription on a mortuary stone at Thebes from the troubled times in which the Palestine Exploration Fund began its activities. Addressed to the

PEF's secretary, George Grove, it was dated 22 August 1867:

My dear Sir,
We completed our travels on the other side of Jordan by a thirty-six hour ride
into Jerusalem ... I wrote to you from Ain Hemar, near es-Salt, on 3rd inst.,
but on arriving at es-Salt, on 13th., I found that my letter had been buried with
the property of the man to whom it had been entrusted ... I told you in that
letter that I had heard of the march of troops against es-Salt, and was hurrying
on to Jerash ... On arriving there I found that the troops were a day's march
from us, and Shaikh Goblan was in a very nervous state. He has upwards of 200
unwiped-out murders on his hands; among others, that of a Turkish officer
and six men, whose throats he cut while they slept ... I send a leopard by
Corporal Phillips, and also a small hawk – present (for) the Zoological Gardens
... The leopard I got in Moab ...
Very truly yours,
CHARLES WARREN

PS – nearly all my time since my return has been taken up in prosecuting the
consular Dragoman for swindling me ...

Before Warren's appointment, another officer of the Royal Engineers, Captain
Charles Wilson, had begun to probe some of the Jerusalem shrines as part of an
investigation of Palestine on behalf of the War Office in London, involving a
trigonometric survey which was completed in 1878 by Lieutenants Conder and
Kitchener, under the auspices of the PEF. Horatio Herbert Kitchener and Claude
Conder were almost evangelical in the religious enthusiasm of their youth. They
had studied Hebrew together while at the Royal Military Academy, and they, like
most of their contemporaries in the Holy Land, were impelled as much by faith as
curiosity in their determination to implement the aims of the Fund as set forth at
the inaugural meeting under the presidency of the Archbishop of York: 'to repel,
with scientific aids, the onslaught of contemporary science on the foundations of
orthodox religion'. They improved the rate of progress of Wilson's team from 76
to 280 square miles a month, despite several attacks on them by Arab tribesmen
and villagers, in one of which Kitchener was stoned and injured. Altogether,
more than 10,000 sites, many of them of archaeological interest, were mapped and
described in a report of seven volumes. An area of about 8,000 square miles was
covered in an exercise which had as its dual and explicit purpose the strategic
assessment of the region and the 'illustration' of the Bible. Even before the arrival
of Wilson and Warren and a contingent of Royal Engineers, work had been in
progress for three decades.

The Cambridge geographer Dr Edward Clarke arrived at Acre in the summer of 1801. He was the first to apply secular scholarship, it might almost be true to say 'scientific method', as opposed to ecclesiastical tradition, to the study of Palestinian antiquities. He was followed the next year by Ulrich Seetzen, a Swiss physician, who spoke Arabic well and was able to travel in disguise, with commissions from the Duke of Saxe-Gotha and the Tsar Alexander I. He was the first western visitor since the Crusades to record the area east of the Sea of Galilee and along the Jordan to the Dead Sea and beyond. Those journeys were followed in 1804 by the formation in London of a Palestine Association, sponsored by wealthy gentlemen and dedicated to the exploration of Palestine, modelled on the successful African Association. It was short lived, but one of Clarke's Cambridge students, the Anglophile Swiss John Lewis Burckhardt, was able to obtain the backing of the influential African body and so follow his countryman Seetzen, in the years between 1808 and 1812, round the Dead Sea and through the Jordan Valley. He located Petra and recorded, more carefully and accurately than anyone before him, the Greek, Roman and Nabataean inscriptions of Palestine, and the signs of ancient habitation. Lady Hester Stanhope, the imperious protector of British priority in the Holy Land, resented the intrusion of a 'foreigner' into territory she regarded very much as her own, and told the ambassador in Constantinople so.

It was, however, an American classicist and theologian who struck the most resonant note in what was to become for Christian scholarship a symphony of discovery and revelation. Edward Robinson of Connecticut was forty-four years old when he first went to Palestine. He had been a student of the biblical scholar Moses Stuart, and had graduated from that most conservative of theological institutions, the Andover Theological Seminary of Massachusetts. He completed his education in Germany at Halle and Berlin, where he came under the influence of Gesenius and Ritter. He returned to America to become Professor of Biblical Literature at the Union Theological Seminary, New York, where he prepared for his apotheosis, a journey through Palestine. Not since the Hebrew historian Josephus returned from the wilderness to Jerusalem in AD 56, at the age of 19, to gather information for his graphic account of the Jewish Wars, had so complete and earnest a scholar traversed the scriptural paths. His book, *Biblical Researches in Palestine*, published in 1841, had immense influence on both sides of the Atlantic. In his own words it described a journey 'which had been the object of my ardent wishes, and had entered into all my plans of life for more than fifteen years'. Robinson was a good scholar who did not allow his own deep conviction to overrule a natural and desirable scepticism, except when confronted by Roman Catholic 'heresy'. He was the first of the 'moderns' to question the authenticity of one of Jerusalem's most famous tourist attractions, the Church of the Holy

The Revd Edward Robinson.

Sepulchre, though centuries before others appear to have entertained the same doubts. Quaresmius, an ecclesiastical geographer of the early seventeenth century, had lambasted 'heretics' who cast doubt on the traditions of the site. Edward Robinson was fortunate in having as his companion the fellow American Eli Smith, a missionary and brilliant Arabist, whose abilities as linguist and philologist enabled Robinson to make a detailed study of almost the entire country, from Sinai to the Lebanon, in two relatively short journeys in 1838 and 1852, and to note important sites and inscriptions. The route of the two Americans was to be that of the Exodus. Mount Sinai and its fifth-century monastery of St Catherine proved the first of many disappointments. The patriarch of the resident Greek church was venal, and the summit, where Moses had received the Law of God, was marked by a mean and shabby shrine. Neither the appearance of the place nor scrutiny of the biblical text encouraged Robinson to think that this could be the place where the Ten Commandments were adumbrated. Seven years after him came a German theologian, Constantine von Tischendorf, who discovered in the monastery the precious parchment manuscript of the Bible which came to be known as the 'Codex Sinaiticus', dating from the fourth century AD and containing the New Testament and parts of the Old.

The Egyptian governor at Aqaba refused Robinson and Smith permission to proceed along the supposed transjordanian route of Moses and the tribes, and so they struck north-east through the Negev desert to Beersheba. 'Here then is the place where the Patriarchs Abraham, Isaac and Jacob often dwelt!' he exclaimed in his journal. Here was the southern border of Palestine proper – Dan to Beersheba. The experience, as for others before and after him, was electric. 'Here Samuel made his judges; and from here Elijah wandered out into the southern desert . . .'. The travellers made their way through Judea on horseback towards the citadel of their dreams, Jerusalem. 'I had read of and studied the localities of this sacred spot; now I beheld them with my own eyes. And they all seemed familiar to me, as if the realization of a former dream. I seemed to be again among the cherished scenes of childhood, long unvisited, indeed, but distinctly recollected.' Like the country through which he had passed, the Holy city was dirty and degraded. Armed with tape measure and compass, he set out to restore to the world a sense of the splendour of Zion. In particular he explored the Dome of the Rock, its enclosure or Haram revered by Jew and Christian as the site of the ancient Temple, by Moslems as the Haram al-Sharif, whence the Prophet ascended to heaven. Since it was pre-eminently a Moslem shrine he could not examine its exterior. Even so, familiarity with Josephus enabled him to identify projecting stones in the southwest face of the wall as the remains of a monumental arch built by King Herod. The feature came to be called 'Robinson's Arch'. The American concluded that the platform on which the Haram was built was in fact the foundation of the Herodian Temple.

There were inevitable flaws in the American scholar's investigative armoury. He was limited by the general lack of archaeological knowledge at the time of his visits. Despite the western obsession with the area over more than eight centuries, much less had come to light by way of useful information about Palestinian antiquity than had emerged from Egypt and Mesopotamia. As in Greece, most of the distant past remained irretrievably buried, and for the same reason; it was covered by the habitations and accretions of the centuries, often crowned by the shrines of Christianity and Islam. As one of Robinson's biographers observed, 'The value of inscriptions was recognised; but old pots, such as would now be eloquent to an archaeologist, were mere curiosities', in Robinson's time, 'that might be Jesubite, Hebrew, Roman, or Arab for all their possessors could tell'. He devoted himself almost entirely to biblical topography, and even in that he was circumscribed by passionate antipathy to 'Popery' and 'Monkishness'.

The pioneering American went past many a *tel*, but the significance of the flat-topped mounds which dotted the landscape, usually composed of the stratified layers of ancient townships, was unknown to most travellers of the time. Robinson thought that they were natural formations, and though he stared Jericho and Lachish in the face he failed to identify them. Nevertheless, he seems to have understood the need to investigate the curious mounds of the region, though he lacked the means. His *Biblical Researches* published simultaneously in the United States, Britain and Germany, won the approval of the academic world and the general public. Carl Ritter called it 'a classic', and it incited a new wave of archaeological interest.

The German Titus Tobler, an historical topographer, followed hard on Robinson's heels to survey Judea and Nazareth. Victor Guérin made a French contribution in the shape of seven large volumes of geographical and topographical information, but like Robinson he too was unable to appreciate the full significance of the archaeological landmarks which lay all around. Claude Conder, the British army officer who arrived in Palestine in 1872, compounded all the misapprehensions of his predecessors. He thought that the mounds were the sites of ancient brick factories.

In 1842, the American Oriental Society, the parent of much that was to follow throughout the Near East, had been established in Boston. Twenty-eight years later, and five years after the setting up of the PEF in London, the American Palestine Exploration Society (APES) was formed in New York. Robinson and his biographer, Roswell D. Hitchcock, were to play formative roles in its work and, indeed, in setting out its aims:

> The work proposed by the Palestine Exploration Society appeals to the religious sentiments alike of the Christian and Jew; it is of interest to the scholar in almost every branch of linguistic, historical or physical investigation, but its supreme importance is for the illustration and defense of the Bible.

In 1848, an American naval expedition, led by Lt. William F. Lynch, sailed down the Jordan from the Sea of Galilee to the Dead Sea, mapping as they went. In 1860 Napoleon III commissioned the great French humanist Renan to investigate ancient Phoenicia, modern Lebanon, and he excavated at Tyre and Sidon, though the best-known consequence of his mission was the literary masterpiece *Vie de Jesus*.

It was another Frenchman of the Second Empire, Félicien de Saulcy, who began the excavation proper of Palestine and thus inaugurated a systematic investigation which was to lead to unsuspected and startling discoveries concerning the earliest human communities. He went to Jerusalem in 1850 to seek solace after the death of his wife. He also sought Sodom and Gomorrah and

Warren at work under 'Robinson's Arch', from painting by William ('Crimea') Simpson.

Charles Clermont-Ganneau.

thought in error that he had found the scene of biblical devastation. Much of his subsequent work was facile, but at least he was the instigator of true archaeological research where conjecture had been rife. In Jerusalem he was attracted to the rock-cut burial chambers at the north of the city, traditionally known as 'The tombs of the Kings'. He readily accepted the tradition, jumping to the conclusion that each grave he found was that of a pre-exilic king of Judah. The richly decorated fragment of a sarcophagus lid was instantly nominated the 'cover of David's coffin'. That the sepulchre, like the many others around it, might be the vault of a rich family of the Herodian period, did not occur to him. Later investigators were in no doubt, however. The classical decoration of the damaged portico forbade any earlier designation. De Saulcy's claims were treated with some scepticism by those who had seen woodcut illustrations of the sepulchre in Guerin's *La Terre Sainte*, but he returned to the site in 1863 convinced of the correctness of his theory. Several sarcophagi were sent to the Louvre, one of which bore the inscribed name of Queen Sadan or Sadah, written twice in different forms of the Semitic alphabet. No light has ever been thrown on the identity of the lady.

Yet another Frenchman among Palestine excavators, Charles Clermont-Ganneau, was of different mettle. His first find consisted of two boundary markers which established the exact location of Canaanite Gezer, along with a Greek inscription of the first century BC warning gentiles not to enter the court of the temple. Much the most important of his many contributions to ancient history, however, was his recovery in 1868 of the famous Moabite Stone, or Mesha Stela as it is usually called, which tribesmen had smashed to pieces in their pique at having been denied just reward for finding it. He found the splintered fragments and thanks to his efforts it was reconstructed with its inscription commemorating victories by Mesha, King of Moab, over Israel in the ninth century BC, at the time when that land was divided into the northern kingdom (Israel) with its capital at Samaria, and the southern kingdom of Judah based on Jerusalem. Mesha of Moab, known as the 'Mutton King', had rebelled against the king of Israel, according to the Bible. 'And Mesha, king of Moab, was a sheepmaster, and rendered unto the king of Israel a hundred thousand lambs ... But it came to pass, when Ahab was dead, that the king of Moab rebelled against the king of Israel'. Ahab, the son of Omri, would ever suffer the fate of men who marry famous women and be known as the 'husband of Jezebel', rather than the ally of Phoenicia and Judah against their common enemy, or the builder of the ivory house so much frowned upon by the Psalmists, the Prophet Amos and the writers of Kings. Jehu, Ahab's successor, was the usurper king of Israel, who broke from Judah and sided with Assyria, 'Jaua of Bit-Humri (the House of Omri)', whose emissaries were shown bringing gifts to Shalmaneser on Layard's Black Obelisk. Mesha must have been tributary at the time that Israel summoned to her aid 'Judah and the Land of Edom' and marched with her allies to lay waste the desolate land of Moab, only to depart – according to the Old Testament – at the moment of victory, leaving matters very much as they were politically. The stone, which tells a different story, was actually discovered by the Alsatian missionary Frederick Augustus Klein.

The story of the Moab stela illustrates in microcosm the intense rivalry with which Europe and the English-speaking world approached biblical archaeology in the midst of the debate which reached its bitter climax in the last quarter of the nineteenth century. Klein was shown the black stela by his Badu host, Shaikh Ahmed bin Tarif, at the village of Dhiban in the Syrian desert. He measured it, finding that it was 'three feet high', and made a partial copy of the text, which he was unable to read. He then proceeded to Kerak, the fortress of the Ottoman army stationed between belligerent Arab and Druse factions in the south of the Vilayet or administrative district of Damascus. He went on to Jerusalem where he confided the details of his find to the German Consul, Heinrich Petermann, a linguist who from Klein's rough copy of part of the inscription was able to determine that it was in early Phoenician idiom. There could, he thought, be little doubt that the missionary had discovered a most important inscription of biblical times. The Arab tribes of the stony desert region in which the stela lay had been alerted to its value by Klein's display of interest. Now Europe was alerted. A battle royal ensued between the governments, libraries and museums of the countries concerned. The French claimed that Klein had betrayed the country of his birth, the British for some reason thought that the secret should have been conveyed to them, and Prussia, recognizing neither that a citizen of Alsace was a natural-born Frenchman nor that Britain had any priority in the matter, authorized Professor Lepsius, the Keeper of the Royal Library, to purchase the stone.

The year 1869, when the matter came to public notice, marked the opening of de Lesseps' Suez Canal. France basked in a glow of achievement and precedence. Britain, fearing the strategic implication of the French engineering feat, was in a sensitive mood. Germany upstaged everyone by sending the Crown Prince Frederick to Jerusalem. In an atmosphere of international vainglory, ownership of the stela of King Mesha became a matter of national pride, though no one knew what its inscription said and the tribal shaikhs had made it clear that as far as they were concerned it belonged to them. Warren, hard at work at Jerusalem for the Exploration Fund, which was deep in financial crisis and unable to pay the mounting debts of its Jerusalem employees, was advised by the German consul to keep out of the matter. Warren acted with the utmost discretion, advising Klein to obtain a plaster impression of the stone as quickly as possible but otherwise refusing to intervene. For his pains he was told by Klein that the Germans could get along perfectly well without his help. The price put on the stone by the Badawin grew alarmingly. A young school teacher, Saba Cawar, was sent by Petermann to negotiate with the Arabs. He returned with a contract to purchase it for 120 napoleons. Clermont-Ganneau, who by this time had spent four years in Palestine and, though only twenty-three, was an acknowledged epigraphist, entered the unseemly conflict, sending secret messengers to make a squeeze-paper copy. A tribal affray took place as his representatives were making their copy, and one of them was injured. All the same, the injured man had the presence of mind to secrete the impression in his saddle-bag before galloping off to Jerusalem. Thus Clermont-Ganneau became the owner of an entire but badly mutilated text. The tribal owners of the stone, the Bani Hamadiyya, realizing that they had been cheated of their 120 napoleons, decided to be rid of the *jinn* within the black stone. They heated it over a fire and then immersed it in water, repeating the process until the hard basaltic mass began to crack. It eventually split open, and when the Arabs were satisfied that it contained no hidden gold, a more vital consideration perhaps than the release of the *jinn*, they shattered it, distributing the larger pieces among the tribesmen, leaving the rest where it fell among the ruins of the desert.

Clermont-Ganneau's foresight in obtaining the 'squeeze' of the inscription was vital. The Frenchman went in search of the tribesmen and combed the ground at Dhiban. Painstakingly, he re-assembled the stela, piece by piece, replacing the missing parts with plaster casts obtained from the 'squeeze' of the original. The text ran:

> I am Mesha, son of Chemosh, king of Moab . . . My father was king of Moab for thirty years and I became king after my father: and I built this sanctuary to Chemosh in Qerihoh, a sanctuary of refuge: for he saved me from all my oppressors and gave me dominion over all my enemies. Omri was king of Israel and oppressed Moab many days, for Chemosh was angry with his land. And his son succeeded him and he also said, I will oppress Moab. In my days he said this: but I got the upper hand of him and his house: and Israel perished forever . . . I have had the ditches of Qerihoh dug by Israelite prisoners . . .

Chemosh was the God of Moab who was worshipped in Jerusalem in the time of Solomon. Qerihoh, Kir-Haraseth of 2 Kings 3 : 25, was the ancient capital of Moab, Diban or Dhiban of the present day. Clermont-Ganneau confided in Warren at Jerusalem, where the British army engineer was by now tunnelling deep beneath the city from vertical shafts which enabled his men to examine the various strata of building without damaging the structures themselves or offending the susceptibilities of their current occupants. It was with Warren's help that the Frenchman had pieced together the fragments of stone and arrived at his first, tentative translation. The two men agreed on simultaneous publication in London and Paris. But Clermont-Ganneau anticipated the arrangement by sending a copy to the French ambassador at Constantinople, the Comte Eugène-Melchior de Vogüé, who had himself carried out surveys of the Holy Land some ten years earlier. On 16 January 1870, the translation appeared in the French *Journal Officiel* signed by Charles Clermont-Ganneau. 'La Stèle de Mésa, roi de Moab, 896 avant J.C.'. Next day *The Times* of London reported the French find and gave the translation. The popular press of Europe took up the story. 'Dramatic Proof of the Bible' was a typical headline. 'Like a lucky actress or singer, it took us by storm', wrote one journalist enigmatically. Incensed by the exclusive claims of the French, George Grove, the founding secretary of the Palestine Exploration Fund, though he had retired from active service in 1868, wrote to *The Times* on 10 February 1870 insisting that Warren and Warren alone had found and translated the text of the black stone. At the same time, backed by wealthy and influential friends in England, he wrote one of many testy letters to Warren demanding that he send better 'squeezes' to London than the 'horrid' examples received so far, and that he should try by every means to get possession of 'as much of this unique Moab relic as may survive'. Warren had suggested early in the proceedings, when the Prussian Museum was trying to purchase the stone, that the British Museum should enter the bargaining through the PEF. His advice was ignored. Now he began to receive angry letters in response to Grove's article accusing him of responsibility for the destruction of this 'holy relic' through negligence.

The sapper, who had by now become an accomplished linguist and engineer-archaeologist, had maintained a correct and dignified position throughout, saying that he did not mind which museum it went to, if and when recovered, so long as it was preserved. He had been starved of promised funds in the five years of his work in Jerusalem, yet was expected to entertain in style the many important visitors sent by the Fund to see how his work was proceeding. The affair of the Moab stela was the last straw. He closed down the excavations in the Spring of 1870, wrote a letter to *The Times* setting out the true story, explaining that Klein had found the stone in the first place, and acknowledging the importance of Clermont-Ganneau's contribution. As a final gesture of defiance he handed to his French colleague eighteen fragments of the stone that Arabs had pressed into his own keeping. Dr Petermann protested from Berlin that it was rightfully the property of Germany. The British Government sided with Germany in an argument which was carried on at the highest diplomatic levels. In the year that the Second Empire fell, Clermont-Ganneau, the lion of French archaeology and scholarship, had the Black Stone of Moab restored and sent to Paris. In 1873 it went on show at the Louvre. It remained for the academic world to engage in a bitter contest of words as to its importance, and even its authenticity. There could be no doubt, however, that its carefully inscribed words in the long-extinct Phoenician dialect of the Moabites, and an early form of the Hebrew language, represented the first known Palestinian text. In the battle which centred on the ownership of a piece of evidence so important to the verification of biblical history, no one noticed, it seems, that it in fact contradicted, or at any rate portrayed another side to, the biblical version of events in the ninth century BC.

Many scholars at first cast doubt on the authenticity of the Moab stone, but their reservations were not sustained. The storm which blew up as the result of the multi-national involvement in its discovery and loss had one positive outcome; it stimulated a new bout of enthusiasm for exploration in the Bible Lands. The PEF sent two young explorers to make a final search of Dhiban,

Charles Tyrwhitt-Drake and Edward Palmer. The former had played an important part in the survey of Palestine, carried out in the Fund's name but increasingly subject to the needs and dictates of the military intelligence office of the British authority in Cairo after the Protectorate of 1882. Palmer, a noted Arabist, became Lord Almoner's Professor of Arabic at Cambridge, a grace-and-favour title since the chair of Arabic at that university was already filled. As the British invasion of Egypt was being planned in 1882, he was sent with two staff officers on an espionage mission to Sinai. All three men were murdered by tribesmen while attempting to cut the Turkish telegraph between Suez and Constantinople, and to suborn Sinai tribal chiefs. Warren, by then a staff Colonel, was despatched to Sinai to find the murderers. Before that dramatic affair, Shaikh Ahmed at Dhiban gave Tyrwhitt-Drake and Palmer a basic lesson in human nature: 'If you Franks had come down here twelve months ago and offered me a pound or two, you might have taken all the stones you chose, the Dhiban one included; but now you have taught us the worth of written stones, and the Arabs are alive to their importance ...'.

Rivalry, jealousy and competitive excavation were the inevitable consequence of the insistent transatlantic demand for biblical history. Two American expeditions financed by the Palestine Exploration Society produced meagre archaeological discoveries, though the Congregationalist Selah Merrill, leader of the second party, published some useful geographical data in 1881. Three years later, in 1884, the Society came to a sudden end, the victim of bickering among members which arose from financial crises such as afflicted the British Fund, and from unrealized ambitions. In 1877, German Lutherans set up the Deutsche Palaestina-Verein, in competition with the Fund. Its man *in situ* was an engineer, Gottlieb Schumacher, who during the next twenty years mapped Palestine from end to end, completing the unfinished work of Kitchener and Conder, and Merrill. He also began to excavate the sites of ancient Megiddo and Samaria. But he proved a better geographer than excavator.

As in Egypt, so in Palestine, methodical, systematic archaeology began with Flinders Petrie. Another Palestinian excavator, the distinguished American William Albright, was to say of Petrie that he was 'the greatest archaeological genius of modern times'. He was probably right, yet it was genius of an ambiguous kind.

His arrival had a twofold significance. As the latest acquisition of the PEF, following one of his early differences of opinion with the Egypt Exploration Society, his advent in 1890 added greatly to the prestige of Palestinian archaeology. But it was as the excavator of Tel-al-Amarna, the desolate site on the Nile between Memphis and Thebes chosen by Akhenaten as his capital, that the name Petrie assumes historic, if somewhat oblique, significance. Three years before he began to dig at the mound of Amarna, in 1887, a few tablets inscribed in the Akkadian cuneiform familiar from the thousands of documents discovered in the royal palaces of Mesopotamia, were found among the debris of the site. By that time of rife excavation, so many riches were being unearthed that it became almost impossible to trace the origins of many discoveries. Petrie's own meticulous methods of recording finds had not been adopted generally. Many artefacts and records were wrongly labelled, or not labelled at all. The tablets of Amarna were, however, even by the standards of the time, exceptional in their lack of provenance. They are said to have been discovered by a peasant woman searching on the mound for the broken-down brick dust which, because of its nitrogen content, had been used through the ages as a fertilizer by smallholders along the Nile. No better explanation of their discovery has ever been advanced, though it is substantiated by nothing more than a colourful tradition. By 1891–2, the season in which Petrie began the Amarna excavations, no mention had been made of the documents. Petrie's interest was chiefly artistic and architectural. His notes for the *Illustrated London News*, written hurriedly between the weightier tasks of digging, sifting and writing his *History of Egypt* as he went along, were concerned with the revolutionary art of the Eighteenth Dynasty. There was no mention of the clay tablets which had been found somewhere in or around the mound four years earlier. The newly discovered art of Amarna would surely have occupied a subsidiary place in his thoughts had he known that among the archives of Amenophis III and his son Akhenaten lay hundreds more documents which cast a penetrating light on relations between all the major states of the world in the fourteenth century BC.

Throughout its long history Egypt was an immensely bureaucratic nation. But from an early date, most of its records were written on papyrus, susceptible to fire, water and vandalism. Unlike the records of Assyria and the other states of Western Asia, preserved by the imperishable clay on which they were written, Egypt's records survived by and large only when they were secreted within the protective walls of the burial chamber, or inscribed on monuments. By far the most important evidence of its past came from the tombs, the house-boats of eternity, and from inscriptions on palace and temple walls. But the Pharaoh Akhenaten's palace contained a library of tablets written and preserved in the manner of those of Nineveh and Nimrud.

They seem simply to have emerged, appearing without provenance in private hands and museum collections. Perhaps the peasant lady of the Nile Valley was more perspicacious than anyone imagined. It was not until thirty years later that the Revd. Archibald H. Sayce, Professor of Assyriology at Oxford and Anglican priest, recorded his hearsay knowledge of the affair. In 1917 he remarked that at the time of the discovery he had heard that at least two-hundred tablets had been destroyed, while many others were deliberately broken. Petrie left the site to others, chiefly J.D.S. Pendlebury. Some years after the tablets began to appear, Petrie told another version of the story. He said that the peasants of the Amarna district were looking for building bricks, and while digging in the ruins found a great number of tablets and tried to sell them to the Egyptian Department of Antiquities which, in spite of the dominance of Britain in the country as whole, was still greatly under the influence of the French. Petrie's opinion of the Egyptian governing body was, if anything, less complimentary than his opinion of the French or the EES, a fact which may have coloured his story. At any rate, the Department of Antiquities, as was its practice, said nothing. The peasants, not to be denied, took them to Luxor and sold them in the streets. It is doubtful whether either story contains the entire truth.

Of a total of more than three-hundred tablets known to have found their way into museum and private collections, only thirty-seven have been identified as the fruits of excavation at Tel al-Amarna. Scholastically, they represent one of the most priceless of all archaeological finds, illuminating the condition of Palestine and some of the major powers of the world, and revealing the internal machinations and external relations of Egypt in the period of the Oppression, a time which also witnessed surging population movements throughout the eastern Mediterranean and Asia Minor. How much more complete that picture would be had more of the cuneiform tablets of Amarna survived, is a matter of conjecture.

Petrie told later how he persuaded the finders of the tablets to take him to the place of discovery. This must have been some time after their disposal. He found several bricks stamped with the words 'The place of the records of the palace of the king'. Thus there could be no doubt that the documents were genuinely from the royal archive. Later, six pottery labels were found near wooden boxes in which the tablets were almost certainly stored, together with a seal. The seal bore the name of Akhenaten, the pottery plaques that of his father Amenophis III.

The Amarna letters were accepted by the end of the nineteenth century as indisputable evidence that Egypt's imperial strength was sapped by the effeminate, schismatic regime of monotheistic sun-disc worshippers which came to its end with the death of Tutankhamen, in about 1320 BC. Most are concerned with political and commercial matters, written in Akkadian, the diplomatic language of the day. The 347 documents which survive in their entirety are addressed to or from Akhenaten and his father Amenophis III. The main burden of their texts is the relations of the Egyptian Court with fellow monarchs of Western Asia and with satellite rulers of Syria, Phoenicia and Palestine.

Independent rulers who wrote to Amenophis III and Akhenaten were Kadashman Enlil I and Burnaburiash II of the Kassite Dynasty of Babylon;

Tushratta of Mitanni; Assur Uballit of Assyria; Suppiluliuma of Hatti; Tarhundaraba of Arzawa; and the unnamed king of Alashia. Even the identities of some of these kingdoms are uncertain. The people of Mitanni, a northern kingdom which straddled Syria and Mesopotamia, were known widely as 'horse lovers', racing their steeds on the banks of the twin rivers, expert charioteers whose ruling aristocracy was called Maryannu, a term related to the Indo-Aryan word Marya, meaning 'young warriors'. Hatti was the land of the Hittites. Arzawa is unknown. Alashia is an archaic name for Cyprus. There can be no doubt as to the identities of the kings of Babylon and Assyria, or of the Hittite domains.

Correspondence over such a broad sweep of territory between powerful heads of state affords a clear picture of regal affairs and political conditions throughout the Near East. Even the transmission of the letters would have been virtually impossible unless there was some kind of law and order in the intervening lands. Both Kadashman Enlil and Burnaburiash say that Amenophis III was in communication with their fathers. Amenophis is shown to have married one of Kadashman Enlil's sisters, and at a time of strained relations between the two empires the Babylonian accuses his brother-in-law of breaking the word of his father, Tuthmosis IV. Burnaburiash confirms that Akhenaten's messengers have paid three visits to his Court, and the Babylonian declines to send one of his daughters to Egypt as a bride, considering the proposed escort of only five chariots insulting. Indeed, the Amarna correspondence opens with acrimonious exchanges between the prospective fathers-in-law, Amenophis and Kadashman Enlil, about the projected wedding. The Babylonian king complains that his messenger has been detained in Egypt for six years in the course of nuptial negotiations. Amenophis was not without influence in his relations with Babylon, or with Tushratta of Mitanni, it seems, for both received annual allowances of gold from him. The marriage did eventually take place, for a later tablet lists the presents sent back and forth. Such letters illuminate the rivalries and attachments of the royal households of the fourteenth century BC in intimate and fascinating detail. In connection with Palestinian history, however, their significance lies in the accuracy with which they enable us to date reigns and events, and assess the stability of the Egyptian dominions.

The vast archives of the Babylonian dynasties began to emerge from the mounds of Mesopotamia soon after the discovery of the Amarna letters, and thus the historical record of the time could be looked at from two essential sides. Kadashman Enlil, according to the Babylonian record, ruled for 'at least' fifteen years, and he vacated the throne in favour of Burnaburiash II a year before his own death, in 1359 BC. Burnaburiash was king for twenty-seven years until 1333. The Assyrian Ashur-uballit I, ruled for thirty-six years, from 1363 to 1328, thus providing a useful check period. The Egyptian side of the story is not as clear. The reigns of the two Babylonian kings spanned at least the forty-two years from 1374 to 1333. The long-living Amenophis III is known to have ruled for at least thirty-nine years, the last twelve of which embraced a co-regency with his son Akhenaten. Akhenaten ruled for a further four to five years after his father's death. There is evidence that part of this period involved another co-regency, with Akhenaten's reputed son, Smenkhkare. A different relationship is suggested, however, by the discoveries of an expedition of the German Archaeological Institute which began to dig at Amarna just before the outbreak of the First World War. It unearthed in the workshop of the royal sculptor, Thutmose, a statue showing the deformed figure of Akhenaten in intimate kissing pose with a young man, along with a relief showing the dual monarchs sitting together clotheless, one with his arm round the other and 'chucking' him under the chin with his free hand. The suggestion that Smenkhkare was the homosexual partner of Akhenaten is lent support by the effeminate looks of the senior partner of the kingship. That the royal city of Amarna, or Akhetaten, to give it the name of its time, was a place of sensual delights as well as religious unorthodoxy and political intrigue may safely be inferred from the obloquy which followed the death of Akhenaten. The fascination of court life at that ephemeral and elusive moment of Egyptian history is highlighted by another famous discovery of the German team – the sculptured head of the beautiful Nefertiti, Akhenaten's wife, one of the artistic wonders of the world.

The letters make frequent reference to the death of Amenophis and the accession of Akhenaten. None can be dated with assurance later that Akhenaten's sole reign, which lasted little more than two years, followed by two and a half years of the second co-regency. But a letter from Tushratta, King of Mitanni, refers to messengers held by Akhenaten for four years after the death of his father, suggesting that the correspondence runs to almost the end of Akhenaten's reign. In short, the documents relate entirely to the period, roughly fifteen years, from the occupation of the capital in about the seventh year of Amenophis's co-regency, to its abandonment under Akhenaten's successor Tutankhamen. There are other events which help to anchor us in time. There are several letters from Zurata and Zatana, vagabond princes of Acco. The internal evidence of the correspondence shows that they were father and son and that Zurata the father was a contemporary of Amenophis III. These two turn up in other tablets as Shutatna and Sharatum. But it is Burnaburiash who complains to Akhenaten that one of his caravans has been waylaid at Hinnatuni in Palestine by 'Egyptian subjects', naming Shutatna the son of Sharatum. If the son was contemporary with Burnaburiash and Akhenaten, it is not ureasonable to suppose that a letter from the father to an un-named Egyptian king was in fact addressed to

Amenophis. Then there is a letter from Biridiya of Megiddo to an un-named Pharaoh, announcing the capture of a city king named Labaia whom they had been ordered to deliver to Egypt. Zurata took charge of the prisoner, promising to put him on a ship to Egypt, and promptly released him on receipt of a bribe. Before Biridiya and his brother could recapture the man he was killed. Zurata's involvement again suggests that the events took place in the reign of Amenophis, or perhaps during the first co-regency.

More than fifty letters emanate from Ribaddi, prince of Gubla which is identifiable as the Byblos of Rome, Jubail of modern Lebanon. One of these refers to the accession of a new Pharaoh, and goes on to say that Aziru, king of Amurru, has captured Sumur, a city which had formed part of his own Syrian territory. From this it is deduced that Amenophis reigned until the capture of Sumur, and was succeeded at that time by Akhenaten. The same kind of detective work led to the gradual apportionment of the letters to the reigns of Amenophis and Akhenaten respectively. Of 347 whole documents, 138 can be attributed to the father Pharaoh, 78 to the son and 5 perhaps to the periods of the co-regencies. All in all, the most convincing of expert conjectures is that the Amarna letters cover the last ten years of Amenophis's rule, and the entire five years of Akhenaten's. As that fifteen year period covers also the accession of Burnaburiash in 1359, and the majority of the correspondence was conducted with his predecessor Kadashman Enlil, probably in the last half of his fifteen-year reign, it is fair to estimate that the letters and the period of the Amarna 'heresy' fall substantially between the years 1367 and 1352 BC.

Many of the letters from subject rulers are written in the Canaanite form of the Akkadian language. One, Suwardata, prostrates himself before the Pharaoh 'on my belly and on my back', and proceeds to matters of political concern to both: 'The King, my Lord, should know that the Hapiru have risen in the land which the God of the King, my Lord, has given me, and that I have beaten them, and the King, my Lord, should know that all my brothers have left me; and that I and Abdu-Kheba alone are left to fight the Hapiru . . .' The Hapiru again. Or Habiru: Hebrew?

The letters anticipate the scene reported by the Spies of Moses of the fearsome fortifications of the Canaanite cities, 'walled up to heaven', of 'cyclops walls' so menacing to the tribes who sought the Promised Land. Zurata appears again. 'Zurata, prince of Acco and Indaruta prince of Achsaph, were the ones who hastened to my help in return for fifty chariots of which I have now been deprived. But behold, (now) they are fighting against me and may it please the King, my Lord, to send the Ianhamu (the Egyptian military chief in Palestine), so that we may wage a proper war and restore the land of the King, my Lord, to its old frontiers.'

Suwardata is an Indo-Aryan name; so is Indaruta. It is estimated that a third of the princely correspondents named in the Amarna Letters are of Indo-Aryan descent, suggesting a dominant aristocracy whose passage across the steppes of central and western Asia towards the Mediterranean had occurred long before the palace of Akhenaten was built as the show place of a new faith and the transitory centre of political and commercial administration. Abdu-Khedba's people, the Hurri or Khuru of Canaan were the biblical Horites of the time of Abraham.

As archaeological discovery gathered momentum, further archives spread across the fertile crescent filled more gaps, showing the closest political and commercial ties between nations from the Aegean to Elam, at a time when the Babylonian Empire reigned supreme under Hammurabi, in the eighteenth century BC, and for the six centuries which followed until the old order began to break up.

Papyri even earlier than the Amarna letters add to the picture of Palestine, ancient Canaan, in the days of Egyptian hegemony. Three hundred years before the capital of Egypt was moved to the newly built city of Akhetaten, Egypt had confronted the terrible force of an invading army of Semites, the Hyksos, 'Rulers of Foreign Lands'. The lesson endured for a thousand years and more. The Egyptians knew them as 'The Robbers'. Manetho recorded their deeds: 'Unexpectedly from the regions of the East, came men of unknown race. Confident of victory they marched against our land. By force they took it, easily, without a single battle.' The historian who had at his disposal the records of the past described the bloodshed and cruelty of their rule, and the eventual move from Memphis to Sais, their fortress capital of Avaris guarded by 240,000 men. That the Hebrews were in Egypt at about the time of Hyksos rule there can be little doubt. Whether Joseph, after being sold off to Potiphar, became the Pharaoh's viceroy and rode in the 'second chariot' of the royal procession is far from certain, but if he did it was surely in a Hyksos chariot with a Hyksos king, for such vehicles were not used ceremonially before their advent. For the rest, clay tablet, stone and papyrus are silent. One twentieth-century scholar, observing that Jew and Egyptian crossed each other's paths in the turbulent times between the wanderings of the Semite Abraham and the tales related in Exodus, asks us to note that Sinuhe was successful in Canaan but was buried according to his wish in Egypt, 'even as Joseph is successful in Egypt but buried in his native Canaan'.

There is no weighty evidence in the Amarna correspondence for the widespread theory that Egyptian control of its adjacent provinces and its influence in Western Asia collapsed almost as soon as the Eighteenth Dynasty came to its end. There were difficulties, but not more so than any great power has experienced in recorded history. There were many achievements in store and great battles to be fought in the ensuing century of the Ramesses and the Setis. But the seed of decline had been sown. Assyria was ascendant in Western Asia and the days of Egyptian supremacy were numbered.

Sometime between the collapse of the Eighteenth Dynasty and the end of the next, the Israelites arrived in Canaan to a less than enthusiastic welcome. They found there a culture which had been established for some seven-hundred years, since the Middle Bronze Age in about 1900 BC. They arrived, as we know from the Merenptah inscription at Thebes, before 1229 BC. Some believe that they left Egypt with the Hyksos in the late sixteenth century. It is probably safer to assume that the exit of the Jews occurred in stages and reached its peak in the middle years of the fourteenth century, after the demise of Akhenaten's capital. But the records of Egypt, Babylon, the Anatolian and Syrian kingdoms, and evidence found subsequently in ancient Greece, showed that the movements of the tribes of Israel were coincident with massive population shifts and invasions. The strip of coastal land between Egypt and northern Syria was subjected to the increasing pressures of migration and the intrusion of alien peoples. As to the 'Exodus', the reputed forty years in the wilderness, and the arrival of the tribes of Moses, the Old Testament and the traditions of the Jews remain our only sources of information. Confirmation of that most solemn of all western traditions, the journey to the Promised Land and the setting up of places of worship to the universal God, was the overt reason for almost all archaeological endeavour in the Near East. But it can offer no independent affirmation. Inscriptions and correspondence subsequently found in Egypt and elsewhere, offer no more than indirect guidance. There is no reason to doubt that the Scouts or Spies of Moses saw a well-armed, if divided foe in front of them, and the tribes halted somewhere on the way. Moses had ascended to the top of Pisgah, 'that is over against Jericho' and the Lord had shown him all the land, before he, Moses, took his leave of the world and handed his mantle to Joshua, one of the twelve scouts and the strategist of the struggle for Canaan.

It was in Canaan that Abraham established himself as a landowner somewhere between 2000 and 1900 BC, and laid the foundations for his descendants' settlement. According to Genesis he commanded his own troops, allied to the Amorites, and successfully defeated a coalition of invaders. Even then, Abraham was called a 'Hebrew' according to Genesis, a word that many scholars equate with *Apiru*, written *ha-pi-ru* in the Akkadian, as in Suwardata's plea to the Pharaoh.

Nearly eight hundred years after Abraham, Canaan was occupied by the Philistines. Israel would have to dispossess them in order to build its own temples and its own empire. Again it is Egypt which provides indirect evidence of the circumstances in which this alien people arrived. Near the Valley of the Kings, where French and British excavators have dug and sifted from the early nineteenth century to the present, the Mortuary Temple of Ramesses III at Madinat Habu has revealed a history of the campaigns of the Pharaoh, written on stone and thus better preserved than the papyrus and painted wall records. These relief tablets show that in the period of Ramesses III, c.1195–1164 BC, Asia Minor and the eastern Mediterranean suffered wholesale destruction at the hands of a sea-borne force which burnt and massacred as it went, until it arrived at the gateway of Egypt. A well-drilled destructive army moved by land and water, marching along the coastal plain of Syria, and probably along the Sinai coast road towards the Delta, at the same time sending a great armada across the water towards Alexandria and Rosetta. One inscription says: 'No country has been able to withstand their might. The land of the Hittites, Kode (Cilicia), Carchemish . . . and Cyprus have been destroyed . . . They march against Egypt.' Another tells of these 'Sea Peoples' entering 'the mouths of the river' and of Ramesses III hastening by swift chariot to engage them. The Egyptians repulsed the all-conquering army, and the invaders suffered terrifying losses if the engraved-stone record is anything like correct. Who were these 'Sea Peoples', destroyers of some of the most warlike nations of the East in their bloody and brief excursions? Nobody has ever been able to say for certain. But after their retreat from the Egyptian onslaught, the Philistines had taken possession of much of Canaan. A large part of the land to which the Israelites believed they had a pre-eminent title, was occupied by warriors who almost certainly came with the 'Sea Peoples'. The depredations of the seafaring marauders of the twelfth century would impress themselves on the students of other lands as archaeological field work proceeded into the twentieth century AD.

In the unfolding story of the division of the biblical lands, legend was still woven into the tapestry of history. Samson and Delilah, David and the Philistine giant Goliath, Saul and Jonathan, were but part of the colourful cast in a drama which would engulf the conscience and consciousness of East and West. Yet the Israelites had hardly settled to enjoy their lordship of the territory promised by God and won in battle, before they built sanctuaries to traditional gods and placed images in the temples of David, and demonstrated that their flesh was as weak as any other by fighting among themselves for power and glory.

David assumed the crown of Israel in c.1025 BC, and made Jerusalem his capital, and Solomon the son of David became the financial emperor of the world. With the death of Solomon in c.926 BC, the vision of a united Israel died, and Assyria became the dominant power. 'So Israel rebelled against the House of David . . . there was none that followed the House of David, but the tribe of Judah only.' In the time of David and his son, the Israelites had exhibited a taste for the Egyptian fleshpots. The convent of the cult prostitutes was in the temple precinct. The sun-god was high on their list of deities. Had the children of Israel perhaps learnt in Egypt, at the heretical court of Akhenaten, the notion of a singular omnipotent God, and adapted it to their own pressing needs on the desert crossing to the Promised Land? And had they perhaps reverted to older and more comfortable forms of worship once they had achieved their territorial objective?

An Egyptian document that has given rise to much conjecture among biblical scholars and those who seek a neutral position in Palestinian archaeology, was published by the British Museum's Wallis Budge in 1922. Called the *Wisdom of Amenemope*, the composition was written on papyrus by the scribe Senu in about 750 BC, but it is a copy of a much earlier document, probably c.1250 BC, in which an official named Amenemope, son of Kanakhte, writes down the words of the wise man to his son. Such compositions were popular during the Middle Kingdom, about 2000 BC, and the words in this case have a remarkable similarity to sayings in the Book of Proverbs: *Amenemope* says, for example:

> Give thine ears, hear what is said, give thy mind to interpret them; to put them in your heart is good.

And Proverbs:

> Bow down thine ear and hear the words of the wise and apply thine heart unto my knowledge (22:17).

There are many like examples, which prove nothing but suggest at the very least an Egyptian influence.

It was not until the eighteenth year of King Josiah, 621 BC, that Hilkiah the high priest told Shapham the secretary, 'I have found the book of the law in the house of the Lord'. It was too late to cleanse the sins of the past:

> And the king commanded Hilkiah . . . to bring out of the temple of the Lord all the vessels made for Baal, for Asherah (Ishtar), and for all the host of heaven; he burned them outside Jerusalem in the fields of Kidron, and carried their ashes to Bethel . . . Moreover Josiah put away the mediums and the wizards and the teraphim and the idols and all the abominations that were seen in the land of Judah and in Jerusalem, that he might establish the words of the law which were written in the book . . .

The God of Israel was not to be appeased. The temples were destroyed, Jerusalem was sacked and the people taken into exile by Nebuzaradan, the captain of Nebuchadnezzar's bodyguard.

Samaria ivory, winged sphinx with human head, 9–7 centuries BC.

Twentieth-century discoveries on the Syrian side of the Euphrates would reveal further hints as to the possible origins of biblical legends, even of proper names; for example, that the name 'David' in the old cuneiform texts was used to denote 'General' or 'Commander' and was not in the days before Israel a proper-name at all.

By the beginning of the twentieth century, archaeologists had begun to investigate the site of Joshua's victory at the crossing of the Jordan – Jericho – where at the sound of the trumpet the wall fell flat, 'And they burnt the city with fire and all that was therein'.

Jericho would provide the key to a past which transcended all existing concepts of urban habitation. Excavations conducted by John Garstang, Petrie's 'promising young student' in Egypt in 1899, and the British woman archaeologist Kathleen Kenyon, daughter of a prominent director of the British Museum, would lead to a walled city which was occupied as far back in time as the ninth millennium BC. At a higher level, representing eighth-millennium habitation, she unearthed a remarkable object which, when cleaned and closely examined was seen to be a primitive man-made sculpture, a flattened skull with its jaw-bone removed, painted at the level of the forehead with broad coloured bands, possibly imitating a headdress. Facial features were delicately moulded in plaster. Sea-shells were used as eyes and ears. Altogether, seven such sculptures were found in the same trench. Others were found at sites in Palestine and Syria in the late twentieth-century. These Neolithic ancestors of the sculptor's art, were created from the heads of the departed. Decapitated bodies in nearby graves suggest that it was a popular art in its time; understandably, for it enabled succeeding generations to keep in touch with each other in a very tangible sense. It was through artefacts such as these that the full-blown three-dimensional arts must have developed, in Sumer and Akkad, Egypt and Greece, to be transported across a time-bridge of some seven-thousand years, to the modern world.

Petrie, in 1897, married one of his students, Hilda Mary Urlin, and from then on they worked in tandem. She proved a capable if divisive excavator and site manager, and a hopeless housekeeper. Among their joint achievements was a series of massive excavations in Palestine. Work there began for Petrie in 1891, as he became increasingly disenchanted with the British in Egypt. From 1926 he and Hilda devoted the rest of their lives to that region – apart, of course, from teaching and organizing annual exhibitions of work which were held under several auspices since Petrie fell out with sponsors one by one. At Tel Abu Salima, an insignificant mound between Gaza and Al Arish, close to the present border of Sinai with Israel, they excavated a mud-brick building which Petrie identified as Assyrian, comparing it with a temple within the palace of Sargon at Khorsabad, which Frankfort excavated: though Petrie believed that part of the Palestinian building was attributable to Nebuchadnezzar. Modern Israeli scholars have identified that outpost as the commercial centre which is referred to in one of the most famous, and most puzzling of Assyrian inscriptions. Following the death of Shalamaneser V, the Philistine (Palestine) cities were joined by the Egyptians in rebellion against the Assyrian Empire. In 720 BC, Sargon II crushed the rebels and their supporters and set up a provincial capital at Gaza. A tablet and a prism, found at Khorsabad and Nimrud respectively, have made it possible to reconstruct Sargon's pronouncement: 'I opened the sealed *karu* of Egypt. Assyrians and Egyptians I mingled together and made them trade with each other.' Scholars have generally believed 'karu' to be the closed harbour of the 'Brook of Egypt', or Wadi Arish. Recent research suggests that Petrie's Tel Abu Salima, which its excavator thought hardly worth recording, was the site of Sargon's great commercial centre, the 'Sealed Karu of Egypt'.

It was for Charles Clermont-Ganneau to link the nineteenth and twentieth centuries with a tragi-comic intervention. Clermont-Ganneau was a mere twenty-three years of age when he became embroiled in the Moab Stone controversy in 1869. He was in his late twenties when a post-script to that affair brought him into the forefront of dispute once again. By then his reputation was established. In 1873 an Arab named Salim al-Gari visited the Jerusalem antiques shop owned by Moses Wilhelm Shapira, a Russian Jew who had emigrated to Palestine thirteen years earlier and had adopted the Anglican faith. Al-Gari offered him a collection of antiquities which included pottery vessels and figurines, stone statues and other items, most of which bore inscriptions whose lettering was remarkably similar to that of the Moabite Stela. Shapira was assured that much more material of a similar kind was available, obtained from a place close to Dhiban. The German museums and universities, anxious to repair the damage to their prestige inflicted by France over the stela, grasped at Shapira's offer of an almost unimaginably prestigious hoard. Inscriptions and figures were studied earnestly by leading Prussian scholars, and their findings were published in dozens of academic articles. The German consul at Jerusalem was instructed to send as much of the material as he could purchase to Berlin. In the last weeks of 1873, the wretched Frenchman who had meddled so embarrassingly in the Moab Stone saga, now ventured an opinion on the Moabite pottery. At a glance he pronounced it a gigantic fraud. He went further. He forced Al-Gari to admit that the pieces had been manufactured in Jerusalem under his supervision. The German consul had tried to prevent the Frenchman from seeing the pottery, but faced with a clear admission of guilt on the part of the Arab, he and the German academic world had to admit defeat for a second time. It was not only Germany that was proved wanting by the Frenchman.

In 1878, a year in which archaeology was preoccupied with Rassam's discovery of the Shalmaneser Gates at Balawat, Shapira was again visited by Arab fortune hunters, this time a group of tribal shaikhs who mentioned that they knew of some blackened skins bearing unintelligible letters. Shapira eventually acquired fifteen strips of parchment from his Badawin visitors. Again, the lettering was exactly like that of the Moab Stela. With a little acquired knowledge of ancient Hebrew, he deduced that he had in his possession the Book of Deuteronomy, and sent copies of the 'scrolls' to Professor Schlottman at Berlin. Twice bitten, the Germans were understandably shy of Mr Shapira. They declared the scrolls from the region of the Dead Sea a transparent forgery. Shapira placed the parchment strips in a bank vault in Jerusalem and concentrated on selling Yemenite Bibles, his chief stock in trade. In 1883 he took the strips from his bank and started to re-examine them, dampening them with water and alcohol to make the letters more legible. He was convinced that he had a version of Deuteronomy that, if not written by Moses himself, was early and complete enough to solve the textual problems that had worried scholars over the years. The Germans became interested. Shapira, an ambitious man, was fêted in Berlin, though Professor Lepsius was sceptical. Leipzig was less cautious, however, and within a few weeks of Shapira's arrival there a pamphlet was published in the name of the scholar Hermann Güthe, entitled 'Fragments of a leather manuscript, including Moses' last speech to the children of Israel'. Shapira left for London, where Walter Besant, the Secretary of the PEF, and Captain Conder, who was on leave in London, arranged for him to see Dr Christian Ginsburg of the British Museum. The entire staff of the Manuscript Room of the museum awaited his arrival. Ginsburg was impressed with the scrolls. He wrote in *The Times* of 3 August 1883 that the British Museum intended to purchase them. The *Illustrated London News* published facsimile strips. The Queen, excited by the prospect of the purchase, offered to underwrite it. A million pounds was the sum mentioned. For a brief moment, Shapira was the most famous man in the world.

On 15 August, Clermont-Ganneau arrived at the museum. He was not a welcome visitor, either to Ginsburg or Shapira, but he was by now a distinguished scholar and entitled to a courteous reception. Professor Sayce had already described the scrolls as forgeries in the *Academy*. But Shapira had the popular press on his side and the Museum could not easily turn its back on assertions and promises, made in the heat of the moment, which would bring the Bible in its original form to England. Clermont-Ganneau was allowed to view the leather strips only through a glass case. He declared then to be 'without hesitation or discussion', the work of 'a modern forger'. In an open letter to *The Times* he offered to produce exactly similar texts for Leviticus or Numbers on strips of synagogue roll, adding that he would not charge 'a million pounds sterling' for them. Ginsburg conceded defeat in another letter to *The Times*. Shapira's business was ruined, though he himself was the chief victim of the 'fraud'. In 1884 he shot himself, a year before his 'Deuteronomy' was sold in London for ten pounds. Conder had insisted during the dispute that parchment scrolls could not survive the atmosphere of the Dead Sea. More than fifty years later, in 1947, scrolls were found on the other side of the Sea, containing parts of Genesis, Deuteronomy and Judges. With them were potsherds. They were taken by the tribesmen who found them to Bethlehem from where they found their way to the black market. The leather scrolls contained incised lines and other features by which Clermont-Ganneau had condemned Shapira's collection. The lettering was similar in some cases. But this time the scrolls were declared authentic by experts of the Oriental Institute at Chicago, working in collaboration with the Chicago Institute of Physics (it was the latter Institute which, by 1952, had developed the Carbon-14 method of dating). By 1947, however, Shapira's name was forgotten and his scrolls had disappeared. Perhaps they will turn up again one day.

───── 7 ─────

Lands of the Twin Rivers

When Layard visited Babylon in the autumn of 1850, while on his last visit to Mesopotamia, he took the opportunity to look at a number of possible sites in the marshy territory which lies between Baghdad and the junction of the Tigris and Euphrates. He made several tentative probes, but he recognized that excavation was beyond his means, technically and financially. Nothing short of a Parliamentary vote of twenty-five thousand pounds would, he thought, be sufficient. In a statement published in the *Journal Asiatique* he added a heartfelt rider: '. . . if ever this sum should be voted, I would solicit the favour of not being charged with its application'.

On his way to the southern sites he called at Nimrud where Rawlinson was now in charge. He found the Resident wrapped in a travelling rug, fast asleep. His assistant Hormuzd Rassam, who was returning to England with his chief, was taken ill. Layard himself contracted malaria. Rawlinson returned to his duties as Consul-General and Resident at Baghdad, after preparing a paper for the Royal Asiatic Society on the continuing excavation of Nineveh. Before it was read at the Annual General Meeting of the Society on 5 June 1852, the Secretary said: 'Colonel Rawlinson, in a letter dated at the camp of Nineveh, 11 April 1852, states that the paper was drawn up . . . in great haste, amid torrents of rain, in a little tent upon the mound of Nineveh, without any aids beyond a pocket Bible, a note-book of inscriptions, and a totally retentive memory'. Rawlinson's tract began: 'Every new fact which is brought to light from the study of the cuneiform inscriptions tends to confirm the scriptural account of the primitive seat of empire having been established in Lower Chaldaea, or in the neighbouring district of Susiana.' The excavations of the great Assyrian cities at Khorsabad, Nineveh and Nimrud were left in abeyance, to await the return of Rassam. Temples, palaces, winged bulls and lions and other colossal sculptures were abandoned, exposed to weather and tribes.

While attention turned southward to the Babylonian and Sumerian mounds,

Christian Rassam, British Vice-Consul at Mosul and eldest brother of Hormuzd, was asked to keep an eye on the Ninevite sites around Mosul. He and his wife Matilda were in regular touch with Layard in his new capacity as Under-Secretary of State at the Foreign Office. Matilda was the sister of George Percy Badger, chaplain to the East India Company and author of *The Nestorians and their Rituals*, published in 1852. Some work proceeded at the Kuyunjik mound under the Vice-Consul's aegis, not at the level of Nineveh but at a later cemetery site which turned out to be Parthian and to contain in its tombs bodies, jewelry, gold face masks and other artefacts from the first century of the Christian era. Matilda wrote to Layard on 21 April 1852, announcing the first finds, 'the body of a young female . . . a thin gold mask for the face – a pair of gold scales laid across the breast – necklace of small gold beads – two pairs of gold earrings, a number of small gold studs . . . two rings, an Assyrian cylinder and an *aureus* belonging to Tiberius. . .'.

Early in July she told Layard of more discoveries, another gold mask and more jewelry. She addressed him affectionately, 'I really believe that were it not for the love which you have for the excavations, that you would forget your old friends entirely', she had written in the previous February. But her letters cast a light on another side of Rawlinson's character. 'I am rather astonished that Col. Rawlinson does not write to you occasionally about the excavations knowing that you must take great interest in everything connected with the mounds' (5 July 1852). In the same letter: 'Hormuzd writes me that the papers are full of the discoveries, but giving all the credit and honour to Col. Rawlinson, whereas he had nothing to do with it . . . when we informed Col. Rawlinson of the discovery he seemed to turn up his nose . . .'. Then, 'I will tell you, confidentially, that whatever we do, and however much interest we may take in the excavations, it does not seem to please him . . . I don't think I ever met with such a fickle person'.

In Layard's absence in 1848–9, Rassam had proved so capable of managing the sites that Kennett Loftus, who had taken over as local representative of the Assyrian Society, felt able to leave them in his care while he went off to 'make certain geological investigations' in the company of troops under the command of the British frontier commissioner, Colonel Williams. In the course of that shadowy mission (even archaeological details were not released by the Foreign Office until seven years later), Loftus made the first scientific survey of Babylon itself, close to the modern Arab town of Hillah. He did not think it necessary to dwell on that part of the journey, however, in the report which was submitted to the Journal of the Royal Geographical Society. He made his way through territory 'thinly inhabited by a rude and almost savage race of nomad Arabs, who are continually at war with each other and with the Turkish authorities'. Loftus and the troops, together with Harry Churchill, a career diplomat who served in Stambul and Tehran, went across marshland from the Euphrates to Nufr (Niffar or Nippur). Loftus had been persuaded, wrongly, by Rawlinson that this was Old Babylon; that there were, in fact, two Babylons, an original city at Nippur and Nebuchadnezzar's later metropolis, of which its proud builder is reported as saying: 'Is this not great Babylon, that I have built for the house of the kingdom, by the might of my power, and for the honour of my majesty?'

His description of the entire region of biblical Chaldaea was precise, couched in the language of the surveyor. His measured words were aptly illustrated by the versatile Churchill who, as well as being a competent artist, tried his hand successfully at journalism during his career in the East. Nippur was approached along the bed of one of the ancient canals which had imparted life and wealth during thousands of years of greatness.

We had but a short time to examine [the ruins]; they consist of an elevated platform divided into two nearly equal portions by a deep channel 36 or 40 paces wide, running in a direction 33 E. of S. The extent of the platform is about 1m. from E.N.E. to W.S.W ... The whole surface is covered with fragments of pottery, bricks with cuneiform inscriptions, and glass ... The bricks are both sun-dried and kiln-baked: the building constructed of the latter is pierced with similar oblong apertures to those observed at ... other ruins of the Babylonian age ... At a few hundred yards on the E. side of the ruins, fragments of what we supposed to be the exterior walls of the ancient city could be traced in a series of low continuous mounds ... I may here mention, for the instruction of future travellers, that the best period of the year for visiting ... is from the middle of October till the middle of December ... .

It was not the stuff of the current popular enthusiasm for archaeological discovery, but very much the kind of information which would assist aspiring diggers. 'We were rather too late, as the ground for 3m. before we arrived at the ruins was so soft that our horses sank above their fetlocks', wrote Loftus. He moved on to Warka. 'We had now attained the Muntafik country, and, as we advanced, a half-naked race of savages – wearing no covering but a loose abba (cloak), their long locks streaming wildly in the wind – rushed out, spear and club in hand, to meet our little party, who, they supposed, were going to plunder them ...'. The intruders were allowed to proceed, sixty warriors performing a war dance, Maori-fashion, as they went on their way.

'After crossing the outer walls of the city, each step that we advanced convinced us that this was one of the most important ruins in Mesopotamia.' Warka, biblical Erech or Uruk, is one of the great necropolis sites of Chaldaea. Its walls, stretching for nearly six miles in circumference, enclosed an enormous platform of mounds and ruins. Three principal structures – temples or tombs –

[178]

could be made out even without excavation. Buttresses of brick masonry bore cuneiform legends of Uruk, which Rawlinson, with whom Loftus was in constant correspondence, assigned with confidence to a king of 2300 BC. 'Warka was a sacred burial-place from the very earliest times till about the commencement of the Christian era', wrote Loftus. In less than three days spent 'in rambling over and examining ruins' he found slipper-shaped coffins of glazed earthenware, extending down for more than thirty feet, at the Parthian level of a vast burial ground. There was a Parthian temple too, but Loftus had no means of dating it. He unearthed a wall section with a coloured mosaic of terracotta. It was of the early Sumerian or Uruk period of the fourth millennium BC, but such terms were unknown in Loftus's day. He visited many other mounds, some of which have never since been investigated. Most were inhabited by lions which naturally enough resented the intrusion into their peaceful lives. In retribution, they ate Loftus's guard dogs, one by one. 'Poor Toga', said Loftus of the last dog to be devoured.

At Sankara (Senkereh) on the bank of an ancient canal, the Shatt al Kor, he found inscriptions that enabled Rawlinson to identify it as the site of Larsa, Ellasar of Genesis. The last mound to be examined in any detail on his journey was Muqayyar six miles from the right bank of the Euphrates. The ziggurat mound, situated in the north-west corner of an extensive group of low mounds, consisted of two distinct building levels. He searched for the canal of Pallacopas which Alexander the Great cut between the river and the ancient city (shown on several old maps), but without success. Neither Loftus nor Alexander before him could have known that they were at Ur of the Chaldees, the reputed birthplace of Abraham. Loftus noted structural similarities between the kiln-brick buildings here and at Warka. Churchill found three large blocks of black granite, which were thought to belong to a large statue or perhaps a sacrificial altar, but with all the strength of a military escort at his disposal the blocks proved too heavy to move.

Two years after his tour of Chaldaea, Loftus went back to Warka to undertake three months' excavation, accompanied by the artist Boutcher. It was time enough for him to come to terms with the immensity of the task. Vast palaces, temples and libraries awaited discovery within the great circle of the city which was among the oldest of urban developments, with a continuous occupation of some 4,000 years. Cuneiform inscriptions found by Loftus and his successors would show Uruk to have been the birthplace of primordial legend; the centre of an empire which existed before Babylon, inhabited by the Sumerians, a people whose origins and language would defy attribution. A second visit to Sankara produced neo-Babylonian cylinders inscribed by Nebuchadnezzar, concealed within the foundations of a temple dedicated to the sun-god Shamash. There

Kneeling worshipper, statuette dedicated on behalf of the life of Hammurabi by the worshipper, Awil-Nannar. Hands and face are decorated in gold foil, c.1760 BC.

were also hundreds of tablets in clay envelopes which Rawlinson dated c.1500 BC, one of which contained a list of square roots, confirming the statement of Berosus that the first Babylonian empire employed both sexagesimal and centesimal notations.

Loftus, the surveyor turned naturalist and geologist, was the most underestimated of nineteenth century explorers and excavators. His work was thorough and his interpretation of finds scholarly. His book *Travels and Researches in Chaldaea and Susiana*, published after his investigations at Warka, Sankara and Muqayyar, was the cause of a new burst of enthusiasm in America, France and Britain for properly financed and organized excavation in the lower regions of Mesopotamia.

For reasons more to do with politics than archaeology, however, a systematic assault on the mounds of Babylonia was delayed for nearly thirty years after the completion of Loftus's work. He was appointed to the Survey of India when the

Frontier Commission completed its tasks, and was affected by sun-stroke. At the end of 1858 he was ordered home to rest and died on board the ship *Tyburnia*, at the age of 37. There was one other serious appraisal before work came to a halt.

In 1854 the British Consul at Basra, J.G. Taylor, visited Tel Muqayyar, hired a labour force and dug for several weeks among the ruins which Loftus had described. Loftus had questioned the observation of an earlier visitor, Baillie Fraser, that there was a circular hole at the top of the mound, but he commented that between the two sections or storeys of the central building there was an inclined plane. '. . . probably, a flight of steps, as I observed at the W. corner eight rows of bricks, the lower ones of which project six inches beyond those above. A similar arrangement is observable at the top of the upper storey.' Taylor showed that the conjectural 'flight of steps' was a *ziggurat*, priestly way to the heavens, an architectural feature which would become increasingly familiar to archaeologists. He found at each corner of the ziggurat a *khazna* or chamber within the building's foundations, in which were concealed inscribed cylinders. They were sent to Rawlinson whose translation showed that they had been placed there by King Nabonidus, the last ruler of the Neo-Babylonian dynasty (555–539 BC). It was apparent from the work of both Loftus and Taylor that it was the habit of ancient kings to conceal their histories and genealogies within the foundations of their palaces and temples at the time they were built or restored, thus preserving them from the caprices of men and nature after their death. Similar 'foundation' cylinders were later found at another mound, twelve miles away and visible across the Babylonian plain, which Loftus had looked on but did not examine: Abu Shahrain, or ancient Eridu.

Taylor's work, brief though it was, marked a new stage in the investigation of the ancient civilizations of Mesopotamia. It was clear from the tablets and cylinders which he discovered and sent to Rawlinson and the British Museum, that the mounds of Muqayyar and Abu Shahrain constituted the site of a civilization older than Babylon itself. Their importance was not appreciated in London, however. All attention was then focussed on the colossi of Assyria, by far the most popular attraction the Museum had known, and even they had become something of an embarrassment of riches. Many of the winged bulls and lions and bas-reliefs which Rassam despatched after his return to Nineveh in 1852, were given to the Crystal Palace, when the Great Exhibition was moved from Hyde Park to Sydenham. Other sculptures were given to provincial and European museums, though the British Museum did keep the fine relief carvings which lined the walls of Ashurbanipal's palace at Nineveh, Rassam's most important discovery. No one, it seems, realized that Taylor and Loftus between them had uncovered the most ancient of Mesopotamian civilizations, Sumer and one of the great cities of its kings, Ur of the Chaldees. Was this, as Rawlinson,

Layard and others had suggested, the true cradle of mankind?

The name had echoed in synagogue, church and mosque for 2,000 years, yet it was 2,000 years before the advent of the Christian faith that Abraham and his fraternity had, by biblical tradition, set out on the journey to Egypt. Genesis was not an easy guide for those who went in search of patriarchal routes. Haran, it records, died in the presence of his father Terah in the land of his nativity, Ur of the Chaldees. Terah took his son Abraham, and Lot the son of Haran, along with other members of the family 'to go into the land of Canaan'. They came to Haran, where Terah died. Abraham left Haran with his family and 'all the souls that they had gotten' to go into Canaan, and thence to Egypt. Thus, Haran was a person and a place. But where was Ur? Ur of the Persians was some 300 miles to the north, at Kalat Shargat, which would be shown to be the site also of Assur, the capital city of Assyria at the juncture of the Tigris river and its tributary the Great Zab. Some authorities believed Al Hadhr, Hutra of the Chaldeans and Hatra of the Romans, about thirty miles into the desert from Kalat Shargat, to be the domicile of Abraham. Others believed Urfa, more than 200 miles to the north-west, to be the place. Little more than a decade before Taylor made possible a positive identification of Ur of the Chaldees, William Ainsworth, in the course of his duties as leader of the Survey of Mesopotamia, went with Layard, Mitford and Rassam in search of Ur of the Persians. Ammianus Marcellinus, historian of the Roman campaign in Persia, called it a 'castle of the Persians', and said that it was some distance from Al Hadhr. He also observed that Jovian's army had retreated within sight of Ur in AD363, *Properantes itineribus magius prope Hatram venimus*. Near Hatra, and not at it. Ainsworth concluded: 'In any attempt to identify the Ur of the Persians, now called Kalat Sherkat (Shargat), with the Ur of the Chaldeans, there is only, till farther evidence can be obtained, the character of the remains, and the narrative of the historian of Jovian's retreat, to be placed in opposition to the testimony of certain Oriental historians in favour of the identity of Ur of the Chaldeans with Urfah, and the existing traditions which have consecrated that city as the birth-place of the father of Isaac.' Harran, the city of Abraham, to which the last Assyrian king withdrew in 612 BC at the fall of Nineveh, was in fact close to Urfah. Taylor produced evidence that the probable site of Ur of the Chaldees was far to the south, at Tel Muqayyar.

John G. Taylor was the son of the self-effacing Robert Taylor, who occupied the Baghdad Residency between the years of Rich and Rawlinson. During the regime of Taylor senior, between 1826 and 1835, there had been a great deal of interest in the Babylonian sites and in those further south, and Captain Robert Mignon, commander of the Residency escort, was sent on an expedition to the Euphrates in the course of which he visited the mounds of Sankara and Muqayyar without being able to identify them as ancient Larsa and Ur.

The Taylors, father and son, were in marked contrast temperamentally to Rich the 'Magnificent Nabob', and the imperious Rawlinson. They were unobtrusive administrators; devout and knowledgeable men. The father stayed at his post in the plague years of 1830–31, when two-thirds of Baghdad's 150,000 souls died from the disease or from the Tigris floods which followed it. His son was Consul at Basra from 1851 to 1858.

Within months of John Taylor's visit to the southern extremity of the Euphrates, 'that sea of brown-brick ruins', the first of two events occurred which were to bring further work to a halt for generations. The Crimean war between Turkey and Russia was the culmination of centuries of rivalry between Tsars and Sultans. It was also the starting point of European conspiracy to redistribute the ossified yet strategically important remains of the Ottoman Empire. Russia, Britain, France, Prussia, and Austria-Hungary were the leading participants in a protracted political and commercial drama which brought about the British occupation of Egypt, the dismembering of Turkey's European empire, and the undermining of British sway in those parts of Asiatic Turkey which had been dominated for so long by men such as Rich, Taylor and Rawlinson. These events would influence the nature of archaeological work when it was able to start up again, just as they influenced trading agreements, railway building and many day-to-day matters. The Indian Mutiny of 1857, also had an effect, albeit indirect, on archaeology. The political authority of the East India Company was usurped by Whitehall. An Empire which had been directed by a Board of Governors in London through its civil and military representatives in Calcutta and Bombay, became the responsibility of a government in London which was elected every four or five years and was liable to veer from moment to moment between policies of ardent imperialism and advocacy of home rule. There would be no more Britishers of self-determined power and individuality in Baghdad or Basra. No more entrepreneurial excursions into Persia, Mesopotamia or Anatolia. Foreign Office permission became necessary. Political rather than academic considerations dictated the response.

Rassam finally left Mosul for England in 1854, preceded by the magnificent collection of hunting scenes and other relief sculptures from the Palace of Ashurbanipal. He was converted from the Nestorianism of his birth to Protestantism. He had flirted briefly with the Roman faith in his youth and another brother, George, had been excommunicated from the Catholic church. Hormuzd Rassam – his name in Arabic means 'engraver' – entered British government service, and after his famous excursion to King Theodore of Abyssinia in 1864 he returned to England, married an Englishwoman and settled to a respectably quiet suburban life. He had made an enormous contribution to the archaeological study of ancient Mesopotamia through his work at Nimrud and Nineveh. Though his health had suffered from confinement during his 'military' mission to East Africa, he would be called again to dig in familiar ground; archaeology and Mesopotamia had not yet done with him.

Rawlinson left Baghdad in 1855. He returned home to great acclaim and a knighthood, entered Parliament as Conservative member for Reigate in Surrey and was elected to the Council of India. There was a brief spell as Minister in Tehran, but his views on Persia and his anti-Russian policy were too pronounced for diplomatic nicety and he gave up the appointment after less than a year. There was a second period in the House of Commons, from 1865 to 1868, but by then the tasks of Assyriology were his preoccupation. From 1861 until his death in 1895 he worked in his own room at the British Museum, translating the countless cuneiform tablets which had arrived from Assyria. His approach to that work, as tasks which yet awaited him were to demonstrate, was bold, and sometimes led to hasty judgement. He chaired innumerable committees, presided over the Royal Asiatic Society and the Royal Geographical Society, lectured and wrote learned papers, received the Order of Merit of Prussia (but not of his own country), became foreign member of the French Académie des Inscriptions et Belles Lettres, and in 1875 wrote the controversial book *England and Russia in the East*.

When he first took up temporary residence at the British Museum, Rawlinson opened a cupboard to find his famous 'squeezes' of the Behistun inscription tucked away and mostly eaten by mice. He had, of course, many years earlier made plaster casts of the Darius testament which led to the decipherment of the Babylonian and Old Persian languages. Between 1861 and 1880 he completed for the museum six volumes of *The Cuneiform Inscriptions of Western Asia*. During that time of intensive work, thousands of tablet inscriptions, often fragmentary, were translated, married together and systematized into that unique corpus of history which the royal libraries of Khorsabad, Nineveh and Nimrud furnished. But Rawlinson was not without assistance. At a time when the Oriental departments of the European museums were being swamped by the papyri, scarabs, stelae, tablets, cylinders and seals of Egypt and Mesopotamia, an increasing number of scholars was coming forward to learn and translate the ancient tongues. Since the publication of Assyrian texts in the *Monuments de Ninive* of Botta and Flandin in 1849–50, and Rawlinson's *Memoirs* in 1851, Hincks in Ireland, Place and Oppert in France, and Lyon and Winckler in Germany had produced numerous edited and re-edited versions. It was generally believed that 'final' versions had been established of the most important texts of Sargon II, Ashurnasirpal II, Shalmaneser III, Tiglath-pileser III, Sennacherib, Esarhaddon, and other Assyrian monarchs. But there was a long way to go, both in discovering more texts and in translation, before history and chronology could be regarded as

George Smith.

reliable. Rawlinson had three assistants in the period of his honorarium at the Museum – Edwin Norris, George Smith and T.G. Pinches. The second, George Smith, who came from a relatively poor and unpropitious background, stole the thunder of all around him.

Smith was born into an impoverished London family in 1840. He was apprenticed to bank-note engraving and with little or no formal education but such parental encouragement as could be afforded in a home where every penny counted, he became passionately interested in the achievements of the early Assyriologists. He somehow taught himself to read the cuneiform inscriptions and before reaching the age of twenty he was a familiar figure in the British Museum where he familiarized himself with the ancient languages of the East. Rawlinson was attracted by the young man's earnestness, and eventually allowed him the use of his own room at the Museum so that he could work on the tablets and inscription 'squeezes'. He quickly justified Rawlinson's generosity by translating a tablet of Shalmaneser III, showing payment of tribute to him by Jehu who, in 844 BC, drove out the Omri dynasty from Samaria and presided over the slaughter of the Baalist idolaters whom Queen Jezebel had cosseted.

Almost every day of the 1860s witnessed new translations from dozens of hands, confirming the existence, and often more besides, of the kings and warriors of biblical and classical history. The early kings of Assyria ruled as viceroys and regents of the rulers of Sumer and Akkad. The very earliest had non-Semitic names, suggesting a synchronous thriving of civilizations from the Persian Gulf to the Anatolian mountains, and perhaps beyond, in the third millennium BC. 'The temple of Belat-ekallim, his lady, for the life of Amar-sin, the mighty, King of Ur and king of the four quarters (of the world), Zariku, Viceroy of Assur, his servant, for his life, has built.' So read the first datable inscription of Assyria. Amar-sin, the mighty King of Ur, ruled during the Third Dynasty of Ur in the twenty-first century BC. The names of thirty-eight kings of Assyria are known before the first reign can be dated with certainty, that of Shamsi-adad I, 'builder of the Temple of Assur', who ruled from 1813 to 1781 BC. Another twenty-six reigns pass into the records before the Kingdom of Assyria can be said to exist as the centre of an independent empire, its seat of administration shuttling back and forth from the original capital, Assur, to Nimrud, Nineveh and Dur-Sharrukin (Khorsabad). It is Enlil-nasir II, who ascended the throne in 1432 BC, who begins an unbroken chronology of Assyrian monarchs which lasts until the destruction of the empire in 612 BC and the defeat of its last king, Ashur-uballit II, in 609 BC.

Even as far back as the end of the third millennium there seem to have been strains in the relationship between the mighty kings of the south and their northern viceroys. The first Assyrian rulers always acknowledged their debt to temporal masters. But by the time of Irishum, who probably sat on the throne around the turn of the third millennium, tribute to the gods of Assur begins to replace obedience to the kings of Ur. The temple of Assur, says an inscription, was built by Irishum, son of Ilu-shuma, in the name of 'Adad (the god), my lord . . .'. Royal inscriptions of later date reflect historical events and allegiances which carry the annals of the ancient world farther afield. In the annals of Sargon II – along with the accounts of conquests and skirmishes in Babylonia, the deportation of the Israelites, the bloody victories over the Mannaeans, Neo-Hittites, Urartians (Armenians), Medes, Elamites, Arameans, and desert tribes – bellicose asides indicate the existence of other lands and peoples. 'I bespattered his people with the venom of death', he says of the Arameans who had proved troublesome in the dependency of Babylonia. The king, whose name is not clear from the damaged tablet, fled. 'Dur-Iakin, his stronghold, I burned . . . its foundations I tore up . . . The people of Sippar, Nippur, Babylon, Borsippa, who were imprisoned therein through no fault of theirs, – I broke their bonds . . .'. The borders of Sippar were restored. The captured gods of Ur, Erech, Eridu, Larsa,

Kisik and Nimid-Laguda were restored to their rightful cities. In a catalogue of the city states and captive peoples of southern Mesopotamia and Persia, Sargon tells of the resettlement on the Elam border of the Kummuhu tribes captured in the lands of the Hittites. 'I settled (them) therein and made them occupy all of its waste places'. He put the region, Dur-Iakin, under the control of his 'officials', the viceroys of Babylon and Gambilu, indicating something of the strength and extent of Assyria in the vainglorious century which preceded its downfall. Its influence was wider still, as it transpired from the same records of the campaign on the borders of Elam and Babylonia: 'And Uperi, King of Dilmun, who lives like a fish, 30 *beru* ('double hours') away in the midst of the sea of the rising sun, heard of my lordly might and brought his gifts'. It was the first known reference to the yet undiscovered civilization, somewhere in the Persian Gulf of Dilmun (or Tilmun), as it was in Akkadian, Niduk-ki in Sumerian.

Smith worked for more than ten years alongside Rawlinson, in which time he assisted in the preparation for publication of the *Cuneiform Inscriptions*, found confirmation of the date of the total eclipse of the sun in the month of Sivan (May) 763 BC, and the date of the invasion of Babylonia by the Elamites, 2280 BC. In 1867 he was appointed an assistant in the Assyriology section, and in 1871 he published the *Annals of Assurbanipal*, and communicated to the newly-fomed Society of Biblical Archaeology a paper entitled *The Early History of Babylonia*.

It was too soon, in reality, to write a coherent history of Babylon, but the tablets and bricks which had accumulated since the pioneering journeys of Niebuhr and Rich led to the kind of conjecture which, like the first archaeological discoveries of the nineteenth century, could be relied upon to arouse the interest and stir the imagination of ordinary men and women.

The messages contained in the new tablets and cylinders were in the same wedge-shape hand that characterized the earliest brick inscriptions from Babylon, and the tens of thousands of tablets from Assyria. But the language was sometimes that which had been recognized by Hincks, Rawlinson, Oppert and others as characteristic of a pre-Babylonian civilization; sometimes the inscriptions were bi-lingual, enabling the Assyriologists to supplement the provisional syllabaries already compiled. Muqayyar could be identified as the site of Ur of the Chaldees; names and legends of 2000 BC and beyond could be established. The tablets from Ur spoke often of the 'flight of birds', from which their composers prognosticated exactly as did the Romans in their Auspices, the *avispicia* of two millennia hence.

The inscriptions of Ur, Uruk, Nippur and Eridu, in a language which dominated the fertile crescent before Semitic tribes came from the desert to superimpose their tongue and culture on the region, were sufficient for the moment. Historians, ecclesiasts, archaeologists and other interested parties

A

B

E

F

Impressions from cylinder seals. A, Sumerian, Early Dynastic I period, c.2900–2750 BC with two bearded goats; B, cylinder inscribed with the name of Ur-nammu, king of Ur, Sumerian goddess in striped robe and horned headdress raises her hands as worshipper is led by another goddess towards deified king, 3rd dynasty of Ur c.2100–2000 BC. c, royal seal of Darius found at Thebes in Egypt, showing king hunting lion from chariot; D, official with mace under arm worships goddess Ishtar who stands on a crouching lion,

started to look in new directions for the aboriginal peoples of civilization; for the Garden of Eden, Adam and Eve and Noah. Myths and legends began to surface which had infused all civilization through the writings of the classical world and the teachings of the great religions. The Assyrian tablets by now constituted a library of the ancient world against which all other discovery and conjecture must be checked.

C

D

G

Assyrian 8–7 centuries BC. E, Akkadian seal of scribe Adda, with sun-god (rays shining from shoulder), rising between two mountains, while Ea, god of the deep, steps over a rampant bull, and Janus-headed attendant stand by, c.2300 BC; F, rounded stamp seal with bull motif from Indus Valley; G, impression from Dilmun seal, also rounded and often portraying the bull and Sumerian gods.

Some of the bilingual texts from Assyria were shown to be copies of documents which were more than 1500 years old at the time of their duplication. One royal title to emerge was that of 'King of Sumer and Akkad'. The Sumerians were already established in the south of the Mesopotamian plain, at the convergence of the two rivers, in the early part of the third millennium BC, occupying walled cities surrounded by villages and farms; each a city state ruled by a prince or *ishakku*. Eventually the Sumerians were overwhelmed by the Semitic desert peoples who occupied the adjacent land to the north, the Akkadians. Rivalry inevitably gave rise to a dominant *ishakku* and thus was established the kingship of Sumer and Akkad, the 'Shepherd of the Black-Headed People', a term that has never been explained by the contemporary legends that have come to light. Kings of the city states gradually came into historical context: Uruk, Ur, Nippur, Kish, Lagash, Eridu. Names briefly foreshadowed in biblical stories came into focus. The journey of Abraham from his birthplace into the Syrian desert, the beginning of the story of the patriarchal wanderings, was hardly less charismatic to the public mind than the route of the Exodus. But even earlier events, striking the most primitive, most primal chords of the imagination, began to unfold.

In 275 BC, Berossus, a priest of the temple of Marduk, or Baal, in Babylon, wrote a history of his country in the Greek language. In it he told the story of the 'Babylonian Flood'. He had drawn his detail and characterization from the much earlier texts of Sumer and Akkad, which would certainly have been at his disposal in the great libraries of Babylon. His book, *Babyloniaca* (or *Chaldaica*), related the history of Babylonia from 'the creation of the world' to Alexander's 'liberation'. The three volumes of Berossus's history were lost, along with most of the tracts of the ancient world, and it became known to the West only at second hand, through Polyhistor, Eusebius, Josephus and others. A little more than two millennia after it was written, George Smith, while working on the Ninevite tablets from the library of Ashurbanipal, found himself reading a narrative of the Deluge, in the Assyrian cuneiform. He promptly set down on the table the fragmentary inscription he had been reading with the aid of a magnifying glass, jumped up, rushed around the room and began to undress himself. His colleagues, unaccustomed to such behaviour, were astonished, though it was generally agreed that Smith was an odd fellow. He read a paper on his findings to the Society of Biblical Archaeology in 3 December 1872. He told of catching sight of a reference to a ship, resting on the mountain of Nisir, followed by the sending forth of a dove. It was a partial story contained in half of a 'curious' tablet, a portion of a Chaldean account of the Deluge re-copied by an Assyrian scribe. His audience, which included leading lights of biblical and lay scholarship, was aghast. Such meetings were invariably reported in the national press and Smith's recital of a story which clearly reflected, if it did not anticipate, the legend of Noah and the Ark, created a sensation. Demands were renewed for governmental aid for archaeological investigation. The proprietor of the *Daily Telegraph*, Sir Edwin Arnold, stepped in and offered one thousand guineas to the Trustees of the British Museum to allow Smith to go to Nineveh to seek the rest of the story.

In January 1873, Smith set out to trace the missing part of the Babylonian

Narrative decoration, Assyrian campaign against Urartu in the 9th century BC, from the gates of palace of Shalmaneser III at Balawat. Palace and temple were burned down in 614 BC but three sets of doors survived.

legend. By May of the same year he had found it among the debris of Ashurbanipal's library, which was much as Rassam had left it twenty years before. At the same time, he found other fragmentary tablets which recorded some of the most important of the Babylonian dynasties and their duration. He returned to England to complete the translation of what proved to be part of the primary literary masterpiece, the Sumero-Akkadian *Epic of Gilgamesh*, making up the chief part of the XIth tablet of the epic. Gilgamesh hears the story from the mouth of its hero, Ut-napishtim, 'I have found life' and the 'Exceedingly Wise'. The Hellenistic version of the same tradition, derived from Berossus's history, is called *Xisuthros*. The hero of the flood in the oldest Sumerian version, which remained to be found, turned out to be *Zi-u-sudra*, 'Life of long days'. Xisuthros was simply a graecized form of the Sumerian. Smith went back to Nineveh in 1874. The *Daily Telegraph* had done the story to death and saw no purpose in prolonging the exercise, but the Museum this time provided the funds for further searches. By now, Smith had begun to put together an even more prodigal saga from the tablets of Assyria and Babylonia, *The Creation, or The Chaldaean Account of Genesis*. His work at Kuyunjik was described in his *Assyrian Discoveries*, published in 1875. In the following year the British Museum sent him out to complete the recovery of Ashurbanipal's library. He contracted fever at the village of Iksji during his last excavation of Nineveh, and died in Aleppo on 19 August 1876, at the age of 36. His fame was assured by the legends of Gilgamesh and the Creation, and the nation raised a fund for his widow and children.

Like all the archaeologists of Assyria, George Smith had come to know the winter winds which sweep down from the mountains of Kurdistan and Persia. The epic the Babylonians called 'He Who Saw Everything' contains a stanza of the seventh day which Smith might have thought a more suitable epitaph than the one erected to his memory at his grave in Aleppo by the Trustees of the British Museum, 'in recognition of his merit and great services'. Ut-napishtim waited to let the birds out of the ark, to reconnoitre the ground around the mountain of Nisir (Pir-i-Mukurun of the present day), whose summit looked down on the Tigris from 8,600 feet. In the vernacular translation of R. Campbell Thompson, it reads:

'Six days, a se'ennight the
hurricane, deluge (and)
tempest continued
Sweeping the land: when the
seventh day came were
quelled the warfare,
Tempest (and) deluge which
like to an army embattail'd
were fighting.
Lull'd was the sea, (all)
spent was the gale,
assuaged was the deluge,
(So) did I look on the day;
(lo), sound was (all)
still'd; and all human
Back to (its) clay was
return'd, and fen was
level with roof-tree'.

Within a few months of Smith's unexpected death, the British Museum asked Rassam to return to Nineveh in his place. Rassam, now an urbane Englishman to all appearances, who had reconciled himself to retirement after an adventurous adulthood spent in the service of his adoptive King and Country, agreed readily.

The Lion of Babylon restored to its former glory at the site of Babylon in modern Iraq.

The Ishtar Gate at Babylon, restored in conformity with the reconstruction in the Berlin State Museum.

Layard had become ambassador at the Sublime Porte, and there was no difficulty in providing his old assistant with a firman which gave him wide scope. The museum had wanted him to concentrate on the Ashurbanipal archive. Rassam had other ideas. Before leaving London, he had noticed two fragmentary bronze plates with relief decoration which embraced two figures. They came from a Christian burial site some nine miles north-east of Nimrud. Rassam made for the cemetery, known as Tel Balawat, where he found more plates. He also noticed a massive metal structure, partly buried in the mound. Although it was badly corroded, he realized that the plates which had first attracted his attention were part of the same structure, a series of bronze strips which ornamented two cedar-wood gates. Each strip consisted of two registers surrounded by a rosette border, on which were depicted social, religious and battle scenes. In this marvellous example of craftsmanship in bronze, he had discovered the 'gates of Shalmaneser III', but there were no signs of a building to which they might have belonged. Later, while a minor *jihad* broke out on the site between Muslim and Christian workmen, he found a second pair of gates, with a simpler arrangement of plates containing larger figure representations, attributed to Ashurnasirpal II (883–859 BC). Rassam believed these bronze gates to be commemorative monuments. He was unable to find any trace of wall or building, however. He later found a marble or alabaster coffer containing inscribed tablets which had a bearing on the matter. Theophilus Pinches, Smith's successor, described yet another 'sensational' discovery at a meeting of the Society of Biblical Archaeology in November 1878.

Balawat was, he said, 'the site of an ancient Assyrian fortress, which had borne a different name before the reign of Ashurnasirpal I, father of Shalmaneser II, whose reception of tribute from Jehu, King of Israel, is recorded on the famous black obelisk'. (In fact, the kings in question were Ashurnasirpal II and Shalmaneser III, though the Assyrian king lists were incomplete at the time). Pinches went on to explain the events which led to the taking of the fortress by the Babylonians during a period of Assyrian decline, even though it was so close to Nineveh and Nimrud, 'perhaps during the epoch of Hebrew ascendancy'. Ashurnasirpal had recovered the place and renamed it Imgur-Bel, and built there a temple to the god of war, near the city's 'north-eastern wall'. A small mound which began the lecture as a fortress had become a city. The provenance of the place and of Rassam's unquestionably beautiful gates (or doors) seemed to rely on their compatibility with Layard's black obelisk from Nimrud, which, with the Mesha stela, of Moab, related events connected with the wars of Syrians and Assyrians against each other and against the despised Israeli house of Omri. There was, however, another source of information. 'These facts are recorded', said Pinches, 'on alabaster tablets found by Mr Rassam in a coffer of the same material near the entrance of the temple itself'. The tablets did, in fact, give the ancient name of Balawat as Imgur-Bel. Whether, as Pinches claimed, they 'shed a fresh ray of light on one of the darkest periods of Assyrian history', is another matter. Pinches described the mound from drawings supplied by Rassam. 'The mound is nearly rectangular and its corners are turned pretty accurately towards the four cardinal points of the compass. The temple ruins lie near the north-east edge, where ran the city wall.' Yet Rassam had said in his official report that he believed the bronze gates to be monuments set up to commemorate the events they recorded. He could find no trace of wall or building. Lastly, the lecturer came to the substance of the inscriptions contained by the plates of the two pairs of gates, decorated in repoussé. It was the customary Assyrian saga of battles, sieges, triumphal processions, the torture of prisoners, and gratitude to the gods who had assured victory to the deserving. The style of decoration was 'fuller' than that of the black obelisk, 'but somewhat carelessly executed'. Then: 'The new document begins with Shalmaneser's Babylonian campaign, when he went to help King Mardaku-Summa-Iddin against that Babylonian Monarch's revolted brother'. There followed descriptions of campaigns around Mount Ararat, against Gozan and Borsippa. Mr Pinches, said the report, held out the hope that in a future paper he would be able to identify among the bas-reliefs 'some Jewish faces of the ninth century before Christ'. Then there was reference to the military campaigns in Syria which led to the conflicts related in the Second Book of Chronicles in which Israel and Judah became fatally involved, 'but at a considerably later period'. Chronicles II, of course, records the events of the first period of the Kingdom of David. The 'later period' was that of the Samaria dynasty of Omri, whose successor was King Ahab.

> Now the rest of the acts of Ahab and all that he did and the ivory house that he built, and all the cities that he built, are they not written in the book of the Chronicles of the Kings of Israel?

Rassam's own account of the matter was amusing and contained enough detail to suggest that he told the truth. The wooden part of the gates had long since rotted away and he described the find as resembling a 'gigantic hat-rack with the top rising to within four feet of the surface of the ground, and the lower portion gradually descending to about fifteen feet deep'. He indicated that the second pair of gates was found about sixty feet to the north-west of the first, and that in the discovery of the 'coffer' with its inscribed tablets, which recorded the building of a temple dedicated to the god Mamu, he had been obliged to dig in tunnels nearly two metres below the level of the graves which could not be disturbed and which inevitably restricted his work.

Pinches' lecture was anomalous. The description of the site was at variance with Rassam's own statement. Nevertheless, the Gates of Balawat, among the finest of all the architectural monuments of the ancient world, echoed the events and scenes depicted on the black obelisk which Layard had found at Nimrud in 1845.

While the public flocked to London's Museum Street to see the magnificently restored gates with their sculptured reliefs of king and warriors in two-horse chariots, which some compared with illustrations of Homer's heroes at the siege of Troy, Rassam found himself at the centre of a very unpleasant dispute. Wallis Budge, head of the British Museum's Oriental Department, declared that no large-scale excavation had ever taken place at the site and that the mound could not have contained a building such as the gates must have belonged to. Dr L.W. King, an academic assistant in the department went further. In a publication on the 'Shalmaneser III Gates' for the Museum, he declared unequivocally that Rassam's account of their discovery was 'an absurdity'.

Rassam's excavations were always chaotic. He was the Ulysses of archaeology, ever wandering in stormy seas, with Scylla and Charybdis prowling at his side in the shape of his employers, the British Museum, and his employees, a divided Arab-Moslem workforce. He became increasingly didactic in his Christian faith and eventually turned to evangelism of a kind which did not commend him to the orthodox church movement of England. It did not gain much sympathy either among the Moslems of the Ottoman territories. Sectarian clashes at Nineveh, Nimrud and now Balawat were notorious. The theft of valuable articles, some of which doubtless appeared in the salerooms of the west after his death, was commonplace.

Pinches was willing to give public utterance to his conviction that the Shalmaneser treasure had come from Balawat, as Rassam claimed. But Wallis Budge, his senior, was suspicious from the first. 'If these two sets of gates were found at Tell Talawat [sic] there must have been a palace at this place', he wrote, 'but this is impossible for there is no room in the mound for a temple, still less for a temple and a palace, however small'. Budge was perfidious in his relationships. He was a man of easy charm and mailed fist. He had made life at the British Museum so difficult for Layard as to contribute in large measure to the great man's subsequent loss of interest in Assyrian discovery. And he took a positive dislike to Layard's now famous successor. Rivalry and jealousy were compounded by Rassam's finds soon after the Balawat episode. He went on to Babylon and the Sumerian sites and extended his search to the Anatolian region by the shores of Lake Van. While passing through Deir az-Zor on the middle Euphrates in 1882, he had heard that important antiquities had been found near Ras al-Ain 'or the source of the Khaboor, in northern Mesopotamia on the river

Jirjib'. In reports to his employers, the British Museum, he said that he had at once sent an agent to examine the spot but that the local governor had stopped work there and had confiscated the 'head of a black statue'. Later reports from Rassam spoke of 'some statuettes in black basalt and bas-reliefs representing, I believe, hunting scenes ...', and 'sculptures in black basalt in which are represented antelopes, horses, armed men ...', etc. When Rassam wrote an account of the events which led to the confiscation of the Khaboor (Khabur) relics, in his book *Asshur and the Land of Nimrod*, he referred to 'a mound at the junction of the Jarajir River with the Khaboor'. The head of the statuette had been taken away from his agent, but the man had brought with him a broken piece of bas-relief with 'hieroglyphic characters', which had been forwarded to England. This unimportant fragment was lost, or more probably confused with another basaltic stone from Carchemish, where a contemporaneous British dig was under way. To ensuing doubt about the statuette head and the missing inscribed stone was added confusion as to the location of the finds. The Arabic consonant 'gh', pronounced like the French 'r', in all probability led to confusion between Rassam's *Jarajir* (Jaghjagh) and *Jirjib*, since both are tributaries of the Khabur river, though some sixty miles apart.

The year 1882 marked the resumption of systematic digging in Mesopotamia. As Rassam made his way to the southern mounds of Babylonia, a British team began to dig at Jerablus, the site of Carchemish of the Hittites, on which Layard had purchased a lease in his Nineveh days. His successor would have liked to dig at the mound of Nabi Yunus where he (Layard) had identified the palace of Esarhaddon, Sargon's grandson. But though Rassam purchased some houses to give himself digging space, Turkish officials refused to allow excavations.

Rassam's first major dig in the south was at Babylon itself. He was disappointed. Birs Nimrud too, ancient Borsippa, the place with the crumbling tower which travellers regularly confused with 'Babel', was no more rewarding. He went on to Tel Ibrahim the site of Babylonian Kutha, where he found a few inscribed bricks bearing the name of Nebuchadnezzar, but he imagined that they were maverick evidence, brought from elsewhere. Disconsolate, he turned towards the Tigris and made his way up river towards Baghdad. He decided to dig at Abu Habbah, reputed to be the site of biblical Sepharvaim, where several small mounds encircled a ziggurat. He discovered a chamber within the ziggurat mound with a bitumenized pavement. Below he found a closed terracotta box. When he opened it he saw a marble tablet inscribed with the name of King Nabu-apla Iddina, a ninth century monarch of Babylon, and containing a beautiful relief of the sun-god Shamash. A shrine in the chamber bore the inscription 'Image of Shamash the Great Lord, dwelling in Ebabbar in the City of Sippar'. He had uncovered one of the most ancient cities of central Babylonia; a city with the

Theophilus Goldridge Pinches, *left*, and Sir Ernest Wallis Budge.

closest ties with the epics of the Creation and Gilgamesh, where the gods Nergal and Tammuz, and Nergal's spouse Ereskigal, the 'Lady of the Underworld', presided atypically. Working with remarkable speed, Rassam traced something like three-hundred chambers, grouped in a series of courts. He excavated about 170 rooms and amassed between forty and fifty thousand inscribed tablets. One of those ancient records was in the name of Nabonidus, the last king of Babylon and father of Belshazzar, whose foundation cylinder Taylor had found in the *khazna* at Tel Muqayyar. It told of the King digging beneath the same chambers that Rassam had penetrated, and coming upon a foundation-stone laid by Naram-Sin, the grandson of Sargon of Akkad. No previous king could have seen the stone for two millennia before Nabonidus fingered it and read the name of his ancestor. A rather longer interval of time separated Nabonidus from Rassam. Other tablets told of trade and craftsmanship in the 2,000 years or more that Sippar had stood as a great city in the fertile valley of the Euphrates.

Fighting had broken out again among Rassam's workmen when he abandoned Sippar to return to England. Venerable, grey-haired, he left the lands of his birth for the last time for a bitter-sweet welcome, accompanied by a veritable treasure-chest of close on a hundred thousand items. He was acclaimed throughout Europe and North America. The Royal Academy of Sciences in Turin awarded him the Braza Prize, worth 12,000 francs, for his work during the years 1879–82. But in Britain there was a suspicious silence, followed by growing rumours that his excavations were not all that they seemed, that his large family in and around Mosul had helped him to secrete valuable finds which were rightly the property of the British Museum. He retired to his Brighton home where he spent much of his time writing about the Christian sects of the Near East and engaging in domestic religious controversy.

Rumour became open accusation. Budge was in the forefront of a campaign which had begun with doubts about the origin of the Shalmaneser gates but which soon broadened into assertions of large-scale theft. Silence could only be taken as signal of guilt. Rassam began to seek redress in letters to journals and antiquarian authorities. But by 1886 the attacks on his probity had become so open that he felt compelled to start legal proceedings. It took six years for the case to come before the Queen's Bench Division of the High Court. Meanwhile, in 1887, Budge visited the Balawat site, together with Rassam's cousin Nimrud. 'None of the natives had ever heard of the discovery of the bronze plates', he reported, adding, 'someone had made a mistake'. Budge was enchanted with Mesopotamia and the milieu that had provided the pioneers with their first vision of true antiquity, but the personal vendettas which seemed to accompany him wherever he went were not absent from the lands of the two rivers. Although armed with letters of introduction to the Turkish authorities from Lord Salisbury and Rawlinson, he succeeded in putting up the back of the Sultan's director of antiquities, Badri Bey. He made several important purchases for the Museum, despite Badri's insistence that valuable items could not be taken out of the country without permission. The Resident at Baghdad, Colonel Tweedie, was uncomplimentary about the Trustees of the Museum and its representatives on the spot. 'Be not sad of heart', the Arabs told Budge when he went to investigate Tel ad-Der, a suburb of Sippar which was thought at the time to be the site of Akkad, the city of Sargon the Great, founded in about 2300 BC. Budge had heard that some 10,000 tablets had gone missing from the site, sold to Baghdad dealers. He persuaded the traders of Baghdad to sell him 9,500 tablets and seals with which he returned, triumphant, to London. His eventual report cast further suspicion on Rassam. Doubt about the Baghdad haul and the whereabouts of the Balawat finds fuelled mistrust in work which had spanned nearly forty years and had enriched the British Museum to the point where it could no longer accommodate any substantial Assyrian treasures.

Rassam's action for libel and slander against Budge was eventually heard in the summer of 1893. Budge was supported by the Trustees and almost the entire academic staff of the Museum, including Rawlinson. Only Pinches, who was a close friend of Rassam, and the Egyptologist Sir Peter Le Page Renouf, broke ranks to support the plaintiff. But Rassam had a powerful ally in Layard, who came from his retirement home in Venice to give evidence on behalf of his sometime assistant. The trial proceedings were bitter and it has been said that the acrimony hastened Layard's death in the following year. Judgement was made in Rassam's favour but the damages he received, fifty-pounds, were hardly punitive. Accusations of theft would never be proved or disproved satisfactorily, but nothing was ever alleged against Rassam which could not with as much substance be levelled against any other archaeologist of the time. Site thefts were so common that in the bazaars of Cairo and Baghdad priceless objects could be purchased for a few copper coins. Many of the items would come up time after time in the salerooms of London, Paris and New York, in the course of the following century.

Not for another fifty years would the likely origin of the Shalmaneser gates be decided. In 1942, one of the inter-war generation of archaeologists, Seton Lloyd, made a close inspection of the Balawat site. At a mound some 300 yards in diameter he found the graves of which Rassam had spoken, and evidence of the digging which had given rise to that famous and disputed discovery. Rassam was finally vindicated in 1956 when Sir Max Mallowan excavated the Balawat mound, circumventing the graves much as his predecessor had done, to reveal a small temple and shrines, together with the eroded remains of rooms which had once served administrative purposes. Forty more tablets were found in the shrine where Rassam had discovered the coffer of Ashurnasirpal II. To the great delight of Mallowan's expedition from the British School of Archaeology in Iraq, the remains of a third pair of gates was found. The tablets of Ashurnasirpal had referred to them. In the temple of Mamu he had 'constructed cedar doors' and 'fastened them with bronze bands' and 'hung them in its doorways'.

In modern terms the old Ottoman vilayet, or administrative district, of Basra is roughly defined by a line from Kut on the Tigris to the Shi'a holy city of Najaf on the Euphrates, and thence to the point where the converging rivers become the Shatt-al-Arab and pass through marsh and bog to Basra at the head of the Gulf. This was the area of ancient Sumer and until the First World War it was administered separately from the Pashalik of Baghdad. British representation was also separate, due to long-standing suspicion between Whitehall and India, so that the Consul at Basra was always of the Levant Political Service and was independent of the Indian Government's men in the Persian Gulf and Baghdad. Thus, access to Sumerian sites such as Lagash, Erech, Ur and Eridu, which had attracted the attention of the major archaeological powers since the surveys of Loftus and Taylor, demanded separate approaches.

Votive figure dedicated by Gudea, Governor of Lagash, from Telloh, c.2140 BC.

The French Vice-Consul at Basra in 1877, Ernest de Sarzec, sensed the delicacy of the position. He applied to the Wali of Basra for permission to dig at Tel Telloh, more or less at the centre of the Basra vilayet. He knew that an application for a firman in Constantinople would reach the ears of Rassam. Tel Telloh was thought at the time to be the Sumerian city of Lagash, but late twentieth-century excavations have shown it to be the site of the adjacent city of Girsu. Whatever its true identity, de Sarzec had made an auspicious choice. In two seasons of digging he produced a large haul of magnificent diorite statuettes and thousands more of the inscribed tablets and cylinders which came to represent the largest imperial library of the ancient world ever assembled. The sagacious Frenchman sold his finds to the Louvre for 130,000 francs. While de Sarzec was negotiating lucratively in Paris, Rassam made a hurried visit to the site with a team of workmen. Within hours they unearthed a fine statue which de Sarzec had re-buried to await his return. Rassam's men also came away with the inevitable collection of tablets and cylinders, before renewed fighting among them caused their employer to withdraw. Shortly after, de Sarzec returned with an official firman from Constantinople.

The black statue, representing Gudea, governor of the city-state in the third millennium BC, was only the first of a massive and sensational haul of statues and stelae to come from the site. Gudea was the third of the Akkadian or Semitic governors of Girsu, and his influence seems to have extended to neighbouring Lagash and to other city centres of Sumer. Inscriptions told of gods and religious rites, of the building and rebuilding of temples. There were details of trade with every known civilization of the time – in diorite, carnelian and timber from Magan and Meluhha by way of Dilmun; distant places which would not readily yield to attempts at identification. The names of craftsmen brought in from Elam and Susa to decorate the great Eninnu temple were recorded. Two clay cylinders contained a literary composition of nearly fourteen-hundred lines, commemorating the rebuilding of the Eninnu; a hymnal and ritual narrative, the longest literary text ever recovered from the prodigal archives of Mesopotamia. Only one military victory is recorded, over the city-state of Anshan, Elam's eastern neighbour. But cultic and symbolic weapons, such as maces with fifty heads, are described. The polished black statues of Gudea – many more were found at Early Dynastic and later levels at Girsu and Lagash – were the first examples of large-scale sculpture to come from a pre-Babylonian society. The solemn-faced governor, or *ensi*, is shown in many poses, standing and seated, hands always clasped in front of him as though he is delivering a lecture, often with cuneiform texts on his skirt, or a plan of a building on his lap. On the whole, the records of Girsu speak more of artistic endeavour, of the construction of temples and worship, than of war and conquest.

De Sarzec excavated for eleven seasons at Telloh, and for much of the time he was harassed by gangs of Arabs who had learnt their ways in Rassam's disorderly school. At this, one of the richest of all the Mesopotamian sites, anything up to 40,000 pieces are said to have found their way to dealers operating through Baghdad, Mosul, Basra and other centres of illicit antiquarian trade. It is believed that even at the present day, a century after de Sarzec's first secretive sounding, many priceless items remain in private ownership, unknown and unrecorded.

The treasures of Telloh revitalized western interest in the Mesopotamian civilizations, which had been diverted to Greece and Egypt in the forty years between Layard's and de Sarzec's discoveries. And they revived the ardour of debate. That concern for magic and the occult, for metaphysical speculation, so firmly rooted in European culture, found fertile ground for renewed debate in Sumerian myth and history. Here and in Egypt ideas were first made articulate. From here, as in Egypt, material evidence and social and intellectual abstraction appeared in vast, almost unmanageable quantity. Ritual, manners, worship and prayer, gods and heroes, literally cascaded from the ground in the shape of exotic idols, beautiful works of art, and written history and legend. Here were the founders of astronomy, astrology and mathematics, the birthplaces of civilization. The shaping of human history and values took on a new perspective. Gilgamesh and Ut-Napishtim were joined by new pantheons and king-lists, new heroes and battles, unsuspected superstitions and death rites. Egypt, already familiar to the West, had its dark side, its mystery. So had Sumer. Yet, as far down as he was able to dig, the archaeologist remained in the realm of history. Still the craftsman worked with the potter's wheel to produce vessels of accomplished finish and decoration, often of outstanding beauty. Even at the earliest levels of community life, the so called 'proto' stages of development, the metal-smith and sculptor, jeweller and weaver, worked with sophisticated skills, using methods which would not be improved upon substantially in five-thousand years. Bronze ornaments were fashioned from the first by the complex processes of sand and 'lost wax' casting, while others were hammered expertly. The sculptor's chisel was wielded with assurance. The cylinder seal, the illustrated imprimatur of king, priest and merchant, was carved from steatite, rock crystal or ivory or any workable material that came to hand; carved in negative by copper tools, often on substances of immense hardness. It was as if communities had formed almost spontaneously out of the nomadic, semi-barbaric tribes and family groups which had wandered towards these alluvial plains from beyond the mountain ranges to east and north and the deserts in the west and south, replete with a knowledge of the craft processes, building techniques and agricultural sciences needed to sustain an urban community.

Although the first texts to come from Telloh, and from nearby mounds such as

Lagash and Tel Jokha (ancient Umma), were concerned chiefly with gods, priesthood and the arts, they nevertheless spoke too of military campaigns as these city states competed for ascendancy. But the battlefield and the vainglory of the victor seem not to have inspired artists and craftsmen in early dynastic Sumer as such things inspired the boastful Assyrian sculptures and the rigidly formalized wall paintings and massive stone portaits of Egypt. Yet in one rare example, Sumer surpassed the most bellicose of its successor states with a military scene of great poignancy. The 'Stela of the Vultures' from Telloh, portrays military discipline at its birth, and some 4,500 years after its creation it was to give H.G. Wells the image he needed to convey the meaning of that term: 'There you see him in a sort of phalanx, advancing with his shield locked with that of the next man and their spears at a level making an invincible line.'

In the enthusiasm of the Sumerian discoveries, the American Oriental Society broke out of the isolation in which it had been placed by its preoccupation with biblical archaeology. With funds provided by the philanthropist and art patron Catherine Lorillard Wolfe, a reconnaissance mission was sent to the 'Babylonian' sites in 1884 under the improbable leadership of William H. Ward, the editor of the New York newspaper *The Independent*. In fact, the appointment was not entirely fanciful. As a collector and keen enthusiast, Ward knew a great deal about archaeology and was a leading expert of his time on the cylinder-seals of Assyria and Babylonia, those miniature wonders of craftsmanship which were the first pictorial-reproduction devices, anticipating by several millennia the discovery of lithographic printing. He later became President of the American Oriental Society. As the result of his mission's tour, Ward recommended that a full-scale excavation should be undertaken at Nippur, and in 1888 a University of Pennsylvania archaeological team under the direction of John P. Peters began work at that site. The expedition promised much. It was well financed and had among its junior members several men who were destined to become famous in the annals of what, for want of a more apt word, must be given the generic name 'Assyriology'. All the same, it was a disaster. The only experienced field archaeologist among them was Herman Hilprecht. Peters, a professor at the Episcopal Divinity School of Philadelphia, concerned himself almost exclusively with elaborate budgetary details. He adamantly refused to take the advice of the knowledgeable Hilprecht on archaeological matters. The Americans had no idea how to control an Arab workforce. Marauding tribesmen were shot at by camp guards, and one raider was killed, thus inviting more serious attention on the part of the Badawin in a notoriously hot-headed region. Peters took the worst possible action – he sent for a Turkish police patrol. The mound was besieged, the reed huts of the expedition were set ablaze, and the camp laid to waste. After the disaster came inevitable dissent. Peters accused Hilprecht of claiming credit for discovering tablets which another member of the team, John H. Hayes, had uncovered; Hilprecht questioned Peters' ability as an Assyriologist; hardly one member of the unhappy band talked to another. In the confusion, the Arabs marched off with rich pickings. Compared with the first American expedition to Babylonia, Rassam's digs were models of order and calm efficiency. The rift between Peters and Hilprecht lasted for the rest of their lives. Nevertheless, the Americans returned in 1890, and from then on began to make important discoveries. They used tried and tested transatlantic methods of impressing the natives. They held spectacular firework displays which convinced the Arabs that the devil was at liberty among them, and paid most tempting wages.

At his first sight of the ziggurat at Nippur, Hilprecht was struck by the dominant religious connotations of the city. Like Girsu, the religious suburb of Lagash, Nippur was a place not of temporal power but a centre of art and learning and of veneration of the gods; the abode of Enlil, the chief deity of Sumer. Among the 30,000 or more tablets which the Americans took home with them were some of the most important of all ancient texts, providing a kaleidoscopic picture of the history and mythology of Sumerian civilization.

──── 8 ────

Egypt and the Israelites

While the teams of many nations dug at every available site from Lower to Upper Egypt in the last two decades of the nineteenth century, Petrie and others worked their way gradually eastwards across the Delta to Sinai, and beyond to the Palestinian sites of Lachish, Gezer, Megiddo and Hazor. Archaeology and literary evidence came closer together. Citadels, temples and artefacts affirmed the geography and much of the history of the Pentateuch, and, as Kathleen Kenyon, the prime archaeologist of Palestine, was to write in the twentieth century, 'produced almost as many theories as there have been writers'. With a century's evidence at her finger-tips, Dame Kathleen could add with confidence, that the Egyptians may have looked upon the flight of the Jews ambivalently, as 'a tiresome disappearance of a useful source of forced labour' and an expulsion 'of rebellious slaves or of infiltrating foreigners'. The only plausible historical background she could find for the Exodus was the reign of Ramesses II (1304–1237 BC), the period when the royal residence was in the Delta.

The Children of Israel took leave of their host laden with divinely sanctioned plunder – 'jewels of silver, and jewels of gold, and raiment' – and proceeded from Raamses to Succoth. 'And God dealt well with the midwives: and the people multiplied, and waxed very mighty.'

And God spake unto Moses, and said unto him, I am JEHOVAH.

The pastoral people whom the pharaoh of the Bondage had turned into bricklayers at Pithom and Raamses were finally persuaded to heed the injunction to Aaron and Moses: 'Bring out the children of Israel from the land of Egypt . . . speak thou unto Pharaoh king of Egypt all that I speak unto thee'.

'Yahweh', the Hebrew word, transliterated by European scholars as Jehovah, carried from Egypt across Sinai to Palestine, and from there to the four corners of the earth. It contained a concept new to human understanding. Monotheism. The singular Jehovah of Judaism and Christianity, Allah of Islam, subject and object of *The Word*, was beautifully rendered in the Koran, nearly 2,000 years hence, when the world was assailed by a new version of the divine message: *La illah il allah*. There is no God but God.

'I am the Lord thy God. Thou shalt have no other gods before me.'

The route of the Exodus might be debated, the accuracy of the Hebrew version of events which led to the long journey to the holy land of Judaism, Christianity and Islam might be questioned. Here, more than a thousand years before the era of Christianity, the multiplicity of deities which had served the ancient world for countless centuries began to make way for one God of masculine gender. That was the overriding significance of the journey out of Egypt into Canaan and the Promised Land.

Another twelve hundred years would pass before the collapse of Rome and the spread of the Hebrew cosmogony. Despite – perhaps because of – the momentous achievements of the nineteenth century, archaeology was as much an academic Janus at the end of its period of initiation as it had been at the beginning; child of the Enlightenment and of the demand for biblical verification. The detailed picture of human society during the thousands of years of urban life before the tribal procession out of Egypt remained obscure, as did much that went with the recorded events of the Old Testament and classical and Jewish literature. Much work was still needed to bring order to the chaos of pantheons, king lists, often overlapping and coexisting dynasties, and the misty ages of nomadic life which preceded history.

Written accounts of events and attitudes were valuable. But they were often defective by intent or lapse of memory. Inscriptions on tomb walls and commemorative statues provided indispensable punctuation marks in the developing grammar of the ancient world. Smaller, less sensational but in many ways more vital clues came from tombs, palaces and burial grounds as multi-national teams flooded into Egypt, the Aegean islands, Mesopotamia and the adjacent territories of Sinai and Palestine to capitalize on and extend the work of the pioneers.

Naville, resolute as ever in his search for biblical history, turned to the delta region of Egypt in 1887 to excavate the 'Mound of the Jews', Tel Yahudiyah. The historian Josephus, so often proved right, was vindicated again. Here it was that in the second century BC Onias, a high priest of the Jews, set up a Levite colony and built an unauthorized temple, thus provoking the wrath of his orthodox brethren at Alexandria. The colony had, according to the historian, survived for 343 years, into the Roman occupation, before Titus sacked its temple, closed its gates and expelled its citizens. In the meantime, the Jews had been tormented under the reigns of both Ptolemy and Caligula. Four centuries before the arrival

Left, unfinished relief of Amenophis IV-Akhenaten, Pharaoh of the 18th dynasty in British Museum, and another in the expressionistic early phase of Amarna art in the Berlin Museum.

of the Jews, the site had been known as Pa-Bast, the 'Abode of Bast', Bubastis of the Greeks, according to Herodotus. Naville, assisted by Petrie's early companion Griffith, found three mounds in close proximity, Yahudiyah, Karmus and Basta, and they excavated one necropolis after another to find Egyptian, Greek and Jewish graves. A few bodies were buried in clay 'slipper' graves such as Loftus found at Sumerian Uruk. Large holes were cut at the head-end for the body to be inserted, and these cavities were afterwards covered with moulded heads of the occupants adorned with rude pottery headdresses. Another aperture enabled the arms of the deceased to be drawn through and folded in the approved manner. Some coffins were covered in painted hieroglyphs and figures of gods, particularly the feline figure of Bast, and striped in glaring colours in imitation of the outer bandages of mummified corpses. Every grave contained two or more ceramic food jars.

In the honeycomb tombs of the Greek and Jewish cemeteries there were touching epitaphs on many a broken limestone slab. One read: '... my father, consumed by affliction, to his soul-kindred and friends. But if thou wouldst know how (great) were his faith and grace, come hither and question his son ...'. Even in the absence of a date, the words 'faith and grace' could be identified as the language of Alexandrian Jews, and probably marked a small tragedy among many in the time of the persecutions under Cleopatra and Ptolemy Physcon, 'Big-Belly', between the years 146–117 BC.

The colourful description by Herodotus of Bubastis and its temple was borne out too. Within a week of digging, Naville and Griffith had found the entire remains of a Thirtieth Dynasty temple, a red-stone building which might well have excited the Greek writers to glowing prose. Its hypostyle hall was constructed with columns terminating in lotus-bud capitals. Stone surfaces were polished to a glass-like finish. Columns and architraves of hall and sanctuary were inscribed with the names of Nectanebo I of the Thirtieth Dynasty and Ramesses II of the Nineteenth, a gulf of almost exactly a thousand years. But Naville ascribed the part of the building containing the hypostyle hall to the period of Amenemes III of the Twelfth Dynasty, reaching back almost to the end of the second millennium. A central hall proved to be of the Bubastite or Twenty-second Dynasty, the work of Osorkon II, the great-grandson of Sheshonq, biblical Shishak. Osorkon has been identified with 'Zerakh the Ethiopian' who invaded Judaea and was defeated in the valley of Zephatha, according to the Book of Chronicles. He was the founder of the Bubastite Dynasty.

The walls of the great red-building, now rubble beneath the remnants of later buildings, had been lined with tableaux in bas-relief. These extraordinary decorations consisted of massive panels each of which contained an intrinsic part of the overall scene of religious festival. Osorkon and Bastet are surrounded by all the gods of the Egyptian pantheon, in procession or dancing with priests, or taking part in acts of adoration and offering. Bastet is always at the side of the King, though sometimes the Queen, Karoma, is permitted to join them. Above, below and between the figures, hieroglyphs are inscribed by the tens of thousands, mostly paying tribute to the great goddess, adopted into the Heliopolitan pantheon as the daughter of Ra, at the time of the Fifth Dynasty, though she had a place in the first as Ba-Ist, 'the soul of Isis'. Most of the hundreds of panels or blocks had fallen face down, and it took four-hundred workmen several days to right them, and Naville many months to make 'squeezes' of the relief carvings and inscriptions. There was a bonus of sculpture, too, among the

Lower part of palette showing Egyptian version of the lion hunt, Late Predynastic, 4th
millennium BC. Mesopotamian influence is suggested by robe of figure at top right.

rubble. Immense statues bearing the name of Ramesses II, sometimes in groups
showing the Pharaoh sitting between gods, and a fine black granite figure almost
life-size, inscribed with the name of the son of Ramesses II,
Mentuherkhopshef, 'General of Cavalry of his father'. But an inscription,
running horizontally across the legs, was a usurpation. The style of the statue is
that of the Twelfth Dynasty and probably represents a noble at the Court. Some
of the figures – in black, red and green stone – are of such size that an eye
measures seven inches across. The hall at the eastern end of the temple of Tel Bast
was one of Naville's most spectacular finds. He called it the 'Festival Hall'.

But it is to Petrie that are owed some of the most crucial of late nineteenth-
century finds. The encaustic portrait-paintings of the Roman period bound to
sarcophagi at Hawara, the Greek and Jewish colonies of the Delta region, the

royal tombs of the earliest dynasties at Abydos, the labyrinth of the temple of Amenemes III at Fayum; such discoveries were enough to occupy almost any academic lifetime. For Petrie, they were simply milestones along a sixty-year journey, a scholastic life-essay which included a prolific output of books and papers, teaching duties which embraced world-wide lecture tours, and further field work which produced finds such as the temple inscription of Merenptah from Thebes, the disclosure of fourth-millennium Naqada in Upper Egypt (the first predynastic site to be excavated), the uncovering at Tel al-Amarna of the Eighteenth-Dynasty city of Akhanten. Those achievements were interrupted by a season's work in Sinai and capped by twelve profitable years in Palestine.

Following a dispute with the Egypt Exploration Fund in 1886 Petrie had carried on his work with the financial aid of the Manchester businessmen Jesse Howarth and Martyn Kennard, and his own limited resources. A few years later he formed his own money-raising institution, the Egyptian Research Account, the embryo of the British School of Archaeology in Egypt, established in 1904. By the end of the century he was excavating at Abydos, Tel al-Amarna, Fayum and other sites. The Petrie regime was stringent to the point of austerity. It had to be. By the end of the century he was only able to carry on 'thanks to a donation from Oxford', arranged through Mr Arthur Evans. Early assistants like Griffith, Grenfell, Hunt, and Garstang – all to gain distinction in their own right – were willing to endure the hardships of their chief's notoriously pennypinching policy. But Petrie's marriage in 1897 added an element of petticoat government to economic stringency, and there were rumblings of discontent.

In 1890 Petrie revealed the interior decoration of 'ordinary' Egyptian homes at Kahun, dating from about 2,500 BC. Two years later he brought to light the contrasting wall coverings of Akhenaten's palace at Amarna, more than a thousand years later than those of Kahun. Petrie was not of course alone in exposing the wonders of Egyptian art and craftsmanship, but more than anyone else he documented and detailed works ranging from the most sophisticated wall paintings of the Pharaohs and palace officials to the humble pots and pottery idols of townsfolk and peasants. In this fertile period of British discovery, the French under Maspéro's leadership concentrated their efforts close to the pyramids of Lower Egypt and the Valley of the Tombs of the Kings some four hundred miles to the south.

Petrie moved to Naqada in Upper Egypt in 1894. His assistant J.E. Quibell, digging further along the river at Edfu on the site of Hieraconpolis, had found evidence of Selk, 'the scorpion', the immediate predecessor of the First Dynasty kings, and of Narmer the monarch of the united kingdom. Another Frenchman, Émile Amélineau, was working among the royal tombs at Abydos to the north. Petrie, the irascible perfectionist had already come into conflict with de Morgan, a mere businessman, and soon he would vent his wrath on Amélineau who, in searching for the tombs of the First and Second Dynasty pharaohs, smashed to smithereens many priceless objects which were not directly in his line of enquiry. Petrie regarded his work as 'scandalous'. He looked on the French generally as 'savages' who could not be entrusted with the simplest task in field archaeology.

At the necropolis of Naqada – and at nearby sites such as Ballas, Abadiyeh, Hu and Hieraconpolis which were excavated by J.E. Quibell and F.W. Green – the British under Petrie's leadership unearthed the first recognisable signs of prehistoric Egypt, stretching far beyond the earliest dynasties into the periods which came to be known from Petrie's discoveries at the sites of al-Amra and al-Girza as the Amratian and the Gerzean. Embracing almost the entire fourth millennium BC, these periods were subdivided into the sequences established at Naqada; Naqada I (Amratian) from c.4000 to 3500, Naqada II (Early to Late Gerzean) from c.3500 to the first dynastic period.

At the commune of the dead at Naqada, the tenacious Petrie recorded every essential detail of 2,149 graves. Some – separated from the commonality – were of a size and opulence which suggested royal or aristocratic ownership. Most were the resting places of ordinary citizens. The burial sites of the late Gerzean period (Naqada II, c.3300 BC), displayed great differences in wealth and social position, marked by types of pottery, jewelry and other personal possessions. In the common graves, the dead were packed side by side, head at the south end of the tomb, face to the west, anticipating later legends of the *Land of the Dead*. In the larger tombs, human bones often bore clear indications of teeth marks. More thorough investigation showed that bone marrow had been scooped out with tools. The immediate conclusion was that these early rural communities practised cannabalism. But there were no signs of burning. It was evident that the large, princely tombs witnessed human sacrifice on a mass scale, slaves and servants following their masters and mistresses to the death pits. Discoveries at the royal tombs of Abydos showed that the practice survived into the earliest dynastic period but that it was soon abandoned, probably on economic grounds. The Egyptians were a practical people, and the wastage of useful resources in this way, particularly of craftsmen, must have offended against their acute sense of civic responsibility.

To Petrie's chagrin, it was the flamboyant Frenchman de Morgan who drew attention to the prehistoric connection between the finds of his countrymen at Abydos and those of Naqada. From the Englishman's point of view it was no more than a 'happy guess'. Serious scholarship could hardly be expected of a man who was afflicted by a more dangerous curse even than his somewhat dubious Gallic nationality. He was a cavalier excavator who subscribed to the unspeakable notion of 'industrial' digging and site clearing methods in archaeology, an idea he had picked up while working with the French team at Susa in Persia. According to Petrie, de Morgan, director of the Egyptian Antiquities Service since 1891, was the son of a Welsh mining engineer, Jack Morgan. He had acquired French nationality along with his brother, a Parisian antiques dealer. For his part, de Morgan was quite content to leave xenophobic outbursts, along with the analysis of the Abydos and Naqada finds, to his austere rival.

It was on the strength of the Abydos and Naqada pottery finds that Petrie was able to establish his elaborate system of sequence dating. At Naqada he followed the evolution of a pottery style which began with a wavy moulded handle, reaching a high point of accomplishment at an early stage of its development and gradually deteriorating until a degenerate wavy line became the primary motif of body decoration. He also identified a burnished redware with white-line and black painted decoration with the earliest (Naqada I) period, and a buff-bodied pottery with pictorial and geometric decoration in a reddish colour representative of the later Gerzean (Naqada II) period. He was able to relate social changes reflected by the other contents of the graves to the pottery sherds which became his chronological sheet anchor. He found, for example, that pots by the sides of even the poorer occupants had contained scented fat early on, in the fifth millennium. But by the end of the predynastic times the pots contained only mud, a symbolic offering which demonstrated a persistent trend in human society. 'The rich had become richer and the poor poorer.'

In 1896, when Petrie left Naqada, de Morgan took his place and with what Petrie doubtless regarded as the luck of the devil, found there the tomb of Queen Nit-hotep of the First Dynasty, though the Frenchman thought at the time that he had found the sepulchre of Hor-aha, Nit-hotep's son. It was de Morgan who intuitively pointed the way to the discovery of prehistoric Egypt. It was Petrie's patient method which made possible an eventual understanding of the true nature and time-scale of a society which existed for two or three thousand years before the invention of writing. As a recent occupant of the Edwards Chair at University College, W.B. Emery, has written: 'Before 1895, our knowledge of Egypt's history did not extend back beyond the reign of the Pharaoh Senefru, first king of the Fourth Dynasty (2680 BC), and to the historian of that day even he was a somewhat shadowy figure'.

Through Petrie's insistence, the systematic classification of pottery became an accepted tool not only of dating but, just as importantly, of comparative social study. It was Champfleury who, at the moment when the archaeological significance of ceramics had come to the fore, coined the descriptive if melodramatic phrase 'history frozen by fire'. More than any other creative activity, pottery has reflected commercial and political surges, social ups and downs, and domestic habits and manners through every stage of civilization. It is the eternal mirror of society which, excepting the essentially contemporary possibility of nuclear cataclysm, is incapable of distortion. Other artefacts added to the role of pottery, however, in the nineteenth century systematization of ancient history, particularly the seal. Often of splendid craftsmanship, these personalized signature stamps of kings and commoners are found in abundance in Egypt and Mesopotamia. Like pottery, they had utilitarian and decorative functions, sometimes amuletic and magical uses. The Egyptians used cylinder seals until the Eleventh Dynasty, about 2,000 BC, when a stamp variety was preferred. It was usually made of steatite or ivory, occasionally of wood, and known as the scarab, after the sacred beetle *scarabaeus sacer* which pushed an excremental ball in front of itself, a process likened to the sun traversing the heavens, mystically propelled by an unseen power. Scarabs were often worn as rings or necklet appendages. They bore the names of their owners, and sometimes references to relatives, loved ones and anniversaries, as well as details such as occupations and residences. Thus a composite picture of domestic and working life emerges: *Lady of the House, Dadet-Mut*, for example; or *Sonb, occupant of the brewery*. Others conveyed the names and titles of kings and princes and the gods sacred to them. Scarabs appear to have been more common among ordinary folk than royalty in the early years of their use, until the middle of the Twelfth Dynasty when the name of Sesostris III (1878–1843 BC) is encountered on thirty or more known examples.

Thus, through the written word and the material evidence of many centuries, dynasties and individual sovereigns, gods and legends, conflicts and political arrangements began to take their places in chronological charts. One piece of evidence could be compared with another. The principal actors in the story of the ancient world could be named and assembled with increasing accuracy from cumulative sources.

The basic document was the well-known Ptolemaic composition of Manetho, a priest of the early part of the third century BC. His systematic history of the dynasties was composed in reply to what he believed to be the conjectural nature of Herodotus's history of Egypt. Manetho, unlike the Greek historian, spoke both Greek and Egyptian, and he had access to ancient records, many of which disappeared after Ptolemaic times. He wrote a pamphlet in refutation of Herodotus's errors, and a history of dynastic Egypt. Unfortunately, they disappeared too, but Africanus in the third century AD preserved a complete copy of the lengths of the reigns of the first three dynasties from Manetho. It confirmed the traditional belief that the first monarch was Menes. Eight kings are named in the record of the First Dynasty, their reigns totalling 263 years. Nine kings are shown in the Second Dynasty, reigning for 302 years between them, and nine for the Third Dynasty lasting 214 years. Of course, the Egyptian Sothic calendar had no precise starting point, so there is no indication of when the dynasties prevailed or when their twenty-six kings reigned. Neither is there any suggestion that Menes is coincident with the start of recorded history. As Petrie remarks, the inauguration of the First Dynasty is no more significant than is 776 BC to Greek history because it happened to be the date of the first Olympiad, or 753 BC to Rome because it marks the reputed foundation. Nonetheless, Manetho's list takes the recorded history of Egypt as far back as it is ever likely to be taken.

It has been argued that Manetho's history is in some respects fantastic and that his reign-spans are inordinately long, like the unnatural life-spans of the Old Testament patriarchs. In following an argument as to the chronological order of the Egyptian dynasties it has to be remembered that when Manetho compiled his history he was probably working from papyri which went back no further than the reigns of Seti I and his son Ramesses II, a thousand years before his own time. His sources for earlier history were more distant from him than he from the reader of these words. In fact, he gives the twenty-six named kings of the first three dynasties a span of 779 years, a perfectly acceptable average of twenty-nine years each, though later reigns are of arbitary and impossible length. According to the Manetho system, the dynasties numbered thirty, from Menes to the Macedonian conquest of 332 BC and the Ptolemaic rulers. By the time that Petrie, de Rougé and others came to compile their reign charts, other sources had been discovered in the tombs and palaces. In the temples of Ramesses II and his father Seti at Abydos, two stone-inscribed king lists had been found. The Ramesses version was removed to the British Museum. It contained only those kings 'adored by Seti' or thought to be worthy of offerings at the hand of his son, Ramesses II. The slab is badly damaged in parts. Its opening lines contain the kings from Menes to Userkaf, first sovereign of the Fifth Dynasty. There is then a gap until the Twelfth Dynasty, where we have the kings Sesostris II and III, and Amenemes III and IV; another gap until the Eighteenth Dynasty where we have kings Amosis I, Amenhotep I, Tuthmosis I, II and III, Amenhotep II, Tuthmosis IV, Amenhotep III, Horemheb; and in the Nineteenth Dynasty, Ramesses I and the signatory kings Seti I and Ramesses II. Other documents help to check still more closely the names and dates derived from the Manetho and Ramesses lists. A Fifth Dynasty stela, the 'Palermo stone', lists the kings of that early period. Another source, the 'Turin Papyrus', gives the kings from Menes to the Eighteenth Dynasty, and a tablet in the Louvre taken from the temple at Karnak covers much the same period. A tomb tablet from Saqqara, now in the Cairo museum, lists fifty-eight kings up to the Nineteenth Dynasty.

By the end of the nineteenth century, the cumulative finds of the past fifty years could be applied as checks to the surviving evidence of ancient historians and to mathematical reasoning based on the Sothic cycle. Many scholars in Europe

Granite sphinx of Kushite, 25th dynasty, king Taharqa wearing double *uraeus*, symbol of the cobra goddess, on forehead. Found at Kawa in Nubia.

poured scorn on the Petrie system. Either the Sothic system or the king lists must be thrown overboard it seemed. In 1905, however, his work in Sinai reinforced his own unshakable conviction that his arithmetic was right. He excavated the turquoise mines at Maghara and Serabit some half way down the coastal region of the peninsula between Suez and the pilgrim station of Tor, found there monuments and stone sculptures cut in the rocks of caves, built by workmen, who for thousands of years had visited the area each winter season to mine the precious ore, which provided the colouring for the beads and other jewelry so much prized by royalty.

Petrie believed, mistakenly, that the earliest of the monuments represented the seventh king of the First Dynasty, Semerkhet, carved on the smooth face of sandstone rock nearly 400 feet above the valley floor. There were, in fact, three figures of the king: the first with his *ka*-name, *horus*, with the crown of Lower Egypt; second, as king of Lower Egypt but without a name; third, as king of Upper Egypt, with *ka*-name again, but without a crown, shown in the act of 'smiting a Bedawin chief'. The last was a finely drawn monument, simple and true in outline, confident and summary in execution; and significant to Petrie's chronological scheme. The carvings proved to be of Sekhemkhet, however,

[215]

Pharaoh of the Third Dynasty, whose pyramid stands in the south-west corner of Zoser's complex at Saqqara. Petrie thought the figure strongly Ethiopian in appearance, familiar from the Sudanese of the modern Egyptian army, 'dark brown skin and very truculent character'. Here was another indication of political change, the declining civilization of the Second Dynasty being replaced by an alien Ethiopian ruling caste, progenitors of the great flowering of art and creative achievement which characterized the Fourth and Fifth Dynasties. Other groups showed royalty in its favourite pose, swiping the Badu, often rudely cut and hardly intelligible. But many monuments were astonishingly fresh in their sandstone outlines, as if newly carved. One of the finest scenes was of Sneferu, last king of the Third Dynasty, with pleated kilt and collar, tall plumes and a pair of horns forming the headdress, and an inscription below which read magniloquently, like an Assyrian stanza:

> Sneferu, the great god, giving power, firmness, and life, all satisfaction of heart forever, smiting the countries.

Stone relief carvings and wall paintings such as the famous Punt scene from the Temple of Hatshepsut at Dair al-Bahari near Thebes, exemplified the use of punitive expeditions in Sinai, Nubia and Somaliland, the Lebanon and even further afield, in search of minerals, ivory, timber and copper.

At Serabit the finds were no less magnificent than those of Maghara. Everywhere within the workmen's caves and the mines themselves, and between the two sites, were to be found stelae and inscribed stones recording the kings of virtually all the Egyptian dynasties who had visited the region or who had been honoured there by loyal citizens. Serabit was a sacred site, signalled by a large black stela of Seti I. On the path leading to it was a knoll of black haematite, the broken stela of Senusert III which once surmounted it now scattered. At the approach to the temple were stelae of Amenophis III and Ramesses II, and everywhere tributes to the goddess Hat-Hor. Within the temple was a beautiful black steatite statuette of Amenophis's favourite wife, Ti, a commoner from the far south of Egypt, or so Petrie thought, but her origins have always been in some doubt.

Even among the sandstone monuments and the fine examples of early craftsmanship which littered the caves and mines of the wilderness of Sinai, it was chronology and technology that most concerned Petrie. Some of the stelae contained mining records with months and days, and these could be compared with the reign years given for several kings recorded nearby. For example, a reference to the Egyptian date on which Amenophis III celebrated his thirty-sixth year enabled Petrie to make a dead reckoning of 1379 BC, 'when Mekhir 9th fell on

Nefertiti, wife of
Akhenaten.

January 19th'. Of Ramesses II, in his 3rd year, month of Phamenoth, day not
stated; 'this was in 1298 BC when Phamenoth was from January 12th to February
11th'. And so on. Petrie the mathematical wizard further examined the records of
the mining seasons, and of the year spans in which they could have occurred. As
his earlier calculations showed, it was his insistence on the addition of an entire
Sothic cycle which led him astray. The Sinai calculations produced an extra nine
hundred years, which he accounted for between the First and Seventeenth
Dynasties. He finally initiated the dynastic period at about 5510 BC. Almost all
other scholars of note for more than half a century accepted c.3300–3100 BC as the
likeliest starting point, but nothing would move the great man of Egyptology.

He was not entirely alone, however, among archaeological exponents of the
numbers game. Support came for Petrie's chronology from an unexpected
quarter. By 1905, Sir Arthur Evans had made important discoveries on the island
of Crete; important not only in the unravelling of Bronze Age Greek history but
also in establishing the dates of early contacts between pre-Ionian communities of

Greece and Egypt. His work seemed to lend support to Petrie's theories, but events would show that the two men shared the same impenitent weakness, a passionate and romantic attachment to their own archaeological patches and a determination to establish their priority in time and influence.

There can be no such reservations about Petrie's contribution to the understanding of Egyptian civilization through the discovery and assembly of its artefacts. To statues and busts of Hat-Hor and the head of Queen Ti in Sinai alone, in just one season's digging, he added innumerable figures of gods and goddesses, priests and officials, copper and bronze tools, tablets inscribed in the proto-Semitic language of the Phoenicians. To the knowledge of everyday life in the Egypt of the Pharaohs, Petrie contributed far more than any other archaeologist. He was fascinated by the ordinary – by the decoration of common homes, the lives of artisans and artists and labourers. Others might devote themselves to the pursuit of palaces and rich treasures. He preferred the humble terracotta figure, the roughly carved piece of stone or alabaster, the inscription of the wayfarer on some obscure byway, the tell-tale sherd sifted from someone else's heap of rubbish. From such details he built up his unequalled social and political picture of Egypt and its surrounding states, always believing its dynastic history to be much longer that it really was, yet putting flesh on the skeleton as no one before or after him, in hundreds of books, articles and lectures.

Documents found at almost all stages of Egyptian civilization, written on papyrus and stone, testified to the part played by the gods, myths and religious precepts of the people in everyday life. Priestly and political commands such as the vizier Ptah Hotep's *Instructions* issued in the period of the Old Kingdom, about 2400 BC, dealt extensively with such matters as wisdom and decorum. Obedience to authority and the sanction of each man's god was summed up in the pithy injunction 'An obedient son is a follower of Horus'. From the end of the Sixth Dynasty, about 2200 BC, so-called coffin texts which had been inscribed to the god-kings of the pyramids began to appear in the burial places of ordinary citizens. From the Eighteenth Dynasty, c.1600 BC, such texts were the almost invariable accompaniment of the dead, written on papyrus scrolls. They were known collectively as the *Book of the Dead*.

There was much excitement in Europe when these compilations began to emerge from burial tombs along the entire length of the Egyptian Nile. Here, as the American Egyptologist Breasted put it, was 'the dawn of conscience', the right of everyman to his own soul, to his own judgement day. De Rougé, in his introduction to a hieratic version of the *Book of the Dead*, saw an absolute connection between the cults of the Nile Valley and the religion of the Hebrews. In what amounted to a paraphrase of Newton's *Principia* he declared that the Egyptians believed in one supreme, eternal and almighty God, who created the world and everything in it, and endowed man with an immortal soul. De Rougé was writing before the discoveries of the coffin texts which found their way to the Louvre and the British Museum from about 1876. Scholars were still 'groping through the hieroglyphic texts' in an effort to understand them in a literal, much less spiritual, sense. De Rougé's view nonetheless received a warm welcome in some theological quarters as showing that the God of Judah and Christianity was an integral part of human consciousness from the earliest recorded times. Others saw it as an admission of the adulteration of belief in the one true God by what was clearly a worship of zoomorphic and anthropomorphic images. The Egyptian god, the 'One' or the 'One One', of the very earliest texts, was certainly singular: the god of the heavens from whom light, warmth and the good things of life derived. The sun-god. But it was a composite, the 'One' of several parts. It cannot be taken as a monotheistic precedent. It is true that the metaphor of light is at the heart of most religions, and is central to the Talmudic texts. But it does not follow that one derives from another. It is a common error of theological reasoning to suppose that the existence of one version of a belief or legend, anterior or posterior to another, is proof of the authenticity of either.

All the same, it is likely that the long contact between the Jews and the Egyptians from Abraham's first sojourn to the Exodus, gave rise to the adoption of common theological themes. The *Song of Solomon* has a marked similarity to Egyptian wedding songs. Moses, learned in the wisdom of the Egyptians, followed Egyptian magico-religious ritual in the construction of the Tabernacle, and the regulations he drew up concerning offerings, equipment and priestly dress. Indeed Moses declared that Yahweh, like the God of the Egyptians, was 'One', suggesting an affinity with the Amarna heresy. Sir Gardner Wilkinson was one of the first scholars to point to the resemblance between Egyptian and Jewish religious rites. Manetho and Josephus both believed that Moses was a priest, and according to Josephus the rebel Hebrews elected a priest of Heliopolis named Osarsiph to lead them. After framing their code of laws and drawing up a constitution that priest changed his name to Moses. To draw from another culture which doubtless filtered into Egyptian folk-lore, the Akkadian account of the infant Sargon languishing in the reeds of the Tigris, has obvious parallels with Hebrew legend. The folk tale of two brothers, Anubis and Bata, in which the younger is falsely accused of adultery with his kinsman's wife, has undertones of the story of Joseph and Potiphar's wife.

The story of the Deluge, of mankind's survival of the primordial catastrophe, of which Egypt is alone among early civilizations in lacking an example, points to perhaps the most universal of the legends which Judaism borrowed from pre-Semitic culture, but again it avails nothing to try to show that one proves the authenticity of the other. If an examination of Egyptian theology proves

anything, it is that the priests gradually extended the belief in immortality and judgement after death from the god-kings to the common people.

In the Book of the Dead, the scribe Ani says to Osiris:

Hail, One, rising (shining) from the Moon! Hail One, Shining from the Moon.

Osiris, the Moon-god, is deputy to the all-powerful sun. Plurality derived from the division at an early stage of the heavenly god into the gods and sub-gods of sun and moon. Before them came the gods of creation.

'I am he who came into being as Khepri.' The opening lines of *The Book of knowing the Creations of Ra and of Overthrowing Aphophis* are laden with doubletalk: 'When I had come into being, being (itself) came into being, and all beings came into being, before earth came into being, before the ground and creeping things had been created in this place . . .' Like the Hebrews, the Egyptians were fond of the explanatory pun. Khepri, the morning sun-god, was conceived as a scarab beetle; and *Kheper* means 'come into being'. There is much play on such words in the Egyptian Creation stories.

In the very beginning, the Egyptian legends tell us, there was only an oceanic waste, Nu (or Nun), from which came Atum, *Neb-er-djer*, lord of the world. Atum, finding no resting place among the waters, created a hillock and vomited forth the twin divinities Shu, the goddess of air and his sister-wife Tefnut, the goddess of moisture. In the mythological dark waters of chaos, Nun became Atum's eye, and Shu and Tefnut were cared for in infancy by the ophthalmic parent of mankind. Atum grew a second eye, brighter than the first, and jealousy ensued. To placate the first Eye, Atum wore it on his forehead, symbolic of the burning power of the sun with the help of which Atum created the world. The Eye became associated with the cobra goddess Buto, the symbolic serpent which the Pharaohs wore as an emblem of power. Atum's Eye had been sent in search of the infants Shu and Tefnut, and when it returned with them Atum wept with joy and from his tears came men. The twin gods Geb (the earth) and Nut (the sky) were born of Shu and Tefnut, but they were separated, because, it was said, of Shu's jealousy of his children's love. The heavens were made dark so that Nut could descend to earth to visit Geb, and so day and night came about. Wall paintings and papyrus drawings depicted Nut as a cow or sometimes as a sow suckling her piglets, Geb as the earth-bull or as a goose, the Great Cackler. Nut

Upper part of statue of Ramesses II, 19th dynasty, with false beard of the pharaohs.

Marital bliss? Perhaps man and wife, but no proof. Tomb figures of Katep and Hetepheres.

swallowed the stars each morning and bore them again at dusk. Another tradition said that stars were the winged *ba*, souls of the dead which lay in her bosom.

Heliopolis was the home of Atum, and it is said that Atum gave birth to Ra there; though it is more commonly written that Ra, the sun at its Zenith, created himself, and became Atum-Ra. There were other versions of the Egyptian story of the Creation. There is the Hermopolitan story of Ra emerging from a cosmic egg laid by the Great Cackler Geb on a hillock rising from the sea of the Two Knives, the sacred lake of Khemenu (Hermopolis), symbolizing the primordial waters. Hermopolis was also the centre of the cult of the hare, *Uno* of predynastic times (the 'springer-up'), a form of Ra. The same creature by the name of *Un-Nefer* was held to be a form of Osiris. Another version tells of the egg being laid by an ibis, the emblem of Thoth. The cult of Ra was established at Heliopolis long before Menes and the united kingdom of Upper and Lower Egypt. According to the pyramid texts Ra, the most popular of the solar gods throughout Egyptian history, masturbated in order to produce Shu and Tefnut and the peoples of the lower region, Nubia and the Sudan. He was the god of virility, fecundity, robustness. His followers made abundant offerings to him. Traditionally, Ra was the first Pharaoh, ruler of the earth from the beginning, journeying from his temple at Heliopolis attended by Shu to the twelve *nomes* or provinces of the land. When he came too close to his people he burned them, and he invoked the enmity of the serpent Apep (Apophis). Sometimes Ra assumed the form of the cat and bit off the head of his pursuer. One god gave rise to another, and in the telling of Egyptian lore there are echoes of the borrowed mythology of other religions. Bastet, the goddess to whom the cat was sacred, was a deltaic deity, perhaps Libyan in origin, adopted by the Heliopolitans as a daughter of Ra at the time of the Fifth Dynasty. But as Ba-Ist, the soul of Isis, she has a place in the First Dynasty. Her city, Bubastis, was known in the Second.

She is found at every stage of Egyptian history, lion-headed at first, sometimes with human limbs but mostly with cat's features entirely, and short-skirted. So the pantheon burgeoned. Isis and Osiris, deeply embedded in Greek and Roman mythology, were fathered by Ra and Thoth respectively. 'The lord of all things comes towards the light ... a great and benevolent pharaoh is born'. Isis and Osiris loved each other even in the womb, and the grief-stricken Isis wandered over the earth in search of her love after her brother Set and the Ethiopian Queen Aso had disposed of his body in the beautiful casket which became his coffin. She finally succeeded in her mission with the help of divine Astarte, carrying the body of Osiris back to Egypt, conceiving a child by her dead husband on the way. Set in his anger cut off the dead Osiris's phallus and fed it to fish of the Nile which were cursed forever. Green-faced Osiris chose to remain in the world of the dead, and so became Khenti-Amentiu, King of the Dead; Isis gave birth to Horus in secret, hiding him in the reeds from the 'poisonous snake', Set, but to no avail. Thoth, in Ra's name, declared that the solar boat would remain at anchor and the world in darkness until the infant Horus recovered. And the infant recovered to become the sky-god, the falcon, the Divine Pharaoh whose eyes were the sun and the moon, who conducted the souls of the dead to his father Osiris in the halls of the underworld. Thus, in a gallery of human-animal figures, each of clearly defined sex and character, was set out the pantheon of Egypt. As the Egyptologist H.P. Cooke remarked, 'if only we could regard them as "he-shes" we should cut their number by half'.

In the years 1892–7, Petrie at Tel al Amarna, Thebes and Deshasheh, and the Frenchman Jacques de Morgan at Dahshur on the outskirts of Cairo, had unearthed tens of thousands of stone, pottery and bronze figures, as well as the royal tombs which added hugely to the historical, religious and artistic narratives. De Morgan's discovery at Dahshur, close to the stepped pyramid of Saqqara, of the tombs of princesses of the Twelfth Dynasty was spectacular. Jewelry exhibiting the fine cloisonné work of the goldsmith at a period of mastery of the applied arts, was ablaze with cornelian, turquoise, and lapis-lazuli, on crowns, bracelets, necklets, pendants and all the panoply of royal attire. These glittering baubles had lain alongside the sarcophagi of the Princesses Ita and Khnemit since their burial some 4,000 years before, yet were so well concealed that they had escaped the notice of thieves during that time. Similar jewelry was found by Petrie at the Middle Kingdom pyramid township of Lahun in the Fayum.

The stone-inscribed king lists of Seti and Ramesses II from the temples of Abydos had omitted the names of Hatshepsut, the queen-regnant, and several of the male monarchs of the Eighteenth Dynasty. There had crept into the quiescent recollection of Greece the names of King Amenophis III and his queen. References to them were found in the records of pre-hellenic Greece. But of the rest of the dynasty, the ancient world, it seems, knew nothing. The fact is hardly surprising since all reference to the 'heretical' years of that dynasty were removed from public monuments. Their names were seldom uttered by Egyptians after their demise.

Akhenaten introduced to the Court and to Egyptian society a new concept of religion, that of Aten worship, or the cult of the sun disc. For almost 2,000 years Egypt had been a land of polytheistic worship; devout, conservative, and resentful of revolutionary ideas. Its art, like its religion, was comfortable, stable and, except for brief periods of unexceptional experiment, stylistically uniform. Amenophis IV had been crowned with the cult name of his own deity, Amun. The rejoinder of the people, 'Amun is pleased' was, in effect, his coronation hymn. He succeeded to a father, Amenophis III, the monarch of what has been

Harp player from tomb of Amenemhat, colour drawing by N. de G. Davies.

Alabaster portrait of Amenophis IV (Akhenaten) and his queen Nefertiti.

Temple statue of Ptah-Ankh with offering basin, New Kingdom, sold at Sotheby's in
July 1981 for £68,000–$136,000.

called 'Egypt's golden age', a king pacific by nature who was inclined to a policy
of neighbourly understanding based on diplomacy and trade, as we see in the
elaborate correspondence preserved in the tablets which were found at Tel al
Amarna in 1887, before Petrie had begun serious excavation of the site. There is
evidence that the monotheistic cult of the solar-disc, with its legend of rays
terminating in hands representative of the divine power, ascendant over all men
and all things, had flourished under Amenophis III. Indeed there is evidence that
Hatshepsut, the female monarch who called herself 'king' was the instigator of
the unorthodoxies which beset the land after the reign of the youth Tuthmosis II,
whose predecessor Tuthmosis I had stretched the frontiers of empire to the
Euphrates in the sixteenth century BC. Be that as it may, Amenophis IV made
Aten-worship the official religion and changed his name to Akhenaten, the
Servant of Aten. Such an affront to the priesthood was unlikely to go
unchallenged. Perhaps the heresy of Aten worship had its origin in that obscure

period of Hyksos rule which followed the Twelfth Dynasty, the period of feudal kings who controlled the Nile flood, conquered far and wide, pacified almost all the known world, and whose name – Khyan – would yet be found on an imported alabaster pot-lid in the royal Palace of Knossos at Crete. According to early chronologers, the Hyksos, the 'Shepherd Kings', ruled for 929 years. But according to Josephus, quoting Manetho, they ruled for 518 years. Whatever the truth of the matter their influence was widespread. The name of Khyan, the third recorded monarch of the dynasty, appears on a lion sculpture at Baghdad, on stone objects in the Hittite capital of Hattusas (modern Boghazkoi) and Upper Egypt, a seal impression found in Palestine, and a statue in the Nile Delta, as well as on the jar-lid at Knossos.

The early chronologers were almost certainly wrong in their estimate of the dynasty's duration. The Hyksos established their capital at Avaris in the Delta and their rule probably lasted no longer than a hundred years, somewhere between 1680 and 1580 BC. Josephus equated these 'accursed' invaders with the brethren of Joseph. Others connected them with the Hittites (a once popular theory now discarded), and translated their name as meaning simply 'rulers of countries'.

Economic forces inevitably played a part in bringing about these dramatic changes in Egyptian civil, military and religious fortunes over a period of almost 400 years until the old orthodoxy was revived under Ramesses I, the founder of the Nineteenth Dynasty, in about 1320 BC. Gold, levied from Kush and Nubia as tribute up to the reign of Tuthmosis III, had sustained the glory of Egypt in life and death for a thousand years. Copper, the essential ingredient of bronze and of civilization, always posed a problem for the Pharaohs since there were no deposits in Egypt itself. This vital raw material came chiefly from Cyprus, the island which either gave to or received its name from the metal. Tin, the other ingredient of bronze, was also imported, perhaps from as far afield as England or Afghanistan. As long as the gold mines were productive and supplies of tin and copper could be assured, expansionist policies at home and abroad were possible. But the Egyptians were extravagant people, especially in matters of religion and comfort in the after life. Pyramids were costly. So were gold encrustations on tomb furnishings finely carved and painted palace walls. The Nubian mines became unproductive because of the absence of water necessary for panning the metal and keeping the miners alive. Not until the twelfth century was the matter taken seriously, when wells were dug close to the mines. By then, rivalry with neighbouring states and the threat of invasion by the marauding 'Sea Peoples', threatened the country's most vital supplies.

The Eighteenth Dynasty had begun under Amosis, who finally expelled the Hyksos, with the revivalist urge of a ruler who had seen enough of decay and

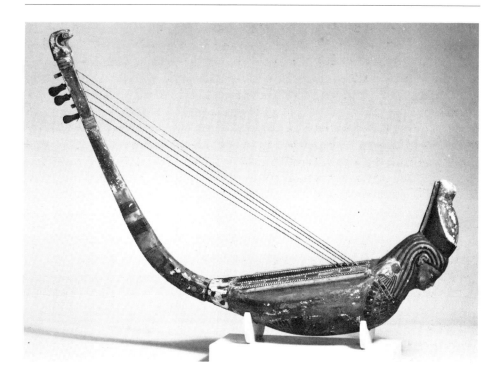

Harp from the tomb of Ani at Thebes, New Kingdom.

degeneration under foreign imposters and 'non-people'. Kamose, brother of Amosis, had declared while under the foreign heel: 'No man can rest in peace while he is racked by the taxes of the Asiatics! I will seize the Asiatic and cut open his belly. My policy is to save Egypt and smite the Asiatics!'. The return of imperial pride went hand in hand with a return to the old gods. The heresy which probably began conspiratorially under a woman 'king', continued briefly under Akhenaten's co-regent and successor Smenkhkare. But under the next Pharaoh, the boy-king Tutankhamen, normality was restored, and the nation reverted to its many gods. Egypt was never strictly speaking a colonizing or warmongering power, though it had its moments of military adventure. There was, all the same, a strong sense of conservatism and imperial pride in its make-up.

The generations which came after the adoption of Aten execrated the memory of the heretics, doubtless for reasons of innate traditionalism and fear of being thrown off balance; a fear common enough among all the nations that have followed. There was enough in the literature and life of Egypt in the years of the Bondage to suggest that the Children of Israel took many a lesson and tradition with them into the wilderness. Thutmosis III, the conqueror who set out the first list of Asiatic and African dominions, led an expedition to the Lebanon sometime in the mid-fifteenth century BC to secure cedar wood. 'They were sharper than the beard of grain, the middle thereof as thick ... I brought them down from the highland of God's Land. They reached as far as the forest preserve ... I sailed on the Great Green Sea with a favourable breeze ...'. And some two centuries later the Jews went into Canaan, where 'The trees of the Lord are full of sap; the cedars of Lebanon, which he hath planted ... O Lord, how manifold are thy works!'.

—— 9 ——

Mycenae, Troy and Knossos

Evans in Crete

The death of Schliemann in 1890 brought to an end the romantic chapter of nineteenth-century archaeology. Troy, Mycenae and Tiryns would be associated with his name almost as intimately as with the heroic legends that inspired his frenzied assault on them.

His reputation would rest uneasily on the unquestioned magnificence of his finds – on 'Priam's' jewels and 'Agamemnon's' mask, on all the 'golden riches', jewel-studded bronze and silver weapons and kingly tombs of Homeric Greece – and on the very questionable methods he employed to unearth such splendours. It could never be said with certainty that some at least of his discoveries were not the possessions of the heroes and heroines of legend. Neither could it be asserted positively that they were. But in the years which followed his spectacular treasure hunt at Mycenae and Troy, his methods of dating and of 'literary' judgement had come under the scrutiny of his assistant Döerpfeld, and of scholars who dug in other lands. Schliemann had looked on the palaces and temples and graves that he unearthed with a simple precept: they must conform to, and thereby prove, the Homeric story of a glorious and passionate bronze-age people who lived a thousand years before Marathon and the building of the Parthenon, or they must be discarded as insignificant trivia. Homer could not be doubted. It was as if the history of imperial Rome were to be deduced from excavation of the Julian graves, and every likeness, every event, judged in accordance with its fidelity to Virgil's epic verse. Archaeology can itself mislead. Thucydides in his *Peloponnesian War* anticipated the dilemma which might face the excavator of the Peloponnese, where Argos of the mythical period was succeeded by Lacedaemon (Sparta), which occupied almost half the region and ruled the rest in the fifth

Stemmed goblet with octopus design in fine chapagne-coloured clay with brown-black
painted decoration; and pot of same period. Late Mycenaean.

century BC. Lest others should be deceived by appearances, he warned: 'But as
their city was not adorned with sanctuaries and fine buildings, and as it was
composed of hamlets in the manner of ancient Greece, it would appear very
humble'. In those circumstances he did not think that future generations would
believe Sparta to have been as powerful as it was reputed to be. Yet if the same fate
should befall the Athenians, to be judged by the posthumous appearance of their
city, 'their power would seem to be twice what it really is'. Schliemann was not
alone among the great figures of archeological discovery in ignoring the spirit of
that prescient warning. But he was the most remarkable in his single-mindedness.
To the end of his days he believed that the shaft graves he had unearthed at
Mycenae contained the bodies of Agamemnon and his companions, victims of
that treacherous night's work by Clytemnestra and her paramour. His momen-
tary response, as he beheld the golden masks of the men, 'two women with golden
frontlets', and two children 'wrapped in sheet gold', was one of certainty that he
had rekindled the flame which was extinguished with the destruction of Mycenae.

Döerpfeld, trained as an architect, patient and painstaking in field work and conservative in judgement, went over his master's digs at Troy and Mycenae and came to the conclusion that the real site of Troy was three layers above the level at which Schliemann had found his 'petty little town with its brick walls' (level VI from the top, a well-fortified city in its eighth building stage and denominated VIH). The German Rudolph Virchow, Professor of Medicine, and Emile Burnouf, director of the French School at Athens, dug with Schliemann at Troy in 1879, going over old ground, but nothing would dissuade him from his original conclusion that only the lowest of the nine strata he had uncovered could be Homer's Troy. Later work by an American team under Professor Carl Blegen would fix the *Ilios* of the Trojan War at an even higher level, VIIA. Unfortunately, Troy VIIA occupies the same ground as Troy VI. Blegen also excavated Pylos in the far south-west, which was seen to be an open city free from the fear of invasion which preoccupied the fortified cities to the north and east – Mycenae, Orchomenos, Tiryns, Athens, Thebes and other mighty kingdoms. The American believed that Troy VIIA was destroyed after Pylos, in the so-called Late Helladic IIIB period, c. 1260 BC. But Blegen's Troy was a poor city with little to suggest Homeric fortifications. Whatever may be the actual site of Troy, most twentieth-century scholars prefer the evidence of pottery which suggests c. 1200 BC as the date of destruction; close indeed to the date of literary tradition, 1180 BC.

As for Mycenae, the shaft graves and their contents were some five hundred years older than the events of the Homeric saga, dating from about 1600–1500 BC. Mycenae was not simply a royal stronghold of mainland Greece. It was the centre of a great Aegean empire, with wide trading links. Mycenaean decorative pottery has been found throughout the Levant and Syria. Among the many vital clues to the ancient world found at Tel al Amarna in Egypt, there were some eight hundred Mycenaean vases, and there were signs in the paintings of the Amarna period that Egyptian and Aegean art exerted a temporary influence on each other. Schliemann failed to see much that would have brought him and the world closer to a true understanding of ancient Greece, had he been able for a second to detach himself from Homer. Even at the largest of the *tholoi*, or beehive tombs of Mycenae, the 'Treasury of Atreus', he hardly noticed the great doorway. Yet it was a work which vied with the mightiest mechanical achievements of Egypt and Babylon, its massive lintel weighing 120 tons yet was somehow manhandled into position with such accuracy that it remained intact for nigh on four thousand years. Two headless rampant lions supported a central pillar, sentinels of the Lion Gate through which Agamemnon and Menelaus may well have passed. And all protected by the huge 'Cyclopean' walls of the acropolis, each rough block of stone so huge that later Greeks thought only *cyclops*, giants, could have put them in place. The lions which looked down from the great gate on the hilltop of

Mycenae were, at the time of Schliemann's discovery, the oldest known statuary of European origin.

It was Schliemann's Greek successor, Stamatakes, who cleared the debris from the *tholos* of Atreus. Other Greeks and the Englishman Alan Wace, systematized the work which the German had started so famously, applying the methods of comparative dating from pottery and other material finds which the Egyptologists and Assyriologists had developed so successfully, though not always with unanimity of view. Döerpfeld detected the most significant of his chief's errors. Schliemann had insisted that all the bodies in the shaft graves at Mycenae were buried at the same time, in conformity with Homeric tradition. They were covered with clay and stones. The sides of each grave were lined with small quarry stones and clay, forming walls of up to seven feet in height. In some cases slabs of slate were leaning against the 'walls', other slabs lay crosswise over the bodies. The bodies themselves were close together, each piled high with ornaments and arms. Schliemann argued that they must have been buried at the same time. It would, he thought, have been logically impossible to dig down through one grave with its incumbent body in order to make a subsequent burial without disturbing the corpse. He also found at the site 'little boxes of stout sheet copper', filled with wood. He thought they might have been head rests. At any rate, they complied with the requirement of a single mass burial of Agamemnon's tragic family, with all the glittering paraphernalia of what Wace described as 'one of the richest archaeological discoveries ever made'.

But Döerpfeld was suspicious. He examined the little boxes of sheet copper at the Athens Museum. He realized that the slate slabs had originally lined the roofs of the tombs, held in position by timbers which were strengthened at ground level by copper sheaths, Schliemann's 'boxes'. The tombs were not filled with clay and stones. The graves were not 'walled up'. The timbers had rotted in the course of time, the slabs had crashed down on the bodies, bringing clay and stones with them. The young assistant, by the kind of diligent investigation that is at the heart of good archaeology, had done more than iron out the faulty hypothesis of his chief. He had shown that the shaft graves had been the site of royal burials for a period of a century or more, from about 1600–1500 BC, and that the objects accompanying the bodies represented different periods. Each 'grave' had been a family vault in which several interments were possible without disturbing the existing bodies. Agamemnon, whose traditional kingship could not possibly have fallen within the period of the royal burials in Schliemann's shaft graves, remains as substantial as ever in the collective imagination, and yet as archaeologically intangible as Abraham and Moses in another context. Eighty years after Schliemann, in 1952, Greek archaeologists working under Dr Papadimitriou found a new Grave Circle in an area which Wace had pointed to

Bronze bull and acrobat. Late Mycenaean, c.1550 BC.

when digging at Mycenae at the instigation of Sir Arthur Evans. The Circle within the Citadel which Schliemann had found was two-hudred years older than the graves it enclosed. The newly-discovered Circle belonged to the same period as the graves within. In the new shaft graves were several skeletons. One had its legs apart and its hands in the position of a man stretched on a sofa. Others were laid facing the centre of the grave. It was a family sepulchre, and as one interment followed another, bodies were moved aside to accommodate their successors. Much fine pottery and funerary gifts of gold and silver were found, such as the famous rhytons or ritual drinking vessels which would also turn up in the same bull's-head shape in Crete. Papadimitriou wrote of a vase 'belonging to a period of at least fifty years later than that of other vases, 'let us say about 1550 BC'. It proved 'that the last burial was committed to the grave at the beginning of the Mycenaean Age', and it must be considered certain therefore that the skeletons 'belong to a royal Greek tribe which established itself at Mycenae and built a strong State at an earlier period than that to which our heroes of the Trojan War belong. These were the first Greeks who, from about 2000 BC, were coming down from the north into continental Greece, were established also in the Peloponnesos, and thence came into contact with the people of Crete and of the islands'.

Had Homer been alive in Mycenae at the time of the Trojan war, the bodies in the tombs within the Cyclopean walls would have been as remote from him as is Queen Elizabeth the First or Ivan the Terrible from the reader of these lines. The man who made a fortune from the Crimean War and devoted it to uncovering Homeric Greece, would yet be the object of critical scrutiny, even of ridicule. One way or another, however, he had taken back the known history of Greece for the better part of a thousand years, from the Iron Age which came with the Dorian invaders of the Aegean sometime after 1100 BC to the Middle Bronze Age.

Döerpfeld, Wace, Blegen and the new generation of Greek archaeologists gradually corrected Schliemann's chronology. Their primary source of 'anchor' dates was information gleaned from sites in Asia Minor and Egypt, where pottery such as had been found at Mycenae, Troy and Tiryns often turned up, along with equally revealing stamp-seals and cylinders. The fact that 'dating' was necessarily arrived at by indirect means pointed to the great difference between ancient Greece and those other lands which had been systematically probed in the second half of the nineteenth century. They – Egypt, Mesopotamia, Syria and Anatolia – contained in their vast libraries and decorated chambers their own revealed history; the culture of every period manifested in all its forms and often dated by reference to the royal personages or events depicted. So far, the revealed past of Greece offered no such convenient short cuts to accurate dating. There were no elaborate inscriptions on the buildings or sculptures of Mycenae and Troy. Written records were few and far between. Where writing had been found, it was in a language which no one understood, though scholars inclined to the belief that it was Hittite or Etruscan in origin.

A meeting in 1882, at the Schliemann home in Athens, by far the grandest of inhabited mansions in all Greece, was destined to change dramatically the balance of advantage which the Asiatic and Egyptian worlds enjoyed over Greece in terms of chronology and, indeed, of longevity. The host was still concerned with Tiryns, the sister fortress of Mycenae, where he had been digging at intervals since 1876, and where he had recently found in the well-preserved palace some

The Harpist. A Cycladic figure
c. 2500 BC. Sold at Sotheby's in
December 1980 for £45,000–
$105,000.

tantalizing fragments of frescoes depicting hunting scenes and a youth leaping
over a bull. The visitor, Mr Arthur Evans, was thirty-one years old and unlike his
host had enjoyed a secure youth and academic background. His father, Sir John
Evans, was one of the world's most distinguished numismatists and an
archaeologist of repute. Harrow and Brasenose, editorship of the *Harrovian* and
of an underground school journal known as the *Pen-Viper* (suppressed by the
headmaster), had left him with a good classical education, a 'first' in modern
history, and a Liberal stance in politics which took a sufficiently radical turn to
attract imprisonment and a sentence of death from the Austrians during the
Balkans crisis in the year of his visit to Schliemann. The German, inevitably,
talked of Homer and Troy. Evans listened politely while training his gaze on the
objects in the room. The jewels and golden ornaments of Mycenae and Troy were
everywhere. But Evans was interested in the smaller objects, particularly some

tiny engraved bead-seals and signet rings. They reminded him of gems he had seen from Egypt and Assyria, but many of the designs contained an 'octopus' theme which was assuredly Aegean. Schliemann announced that he intended to dig next in Crete, whence at the siege of Troy, 'came forth the men from Knossos' along with warriors 'from Gortyn of the Great Walls, from Lyctus, Miletus, chalky Lycastus, Phaestus, and Rhytion, fine cities all of them ...'.

Evans, recently married to Margaret Freeman, daughter of a well-known historian, returned to England and the stewardship of the much-neglected Ashmolean Museum at Oxford. A condition laid down by Ashmole in his bequest was that keepers of the collection must combine travel and lecturing with their museum duties. Evans added excavation work at Roman and Celtic sites to those obligatory activities, and in a series of lectures he addressed himself to the controversial subject of the influence of early eastern cultures on those of Europe. Schliemann's work, particularly at Mycenae and Tiryns, and subsequent writings by German scholars based on the Achaean discoveries, with their insistent reference to the distribution of engraved seal-stones, had led to the proposition that the island of Crete was a centre of Mycenaean culture. There was evidence, too, that the Mycenaeans had well-established contacts with the lands which fanned out from their eastern border and the Mediterranean shore to the distant Caspian, the Sea of India and the cataracts of the Nile. In 1889, the explorer Greville Chester presented a 'Cretan' seal-stone to the Ashmolean, and in 1893 Evans found other examples in Athens and in the Berlin collections. In that year also, painted pottery was found in the Kamarais cave on Mount Ida and was removed to the museum at Candia in Crete. At almost the same time, Flinders Petrie announced the discovery of identical painted pottery at the twelfth-dynasty site of Fayum in Egypt. In 1894 Evans acquired a piece of land at Candia. At that time Ottoman law prevailed. Five years later Britain persuaded the Turks to abandon the island to the Greeks and Evans was able to gain full possession of his property. He at once began excavations there in collaboration with the British School at Athens and its director David Hogarth.

Evans had already become a devoted student of ancient Greece, deducing a form of 'picture-writing' from the seal-stones with their pictographic signs. He had also copied a clay tablet containing a linear inscription. He had become an acknowledged Hellenic scholar when the first major tragedy of his life occurred with the death of his wife in 1893 after fifteen years of marriage. It was the year in which they had bought an 'earthly paradise' in the shape of a country estate at Youlbury in Oxfordshire, an alternative abode to their beloved Venetian house at Ragusa, the Casa san Lazzaro. Evans found a new 'paradise' in Crete. Since his youthful travels in the Balkans he had acted as an occasional correspondent of the *Manchester Guardian*. Hogarth, over much the same stretch of time, had combined the duties of running the British School at Athens and digging at Ephesus and Crete, with various journalistic roles, the chief of which was that of correspondent of *The Times*. He wrote prolifically on archaeological matters for the *Illustrated London News* and for learned papers. The two men had much in common, though they did not see eye-to-eye politically. Both were brilliant writers, and in their different ways both exerted a considerable – and not always benign – influence on British policies in the Balkan and Aegean territories of the Ottoman Empire. In 1899 they launched the Cretan Exploration Fund, at almost the precise moment of the declaration of the Boer War. They hoped for five-thousand pounds. In the event they received five-hundred, of which a major contribution came from the Evans family. Prince George of the Hellenes, then entitled to style himself 'High Commissioner for the Powers in Crete', also contributed and became Patron of the Fund. The three directors were Evans, 'Ashmole's Keeper', Oxford; Hogarth, Fellow of Magdalen; and R. Carr Bosanquet, successor to Hogarth as director of the British School.

Hogarth had been digging for twelve years past in Cyprus and Crete for the British School, and had started excavations at Lacedaemon. In March 1900 he joined Evans at the site of Knossos, at the hill of Kefala. A third British archaeologist joined the team at the start, Duncan Mackenzie, who had been digging on Melos island in the Cycladic group. The scene of their new endeavour lay some hundred kilometres off the southern mainland of Greece, a rugged island athwart a myriad family of fragmented lands which emerge like stepping stones from the Aegean and Ionian seas. Crete is a mountainous country cut by deep valleys, in one of which, cleaving the island almost in the middle from north to south, lies Knossos, close to the northern coastline and just inland from Heraklion.

Mackenzie came in response to a telegram from Evans which read 'Personal not School affair terms four months sixty pounds and all expenses paid to begin at once'. It was to this able and sociable Scot, that Evans paid the highest tribute, especially for fostering a team spirit among Christian and Moslem workers whose common sport 'consisted of massacring each other'. And it is to his day-book that we owe the most detailed account of the early stages of the excavations at Knossos.

The entry for Friday, 23 March 1900 was to the point. 'The excavations by Mr Arthur Evans at Knossos began this morning at 11 a.m.' There were thirty-two men at work on the first day. Within a week about a hundred were employed at the site, uncovering the area which had already been designated the 'Palace'. It had been cleared some twenty years before by Minos Kalokairinos, who made soundings in several parts of the west wing in 1878–79. The pottery found by the Greek had been the subject of numerous articles and comments in professional journals. Thus, Evans was well aware of the nature and layout of the site before he began to dig. In 1881, W. J. Stillman observed the work of Kalokairinos and a certain Turkish Bey and reported to the American Archaeological Institute his observation of huge blocks of hewn stone with incised designs on them, and of 'ancient walls'. But Evans was not prepared for the size of the structure just beneath the surface, which had remained undisturbed since the palace was finally destroyed. Within a few days of starting work, his men began to unearth walls with frescoes still hanging to them. The area that Evans had taken as the site of 'the Palace', was a throne-room complex with antechamber and a small shrine. The earth and sherd dumps which had become sizeable within a few weeks of digging were soon seen to be covering a large part of the Palace. They were, of course, removed as the excavations continued. As successive layers were cleared it was seen that the anteroom or lobby was entered by a short flight of steps leading from a central court. The original plaster from walls and ceilings covered the steps and floor. Stone benches were in their original places along the north and south walls. A fragment of fresco containing a bull's hoof hung over one of the south-wall benches. Panels in imitation of veined stone provided a homely twentieth-century feature on other pieces of fresco. Between the benches were found the charred remains of a wooden object. Evans had no doubt of its identity, labelling it in his notebook 'Throne'. The anteroom gave access at its western end to the throne room, with a large stone basin along the south wall. This lustral basin was approached by six steps. Evans dubbed it 'Ariadne's bath'. Work went on smoothly and with amazing rapidity. Almost everything seemed to be in place, as if the royal community of the Palace had been there at one moment and gone the next, with every stone alabastron, every vase, in place, though sometimes upside down. Charred remains of wooden objects indicated fire. Pieces of crystal and other materials found in the lustral basin appeared to have fallen from a loggia above, perhaps as the result of some violent action by man or nature. By 27 March, just four days after the start of the excavations, Evans was able to divert his gaze from the throne room and take stock of the work going on all around. 'The extraordinary phenomenon – *nothing Greek* – *nothing Roman* – perhaps one single fragment of late black varnished ware among tens of thousands. Even geometrical pottery fails us – though as tholoi found near the central road show, a flourishing Knossos existed lower down ... *Nay, its great period goes at least well back to the pre-Mycenaean period.*'

Even in the first weeks of the excavations at Knossos, news spread of sensational discoveries; not of the gold and jewels and entombed warriors such as Schliemann had staggered the world with at Mycenae and Troy, but of mature, sophisticated arts; of palatial halls, of a civilization patently older than Mycenae yet having many features of building method and pottery decoration in common

Sir Arthur Evans, from a painting by Sir William Richmond.

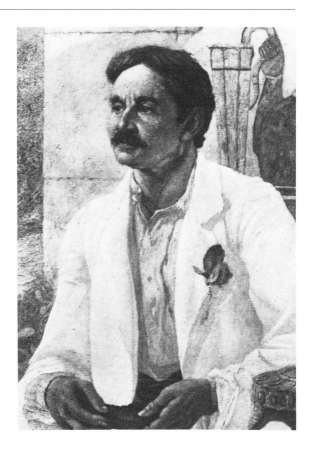

with the ancient habitations of Peloponnesos. Döerpfeld, still digging at Troy and Mycenae, and now director of the German Archaeological Institute at Athens, came down to Crete to see for himself. More professional helpers were summoned. First to arrive was the architect to the British School at Athens, Theodore Fyfe. An experienced foreman was soon needed and Hogarth's sometime helper in Cyprus and Crete, Gregorios Antoniou, was called in: a notorious tomb robber in his youth but now a man of great reliability and experience.

Inevitably there were rifts among the leading men. Evans was accustomed to wealth and like many who are born into riches he was curiously insensitive to those who have to earn a livelihood. He drew no salary and was at a loss to understand Hogarth's need of regular payments, especially since funds were scarce. Eventually, Hogarth was driven to remind the man whom he was shortly to succeed as Keeper of the Ashmolean that 'You are a rich man's son, and have probably never been at a loss for money . . .'. And Hogarth, who knew better than most how to find an adversary's weakest point, reminded his chief that his 'princely' life-style did not encourage possible contributors to the Cretan Fund, particularly when they had the 'frugal example of Flinders Petrie' before them. Another architect, Christian Doll arrived in the fifth year of the excavations and started a diary which told of the continuing flow of visitors and occasional site dramas: 'Profs. Mosso and Pernier on the Excavation quite early. Prof. Gardner and party arrived at 1 o'clock in 4 carriages. Showed him all the unsafe spots to be avoided. Showed Wace over the Palace staircase. Gave the party tea at Candia House.' On another occasion: 'Row between Manolakis and the French officer over their horses being taken onto the Excavation. Manolakis struck by the officer'. Manolakis had arrived to take the place of Gregori as foreman soon after work started, the latter moving off with Hogarth to other pastures. Evans called him 'My mountain wolf', and he was the bravest of men, destined to die fighting on the side of the Allies in the First World War. He protected the site for thirty-five years from graffitists and people who dared to ride horses over it. Doll designed an excavation house – the Villa Ariadne – to replace the residence at Heraklion. It was invariably full of visitors.

Mosso and Pernier, the former an anthropologist, were working at another famous Cretan site, Phaistos on the other side of the island. Wace arrived in Greece in 1902 to join the British School. In 1914 he would become its director, and take part in one of the most bitter of all archaeological conflicts with the man he at first admired greatly, Arthur Evans. Even at the outset of the Knossos dig, Evans began to take a possessive, sometimes blinkered view of the site which was literally his own property. As Schliemann turned his beloved Homer into a positive Achilles' heel, and as Petrie was cursed by a faulty chronological deduction, so Evans was to create a quite arbitary blind spot out of his devotion to Knossos, its palaces and what he believed to be its demonstrable precedence in the history of Greece. Wace was to find himself virtually *persona non grata* in Greece for his temerity in suggesting that the mainland Mycenaeans conquered Crete, rather than the other way round. Wace was to be proved right in the end.

On 30 March 1900, Evans made what was to prove the most vital and frustrating of all his discoveries. While rummaging in an area close to a temple building he discovered a clay bar, elongated in form which he likened to a 'stone or bronze chisel'. It contained writing and, he believed, numerals. A few days later in a nearby area which came to be called the 'Room of the Chariot Tablets', he found a hoard of tablets inscribed with the same ideogrammatic writing.

Alongside them were the remains of carved wood, sealing appendages and hinges. Like the Amarna tablets of Egypt, the tablets of Knossos had obviously been stored in a chest and securely sealed. Were these the Amarna equivalents, providing perhaps an insight into the lives and political alliances of the kings of old? They were not to prove so historically revealing. But they were to become vital pieces in a philological jigsaw.

One of the tablets Evans had seen in 1895, in the course of his early wanderings, contained a similar script, and had probably come from the excavations of the local man Kalokairinos at the same site. Evans called the writing 'Linear B', thus distinguishing it from another form of writing, with hieroglyphic and syllabic components, called 'Linear A'. The former system of writing was used in the later period of Knossos for the keeping of palace records; the latter, and older, script has defied all attempts at decipherment. Unlike its Egyptian and Mesopotamian counterparts it has never been found in association with known languages. Evans made many attempts to understand the languages he had discovered. Others, including the most distinguished classicists, Egyptologists and Assyriologists, tried for more than thirty years to decipher them. In the end it was an unknown young man named Michael Ventris, an amateur philologist, who succeeded where so many had failed. Ventris was present as a scoolboy when, in 1936, thirty-six years after the discovery, Evans gave a lecture in London to mark the jubilee of the British School in Athens. The great archaeologist was then a lively 85 year-old, honoured and knighted. Ten years later the young Ventris, by then qualified as an architect, announced that he had deciphered Linear B. The assumption that the primary language of the region had originated in Asia Minor, and that its roots were probably Hittite or Etruscan, was widespread. Ventris identified elements which were clearly related to ancient Greek – earlier than Homer's Greece but with names recognizable from Achaean syllogisms for gods and pottery vessels, for words such as *ass* and *horse*; the word *tripod* was found to occur in both forms. Ventris published his work in 1953 in collaboration with the philologist John Chadwick. At last, exactly fifty-three years after they were discovered, the tablets of the Temple Repositories and the adjoining area could be read, though haltingly for Ventris's study provided a very limited syllabary and few words. And when their messages became at least partially clear, they were disappointing, dealing chiefly with administrative and financial affairs in the Mycenaean, or Late Minoan, period of the Cretan palaces. Evans' 'chisel' shaped tablet was the first to be translated. It referred to an official of the Court named or styled 'Meunas' and was followed by ideograms for 'corslet', and 'chariot'. Some scholars doubted the validity of Ventris's system. The improbability of 'corslet' and 'chariot' seemed to confirm their doubts, until a bronze corslet was found at Dendra on the Greek mainland in very recent times. It remained for the tablets, pottery, bronzes, and the other artefacts of Knossos and its associated sites to be confined within a framework of dates. More careful digging was needed, however, before a chronology to match the consecutive periods of Egypt and Mesopotamia could be devised.

As work proceeded in April 1900, the American woman archaeologist Harriet Boyd from Boston, looking for a site of her own in Crete, was present when one of the most important of the early finds was made. On the north wall of the Palace they found part of a fresco with 'palms'. Evans decided next day that he was wrong. 'No! reeds'. Next to the fresco they uncovered a tall stone slab. Mackenzie's diary recorded that it 'proved to be the back of a stone chair whose seat was soon brought into view'. The chair or throne was set on a platform and had been covered with painted plaster. Harriet Boyd wrote that Mr Evans dubbed the chair 'the Throne of Ariadne'. Almost all Evans's semi-jocular asides related to Ariadne, the mythological daughter of Minos. He considered that its somewhat 'Gothic' shape was more suited to the ample proportions of a woman than a man. Through the west wall of what was now known as the Throne Room, in the small inner Sanctuary, a large area of fresco revealed seated griffins. Gilliéron père, Evans' French artist, identified the creatures and made drawings of them on 18 April. Evans, alive to the importance of publicity in providing for future funds, reported the discovery to the Press, pointing out that hatched lines were used in the paintings to shade the griffins' bellies. *The Times* misunderstood the syndicated report, and asserted that the griffins on the wall of the Sanctuary were shown 'in the act of hatching eggs'. In the second season at Knossos, the griffin theme was seen to extend to the Throne Room itself when a paw was identified on the north wall.

Gradually human and animal figures came into view which expressed not only an unsuspected and highly developed art but also gave flesh and bones to a society which, from its pottery, and by comparison with contemporary finds from the Egyptian tombs, could be seen to have passed its zenith when Mycenae was born. But Evans was in the Palace of the upper stratum at this time, the latest of the centres of administration which had occupied the site, as it would soon transpire, for three millennia before the final destruction about a thousand years before the Christian era. In April more frescoes revealed the first pictures of the people Evans would label 'Minoan', though at the time of discovery he properly used the term 'Mycenaean'.

> . . . One represented the head and forehead, the other the waist and part of the figure of a female holding in her hand a long Mycenaean *rhyton* or high, funnel-shaped cup . . . The figure is life size, the flesh colour of a deep reddish hue like that of the figures on Etruscan tombs and the *Keftiu* of Egyptian paintings. The

profile of the face is a noble type; full lips, the lower showing a slight peculiarity of curve below. The eye is dark and slightly almond shaped . . . The arms are beautifully modelled. The waist is of the smallest . . . far and away the most remarkable human figure of the Mycenaean age that has yet come to light . . .

The figure was subsequently identified as that of a male. But no matter, Evans' belief that it was synchronous with the Egyptian Keftiu paintings from Thebes of the Middle Kingdom, the period of great disruption by the 'Island People' or the 'People from the Great Green Sea', with whom the Pharaohs traded and warred, was significant. So was the reference to a likeness to figures on Etruscan tombs.

Heredotus believed that all the autochtonous, pre-Hellenic inhabitants of Greece were Pelasgians or 'barbarians'. The only true Hellenes, he asserted, were Dorians. Ephorus, in the fourth century, believed that the Pelasgians originated in Arcadia in the west of the Greek mainland, and thence spread through Greece and beyond. Thucydides suggested that these undeveloped peoples colonized Italy. Hellanicus of Mytilene, the fifth century BC historian, believed that the Pelasgi were to be identified with the Tyrseni, who figure as pirates in the Hymn to Dionysus (probably composed about 600 BC). Thucydides connects the Tyrseni with Lesbos. Hellanicus says that they were driven out by the Dorian Greeks and that they settled across the Ionian Sea and founded Etruria. Another theory was that the Tyrrhenians and Pelasgians were neighbour tribes of the north-west Aegean, and that they were synonymous with 'backward' or 'barbarian' peoples in the classical Greek mind. Following Evans' discovery of the figure on the palace wall at Knossos, another explanation became possible; that the broad-shouldered, curly-haired, slim-waisted prehistoric Cretans were the 'Peoples of the Sea' or of the 'Islands' who caused so much chaos in Egypt and the intervening lands in the later centuries of the second millennium BC. Were they perhaps the *Tursha* who Ramesses II, as crown prince in about 1290 BC, repulsed, when they attacked from Libya along with the 'Shardana' who some equate with Sardinians? In his wars with the Hittites, after he had ascended the throne, the Egyptian records show that Ramesses also had to fight various tribes from Asia Minor who were allied to his main enemy. His son Merenptah had to deal with renewed attacks by these mysterious peoples at the end of the thirteenth century BC, as did Ramesses III a few years later. Being finally repulsed by the Egyptians, did these people withdraw westwards and perhaps settle in Italy, changing their name to Tyrseni, and founding the so far unexplained nation of the Etruscans? It is a plausible theory, but it is as well to recall that the Greeks had two meanings for the word Pelasgi, a people and a condition (barbarian).

What of Evans' fresco? Local Greeks were convinced that it represented a Christian saint. So was Manolakis, who was appointed night watchman over the vulnerable and precious painting. The resourceful young man awoke in a cold sweat at night, to the sound of 'lowing and neighing', according to Evans. 'Something about, but of ghostly kind . . .', Manolakis told him.

The Throne Room, containing the Bronze Age gypsum-stone seat of the earliest royal family in Europe, almost certainly going back beyond the Mycenaean kings of Homeric legend, remained in the van of public interest. Demography and the early shifts of population in the Bronze Age world were a trifle too arcane for the popular press even in the year 1900. By August, the archaeologists of Knossos were following 'Ariadne's thread' with increasing excitement. They were into the Labyrinth of poetic legend. Europe was entranced. *The Times* and other leading newspapers appointed special correspondents at Heraklion. Parties of sightseers came from all over the world. On 10 August, Evans was able to tell *The Times* of 'the most important discovery', the Cretan script. Evans had become the author of the history of European civilization in its earliest stages, the first two-thousand years; and more, for he was already finding pottery, jewelry, tools, which pre-dated the palace culture that he was gradually reconstructing. For the moment he could only assign a rough chronological order to his finds. But by degrees he collected and assessed the pottery and jewelry, the bronzes and the architectural details of his own and other excavations in Crete, and of the Mycenaean finds on the mainland, and evolved a combined chronology and historiography. He devised three geographical areas: Crete whose civilization he called Minoan; the southern mainland, Helladic, and the Aegean Islands, Cycladic. Each of these was divided into three parts according to pottery styles, Early, Middle and Late. These denominations were in turn given three numerical and three alphabetical subdivisions. Thus, a kind of shorthand developed in archaeology by which LM III–C was understood by the cognoscenti as meaning the final stage of Late Minoan, i.e. the end of the period 1400–1100 BC. More graphically, he recognized the Palace as the typical feature of Cretan civilization and so superimposed a 'Palatial' definition on his dating system, related to the periods of construction and destruction of these royal residences. The most important of the dates and facts of the Evans time scale may thus be summarized:

EARLY NEOLITHIC, before 5500 BC, first undecorated pottery
NEOLITHIC, 5500–3000 BC, decorated pottery
EARLY MINOAN (Pre-Palace), 3000–2000 BC
MIDDLE MINOAN, first palaces built 2000 BC; destroyed 1700 BC
LATE MINOAN I, new palaces, 1700–1400 BC
LATE MINOAN II AND III, post-palatial, 1400–1100 BC
MYCENAEAN, 1400–1100 BC

Not everyone agrees precisely with the dates or the reasoning by which they were arrived at. But they serve well as a foundation of understanding in a complex area of study, and no one has ever produced a better or more intelligible system.

Evans' primary reason for deciding to dig at Knossos had been the strange, undecipherable sign-writing on miniature stamp-seals and a single tablet. Now, six months into the excavations, he could write to his family: 'The great discovery is whole deposits, entire or fragmentary, of clay tablets analogous to the Babylonian but with inscriptions in the prehistoric script of Crete. I must have about seven hundred pieces by now ... it is the coping-stone to what I have already put together.'

Whenever he wrote to his family with news of further discovery, his father responded with generous contributions to the Fund. The Boer War continued through the first two years of digging and money was scarce from other sources. Sir John Evans was not the only benefactor, however. Uncle Tom Dickinson, a millionaire paper manufacturer, helped out. Both father and uncle died within a few months of each other eight years after work began at Knossos. Arthur inherited both estates. The financing of the expedition, destined to last for exactly thirty-one years, was secure from then on.

At the end of the first year, Evans wrote to his father acknowledging his help and explaining that he wished to keep 'some of Knossos' in the family. He was reluctant to 'pool' resources through the Fund, 'largely because I must have sole control of what I am personally undertaking'. There was a revealing admission of an autocratic resolve at the end of his letter. 'With other people it may be different, but I know it is so with me; my way may not be the best but it is the only way I can work ...'. He had already embarked on the costliest of individual enterprises in the history of archaeology, the restoration of the Palace of Knossos as he believed it to have been at the height of its power and magnificence. First the Throne Room was covered over and in order to support the flat roof the original columns were restored and replaced under the supervision of Theodore Fyfe. Four years later the roof was replaced by a pitched construction with metal girder supports. A loft was created for storing sherds, a 'kind of reference museum'. The younger Gillieron of the father and son team of French artists, restored an existing griffin in the Throne Room frescoes, and others were added by pére et fils. In 1930 an entire upper storey was added, using reinforced concrete. From first to last, the work embodied Evans' own taste and overall concept. The Central Court, approached from a stepped portico south of the Throne Room, was completely restored between 1900 and 1923. It all cost a great deal of money and expert labour, and gave rise to increasing doubt and controversy as Evans imposed his own judgement on the work of architects and artists. He sought to convey the 'spirit' of the Palace structure and decoration rather than create a literal reconstruction. Many would say that he was right; others that he was grossly mistaken.

Throne Room, Lustral Basin, Sanctuary and Room of the Chariot Tablets represented a good first season's work at the Palace of Knossos. To the west of the archive which had given up the tablets, a corridor ran due north-south, giving access to eighteen narrow store-rooms, or 'Magazines' as Evans called them. Most contained huge clay storage jars, the pithoi which Kalokairinos had noted twenty years before. These massive storage jars, capable of holding some 35 gallons of oil or wine, or an equivalent amount of grain, were found in ever increasing number as the Magazines were cleared in the following six or seven seasons. They became the exemplars of Crete in the world's museums, as typical of their habitat as were the great Ninevite wall sculptures of theirs. Two rare examples were found in the tenth Magazine, with incised horizontal decoration broken up by rows of medallions. The room had been disturbed by treasure hunters and one of them was broken. The other was removed to the Ashmolean. At the foot of Mount Juktas, a few miles west of the excavations, modern potters made similar vessels in a manner which probably differed little from that of their Minoan predecessors. A potter's wheel was slowly turned by an assistant seated in a hole in the ground, while the potter built up the *pithos* from its clay base. Some, in the period later designated Middle Minoan, had been used as burial urns. Others became chimney-pots, dog kennels and hen coops. More Magazines were found beyond a blocking wall at the end of the corridor. In one an alabaster lid was found bearing a cartouche with the inscribed name of a Hyksos Pharaoh, Seuserenre Khyan, who ruled in about 1650–1630 BC. It was used to establish a date for the termination of the Late Minoan Period, but the authority of an imported vase as a method of dating, unless supported by other evidence, is suspect. Other pottery and limestone vessels came in profusion from the same Magazines.

The northern entrance to the Palace consisted of a paved passage with heavy columns supporting its stone ceiling. The west portico of the passage contained fragments of a fresco showing a charging bull. Here was the Bull of Minos, the Taurus on which all the fame and imagery of the Cretan discoveries would fall. The first fragments were discovered late in 1900. Not until 1902 were other crumbled pieces found among the rubble of the site, so enabling the artists and architects of Knossos to reconstruct the probable scene of several framed panels, each depicting an episode in the bull games which were held, in all likelihood, in the Central Court of the Palace. One restored panel showed a girl fighting with a bull, a boy somersaulting over its back while another girl stood at its rear. An artistic convention of the Minoans was the use of white paint for females and red for males, so that they could be easily distinguished. The fashions of the period are revealed marvellously. Girls dressed more gaudily than boys, both with tresses and belts or loincloths, striped socks and pointed shoes. Bangles and necklets were worn by both sexes, and hands were gloved or thonged. The Bulls of Minos were to become its great glory.

A store room of one of the earliest palaces on the site, so full of fine pottery that Evans called it the Royal Pottery Store, showed that in the earliest Minoan period ceramic cups and bowls of the most delicate shape and constitution were made; so delicate that most were broken, though they were restored without great difficulty. Some were polychrome decorated, others impressed. A few black wares were lustre painted.

The technical and decorative skills which they witnessed echoed those used in the painting of the wall frescoes. Empirically, they had discovered the uses of the 'earth pigments', particularly the salts of iron which gave them brownish reds, yellows and greys. As time went on the range of colours used for the wall paintings grew to include a broad spectrum including the magnificent 'Egyptian' blue of the restored panels which, from the time of their completion in the 1930s, became one of the great tourist attractions of the Greek islands. Later investigation revealed that the Minoans became masters of the true fresco technique, painting on wet plaster. The magnificent palaces of the island were show-places of the ancient world, equalling and in some ways excelling Egypt and Babylon in the splendour of their painted halls, every wall, ceiling and floor of which was finely plastered and finished. The ladies of the Court with their many-coloured dresses and elaborate hair styles were joined by dolphin frescoes, octopus and starfish, leaping bulls and bull-acrobats, bulls in stone and pottery, on golden chalices and tiny bead-seals, the young priest-king with bared torso and plumed-hat, and everywhere the sign of the double-axe; sacrifice, sport and worship, the fabulous and mythological, and the actual; yet, remarkably, nothing depicting military or political events, nothing to indicate victory or defeat in battle, or leadership in the affairs of state. It was as if these precursors of the Greeks had invented a luxurious and joyous autocracy; playing games, creating beautiful artefacts, chattering amiably, and engaging in worship and ritual without excessive servility; bothered neither by dissension within nor enemies without. Yet these were the people of the double-axe whom Evans believed conquered the mainland following the destruction of their own Palace kingdom at the end of the fourteenth century BC, whom other scholars believed to have been the maritime marauders of the following century. If so, their art shows them to have been great liars and deceivers. But art, in all its many and varied forms, cannot lie consistently.

Heavy rains and the collapse of tunnels dug by the excavators to expedite their progress caused delays and unexpected cost, but progress was remarkable all the

[247]

same. In six seasons the site of Knossos was virtually laid bare. The meticulous and controversial restoration work on which Evans embarked almost from the outset was to take five times as long as the excavations themselves.

Hogarth left the Knossos dig after little more than a month in order to investigate another legendary site, the Dictaean Cave in Mount Lasithi, at the centre of the island, Dicte of the ancients. It was here that the father of gods, Zeus, was supposedly born. The cavern in the mountainside was sometimes given the name Psychro. Other expeditions, Italian and American, were also digging on the island.

By September 1906, Hogarth was able to deliver to readers of the *Illustrated London News* an account of all the work that had been progressing for the past six years in Crete. He saw the island as a haven fashioned by nature for the evolution of a high civilization in early times, 'with its wide plains, high rain-condensing mountains, and long seaboards; the whole set in a singularly favourable geographical position'. Unlike Schliemann's Mycenae, Knossos and its associated townships had no need of Cyclopean walls or citadels. It was protected by the sea. Now, thanks to Mr Evans, the veil was lifted. With the ending of Turkish rule, for which the Greek occupants of the island were eternally grateful to the British, scholars who had waited patiently till 1900 were presented with the 'chance of a century'. Britons at Knossos, in the Cave of Psychro and at Praesos, Palaikastro and Zakro, the Italians at Phaistos and Hagia Triada, the Americans at Gournia on the Bay of Mirabello, had made full use of the opportunity. But 'Knossos', he said, 'stands first in time and importance'. There Evans had laid open a vast Palace, extending over many acres, built and rebuilt over the ages 'upon a site whose human remains go back at least as far as the earliest Pharaonic dynasties of the Nile'. Until Hogarth summarized the work at Knossos, reports of the excavations had concentrated almost entirely on the frescoes and architectural features, and the undeciphered script. Evans had not yet decided on the name which would be used to describe the culture of Crete, *Minoan*, neither had there been much reference to the necropolis or human remains, or to religious practice. So far, the palatial kingdom of Crete seemed to rest on it extensive labyrinth of buildings and magnificent mural art.

'Its intricate corridors and passages probably suggested the idea of labyrinthine complexity to the later Greeks', wrote Hogarth, 'and we must associate it with the royal dynasty that bore the name of Minos'. He described the ruins as seen from the east, with the royal quarters in the foreground, the Throne Room at the centre, the long rows of Magazines or storerooms behind; the stepped area leading from the north-west doorway, 'which probably served as a place where Kings sat in judgement or council', with its square central pillar the blocks of which each bore the sign of the labrys or double-headed war axe, fetish symbol of

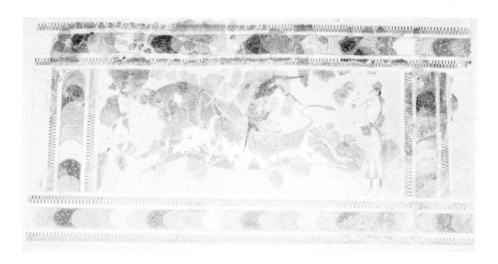

Fresco from Palace of Knossos. Leaping bull and acrobat.

a mother goddess who appears time and again in seals and figurines, sometimes with a boyish figure at her side. Hogarth called her the 'Virgin Mother goddess whom we know to have presided over the religion of the primitive Aegean lands'. Since so much that was discovered at Mycenae, Troy and Tiryns, and now in Crete, conformed in spirit and appearance to the legends which inspired the poets and convinced the historians of classical Greece, was it not reasonable to assume that this was Hesiod's Rhea?

'. . . subject in love to Cronos and bore splendid children, Hestia, Demeter, and gold-shod Hera and strong Hades, pitiless in heart, who dwells under the earth, and the loud-crashing Earth-Shaker, and wise Zeus, father of gods and men, by whose thunder the wide earth is shaken . . .'? Here is the panoply of gods which came down through classical Greece and found its counterparts in Roman mythology, just as it had its antecedents in the pantheons and legends of Asia Minor and Egypt. Here, surely, were Rhea and her son Zeus. Evans thought so, as did Hogarth. To the present day, eminent authorities say otherwise, however. Remarkably similar, though more primitive, clay figures show that the Mother Goddess was wordhipped by Neolithic inhabitants of the Aegean. Many believe that the figures of Knossos represented several goddesses. Evans's lady had

[249]

different dress and hair styles at different periods, sometimes bareheaded, sometimes wearing a tiara, at others with tight bodice or bare breasts. Hogarth described the palaces which had arisen on the same site, all named by Evans: Corridor of the Bays, Grand Staircase, Hall of the Colonnades, Hall of the Double-Axes (otherwise the King's Megaron, the suite of the ruling monarch) and the smaller Queen's Megaron which was connected to the king's chambers by a dog-leg corridor.

Whatever the doubts in matters of detail, it could be asserted by 1906 that Thucydides was right in his belief that the poets had recounted accurately the history of the ancients: 'Minos is the earliest ruler we know of who possessed a fleet and controlled most of what are now Greek waters. He ruled the Cyclades, and was the first colonizer of most of them, installing his own sons as governors. In all probability he cleared the seas of pirates, so far as he could, to secure his own revenues.'

The troublesome seafarers who wrought havoc more than three thousand years before Knossos was excavated almost certainly included Aegean islanders, and perhaps they had a hand in the ultimate destruction of Crete itself. But in its long centuries of precedence, Crete it seemed had been at the centre of Aegean civilization and a stabilizing influence in a trading network which spread from the Mediterranean to the Indian Ocean, from East Africa to the Caucasian mountains.

Hogarth, prolific writer and somewhat careless archaeologist, had little to do with the major excavations on Crete. In 1904, after his excursion to the Dictaean Cave, he crossed the sea to ancient Lydia on the Asiatic seaboard of Turkey, to Ephesus. There he resumed work on the Ephesian Artemision, 'one of the 7 wonders of Hellenistic and Roman Times', which another wealthy and eccentric Englishman, John Turtle Wood, had explored from 1863 to 1874, largely at his own expense. Wood had discovered the temple of the great city known to St Paul, the temple of Diana of the Romans, Artemis of the Greeks, of which Pliny asserted, correctly, that it had one hundred external columns, twenty-seven of which were 'the contributions of kings'. Before he left the site, Wood had three-hundred labourers working for him. Hogarth, assisted by the architect A.E. Henderson, whom he would roundly condemn seven years later for his slapdash work at Carchemish, and by Gregorios Antoniou, 'ubiquitous foreman of archaeological sites in the Levant', dug down to the Hellenistic (fourth century BC) foundations and beyond to the kingship of Croesus in the second half of the sixth century. A vital discovery at the level of the Greek temple was a fine, well-preserved collection of ivories which suggested artistic ties between Crete and Mycenae, and between Aegean, Western Asiatic and Egyptian societies. Ivories found at Mycenae and Sparta by the German teams of the early 1900s were closely analogous in their craftsmanship to Cycladean or Minoan works in the same material. They also resembled in some aspects ivories which Layard and Rassam had found at Nimrud. The French archaeologist and historian Georges Perrot saw Minoan influence in the Nimrud works. Hogarth noted that the Nimrud ivories showed 'identical carving techniques to those of later Ionian artists working in Egypt'. He saw no reason to doubt a mixture of Mesopotamian and Egyptian influences eventually finding their way, through Greek settlers, to Egypt and Asia Minor. With every excavation, the first decade of the twentieth century was throwing up evidence of close cultural and trade intercourse throughout the ancient world.

Hogarth had journeyed back and forth to Crete in the Ephesus intervals, and in 1911, as he prepared to move on to Carchemish, he summarized the first decade of work among the palaces of Crete. An Italian team under the brilliant German-Italian Frederico Halbherr at Phaistos had uncovered a great Palace commanding the plain of Messara. It was even more spectacular than Evans' Palace at Knossos, though less significant artistically. Set in fine surroundings, and having much the same components as Knossos – a central court with open living rooms leading on to it, and a magnificent staircase to the megaron, with the Queen's chamber leading from it – the royal establishment at Phaistos merely underlined the unique luxury and opulence of Minoan society. And some two miles to the west, Halbherr discovered an even more eloquent testimony to that civilization which spanned two thousand years. At Hagia Triada (named after the little church of the Holy Trinity) he found the remains of a princely villa, marvellously preserved by the position of the mound on which it was situated. The rooms, unlike those of Knossos, had not been ransacked after the sudden disaster which brought Minoan civilization to its end. There were artefacts of great value still *in situ*, including two cups made of soapstone, sculptured in relief, among the loveliest of all the treasures of the Aegean. In the neighbouring cemetery the first painted sarcophagus of the Aegean came to light, an invaluable record of early burial practice, and a reminder perhaps of Egyptian influence in its scenes of ritual sacrifice of a bull with a symbolic treatment of the hereafter. The frescoes of the villa count among Halbherr's many magnificent prizes, as does a clay disc from the Phaistos Palace, impressed with untranslatable hieroglyphs, dating from the mid-third millennium BC and regarded as the first example of European printing. Among the 250 characters are ships, arms, men and animals, presumably impressed by a seal-stamp, but their meaning, as with the Linear A tablets of Crete and Mycenae, remained elusive.

Harriet Boyd the Bostonian, moved with relish among the determined, quick-tempered men who dug 'the hundred-citied Crete', until the outbreak of the First

World War put an end to such works. She unearthed many treasures at Gortyna in the south of the island, including a gem of a vase found in eighty-six pieces and re-assembled to show a remarkable painted octopus design. Its dynamic use of a flowing natural motif on a curved plane, exemplifies a freedom in art which was denied to classical Europe by a slavish application of the laws of perspective and mathematical proportion. The serpent, which might have served as well as the octopus in ceramic art, is a favourite Minoan religious symbol, but it is usually made to entwine the arms of women in pottery figurines, or held in the hands of bare-breasted ladies of high society; seldom is graphic use made of it.

Hogarth traced Minoan civilization from its emergence out of the Neolithic into the Bronze Age, 'only a little later' than Egypt, to maritime trade and agricultural sufficiency under the royal house of Phaistos. Thereafter Knossos rose up to dominate the Middle Minoan period, when the Twelfth Dynasty ruled in Egypt. Excavations along the Nile, in the Argolid (Tiryns), Cyprus and the Cyclades had showed that fine works of Cretan craftsmanship were sent to those places. Then, at the end of Evans' Middle Minoan II period, Knossos was sacked and destroyed, while Phaistos survived. But the tell-tale indications of fire found in all the palaces showed that soon after Knossos was restored, Phaistos was put to the flame and the sword. By the end of the first Late Minoan period, about 1400 BC, Knossos was the centre of social and cultural life not only in Crete but over the whole Aegean. Then, as suddenly as in earlier catastrophes, Knossos and all the cities of Crete were utterly destroyed. Certainly fire raged, but whether a natural disaster such as an earthquake struck, as many geologists believe, or a man-made holocaust descended, is uncertain to the present day. Yet the remains of what was there before, culturally, are so like the remains of what came after, that Hogarth and many others believed that the last invaders of Crete, the men of the Late Minoan III, must have been Mycenaeans from the mainland, bringing with them a culture which they had shared with the Minoans in the first place.

> This final cataclysm seems to have happened some time in the twelfth century BC, and it was most likely a phase in that same unrest of peoples, which in the days of Ramesses III, carried the Akaiuasha, or Achaeans, to the confines of Egypt. Knossos now became Achaean, so far, at least, as its rulers went; and Achaean were all its traditions when, two or three generations later, the Aegean world produced its first literary chronicle, the Homeric epics.

Lawrence Durrell, in our own time, remarks on the difficult 'intellectual act' posed by the time scale of ancient Greece, indeed of the ancient world, as archaeology pushes back its frontiers to a grey area of contiguity with the Neolithic world, somewhere between 6000 and 3000 BC, when nomadic hunters became semi-settled villagers and laid the foundations of civilized life. 'What', he asks, 'would be the impressions of a Minoan archaeologist, picking over a heap of mud in a London devastated by atomic attack – a heap which yields him objects as disparate as a teddy bear, a Father Christmas, a Rembrandt, (was England full of monkeys, and at what epoch?), an Iron Cross, an income tax return . . . and so on? How would he sort them out historically and assign a purpose to them? Were the English believers in a bear totem? And was Father Christmas a sort of Zeus? The possible margin of error is disquieting . . .'. We should be on our guard against the 'certain certainties' that T.S. Eliot refers to, adds Durrell.

The two great archaeologists of the Aegean, Schliemann and Evans, were little worried by the doubts which tormented lesser men. They were guided by their certainties, one that Homer's heroic tales of Mycenaean times contained both poetic and historical truth, the other that Ariadne's web stretched out from the island of Crete and embraced the southern mainland, and carried forth its arts, its culture, much as he Evans, 'the great visualiser' as one of his architects called him, had reconstituted it in the Palace of Minos at Knossos.

No two men chosen by fate to reconstruct the beginnings of European civilization could have had more disparate backgrounds. One had made for himself the fortune which gave him the leisure to realize his overweening ambition, and learnt from his beloved Homer all that he needed to know to pursue it. The other, born to wealth and a formal education which came 'of an English paper-making fortune, learnt about archaeology on his father's knee and had no need to waste his useful energies in the harsh world of commerce. Yet they had a good deal in common. They were both arrogant and autocratic in manner, and neither was much inclined to listen to contrary opinions. Yet both won the devotion and affection of those who were closest to them.

Evans – who died at his Oxford home in 1941 at the age of 90 – believed to the end that Knossos and its satellite cities were destroyed by a natural calamity, probably an earthquake. John Pendlebury, his brilliant assistant from 1929 when he was induced from the excavations at Amarna in Egypt to become Curator at Knossos, thought otherwise. He believed that Knossos was sacked, probably by a force from mainland Greece. He and other notable scholars like Halbherr and Blegen, inclined to the view that sometime in its final period, Late Minoan III in Evans' chronology (1400 to 1300 BC), a society that had declined and degenerated in the way of great empires, was attacked and utterly destroyed from outside. Mycenae itself, and the other Achaean cities, were destroyed soon after, and there came the 'return of the Heracleidae', the Dorian neighbours who strode the Aegean from Epirus to the Corinthian Gulf, from the Peloponnese to the Cyclades and Crete, to divide Greece between themselves and the 'non-Dorians', the Ionians. By the twelfth century BC, Aegean civilization was no more, and the

[253]

foundations of a European civilization led by Classical Greece had been laid. Pendlebury believed that Homer's 'bronze-clad Achaeans' were responsible for the destruction of Knossos. By the time of his death in Crete during the Second World War, Pendlebury's view was generally accepted. By the late twentieth century, however, opinion had swung back to Evans' theory, backed by geological evidence.

Yet another architect, Piet de Jong, joined the exceptional band of men and women who worked with and for Evans at Knossos. He arrived in 1922 and played an important part in restoring the Palace, later becoming Curator of Knossos. He and Christian Doll were the two men who did most to realize Evans's vision of the Palace, a monument that would ever crown the island of Crete and inspire the scholar and tourist alike with a unique sense of antiquity. It is, in a way, a pity that the glory of Knossos should so overshadow the other achievements of the Cretan archaeologists – Halbherr's Italians (to whom Evans always paid the highest tribute) at Phaistos and Hagia Triada, the French at Mallia, the Americans at Gortyna, the other British at Praesos, Palaikastro and Zakro – but their achievements are an enduring part of the most spectacular and, from the European standpoint, the most stimulating of all archaeological discoveries.

When Schliemann died in 1890 at the relatively early age of sixty-eight, the controversies of his lifetime were overshadowed by the greater glory of his achievement. After a visit to Petrie's excavations at Fayum, the equally proud Egyptologist described his German visitor vividly: 'short, round-headed, round-faced, round-hatted, great round-goggled eyes, spectacled, cheeriest of beings, dogmatic, but always ready for facts.' Ernest Gardner, found him 'intensely real, full of imaginations and prejudices, of love and hatred', who yet 'regarded all criticism of his views as libels and calumnies, and attacked them in the spirit of the theologian who has to combat an insidious heresy'. Prime Minister Gladstone retained his admiration to the end. 'Either his generosity without his energy, or his energy without his generosity might well have gained celebrity; in their union they were no less than wonderful', he wrote in posthumous tribute.

But there were other views. Ernst Curtius, excavator of Olympia and most respected of field archaeologists, called him a 'Pfuscher und Schwindler'. The contemporary French diplomat, M. de Gobineau, said that he was 'capable de tout en fait de faussetés'.

Always there was a nagging suspicion among those who succeeded Schliemann that his haphazard and secretive methods might have concealed something more sinister than mere pride or idiosyncrasy. Before his death he gave all the magnificent finds of Troy, Mycenae and Tiryns – or those of them that remained in his personal keeping – to the Imperial Museum of Berlin. Many of them were to

Loggia of the Hall of Colonnades, Knossos.

disappear in the chaos of the Second World War, never to be seen again. Others are known to have been taken by the Soviet authorities on the occupation of Berlin and removed to Russian keeping. They and the incomparable possessions of Greece, and lesser treasures distributed among the museums of the western world, are proof enough that Schliemann's methods, however unorthodox, were effective. Priam's treasure was always in most doubt, and despite innumerable biographical studies many of the relevant papers and diaries remained to be studied as recently as 1972. In that year, an article by the American William M. Calder III, pointed out that Schliemann's autobiographical works were 'riddled with false claims and fictitious episodes'. In 1981, Donald F. Easton, a research fellow in archaeology at Liverpool University, reopened the debate. In an article in the journal *Antiquity* he wrote: 'There has always been an enigma over the precise date during the Troy excavations of 1873 when Schliemann found the collection of metalwork which he dignified as "Priam's Treasure"'.

He examined the German's 1873 notebook, containing entries for most days of the excavations which record briefly the finds and events of the moment. But nowhere could he find reference to what for Schliemann must have been the most staggering achievement of his life. There is confusion because Schliemann used both Gregorian and Julian calendars, the latter being twelve days in arrears of course. Schliemann himself had said that he found the treasure at the end of May 1873, though he later averred that it was on 7 June. At that time, the tone of the diary changes markedly. The date *Mittwoch* 28 is crossed out and *Dienstag* 27 *Mai* substituted. Only the numbers of workmen taken on and their cost are noted. There is no reference to discoveries of any kind. Easton is charitable. From a close examination of the 317 page diary he says 'the discovery of "Priam's Treasure" certainly falls within the period 23–31 May (Gregorian). He pinpoints it finally to Tuesday, 27 May, which would reconcile with Schliemann's 7 June allowing for muddled dates because of the two calendars. As to the removal of the treasure, illegally, from Turkey, the author is less benevolent. Published and unpublished documents alike, backed by the evidence of the diary, show that it was smuggled to Athens, probably with the help of the Englishman Frederick Calvert, early in June 1873, just as the famous *triglyph* had been a year earlier. Both were, in plain language, stolen.

The matter did not rest there. In 1983, the same specialist journal contained an article by David A. Traill, a Scot teaching classics at the University of California. Traill spread the net of investigation over a wider area, taking in Schliemann's private life as well as his archaeological claims. Many versions of events in diaries, books, letters to publishers and biographers were compared. At the centre of the enquiry was the famous incident at Troy towards the end of 1873, when he 'exposed the Trojan circuit wall which runs out from the Scaean Gate' and found in one of the rooms of Priam's palace a container full of treasures though, for reasons of security, he was not in a position to disclose 'the number of vessels or to describe their shape'. Traill examined his subject's probity through the autobiographical claims, and his early reports to his publisher in Leipzig which Traill denoted A, B, C and D. He decided that Schliemann's American venture in the 1850s, his claim to have witnessed the San Francisco fire of 1851, his American citizenship and divorce were all based on deception. If those accusations were true, and the evidence seems to be substantial, they would not be too serious. It is a dull person who goes through life without embroidering his experiences here and there, or without deceiving officialdom with a few white lies. But the events at Hissarlik seem on the face of things to involve intellectual dishonesty of an exceptional order. That is a more serious matter.

Schliemann had, in his own published account, divided the treasure into two

Minoan priestess, a familiar religious symbol from
the Cretan palaces, *c.*1700 BC.

Knossos at the present day, with Horns of Consecration on restored west wing of south Propylaeum. Believed to have a cultic significance.

parts, known as 'A and B', and asserted that Sophia was present when they were found. In a subsequent interview with a journalist, the foreman Yannakis also claimed to have been present. Traill finds that Sophia was not at Troy when the treasure was discovered. 'If then Schliemann is lying about Sophia, how much of his story are we to believe?'. Further research showed that Easton's date of 27 May as the likely time of the great discovery could not be sustained. 'The discrepancies regarding find-spot, discovery date, the gold sauceboat and the jewellery strongly suggest that Schliemann's various accounts of the discovery of "Priam's Treasure", like his interview with President Fillmore and his "eye-witness" account of the 1851 fire ... are sheer fiction. It follows that we do not know where, when, or how Schliemann acquired the collection of artifacts which he called "Priam's Treasure"'. As for the employment of Schliemann's finds in the dating of Troy, about which argument and conflicting theories continue to rage in academic circles, even after the diligent work of Dörpfeld and Blegen, Traill is sceptical:

> The treasure is of unparalleled magnitude for a single find from a West Anatolian site at this time. Its very bulk invites suspicion. It seems much more likely that Schliemann pieced the treasure together over a period of months or even years ... if, as now seems likely, 'Priam's Treasure' is a composite, we have no reliable evidence for the provenance of any of the pieces ... it follows that no piece from "Priam's Treasure" can be used for the purpose of dating the end of Troy II.

Even as these words were being written, the dispute over Schliemann's 'treasure' intensified. Not only Schliemann's reputation was under attack now; the argument was as much to do with the critics' own analytical methods as with the reliability of the excavator of the Hissarlik site. In 1984, Easton returned to the attack. The textual relationships set out by Traill could convey a false idea, he wrote. Divergence there certainly was between the four texts which Traill had designated A to D. Easton found discrepancies in the Atlas which Schliemann published with his *Trojanischer Alterthumer*. But there is nothing unusual in an archaeologist revising his field notes when he returns to the calm of his study. Easton points out that texts A and B, on which Traill relied heavily, were written on site. C was written in Athens as a rough draft of an intended despatch. Text D was a reworked version of C and was intended as a definitive account of the treasure. Easton, by no means a wholehearted member of the Schliemann lobby, concluded that 'In the northeast trench ... Schliemann had exposed the (Troy II) citadel wall by the time he wrote the resumé dated 31st May in his diary ... it was at the south eastern end of the trench that Schliemann found "Priam's Treasure"

... The find spot is clearly described'. Traill had seen 'sinister fraud'. Easton now held Schliemann to be guilty 'at most of vagueness or of succumbing to the temptation to "correct" his memory away from the site'.

The provenance of the most famous treasure trove ever discovered was to be debated even more fiercely after its wartime disappearance from the Berlin Museum, than in Schliemann's own controversial lifetime. Easton says: 'The objects concerned clearly derive from the Early Bronze Age ... It is, therefore, inconceivable that they should have been bought by Schliemann or manufactured to his instructions and then set up as a suitable treasure'. The main part of the haul, denoted 'Treasure A', he now believes 'may have been discovered on 31 May, 1873, somewhat in the manner Schliemann describes, only without the presence of his wife'. The claim of the foreman Yannakis to have been present at the discovery, he finds 'very doubtful'. And finally, for the moment, at any rate: the treasure must have been found 'at the southernmost end of the northwest trench', in a corner by the north wall at the level of Troy IX A, 'which probably places it in the debris of Troy II that had spilled over the citadel wall'. He finds 'some evidence', that the cache called 'Treasure B' may have been part of a cist-grave dating to Troy III, or possibly Troy IV. That grave 'may have been only one of several belonging to an E-B II or III cemetery located on the citadel mound of Troy'.

After all the argument, the fact remains that we are still unsure of many things besides 'Priam's Treasure'; we do not know whether there ever was such a king, or who were the people we call – in translation of the Greek – 'Trojans', or whether a Trojan War was ever fought. For that matter, archaeology in alliance with geology, that most disciplined of disciplines, still seeks a cause of the final destruction of Evans' Crete and Schliemann's Mycenae.

The Gates of Ishtar

Babylon and its neighbours

I, Hammurabi, am the king of
                 justice,
to whom Shamash committed law.
My words are choice; my deeds have
                 no equal;
it is only to the fool that they
                 are empty;
to the wise they stand forth as an
                 object of wonder.

From Epilogue to Hammurabi's Code

Still the mounds of Babylon were intact. Close to the township of Hillah on the lower Euphrates, they and the twin mounds of Borsippa nearby challenged the excavators of many nations who converged on the southern sites of Mesopotamia in the last two decades of the nineteenth century. Sumer and Akkad, the proto-civilizations of the Near East, had given up at least some of their ancient secrets; divulged in part the legends and hero-myths, king lists and pantheons which could be cross-referenced with later versions and derivations found in Egypt,

Assyria and Greece. The ancient world had written its own history profusely, in verse and prose, and its dominant themes – the search for spiritual succour, for identity and immortality – would not change greatly in the next few thousand years. The earliest testaments of intellectual and physical achievement, of marvellous feats of construction and creativity, of cruelty and evil, were revealed in a huge and ever-growing library of cuneiform and hieroglyphic documentation. But at the dawn of the present century, the most famous city of the ancient world still wore the veil of two thousand years; little changed from the time of its oblivion, except for the continued removal of its bricks and projecting slabs of stone and plaster by Arab villagers.

In 1894, France renewed the interest in Persia which had begun with the pioneering epigraphic work of Flandin and Coste at the time of Rawlinson's and Layard's youthful travels. Marcel Dieulafoy investigated the ruins of Susa, and in 1897 his country was awarded a permit by the Shah to dig in Persia in perpetuity. At the time, Britain and Russia disputed their respective spheres of influence in Persia. Bismarck's twenty-year old German Empire had already established a firm foothold in the East. It had opened commercial offices on both sides of the Persian Gulf, and was in the process of negotiating 'preferential rights' with the Porte to build a railway which would eventually run from Berlin to Baghdad, and perhaps on to Basra and the Gulf. Imperial Russia countered by proposing a railway from the Caucasus through Persia and Mesopotamia to the Mediterranean. Britain decided that it would be better to allow the French sway in Persia and the Germans in Mesopotamia.

In January 1898 the Deutsche Orient-Gesellschaft was founded in Berlin. Fourteen months later, on 26 March 1899, it took its first spadeful of earth from the site of Babylon. Digging would go on without interruption for another eighteen years, until the First World War intervened. In that time, modern, scientific archaeology came of age, and some of the glories of the ancient world found a new home in the State Museum of Germany.

'No excavations have yet laid bare the buildings of a Babylonian town', said Budge when he left Mesopotamia in 1890. Ten years later, the Deutsche Orient-Gesellschaft team under the direction of Professor Robert Koldewey of Berlin, had begun to uncover the palace and temple of Marduk. Perhaps as important as its revelations, however, was the use of immaculate techniques of digging and the imposition of a strict scientific approach to archaeology. For the first time, the growth of an historical site was revealed in minute detail layer by layer; from end to beginning as it were. The significance of stratification in the uncovering of ancient habitations was elucidated. After the excavations at Babylon, the techniques of field archaeology throughout the world underwent a radical change.

[260]

Tomb of Cyrus at Pasargade, founded as capital of Achaemenid Persia 546 BC.

Herodotus had exaggerated the size of Babylon. By the end of his second season, Koldewey had traced its perimeter walls to the east bank of the river, and then by the span of the gracefully arched bridge of the great temple, Etemenanki (long since ruined), to the other side. The Greek historian said that the Euphrates divided the city 'in the middle', inferring two equal parts, and that its perimeter was altogether fifty-five miles. Koldewey demonstrated that it was just over eleven miles, allowing for a huge but uncompleted extension on the east side which was intended to enclose Nebuchadnezzar's Summer Palace, and that the eastern section was the larger. Not all authorities dismiss Herodotus even at the present day, in favour of the German experts. Some believe that the true extent of the ruins on both sides of the river is an area roughly fifteen miles by twelve, and that it was protected by a wall parts of which may have disappeared altogether, thus leading Koldewey to trace it incorrectly. Whatever the truth about its exact size, Babylon was without question enormous in extent for a city in the time of Nebuchadnezzar, far greater than any Herodotus can have seen in Greece or on his diverse travels.

In fact, double walls surrounded the city, the innermost of which was about twenty-four feet thick, with a gap between of about forty feet, filled to the top with rubble. Herodotus had measured this massive protective shell, and Koldewey's dimensions were more or less in agreement. The top of the wall, according to the Greek historian, was wide enough for a chariot 'to drive round' it. Babylon in its heyday was no easy city for the invader to penetrate. But when the Germans arrived, the massive outer wall of kiln-baked brickwork had disappeared, as had the bricks of the famous tower, the ziggurat, removed by generations of Arabs for their buildings. The inner-city wall of mud-brick had crumbled to dust. Only foundation bricks remained beneath the rubble of the site. Hammurabi's second-millenium city was inaccessible because of a rise in the sub-surface water table.

The first level, that of the Neo-Babylonian Empire (seventh to sixth centuries BC), contained chiefly the monuments and memorials of Nebuchadnezzar II, its second King (605–562 BC), whose feats in destroying Jerusalem between 598 and 586, humbling Egypt at Carchemish in 605, and taking Israel into exile, ensured his immortality. He was reputed by the Greek historians to have made Babylon a great fortress and a city of splendour. He has been called 'the Augustus of Babylon'. As the Germans dug they found that everywhere bricks were glazed in bright enamel colours, many in fragments, others in perfect preservation. Twenty-five metres down they came to the foundations of the Temple of Marduk, which had embraced the palace in which Alexander the Great spent his last days, the Esagila. As palaces and other buildings were gradually exposed, they came to the stump of the great ziggurat, the stepped tower of Babel, within the temple shrine of Etemenanki. A few miles away across the river, on the west bank, lay neighbouring Borsippa, Birs Nimrud to the Arabs of the present, where an almost identical tower rose up, preserved by its upper brickwork (which had been fused to a blue, glass-like state by lightning), from the fate which befell its sister. They would have been similar and could be described as easily by one as the other. Each was about seventy-five metres high and receded in successive stages. The uppermost storey was closest to heaven and the gods, and was adorned with six sanctuaries, all consecrated to particular deities. No one, to date, had begun to imagine the precise purpose which the ziggurats of Mesopotamia served in the thousands of years that they had stood out from the Mesopotamian plains as stairways to the sky. Herodotus tells the story of 'Bel and the Dragon' which appears in the *Apocrypha* and speaks of the deity consuming strange offerings in his sanctuary, and being entertained by a 'human' bride, such as the 'singing women' of the Egyptian temple of Amon.

A German historian of the work of Koldewey's team told of the 'sudden shock' as they came to the north end of the Marduk palace-temple complex, and beheld the gates which opened on to the Processional Way, the great royal thoroughfare of the ancient world. The Ishtar Gate. Its double portals were flanked by mighty towers, ornamented with 575 bulls, dragons and lions, though only 152 were intact, dedicated to the mother-goddess, holy Inanna of Sumer, Astarte of the

Robert Koldewey, photographed by Gertrude Bell at Babylon in 1911.

Phoenicians, Aphrodite of the Greeks, queen of gods, goddess of war, of death and life. The worship of Ishtar was implicit in the life of Babylon and Assyria, and from there it spread to Phoenicia where a temple was built to her at Ashkelon, and thence to Cyprus. Her shrine at Cythera was the oldest in Greece.

Remarkably, the Abbé Beauchamp, when he visited Babylon in the eighteenth century, had found the Ishtar Gate projecting from the central mound and had given the modern world its first partial description of the famous portal. The Germans could be forgiven some elation at rediscovering it, more or less intact, preserved by the very dust and rubble that covered it. They removed it to Berlin where it was one of the most spectacular attractions of the State Museum until its destruction in the Second World War. It was reconstructed after that war, and remains one of the few artefacts that Koldewey and his colleagues removed from their places of origin.

The reports of the Deutsche Orient-Gesellschaft, covering many sites in Mesopotamia, Egypt, Syria and Anatolia in its first fifty years, constitute a massive library of unglamorized fact, amounting to eighty-nine volumes. It is necessary to dig deep into these academic chronicles to follow Koldewey's

The German excavations at Babylon, photographed by Gertrude Bell, 1911.

progress along the processional route of Babylon some twelve metres above the level of the plain, and downward through the foundation walls of Nebuchadnezzar's city.

There was a surprising paucity of sculpture and pictorial art among the surviving glories of Babylon, save the monumental pieces such as the great lion probably Hittite anyway, and the beautifully glazed and coloured bricks of the Ishtar Gate and Nebuchadnezzar's Palace with their reliefs of *sirrush* dragons, bulls and lions. These remnants attested the skills of the craftsman class in the reigns of Nabopolassar, Nebuchadnezzar and Nabonidus. But they were exceptional.

The American Henri Frankfort remarked on the scarcity of creative work 'which makes it impossible to estimate its artistic achievement', while there was intense literary activity. Frankfort points out that while the Hellenistic world derived its astrology and much of its science from Mesopotamia, 'Neo-Babylonian art did not affect the west. It was from Assyria that Greece and Etruria obtained their models during the "orientalizing period", through the intermediacy of the Phoenicians'.

Not all the history of Babylonia was dependent on the findings of Koldewey's team. The Assyrian inscriptions had revealed a great deal. So too had the Egyptian records, often translated into Akkadian. And as the Germans dug at Babylon, the French at Susa found perhaps the most important document of the

[264]

ancient world, the Law Code of Hammurabi. The period of the Amorite or Old Babylonian dynasty was marked by constant wars with its Elamite neighbour, Susa. Sometime about the turn of the thirteenth century BC, an Elamite raider by the name of Shutruk-Nahhunte had returned to Susa with a diorite stela; a trophy of war. It was topped by a bas-relief showing King Hammurabi receiving the commission of the sun-god Shamash, who was also the god of justice, to write the laws. It was dated according to the custom of the time to the monarch's second year. He ruled for forty-three years, but expert opinion differs as to the chronology of the period, some saying that the king began his rule in 1792 BC, others preferring 1728.

The French found the stela at the end of the 1901 season. With none of the inhibitions of their German counterparts across the Tigris, they rushed with their prize to Paris and an eagerly receptive Louvre. The laws were written on both sides and many had been chiselled off by the Elamites, but several copies of the text were discovered subsequently so that scholars could reconstruct almost word for word the preamble, the 282 clauses and the epilogue which formed the basis of law in Babylonia, Assyria, and many of the surrounding states, and ultimately of Talmudic law and the statutes and codes of the Christian world.

From first to last, the laws of Hammurabi foreshadow the Mosaic Law of the Old Testament and the moral precepts of Christianity and Islam. Many have passed almost without change of phrase into the everyday codes of conduct which govern large parts of the world in the present era. So, it must be said, has much of the mumbo-jumbo inherent in all law making.

The law maker 'called Babylon by its exalted name' in issuing his edict for all the world to obey, that justice might prevail in the land and beyond, that the strong might not oppress the weak. And the sanction of all the gods of the Sumero-Akkadian pantheon was set out by him who 'strides through the four-quarters of the world'.

> who made the name of
> Babylon great;
> who rejoices the heart of
> Marduk, his lord ...

Murder was the subject of the first laws. False accusation was as serious a sin as the act itself. If one man accused another of the crime, but was unable to prove it, 'his accuser shall be put to death', said article one. In cases of sorcery, he against whom the charge was made must throw himself into the river and contend with the waters, by way of proving his innocence or guilt. Early on the judiciary was put firmly in its place. If a judge gave a judgment, rendered a decision, deposited a sealed document, but later altered his judgement, and his alteration was proven, he (the judge) must pay twelvefold the claim outstanding, 'futhermore, they shall expel him in the assembly from his seat of judgement and he shall never again sit with the judges in a case'. Theft of property from Church or State was punished by threefold the fine applicable in the case of theft from a private citizen, and death was the penalty of default. Ownership of slaves was regulated severely, and abuse of the privilege punishable by death. Two shekels of silver was the statutory reward for the return of a fugitive slave. The artisan's price is set down exactly; so many pieces of silver per day for the brickmaker; so many for linen-weaver, seal-cutter, jeweller, smith, leatherworker, basket-maker, builder. Larceny, ransom, theft, marital rights, the obligations of wives, husbands, children and parents, military service; all were catered for in explicit terms of right and wrong; of crime and punishment. Tenant and landowner, shepherd, craftsman, farm produce and urban property were covered by ordinances which are reflected in the legal jargon of the modern world. Take, for example, the case of receiving stolen goods:

> When the man whose property was lost, has found his property in the possession of another, if the man in whose possession the lost property was found has declared, 'A seller sold it to me; I made the purchase in the presence of witnesses', and the owner of the lost property in turn has declared, 'I will produce witnesses attesting to my lost property; the purchaser having then produced the seller who made the sale to him and the witness in whose presence

he made the purchase, and the owner of the lost property having also produced the witnesses ... the judges shall consider their evidence ...

The law's delays have a long pedigree. But even the systematized code of Hammurabi had much earlier antecedents.

The excavations at Lagash produced one of the most precious of all ancient documents, dating from the reign of Urukagina in about 2350 BC. It is not a legal code like Hammurabi's but rather a bill of rights or *magna carta*, a reform document which records the sweeping away of social abuses, catalogues the malfeasances of bureaucracy, even including the ruler and his palace hangers-on, and draws an all too recognizable picture of man's conduct towards his fellows on every plane, social, economic, political and psychological. There are undertones of a power struggle between Church and State, in which the citizens sided with the temple, which may have given rise to a new regime. The word *amargi* is used in the literal sense of 'return to the mother' in Sumerian. In the sense in which it is meant, however, it represents the first known use of the word 'freedom'. In criticizing the injustices of the days before the reformer king Urukagina, the document presupposes a need for just laws. 'The oxen of the gods ploughed the *ensi's* onion patches; the onion and cucumber patches of the *ensi* were located in the gods' best fields', complained the historian of 2500 BC, writing figuratively of palace officials who ploughed their own furrows. Levies and taxes were imposed on life and death. The parasites of society made money out of success and out of misery. Making a living from bereavement was common. Come famine or shortage, the tax collector was omnipresent. No wonder the palace officials were fat and prosperous. No wonder the 'big men', the rich, grew richer and the poor poorer. The artisan and apprentice, proud men that they were, had to beg for food. Prisoners, forced into slavery, were blinded to prevent them escaping and put to doing the work of animals in the fields. In one of the several different versions of the document discovered, the Sumerian courts stress the need to 'write down' the nature of the guilt for which the accused was punished. The woman taken in adultery 'must be stoned with stones on which their evil intent is inscribed'. The woman who has sinned by saying to a man 'something she should not have said', must have her teeth crushed with burnt bricks (presumably containing details of her guilt).

The earliest attempts at achieving social justice by statute were not even-handed with regard to class or sex. Neither, for that matter, were their successors. In seeking to right the injustices of the past, Urukagina's reform text promulgated perhaps the first written rules of social conduct. It was succeeded, some three hundred years later, by the code of Ur-nammu (2112–2095 BC), founder of the Third Dynasty of Ur. It began with the creation of the world, and

The Berlin reconstruction of the temple of Marduk at Babylon.

the coming into being of the land of Sumer and the city of Ur. An and Enlil, the chief deities appointed the moon-god Nanna as king of Ur. From that beginning, the other cities and kingships of Sumer developed, but the land had fallen victim over the centuries to the 'chiseller' and the 'grabber'. 'The orphan shall not fall prey to the wealthy ... nor the widow to the wealthy ... the man of one shekel shall not fall prey to the man of one mina'. Fines were set for the cutting off of a foot, for the severing of bones, and the cutting off of a nose. The origins of later moral and legal codes must be sought in the long centuries of response and

reaction to these primordial documents. The notion of 'an eye for an eye and a tooth for a tooth', had already given way to a more practical approach to retribution in which a money fine was substituted as a punishment.

Tablets of pre-Sargonic Sumer recovered from the temples of Lagash, dated from about 2700 BC, record inventories, trade agreements, sales and purchases of every kind. From these, from the Urukagina text, and from later historical documents it has been possible to form a picture of early civilization which is detailed and at times unexpected. An ordered society with well-defined strata of nobles, commoners, clients (dependents) and slaves. Contrary to almost universal belief up to very recent times, all land and privilege was not vested in the king and temple. Commoners and clients owned land and were protected in law. Women

[269]

had well-defined rights. Inevitably, it is a picture also of rivalry between the 'big men' (in predynastic times the term meant city kings), and the states which dotted the Euphrates and Tigris on either side. Early though they are, the surviving documents which tell of Sumerian society from about 2700 BC have an antique flavour. Urban life already had a tenure of a thousand years or more. Sumer was being overwhelmed by Semitic intruders from the surrounding desert lands, language and customs were changing. A new political and cultural order was imposed, and its moment came in about 2300 BC when the dynasty of Akkad was established under Sargon the Great.

Stamp seals of simple design, used well before the invention of writing in the fourth millennium, gave way to more elaborate cylindrical versions. These modest tokens of possession and trade, together with painted pottery, provide the earliest pictorial glimpses of social and natural environment before the written word came to the assistance of the historian.

Dr H.R. Hall, one of the first archaeologists to attempt to rationalize the beginning of civilization in southern Mesopotamia, wrote:

> The Sumerian culture springs into our view ready-made, as it were, which is what we would expect if it was, as seems on other grounds probable, brought into Mesopotamia from abroad. We have no knowledge of the time when the Sumerians were savages: when we first meet with them in the fourth millennium BC, they are already a civilized, metal-using people living in great and populous cities, possessing a complicated system of writing, and living under the government of firmly established civil and religious dynasties and hierarchies.

With the exception of the peep-show provided by a few rather primitive stamp-seals which pre-date the pictographic writing of Sumer, that was a true statement of the position in 1913 when Hall published his *Ancient History of the Near East*. The explanation of this sudden windfall of civilization was obvious. These clean-shaven people with their bearded gods, had come from elsewhere, from the steppes of Central Asia or perhaps beyond, stopping off in ancient Elam to pick up civilized habits and the smatterings of their culture. The theory went further. Hall, and indeed all archaeologists for several decades to follow, believed that the Sumerians settled between about 4500 and 4000 BC, on a few low islands of alluvial land amid the swamps of southern Mesopotamia. Before that time they believed the entire land beyond the confluence of the two rivers to a point just south of Ur, to have been covered by the waters of the Persian Gulf. The gradual receding of those waters, the formation of the river extensions, and the build up of silt deposits from the Tigris, Euphrates and Karun rivers provided the foundations of human habitation – and, most probably, the basis of the Sumerian preoccupation with the flood legend.

That theory went unchallenged until 1952, when two geologists, Lee and Falcon, published a study entitled *The Geographical History of the Mesopotamian Plains*, in which they showed that the land of Sumer was above water long before 4500 BC. It was, therefore, possible – though not of course inevitable – that settlement had taken place much earlier. The fact that no traces of such settlement had been discovered was explained quite simply. The land had been sinking slowly ever since, as the water table had been rising, and the rivers had changed their courses. It is feasible, therefore, that the early remains of Sumer, perhaps going back to Neolithic habitation of the so-called pre-pottery period, are under water and will never be recovered. Archaeologists had been misled by the higher water level into believing that they had touched virgin soil when they delved below the level of the earliest pottery and found nothing. But there is other evidence which tends to suggest that early archaeological guesswork may have been correct. Clues to the likely time of the earliest Sumerian habitations come from ingenious calculations of changes in atmospheric conditions in the Gulf and eastern Arabian regions. It is suggested that there is a detectable cycle of 'moist' and 'arid' conditions which vary from one- to three- thousand year periods between about twenty thousand and one thousand years ago. The 'Neolithic Wet Phase' is known to have occurred between about 9000–6000 BC. Thus, there was a period of three thousand years in which the conditions for the classic 'Neolithic Revolution', based on agriculture and the cultivation of wheat from its wild antecendent, were favourable.

This is almost certainly the period in which semi-nomadic settlement would have taken place and the arts of land husbandry and pottery developed. There were relatively short phases of aridity and moisture from 6000–4000 BC, which, in an area whose rivers and streams were rejuvenated, would have provided ideal conditions for the development of existing Neolithic settlements or for the appearance of a new and virile populace. Such matters, even in the late twentieth century with its sophisticated techniques for investigating the past, remain in the melting pot. In that monumental study of China begun half a century ago by Joseph Needham and carried on by his disciples, *Science and Civilization in China* the same transition is traced from early, pre-pottery Neolithic to that critical phase at which barbarism becomes civilization. The authors challenge Gordon Childe's almost universally approved theory of the transition from nomadic to settled existence, in its relevence to both the Near East and China. They argue that there is no clear archaeological evidence for 'major post-glacial climatic change' in the Near East. Also, in hunter-gatherer societies of the present day, 'numbers

[271]

increase very slowly if at all', though they concede that this might not always have been so. They add more persuasively: 'If something constrained groups of hunter-gatherers to abandon their nomadic life for a sedentary existence, then population pressures might well build up to the point where farming becomes a necessity'. In other words, Childe's thesis of the happy accident of wheat cultivation as the foundation stone of sedentary life is replaced by a more pliable notion in which farming became a necessary activity for communities which, for one reason or another, had been trapped by 'locational restraints'. Why, otherwise, ask the authors, should populations have concentrated in areas where farming first developed? '. . . since hunter-gatherers can live very adequately even in deserts or tundras, why did they not simply wander off into the surrounding emptiness?'. We simply do not know whether the earliest Sumerian communities arrived fresh from some foreign field, or developed as farmers, craftsmen and traders out of an existing neolithic community, compelled perhaps by local constraints on their movement to settle and cultivate plants and animals. Much of the evidence is probably inaccessible under alluvial silt.

Fifty years after the Germans, French and Americans joined the British in Mesopotamia, systematic digging began in the Syrian regions on the other side of the Euphrates. Those excavations were to cast doubt on the idea that Sumer was, in fact, the primary civilization of the Near East, indeed of the world; that the movement of peoples and language was from the southern extremity of Mesopotamia, north and north-west to Syria, and Palestine and even to Egypt. More recent excavations suggest that contemporary or even earlier settlements may have existed, and that transmigration may have been primarily in the opposite direction.

As excavations proceeded at Babylon and the older sites to the south, pottery dating came into prominence much as it had done in Egypt under Petrie's influence. At Babylon, as elsewhere, the vast documentary resource of the inscribed tablet and stela provided a detailed history back through the occupations of the Greek and Persian dynasties to the last native rulers, the 'Chaldaean' or Neo-Babylonian Dynasty inaugurated by Nabopolassar, father of Nebuchadnezzar II, in 625 BC. In eighteen years of sifting and digging the Germans worked backwards through the period of Assyrian domination and the destruction wrought in the eighth century by Tiglath-pileser; the tenth century rule of the Elamites under Mar-biti-apla-usur; the chaotic years of the 'Sealand' and 'mixed' dynasties; the Kassites of the twelfth to fifteenth centuries; to Samsuiluna (1749–1712 BC), Hammurabi's successor. The Germans were unable to reach the lower level back to the beginning of the First Dynasty of Babylon and the first king of the Hammurabi dynasty, Sumuabum, because of the high water table. At the earlier sites in the south, investigations, though not always as systematic as those of the Germans, enabled periods to be dated according to pottery finds at successive levels, places giving their names to periods by reference to the vessels found at the lowest and oldest strata of habitation: from the first dynasties of Isin and Larsa at the start of the second millennium to the Third Dynasty of Ur at the end of the third; from Akkad to Sumer and the early Bronze Age, to the period of Jamdat Nasr in the third millennium, Uruk in the fourth, and beyond to the Ubaid, the Halaf and the Hassuna, into the mists of the sixth millennium.

In 1901 the Deutsche Orient-Gesellschaft began to dig at Abusir in Egypt. Its funds were limited by a Kaiserly hold on its purse strings (on 1 January 1902 it had 34,980 DM in the bank). By careful manipulation of its finances it was able to move on, however, to Assur, the original capital of Assyria. Operations there were under the direction of Dr Walther Andrae. In 1906 more money became available through a grant from the Prussian State legislature, 130,000 marks per annum, and excavations were begun under the leadership of Professors Winckler and Puchstein at another vital site, Boghazkoi in Turkish Anatolia, long suspected to be the ruined city of Hattusa, the capital of the Hittite Empire. Evidence had mounted through the nineteenth century of hieroglyphic and other undecipherable inscriptions spread across northern Syria and Turkish Anatolia. The British theologian and archaeologist A.H. Sayce had given the inscriptions – collected as far afield as Carchemish and Hama in Syria and Gordium, Alaca Hüyük and Boghazkoi in Asiatic Turkey – the general name 'Hittite', but the academic world was sceptical. Similar hieroglyphs had been noticed in the late 1700s by expeditions of the Society of Dilettanti at Halicarnassus, Ephesus, and other places on the Turkish Aegean coast. Several French and German visitors to the ancient Cappadocian city of Boghazkoi had reported tablets, bricks and rocks with inscriptions in the recognizable Akkadian-Assyrian language and in the 'Hittite'. And in 1820, a German named Schultz followed the Frenchman Jean Saint-Martin to the Lake Van region of Armenia. Schultz was murdered by Kurdish bandits but was able to send to Paris copies of inscriptions in Akkadian and another language, subsequently labelled 'Vannic'. The ancient kingdom of Urartu, referred to often in the Assyrian texts, had been located. Urartu was at the height of its power between about 850 and 600 BC. In 1850 Layard had copied more of the inscriptions of Van and he later persuaded the British Museum to allow Rassam to dig at Toprak Kale by the eastern shore of the lake. In the event, the excavations were begun in 1880 by the American missionary Dr Raynolds and the British vice-consul Emilius Clayton. Rassam joined them, but the results of the dig were disappointing. A later German expedition showed that the Anglo-American team had been digging on the site of the temple of the Urartian god Haldi. Layard also urged the Museum, in 1877, to purchase ten bronzes offered by an Armenian. Similar bronzes had been received by the Hermitage at St Petersburg in 1859 and were catalogued as 'Sassanian'. The discovery of Urartu and its rather stereotyped bronzes was not deemed important until the appearance of a Soviet expedition in 1939, after which the art and architecture of the kingdom were assessed. Frequent clashes with Assyria are reflected in a fine Assyrian relief from Tiglath-pileser's Palace at Nimrud showing an Urartian horseman in battle array. Clearly, the national and linguistic elements which had been revealed beyond the frontiers of Assyria and Babylonia were not of a uniform pattern. They were separate national and cultural entities.

The Boghazkoi dig was undertaken in collaboration with the Institute of Archaeology in Berlin, whose director, Professor Borchardt, led the investigations in Egypt. The techniques established by Koldewey at Babylon were to be followed zealously by the new excavators. Their work quickly showed the Hittites, or Hatti, to have been a powerful force in lands stretching from the Assyrian border to the Asiatic coast of Greece from the fifteenth century BC. Mitanni, Syrians, Babylonians, Cappadocians, Assyrians, Egyptians, and many other peoples crossed their paths and learnt to be wary of them. One of Winckler's many important discoveries at Boghazkoi was the inscribed name of the Hittite King Mursil, which led some scholars to relate the name to one of Pelops' charioteers, Myrtilos, thus suggesting a link between Trojans and Hittites, and strengthening the belief that in the fourteenth century Greece was subject to a Hatti ruling dynasty. Hall believed the Hittites to be a unique race, indigenous to Anatolia, art and language pointing neither to Semitic nor Indo-European origins. The discoveries of the Germans gave rise to intense debate about the ethnology and languages of the Anatolian and Armenian regions, which was resolved to some extent by the discovery of the Czech Friedrich Hrozny in 1915 that Hittite was an Indo-European language, though the cuneiform texts of Boghazkoi embraced eight different languages, one of which was Akkadian, and several dialects, one of them written in hieroglyphs. The haul of more than ten thousand tablets found by Winckler's team at Boghazkoi was a rich addition to the vast literature on those Asiatic lands where Semitic and Indo-European cultures came into conflict and proximity.

By the first decade of the twentieth century, the texts of the ancient world had grown into a massive body of cumulative knowledge. By virtue of the permanent nature of the records on clay kept in the course of more than three-thousand years, an incomparably detailed picture could be built up of individual, family and social life. In a miracle of preservation, the painstaking inscriptions of kings, priests and ordinary men and women, made with tools of copper and bronze on an everlasting vehicle, had survived war and civil strife, fire and sword.

The text of Urukagina was six centuries earlier than Hammurabi's law code.

Hammurabi reigned some 1,200 years before his 'Chaldaean' successors Nabopolassar and Nebuchadnezzar. In that time the laws of Babylon had undergone inevitable modification. The marriage dowry had become the subject of tight contractual arrangements, the disposal of female slaves was regulated by stringent financial clauses: 'a man who sold a female slave when there was a claim outstanding against her and she was taken away – the seller shall give money to the purchaser in accordance with the terms of the deed in its full amount; if she bore children, he shall give her one-half shekel of silver for each'. Marital relationships are regulated by the State. 'If a man has a wife and then the man dies, his brother shall take his wife, and then his father shall take her. If in turn also his father dies, one of his brother's sons shall take the wife whom he had. There shall be no punishment.' But if a man sleeps with the wife of his brother while his brother is living 'it is a capital crime'. Again, 'if a man cohabits with several slave girls, sisters and their mother, there shall be no punishment'. As in Hammurabi's Babylon, the prices of goods, chattels and services are laid down by the State. 'The price of 1 acre of vineyard is 1 mina of silver'. 'The price of 5 hides of weanlings is 1 shekel of silver'.

Geography and environmental amenity are reflected in the laws of Neo-Babylonia. 'If a man seize a woman in the mountains, it is the man's crime and he will be killed.' If, on the other hand, he seizes her in her house, 'it is the woman's crime and she shall be killed.' More intelligibly, 'if the husband finds them he can kill them, there shall be no punishment'.

The marvellous network of canals which provided irrigation and transport throughout Mesopotamia from the earliest times imposed obvious legal restraints on the citizen. The man who did not maintain his dike and was responsible for the flooding of another's land or property would pay precisely determined fines in grain or animals. For stealing wood, especially by dismantling a boat, a woman (the usual offender in such cases), would suffer forced labour in the field.

It was in the realm of sexual mores that the laws of the later Babylon excelled in coping explicitly with anthropological and zoological abuse alike. 'If a man does evil with a head of cattle, it is a capital crime and he shall be killed . . . he must not appeal to the king', 'If a man does evil with a sheep, it is a capital crime and he shall be killed.' . . . And: 'If a man violates his own mother, it is a capital crime. If a man violates his daughter, it is a capital crime. If a man violates his son, it is a capital crime.' And: 'If a man violates his stepmother, there shall be no punishment', so long as the husband is not living. 'If father and son sleep with (the same) slave-girl or harlot, there shall be no punishment'. Life could be complicated for the active man. 'If a man does evil with a horse or mule, there shall be no punishment', and 'If anyone sleeps with a foreign woman and her mother (or her sister), there will

[275]

be no punishment'. There remained clause fifteen of the statute, suggestive in its language of the universal prolixity of lawyers:

> In the case of a Seignior who acquired a wife and she bore him children and, when fate carried off his wife, he acquired another wife and she bore him children – after the father has gone to his fate, the sons of the earlier wife shall take two-thirds of the property of the paternal estate and the sons of the later wife one-third; their sisters who are living in the paternal home ... etc.

But it is in their revelation of cultic and religious rites, and the practices of the temple priests that the later texts, copies of much earlier documents, begin to portray the darkest and most secretive aspects of Akkadian and Babylonian society. In doing so, they exemplify, too, practices which have survived in the ritual and dogma of almost all religion.

The temple scene is set in the Akkadian account of the programme for the New Year Festival at Babylon, recorded on tablets of the Seleucid period. On the second day of the month of Nisannu, at two hours before the day's end, the priest is bidden to arise and wash in the water of the river, and then to enter into the presence of the great god Bel. He recites a prayer which speaks in its opening lines of man's preternatural dependence on an omniscient power:

> O Bel, who has no equal
>   when angry,
> O Bel, excellent king, lord
>   of the countries,
> Who makes the gods friendly,
> O Bel, who fells the mighty
>   with his glance,
> Lord of the kings, light of
>   mankind, who divides the
>   portions –
> O Bel, your dwelling is the
>   city of Babylon, your
>   tiara is the city of
>   Borsippa ...

He speaks of 'the secrets' of the temple Esagil. 'Whoever reveres the god Bel shall show them (secrets) to nobody except the *urigallu-* priest of the temple Ekua'. The *urigallu* or high priest opens the temple gate, reciting a prayer as he does so, to admit the throng of lesser priests and singers. A seal is placed in the tiara of the

god Anu. For two more days there are prayers and invocations.' ... The evil
enemies ... the exorcism ... The great lord Marduk (Marodoch or Merodach) has
uttered a curse that cannot be altered ... the god Bel, my lord ... the lord of the
countries ... the city of Babylon ... In the middle of the earth ... the temple
Eudul ... the people dwelling in ... the maidservants ... of the city Babylon ... all
of you dwell ...'. The tablets are so damaged as to make a full translation
impossible, yet the sonorous, repetitive recitation of prayer, the magnificence of
the occasion as the ever-swelling body of priests and choirs assemble is not hard
to imagine. On the third day the high-priest arises again and recites another
prayer to Bel, and opens the doors to *erib-biti* priests and *kalu* priests and more
singers, and then craftsmen are called forth. Metalworkers offer precious stones
and gold from Marduk's treasury to make two images for ceremonies to be held
on the sixth day. Woodworkers provide cedar and tamarisk, a goldsmith gold.
From the third day to the sixth sheep are slaughtered before the god Bel and
distributed in ritual portions to the craftsmen; the tail to the metalworker, the
breast to the goldsmith, thigh to the woodworker, ribs to the weaver. The
portions are offered to the priest and then to the artisans. Imagery, mirror-like,
evokes the eternal analogues of religion. 'Those two images (which the artisans
are to make) shall be 7 finger (-widths) high. One shall be made of cedar, one of
tamarisk. Four *dusu*-stones shall be mounted in settings of gold weighing four
shekels. One image shall hold in its left hand a snake made of cedar, raising its
right hand to the god Nabu ...'.

The Babylonian records take temple ceremony back to Uruk, a thousand years
earlier, and even those copied texts refer to older tablets 'verified and collated' by
the theologians of the day. A procession of priests and choristers offers up much
the same prayers and incantations as it makes its way from the ship of the god Anu
to the temple quay, along the Street of the Gods and through the Royal Gate to
the Akitu, the house of prayer, outside the city. They are accompanied by the city
brewers who are harnessed to a cross beam supporting a moving statue of Anu.
All together on the way to the Akitu House they recite a blessing to the Great Anu
and the lesser deities of the city-state, Enlil, Ea, Beletile, Sin and Shamash, Nergal
and Sibitti, Igigi and Anunnaki. Ritual seems to be centred on the brewery
representation.

From another tablet we follow the same route in the daily sacrifice to the gods
of the city of Uruk. Eighteen gold *sappu*-vessels are arranged on the tray of the
god Anu. 'Of these you shall prepare before the god Anu seven *sappu*-vessels on
the right – three for barley-beer and four for mixed beer – and seven on the left –
three for barley-beer, one for mixed beer, one for *nasu*-beer, one for *zarbabu*-beer,
and one alabaster *sappu*-vessel for milk ...'. And twelve gold *sappu*-vessels must
be set before the goddess Ishtar, and ten before Nana. Other vessels are filled with

food, every constituent measured to the last *sat* (given in decimal). The chef shall supply thirty loaves to set before the goddess Antu, thirty before Ishtar, thirty before Nana, twelve before the seat of the god Anu, sixteen before the temple-tower . . . altogether, one hundred and sixty-eight loaves for the four daily meals of the sacrifice; hundreds more vessels loaded with food for the 'gods' trip' to the heavens. Miller and chef, as they work at the tasks of grinding the flour and kneading the dough and withdrawing hot loaves from the fire, recite verses beginning with the mystical incantation:

Nisaba hengal dussu makalu ellu

Dates from the land of Dilmun, a particular delight, are crammed with 'ordinary' dates into the vessels which will feed gods and men, every day of the year, four times a day.

Then the ritual sacrifice for the gods of the various stages of the temple-tower, the ziggurat, 'every day of the year to the deities Anu, Antu, Ishtar, Nana, and the other gods dwelling in the Resh Temple, the Irigal Temple, and the Esharra Temple, which is the topmost stage of the temple-tower of the god Anu'.

'For the main meal of the morning . . . seven first-class, fat, clean rams which have been fed barley for two years; one fat, milk-fed *kalu*-ram, of the regular offering . . . one large bull, one milk-fed bullock, and ten fat rams which, unlike the others, have not been fed barley . . . While slaughtering the bull(s) and the ram(s), the slaughterer shall recite . . . beginning with the words

Mar Samas belu buli ina seri usabsa ri-iti.

. . . the chief slaughterer shall speak a prayer . . . to the deities Anu, Antu, the Great Star, and the planet Venus [Astarte/Ishtar]; he shall recite it to no other god.

Thus to the second meal of the morning: the usual offering of rams is followed by 'one large bull, eight lambs, five grain-fed ducks, two ducks of lower quality, three flour-fed cranes, four wild boars, thirty *marratu*-birds, three ostrich eggs, three duck eggs!

The vivid processional scene, even at a distance of several thousand years, is not hard to imagine as kings, princes and priests make their way on dressed barques along one or other of the rivers, and accompanied by choirs of a size that Handel might have envied proceed along wide avenues to the temples, and in final view of the populace mount the winding stairs of the ziggurat to secret enclaves where rites might be performed in propinquity with the gods. Incantation, prayer, chanting and hymn singing, wafted on the steam of hot animal blood and the permeating aroma of incense and dung; the gods' repast shared with gluttonous royalty and priests in the high chambers of the heavenly tower. A scene of bloody obeisance, carried on throughout every day of the year in all the temples of Sumer and Akkad, Babylon and Assyria, and beyond in the cities of Elam, Syria and Anatolia. The ritualistic precursor of all the institutional religions, all the idolatry and devil worship, occultism and divinity, which would hold mankind in its grip from the awakening of civilization to the age of space invasion, ever insisting that eye and mind should be averted from the tedium of the knowable and cast fearfully upon the unknowable.

Yet, despite all the revelations of the archives of the ancient world, the true happenings of the temple, and the exact role of the priesthood remain veiled in mystery. The central institution of the ancient world kept its deepest mysteries hidden. The records that have been found are generally concerned with the functions of craftsmen who served the priesthood, and with aspects of ritual which were well-known to the populace. As for the finances of the temples, it is clear that they owned property on a large scale and were not by any means averse to competing in such secular activities as buying and selling. Gifts were a common source of wealth. Not until the Neo-Babylonian period are there indications of small pieces of silver being dropped into collecting boxes at the entrance to the sanctuary. But there are clues in the 'permitted' descriptions which found their way into written history.

Fetish and fad, the theory of 'unclean' meat, have their recorded origins here in the cities of Sumer and Akkad. 'On the sixteenth day of each month, ten first-class, fat, clean rams, whose horns and hooves are whole, shall – after (the sacrificer's) hands have been cleaned – be offered to the deities Anu and Antu of heaven and to the seven planets on the *topmost stage* of the temple of the god Anu ...'; all in addition to the regular offerings, for the daily routine, the festivals, Opening of the Gates ceremony, the Clothing ceremony, the Brazier ceremony, the Divine Marriage, and the obligatory sacrifices of the King, written down in minute detail in all the temples and chapels of the kingdom. 'In the temple of the god Shamash, ram's meat shall never be offered to the deity Shakkan ... In the temple of Sin, bull's meat shall never be offered to the god Harru ... Fowl flesh shall never be offered to the goddess Beletseri. Neither bull's meat nor fowl ... to the goddess Ereshkigal.' The tablet of the Daily Sacrifices to the Gods of Uruk, ends with the words: 'This tablet was copied from tablets which Nabuaplausur, king of the Sea Land (probably seventeenth to fourteenth centuries BC), carried off as plunder from the city of Uruk; but now Kidinanu, a citizen of Uruk, a *masmasu*-priest of Anu and Antu, a descendant of Ekurzakir, an *urigallu*-priest of the Resh Temple, looked at these tablets in the land of Elam, copied them in the reigns of the kings Seleucus and Antiochus, and brought his copies back to the city of Uruk.

Demonology, the exorcism of evil spirits, incantations against ghouls, vampires, ghosts and the kindred spectres of man are represented in the temple inscriptions of almost all ancient civilizations. So are the rites of worship and the assuaging of godly anger and jealousy by offerings at the sacrificial altar. But the evidence of human sacrifice, sometimes regarded as an importation from Babylon into Canaan and Phoenicia, and thence into the religious practices of the Israelites, is speculative. Such practices would certainly have been omitted by the priestly scribes from the written accounts of Babylonian ritual. Frazer in the *Golden Bough* attributed acts of human sacrifice to the Semitic races in general without, it must be said, producing convincing evidence to support his belief.

'Sanctify unto me all the firstborn, whatsoever openeth the womb among the children of Israel, both of man and of beast: it is mine.' Quotations in the Old Testament bear contradictory witness to the demands of God for sacrifice, both human and, in the biblical sense, animal. Frazer's anthropological view was adamant. '. . . we know that the Semites were in the habit of sacrificing some of the children, generally the firstborn, either as a tribute regularly due to the deity or to appease his anger in seasons of public danger or calamity'. Numbers is frequently quoted in support of that tradition, along with the idea of a Bronze Age serpent prototype of the Iron Age Hebrew God Yahweh. 'For all the firstborn are mine; on the day that I smote all the firstborn of the land of Egypt I hallowed unto me all the firstborn in Israel, both man and beast: mine shall they be: I am Yahweh'. 'And Yahweh said to Moses, "Make a fiery fiery serpent, and set it on a pole; and everyone who is bitten, when he sees it, shall live". So Moses made a bronze serpent . . .'.

It is not perhaps surprising that seals have been found in Palestinian graves of the Greco-Roman period with representations of Yahweh with serpent legs; or that the even less palatable idea of the sacrifice of the firstborn should have found it way into perfectly respectable works of anthropological science. Jeremiah is unequivocal in its denunciation of such practices, however. 'For the children of Judah have done that which is evil in My sight, saith the Lord . . . and they have built the high places of Topheth which is in the valley of the son of Hinnom, to burn their sons and daughters in the fire, which I commanded not, neither came it into my mind.' Such acts, though they may have been committed in ignorance, were specifically outlawed.

The burning of children, 'passing the children through the fire to Moloch', was attacked in several books of the Old Testament as a forbidden custom. The name Moloch probably derived from a Canaanite or Phoenician deity, and necropolis finds in Carthage and its colonies show that it was the custom of the Carthaginians, who were colonists of the Phoenicians in the eighth-sixth centuries BC, to burn babies on a pyre, burying the ashes in an urn, a small stone inscription marking the place of burial. Such cemeteries were separate from ordinary burial grounds at Carthage and were called 'Topheth'. Thus placated, it was hoped that the gods would ensure the fertility of the land.

The ambivalent attitude of the Israelites to the precepts of Canaanite and Phoenician cult religions, had its counterpart in Egypt. Manetho in his *History* confirms that in about 1570 BC Amosis abolished the law which permitted the ritual slaying of men at Heliopolis and the incarceration of the sacrificed bodies with 'pure' calves. Such sacrifices were carried out in threes. Amosis commanded that 'men of wax of the same number' should be substituted. Such practices among the Hebrews are confused by biblical injunctions regarding 'unclean beasts' which were the property of God and must be redeemed. The ass must be redeemed with a lamb, or be killed by having its neck broken. Two different traditions appear to have sprung up at a very early time and to have become part of the lore and ritual of the Hebrews, taken perhaps as a legacy from Egypt, and written into the religious texts of Israel. Anthropology on the whole regards the idea of 'unclean' beasts as descending from a time when the Semitic tribes used tabu-beasts as their totems, and their importation from the desert to civilization as being both early and transitory.

Western treatises on magic, satanism and such matters, however, speak of 'incantation', 'divination', 'haps and fates', in the same breath as 'Chaldaeism', of the birth of satanism in Ur, and the 'secret practice' of human sacrifice at Babylon. Evidence is usually scanty. Cannibalism as a feature of ancient civilization has more documentary support. Indeed, it is attested as a response to the threat of starvation in war, particularly in siege conditions. One of the so-called 'prophecy texts' among the Assyrian inscriptions in the British Museum reads: 'That prince shall see woe, his heart shall be grieved; during his rule battle and strife shall not cease, in that reign brother shall eat brother, men shall sell their children for money; the lands shall be raised up one against another. The man shall desert the maid and the maid desert the man; mother shall bolt her door against daughter. The property of Babylon shall come into Subartu and Assyria'. It is a familiar Assyrian threat against a contemporary ruler, perhaps prophetic, perhaps figurative. Another tablet says: 'There came the daughter of Anu to Bel, her father, and said, "Bring me, O my father Bel, what I ask of thee: the flesh of men ... the blood of men ..."'. It is not always easy to distinguish fact from fancy, or cant from incantation, even in the most unsophisticated of texts.

We are on safer ground with the everyday ceremonies and injunctions of the ancients, within and without the temple. In the Hittite texts there is a preoccupation with ritual as a tool not just of appeasement but of war and vengeance. Among the thousands of tablets discovered by the Germans at Boghazkoi, battle oaths and ritual loom large. 'When they perform the ritual at the boundary of the enemy country he sacrifices one sheep to the Sun-goddess of Arinna and to the Storm-god, the Patron-god ... to all the gods, to all the mountains and rivers. But one sheep they sacrifice to Zithariyas.' It seems that the god Zithariyas had let them down in their ongoing war with the mountain tribes known as the Kashkeans. There would be no extravagant sacrifice on his behalf. 'Let Zithariyas win back his place of worship!', wrote the scribe of the Hatti. 'But ye, the gods of the Kashkean country, began war ... The gods of the Hatti land and the people call for bloody vengeance ...'. When they have completed their incantations the soldiers go before the Hatti gods again, 'and they eat up the meat and the bread'. They bring sacrifices 'to the Hatti gods, the Storm-god and the Warrior-god'. The 'master of the gods', the officiating priest, receives the implements used in the feast and the skins of sacrificed sheep. The soldiers return to the battlefield.

The Hittites had rituals for dealing with the bad omen, for healing domestic squabbles, for curing impotence in men, and for many of the other problems and misfortunes of everyday life. 'These are the words of Pissuwattis ... who lives in Parassa: if a man possesses no reproductive power or has no desire for women, I bring sacrifices to Uliliyassis on his behalf and entreat him for three days.' The customary gargantuan feast is prepared, with a pitcher of wine and the shirt of the male sacrificer. A virgin takes the shirt and the sacrificer, having bathed, walks behind her and Pissuwattis, who recites, 'See! I have taken womanliness away from thee and give thee manliness. Thou has cast off the ways of a woman, now show the ways of a man!'. The rigmarole proceeds to a eunuch who is introduced to the bedchamber but can produce nought but excrement and urine. 'Such will not be the case with thee!', the sacrificer is assured. 'See! I am entreating and alluring thee. So come! Bring with thee the moon, the star of the nether world, the sun!' and so for three days the entreaty is made three times a day. 'Let him have thy maid and let her bear his yoke! Let him take his wife and beget children for himself ... Thou, O god, prove thy divine powers.' The sacrificer is told to lie down and 'experience the bodily presence of the deity in his dream'. He must tell whether the deity (the goddess) appears to him, and sleeps with him. He goes off to worship and set up more sacrificial vessels. The outcome is inconclusive. The tablet is mutilated and the secret of fecundity is lost.

Motherhood and the association of maternity with patriotism is expressed evocatively in the Hittite inscriptions. In a vigorous appeal to the Cedar-gods, prayer and sacrifice are directed to exiles of the pantheon, cut off from the homeland by surrounding 'enemies'.

O Cedar-gods, whether in heaven or on earth, whether on mountain or in rivers, whether in Mitanni country or in the country of Kinza (Kadesh on the Orontes) . . . the country of Ugarit . . . Kinahhi (Canaan in the Hurrian tongue), the country of Amurru . . . of Sidon . . . of Tyre . . . Arrapha (Kirkuk) . . . Ashur, Babylon . . . Egypt . . . Alashiya (Cyprus) . . . the Kashkean country . . . or in whatever other countries – come ye now back to the Hatti land! . . . Come ye to the blessed, holy, fine, and wonderful Hatti land . . . Come ye back to your fine and wonderful sanctuaries! Sit ye down on your thrones . . . Provide ye for the king and the queen life, good health, long years, power of procreation, sons and daughters, grandchildren and great-grandchildren! For the man manliness and valour, for the woman womanliness and motherhood!

A hymn to family and country, designed perhaps to succour the exile in a hundred-and-one lands.

The Babylonian tablets show that folklore which persists in the present day has a respectable charter of age. The owl hooting in the night presaged evil in Babylonia. Owl, ostrich and hawk were birds of ill-omen. Hebrew tradition spurns the same birds but the principle, adumbrated in Leviticus, seems to differ.

And these ye shall have in abomination among the fowls; they shall not be eaten, they are an abomination: the eagle, and the gier eagle, and the osprey; And the kite, and the falcon after its kind; every raven after its kind; and the little owl, and the cormorant, and the great owl; and the horned owl, and the pelican and the vulture; And the stork, the heron after its kind and the hoopoe, and the bat.

Great importance was attached by the Sumerians and their successors to the virginity of ceremonial and sacrificial animals. The virgin kid, and even the virgin pig are often specified in the early tablets, though from Akkadian times the latter creature is held in almost total abomination, in anticipation of later Semitic attitudes. The virgin kid was used in Europe in the Middle Ages to provide parchment for the writing of magic spells. And an Assyrian custom, the hanging of plants in the doorway to prevent demons from entering, has survived in the Jewish custom of hanging aloes and cacti in the arches of doorways. Hanging plants may have an even more common, if unconsciously symbolic, manifestation in almost every English suburb.

Witchcraft and black magic are stirred into the Hittite tale of the Old Woman who mends domestic quarrels. 'These are the Words of Mastiggas, the woman from Kizzuwatna', it begins, 'I treat them as follows'. Black wool is wrapped in mutton fat and presented to the sacrificer(s). 'Whatever thou spokest with thy mouth and tongue . . . Let it be cut out of your body . . .'. She takes salt, blood, fat and wax and makes the wax into imitation tongues and waves them over the sacrificer(s). 'In whatever curses you indulged, let now the Sun-god turn those curses and tongues towards the left!' She throws the tongues into the hearth. Red and blue wool are placed upon the bodies of the two sacrificers, and two figures made of dough are put before them. Hands and tongues of dough are placed on their heads and then the Old Woman removes them. She breaks the hands and tongues of dough into pieces. 'Let the tongues of these days be cut off! Let the words of these days be cut off!' She takes a tray and places seven tongues and seven hands on it, and tells the sacrificers, 'Here are the tongues and the hands of that day which is a source of disgust. Let the Sun-god turn them towards the left for thee!'. More incantation, 'Be ye cleansed of your evil tongue!'. More ritual with the dough. A white sheep is driven to the scene. 'Here is a substitute', she tells the sacrificers. 'Let the tongue and the curse stay in its mouth!'. The mouth of the beast is opened and they spit into it. 'Atone ye for those evil curses!'. A hole is dug and the sheep seethed over it and put into it. There are libations of wine, and then a black sheep is driven up. 'For your heads and your bodies the black sheep is a substitute. In its mouth is the tongue of curses.' The sacrificers spit into its mouth. The sheep is slaughtered and cut up, and burnt in the hearth. More dough is kneaded in a clay pan. A small pig is waved over the participants and then slaughtered. Honey, olive oil, blood, fruit and mutton fat are worked into the evil mixture in the 'kneading-pan of Ishtar'. Another black sheep. Seven stone pillars are arranged on the ground and fires lit to their right and left. Bread and wine are taken. The stone pillars are smashed and thrown into the fires. The pottery mixing bowl is smashed. 'Let them break all the words of mouth and tongue in the same way!'. The Old Woman rubs down the limbs of the two sacrificers with hay. Water from an amphora is poured into the horn of an ox, and the sacrificers pour it over their heads, and rinse their hands and eyes with it. Then salt is added and it is poured back into the ox horn, which is sealed by the sacrificers. The scene ends enigmatically: 'On the day when the olden kings return and examine the state of the land, – then, and then only, shall this seal be broken.'

Spittle plays a part in many acts of superstition in the ancient world. In the catalogue of rituals cradled in the temples of ancient Babylonia, the spittle of man helps to achieve affinity with the gods. Among the tablets found at the Sumerian sites, one tells of the priest mixing his spittle with that of the god Ea. Centuries later, in Palestine, Christ 'spat on the ground, and made clay of the spittle, and He anointed the eyes of the blind man with the clay'.

Gertrude Bell at dinner with the German team at Assur, 1911. On her left, Dr. Walther Andrae.

The period from 1900 to 1914 was notable for archaeological enterprise and for remarkable feats of exploration in the Arab lands. Several scholar-travellers appeared on the scene, the most significant of whom were the Czech Alois Musil, professor of Semitic languages and Old Testament studies at several seats of learning in the Austro-Hungarian Empire, and the Englishwoman Gertrude Bell. Railway construction, archaeology and travel under various academic and semi-official guises went on cheek by jowl. Musil and Miss Bell, who was known as Al Khatun or 'The Lady' to the Arabs, moved freely between all the disparate groups, and they made invaluable contributions to the recording of early Christian and Islamic remains in Syria, Mesopotamia and Anatolia.

Getrude Bell made her first modest journey in the region in 1899, just in time to welcome the new century at Jerusalem with the multi-national throng which celebrated at the Greek, Catholic and Anglican churches by the Temple Ground, where Robinson's arch and the tunnels of Wilson and Warren and their successors reminded the visitor of the pioneering works of the Palestine Exploration Fund and the American missions. For the next twenty-six years the wealthy and very emancipated Miss Bell – an Oxford graduate who was not convinced of the desirability of franchise or university education for women – devoted herself body and soul to the Arab lands. She enjoyed the hospitality of the German excavators at Babylon and Assur and her praise of them and their digging methods was unstinting. The elegant white-bearded Koldewey at Babylon and the handsome, dark-bearded Andrae at Assur, became her confidants and hosts at the extremities of Mesopotamian civilization.

Work on the Berlin-Baghdad railroad went on alongside the archaeological enterprises of Anatolia and the Tigris-Euphrates areas. Bustling gangs of workmen came from several European countries to share the work and the spoils. Rail engineers from Germany, Turkey and elsewhere were soon joined at Baghdad, Damascus and Basra by 'travellers' and acknowledged intelligence officials. Prominent among them on the German side was Baron Max von Oppenheim, a member of a distinguished banking family and one of the favourites of the Kaiser and the German Court. In 1893 he had made a journey from Damascus to the Persian Gulf, passing through Mesopotamia *en route*. He combined an enthusiasm for archaeology with his many other activities. He was known in Egypt as 'The Spy' and spent a good deal of time visiting the United States and entertaining at the Kaiserhof. He decided in 1899 to dig at Tel Halaf, a mound which he discovered on his 1893 journey, close to Ras al Ain and the river Jirjib, the scene of Rassam's discovery of the black basalt sculptures in 1882. Digging proceeded at Tel Halaf on and off for the next fifty years. The site's characteristic cream-bodied pottery with reddish brown decoration, found at the lowest level then attained in Mesopotamia, denoted a culture of the fifth millennium, 4000–4500 BC and beyond.

In 1904, two assistants in the Oriental Deparment of the British Museum, R. Campbell Thompson and L.W. King, arrived at Nineveh to resume the excavations which Rassam had abandoned some twenty years before. They had hardly put spade to the rubbish-filled trenches of their predecessors when King was struck down with dysentery and an order came from London for them both to proceed to Behistun to examine the Darius inscription. It was a strange assignation, since the museum had already published the inscription. Campbell Thompson, known throughout his career as 'CT', was given to a pretentious, crab-walk prose style, which concealed his real activities beneath a colourful cloak of classical and native Scots imagery. His epigraphy, much admired by his colleagues, was of the same eccentric quality. A big, bluff, secretive man yet full of bonhomie, he was devoted to the bioscope from the first days of film-making, and he counted his pennies carefully. At the conclusion of the abortive Nineveh dig he settled his account with the British Museum by sending them a postage stamp for the balance owed, a few pence and a halfpence. His translation of a cylinder bearing an inscription of Sennecherib, describing the mountain territory in which the Assyrian king fought many of his battles, is worth quoting for its freakish originality:

[286]

Perch'd like an eagle's aery,
      that king of birds,
High on the ruggedness of
      Nipur's peaks,
Bent not in vassalage beneath
      my sway.
There below Nipur I array'd
      my host
And panoply of valiant
      men-at-arms,
Embattail'd, ruthless; like
      some headstrong bull
I, the forerunner, led them ...

He called his spade 'the handmaid of Clio', and then thought it best to desert the muse and call it simply a 'spade'. He was surely referring to Rawlinson, who died in 1895, just before Thompson entered the British Museum's service, when he wrote of 'those retired gentlemen of a gallant profession, Major-Generals, who can write a washing bill in Babylonic cuneiform, who, relinquishing their life-work, devote themselves to breeding theories, riding a new hobby-horse Antiquity out of Hebrew Translated, and then you shall see wondrous decipherments, miraculous Biblical discoveries'. Perhaps his reluctance to speak or write of his own work in the field is explained in a characteristic aside: 'Truly the most comfortable are those secretive hidalgoes of learning who, all unwedded to their art, risk no progeny of criticized mistakes; and many that hold their peace are counted wise'. An astute anticipation, perhaps, of E. M. Forster's observation that 'the desire to appear weighty often disguises itself as disinterested curiosity'.

'CT' travelled on unexplained missions in Sinai, Anatolia and the Sudan, before turning up at Carchemish in 1911 as assistant to David Hogarth, now succeeded to Evans' position as Keeper of the Ashmolean at Oxford. Hogarth arrived with 'Gregori' the trusted foreman of the Crete and Ephesus excavations, the poacher turned gamekeeper described by Thompson as 'a kind and portly Cypriot, long celebrated as a tomb finder, a dowser of graves with iron probes instead of hazel twig'. Hogarth had been assisted at his last dig at Ephesus by A.E. Henderson, the architect who had been in charge of the British Museum excavations at Carchemish from 1878 to 1881. Neither Ephesus nor the earlier digs assigned to Hogarth at the Dictaenan Cave and Zakro in Crete had been notably successful. At Zakro he failed to find the Palace site which yielded spectacular results to his successors. At the Dictaean Cave he had used characteristically crude methods to open up the allegorical birthplace of Zeus, 'Our blasting charges made short work of the boulders in the upper hill, and luckily the threatening roof held good'. But as was his way he made good the deficiencies of archaeology by vigorous writing which appealed to the academic and lay worlds alike, 'There is a shallow hall to the right and an abysmal chasm to the left, the last not matched in Crete for grandeur, nor unworthy of a place among the famous limestone grottoes of the world'. At Ephesus, the major discoveries were made before his arrival on the scene. Hogarth described himself as 'a wandering scholar of the Levant', and said that he 'looked forward to spending quite a respectable portion of Eternity in talking to Herodotus'. He was a shrewd leader of expeditions whom Lawrence would immortalize in *The Seven Pillars of Wisdom* as the 'Father Confessor' of the military intelligence offshoot known as the 'Arab Bureau' in wartime Cairo.

The decision to resume digging at Carchemish rather than concentrate the Museum's limited resources on the vital Assyrian and Babylonian sites, is a mystery which is perhaps explained by events close to Jerablus, the modern town next to the ancient site. German railway engineers were building a bridge there to take the line from the Syrian side of the Euphrates across the intervening desert and rivers to Baghdad on the Tigris.

Thompson, a fellow of Merton College, Oxford, was joined at Carchemish by two young men from the same university. Leonard Woolley, thirty-one years of age, had left New College with a 'first' in theology and was persuaded by the Warden, the famous Dr Spooner, to take up archaeology rather than schoolmastering as a career. Since then he had studied Greek civilization, returned to Oxford as assistant to Evans at the Ashmolean and, in his own phrase, devoted himself to 'Dead Towns and Living Men'. From 1907 he began his field apprenticeship under Petrie in Egypt, where he found the discordant atmosphere of the camp not to his liking. He went on to work alongside Randall MacIver, another refugee from the Petrie camp, for the University of Pennsylvania expedition in Nubia, where he was employed at the Meroitic necropolis of Karanog and at other non-Egyptian African sites. There was also a brief interlude in Italy where he was greatly impressed by the native archaeologists. 'The Government', he wrote, 'comparatively poor though it be, spends yearly upon excavations and upon the upkeep of national monuments, an amount of money which the British public would grudge in a decade, and for carrying out its excavations, there is no lack of capable men'. Like Thompson he had since come under the spell of Hogarth and thus found himself at Carchemish.

The fourth and youngest member of the party, Thomas Edward Lawrence, was twenty-three years old and very self-confident. All were witty men, brilliant

Golden Lyre of Ur, ornamented with splendid bull's head of gold sheet on wooden core, from tomb of Pu-abi.

Gilded wood figure of Tutenkhamen as harpooner on papyrus raft, one of funerary
objects invoking mystical journeys in after-life.

Woman and child with lamb, Neo-Hittite relief from Carchemish.

raconteurs, and clandestine in their behaviour and writings. Lawrence, a classicist and medieval historian, was a scholarship student of Jesus College. He arrived at Jerablus in 1911 after walking through northern Syria. He had known Woolley and, of course, Hogarth at Oxford.

Campbell Thompson was responsible for the appointment of the expedition's cook and general factotum, Hajji Wahid, who had just been released from jail when the British arrived. Frustrated in his attempt to court a Moslem girl whose brothers objected to the liaison, Hajji had taken matters into his own hands, attacking the brothers and two kinsmen who were sworn to protect the lady, killing four of them. As a government official observed, 'one murder or two might have been overlooked, but four in a night was too much of a good thing'. 'CT' thought him the ideal candidate as camp provider and protector. He was never seen without his gun, even in the kitchen, and on one occasion, when his employers were away, he held the chief engineer of the German rail expedition at gunpoint rather than permit him and his colleagues to remove much needed earth from the site. Much of the Britishers' time at Carchemish was spent in watching the Germans through a telefoto lens, not a common instrument on archaeological sites at that juncture. The expedition house, built by the previous inhabitants and in some disrepair, was made into a pleasant home, and Lawrence carved a 'Hittite' sculpture in alabaster which was fixed above the front door. The expedition was financed by 'an anonymous well-wisher', though carried out in the name of the British Museum. Gertrude Bell called at the site and accused Thompson and Lawrence of 'primitive methods' in their digging, and told them to look to the Germans at Kalat Shargat (Assur) for example. Part of the Carchemish site had been excavated down to the Hittite level by Henderson long before Hogarth's team arrived there. Hogarth spent little time at the site. Thompson left after a year in order to marry. Woolley and Lawrence sent a few neo-Hittite carvings and sculptures to London late in 1913, and many more to Istanbul (later removed to Ankara). Others were crated for transport to England but were stranded by war and destroyed by local treasure hunters.

In January 1914, Woolley and Lawrence closed the site and went off suddenly to Sinai, which an army team under Captain Newcombe was surveying for the Palestine Exploration Fund. They were shown by Newcombe 'the way wherein they must walk, and the work that they must do'. A few months later, all four of the Carchemish diggers were serving as staff officers of the British army in Egypt. Baron Max von Oppenheim became their opposite number in Damascus. The Ottoman Empire joined forces with the German and Austro-Hungarian Empires. Though the Germans in Mesopotamia carried on for nearly two years more, British, French and American archaeology came to an abrupt, if temporary, halt.

Gods, Kings and Legends

Woolley at Ur and Carter in the Valley of the Kings

The faithful servant pleaded,
        clung to life,
Answers his master:
"My master, you who have not seen
        that 'fellow' are not
                terror-stricken,
I who have seen that 'fellow'
        am terror-striken ...
    My master, journey you to
                land,
I will journey to the city,
Will tell your mother of your
                glory,
Let her squeal with laughter,
Then will tell her of your
                death,
Let her shed bitter tears."

From *Gilgamesh and the Land of
the Living* in Kramer's
The Sumerians

The parallels of history had been traced backwards for three thousand years in less than a century of planned excavation, but there remained many still open questions. Did the Hebrews borrow the story of the Deluge and Noah's Ark from

The Sumerian face of evil.
Fragment of terracotta plaque
of Humbaba, demon of the
Gilgamesh epic. Found at Ur.

Sumer, or at any rate from the Akkad of Genesis? Did Greek borrow from Jew, and vice-versa? In pre-Christian Alexandria, pagan critics invoked Greek myths to discredit the Bible of their Jewish neighbours. Twentieth-century scholarship had begun to see a clear stratum of ancient Near Eastern thought and art underlying Greek and Hebrew traditions. Subsequent research would show a 'linguistic alliance' going beyond the twenty-fourth century BC in which Semitic words from the Akkadian infused the language of Minoan and Mycenaean Greece, while identifiably Indo-European words appear at an early stage in the Akkadian records. A western Semitic god, Dagan, mentioned in the Greek tablets, appears in the Mesopotamian pantheon as a patron god of the Akkad dynasty, as Bel's father in the Epic of Kret from Ugarit (part of a critically important 'literary' hoard found at the site of a Mycenaean tomb in Canaanite Syria in 1929), and as a principal god of the Philistines in biblical times. The development of the cuneiform script as the vehicle for so many languages is, of course, a basic proof of linguistic symbiosis. Common themes of art, even of dress, would reinforce the notion of interdependence and the intermingling of peoples, cultures and languages, in the early phases of Near Eastern civilization. Hittite inscriptions at Boghazkoi made vital references to the Aegean kingdoms; and a tablet from the same archive contains an 'apology' of Hattusili III with a prologue written in pure Akkadian, without a trace of the native Indo-European tongue. Hittite and Hurrian translations of the Epic of Gilgamesh underline the widespread nature of cultural cross-fertilization in the second millenium BC.

Terracotta of hero Enkidu, the Wild One, with divine headdress and standard surmounted by sun disc. Found in Anatolia.

The explanations of the early church fathers, that parallels were the work of demons, planted in Greek literature to harass the Church and do the bidding of the devil, were all very well in their day. In the twentieth century AD, more plausible answers were called for. Some theological scholars gave the Phoenicians the role of devil's advocate. Others thought the 'diffusion of the Gilgamesh Epic' explained the most tempting analogues. The western sense of separateness has never been erased entirely. Even at the present day, Old Testament, classical and ancient scholarship are kept in closely guarded compartments in some of the most distinguished universities and museums.

[293]

The American, French and German excavations at Nippur, Kish, Sippar, Uruk, and Babylon, and the Hittite capital at Boghazkoi, had shown that the Flood legend contained in the eleventh of twelve tablets from Ashurbanipal's library at Nineveh, was a resumé of a long and essentially secular epic which originated in Sumer in the third millennium BC. In Sumer, Gilgamesh was the hero of innumerable tales, all of which have taken their names from incomplete cuneiform versions – 'Gilgamesh, Enkidu and the Netherworld', 'the Killing of Humbaba', 'The Bull of Heaven', 'Gilgamesh and Agga', and many more. Like the Homeric legends, Gilgamesh and its associated hero-tales must have originated in days before the written word, handed down by bards, perhaps by father to son. It was not until the fourteenth century that the Akkadian version took the form of a composite epic. It was copied in the seventh century BC on to the first eleven of the twelve Ninevite tablets, ending with the story of the flood. The twelfth Nineveh tablet is a literal translation of an original Sumerian story in which Gilgamesh's mythical friend Enkidu searches the Underworld for his (Gilgamesh's) hoop and stick and is trapped there, returning in spirit to describe the nether regions. The story whose literary counterparts are countless, does not however form an integral part of the Akkadian version.

The title usually given the Akkadian epic of Gilgamesh, taken from its first line, is *Sa naqba imuru*. 'He who Saw Everything'. It is a good name for the first recorded hero-legend. But the suggestion of omniscience is, in a way, misleading, for Gilgamesh was not mythological. He is known from other evidence to have been the real-life King of Uruk, and the opening of the tale shows him as an oppressive, tyrannical monarch whose subjects are only too anxious to be shot of him. 'Two-thirds of him is god, one-third of him is human', it says. The nobles cry out 'He should be our shepherd: strong, stately and wise', yet 'unbridled is his arrogance'. The 'wild-man' Enkidu is created by the gods and set up as a rival. He and Gilgamesh come to blows, then swear eternal friendship. Enkidu was born in the hills, 'with the gazelles he feeds on grass'. The parallel with biblical Nimrod did not escape notice as the tale unfolded. 'Go my hunter, take with thee a harlot-lass', says Gilgamesh.

> The lass beheld him, the
>   savage-man,
> The barbarous fellow from
>   The depths of the steppe:
> "There he is, O lass! Free
>   thy breasts,
> Bare thy bosom that he may
>   possess thy ripeness!

> Be not bashful! Welcome his
> ardor!
> As soon as he sees thee, he
> will draw near to thee.
> Lay aside thy cloth that he
> may rest upon thee.
> Treat him, the savage, to a
> woman's task!

Sated, Enkidu boasted that he would shout to Gilgamesh in Uruk that it was he who was mighty, could alter destinies, 'joyful, radiant with manhood and vigour'.

The first of the Assyrian tablets pronounced the themes of conflict, the search for the after life, redemption and reconciliation, love and lust, which would commend the story as the epitome of Sumerian culture; of that civilization which gave the world the wheel and the art of writing. Although badly mutilated, Tablet I in the British Museum's Assyrian collection permitted a plausible translation. The second tablet from Nineveh, in which Gilgamesh and Enkidu come to blows and then swear eternal friendship, was too mutilated and disjointed to allow of anything like a coherent translation, but the gap was filled in 1917 when Stephen Langdon of Oxford published the text from a Babylonian version found at Nippur by the Americans and known as the 'Pennsylvania Tablet'. The third Assyrian tablet was also fragmentary and was supplemented by another American find, the so-called 'Yale Tablet'. It tells of the reunited Gilgamesh and Enkidu going off to the Cedar Forest in Amanus (Lebanon), the home of Ishtar, to find fame by slaying the evil giant Humbaba. With the aid of eight strong winds sent by Shamash the sun-god, the heroes slew the giant and returned in triumph to Uruk, to the singing and dancing of the womenfolk.

In tablets four to ten we follow the god-king and the Wild One in the marvellous fantasy of their search for an enduring name, culminating in Enkidu's death and Gilgamesh's forlorn quest for the secret of immortality.

The story strikes a recognizable note in Hebrew legend:

And it came to pass as they came, when David returned from the slaughter of the Philistine, that the women came out of all the cities of Israel, singing and dancing, to meet king Saul, with timbrels, with joy, and with instruments of music ... And the women sang one to another in their play, and said, Saul hath slain his thousands, and David his ten thousands ... And Saul was very wroth, and this saying displeased him ... And Saul eyed David from that day and forward ...

Left to right: D.G. Hogarth, C. Campbell Thompson, Leonard Woolley, Max Mallowan.

Ishtar is impressed by the slaying of the giant and offers herself to Gilgamesh in marriage, but the hero spurns her, suspecting her treacherous nature. She persuades Anu to send the Bull of Heaven to kill him but the Wild Man Enkidu slays the creature. The heart is offered to Shamash, a hind quarter is thrown impiously into the face of Ishtar. Gilgamesh and Enkidu are fêted by dancing girls and chanting antiphons, but the rejoicing is short lived. In their anger at the scorning of Ishtar and the killing of the Heavenly Bull, the gods cause Enkidu to die and Gilgamesh sets off alone on the long and dangerous road to eternal life. He crosses the Waters of Death and meets Utnapishtim, citizen of Shuruppak, the first city of Akkad, and the only mortal ever to be granted immortality, who tells him the story of the Flood. Utnapishtim tests his visitor by asking him to forgo sleep, but Gilgamesh fails the test and in his pity Utnapishtim tells him where he can find the Plant of Life. Gilgamesh finds the divine plant but loses it to a serpent. Thus he returns to Uruk, resigned to mortality and to mere kingship.

[296]

The story of the Flood in the eleventh of the Assyrian-Akkadian tablets, showing Utnapishtim as the precursor of Noah, had stirred the imagination of the West more than forty years before the outbreak of the First World War. In literary and intellectual terms, it was perhaps the single most important discovery of archaeology: the spanning of the gulf between the first known civilization and the modern era, the completion of a primordial chord.

Dr H.R. Hall of the British Museum, whose book *The Ancient History of the Near East*, published in 1913, was the standard work of reference of its day, saw Gilgamesh as 'a sort of Herakles'. 'He and other Orientalists realised also that the saga of the Sumerian hero contained interesting precedents for the biblical stories of Noah and Nimrod, and even of the Garden of Eden. Others saw the possibility of a connection in the fourth millennium BC between Sumerian and Minoan civilizations in the analogy of bull grappling and bull acrobatics in the Cretan wall paintings and Sumero-Akkadian cylinder seals. The Epic of Gilgamesh, set alongside the often fragmentary Creation legends in Sumerian and Akkadian, was manifestly the begetter of many a tale.

Sumerian king lists were published in Paris in 1911 by Scheill. They were illuminating but far from convincing, giving as they did the rulers of Kish headed by Queen Azag-bau, a 'drink-seller' who reigned for exactly one hundred years, followed by the dynasty of Opis, and the dynasty of Lugalzaggisi at Uruk. Some forty years later, the American Sumerologist Samuel Noah Kramer came upon the first ten lines of an incomplete text from Tummal, the sacred district of Nippur, dedicated to the goddess Ninlil, and which Poebel had published in his *Historical Texts* in 1911. The Tummal text anticipates the story of the further exploration of Sumer-Akkad, but it is a necessary preliminary to an understanding of early dynastic civilization. Its ten lines reveal the names of the earliest kings and the power struggles which occurred in the time of Gilgamesh. They show that Mesannepadda wrested control of Nippur from Agga, the last ruler of the First Dynasty of Kish, probably by launching an attack on the neighbouring city. He was followed by his son Meskiagnunna as king of Nippur before Gilgamesh wrested power from him. But although Mesannepadda styled himself on his own seal-inscription as 'King of Kish', he was as the founder of the First Dynasty of Ur, and was an older contemporary of Gilgamesh the man-god hero of legend who became by tradition the fifth king of Uruk after the Flood. The latter's kingship could be dated from the internal evidence of the Sumerian king list and the two separately published parts of the Tummal inscription to c.2600 BC.

The end of the First World War found Near Eastern archaeologists conveniently positioned to carry on the tasks which they had dropped so abruptly. Soon after the outbreak of the war, Hogarth, Lawrence and Woolley were sent to Cairo as the nucleus of the Arab Bureau. They took up residence at the Grand Continental Hotel and worked next door at GHQ in the Savoy Hotel. They were later joined by Gertrude Bell. Occasionally, they observed the comings and goings of a red-faced and rather fiery individual named Howard Carter, and were told that he was by repute a fine draughtsman and water-colourist who had dug with Petrie, Maspéro, Pitt-Rivers, Percy Newberry and other legendary Egyptologists, had been befriended and supported in his work by the Earl of Carnarvon, and was currently interested in a site at Thebes. Carter was appointed King's Messenger by the military authorities in Cairo in late 1914 but proved too difficult to handle. He was dismissed before the war was many months old and returned to Thebes and the Valley of the Kings. Woolley detached himself from the Arab Bureau and was put in charge of the intelligence office at Port Said, before risking a 'holiday' voyage in Lord Rosebery's yacht which had been transformed into the spy-ship *Zaida*. The ship was sunk by a Turkish mine off Alexandretta and Woolley was rescued from the water, and taken prisoner of war. He spent the rest of hostilities in Anatolia. Gertrude Bell went from Cairo to Basra in 1916 where she joined Captain Campbell Thompson in the Intelligence Department of Expeditionary Force 'D', before becoming Oriental Secretary to the High Commissioner.

In 1918 Campbell Thompson made preliminary soundings at Tel Muqayyar, the site of Ur which Taylor had investigated in 1853–4, using Indian troops as his diggers. He was followed in the next year by H.R. Hall. Neither can be said to have done more than scratch the surface of Ur, though Hall bared the remains of the palace of Ur-nammu, first king of the Third Dynasty of Ur (2112–2095), a building which its owner had given the name 'E-Kharsag' in Sumerian, the House of the Mountain, and which had been destroyed by fire. 'CT' moved on to another of Taylor's sites, Abu Shahrein or Eridu, where the most remarkable surface debris was found, washed out of the sides of the mound from considerably lower levels by the rains and floodwaters of some five thousand years. Among the finds were lapis lazuli and shell objects, a solid gold nail, rough stone maceheads such as had been used in archaic Egypt, and most importantly sherds of painted pottery characteristic of the period before 3500 BC, exhibiting potting and decorative standards patently superior to those found at succeeding levels.

Hall shifted his attention to a small temple platform at Al Ubaid, a few miles from Ur, which turned out to be the Sumerian prototype of the later ziggurats of the chief Mesopotamian cities, and a structure contemporary with the archaic temple of Ishtar excavated by Andrae at the lowest level of Assur when the Assyrian capital was an outlying province of ancient Sumer. There too, pottery was found at levels earlier than the temple foundations.

In 1922, a joint team from the British Museum and the University Museum of Pennsylvania under the direction of Leonard Woolley arrived in Iraq (the name Mesopotamia was dropped under the British occupation). There and at the other extreme of the fertile crescent, discoveries were about to be made which would contribute the most sensational chapters of all to the story of the past.

Woolley's ecclesiastical backgroud – his father was a clergyman and at Oxford he read theology with enthusiasm – made Ur of the Chaldees an attractive choice. His two years in Turkish captivity at the officer's prison camp at Kastumani in Anatolia had given him time for reflection. By the end of the war he was ambitious to lead a major excavation. The necessary financial support would take time to raise, however, and in 1919 he returned to the Neo-Hittite site at Carchemish which he and Lawrence had hurriedly abandoned five years before. The excavations were surrounded by the warring French army of occupation in Syria and Kurdish tribesmen, and he gave up an unequal struggle after a season's work to join the Egypt Exploration Fund's excavations at Tel al-Amarna. After another season's digging, he was invited to lead an Anglo-American assault on Ur, sponsored jointly by the British Museum and the University of Pennsylvania.

He arrived in the winter of 1922 at Ur-Junction, two miles from Tel Muqayyar, on the Baghdad-Basra branch of the railway that was to have connected Berlin with the Persian Gulf. (The Turco-German workforce had been unable to complete the line from Aleppo to Basra via Baghdad when war was declared and the intermittent gaps which they left were connected by the British Expeditionary Force during and after hostilities.) Several of the most important Mesopotamian mounds were now accessible by train and automobile, chiefly model-T Fords which had been abandoned by British and American troops.

Woolley was greeted by Gertrude Bell, whom he had last seen at dinner in Cairo in 1915. In April 1920 Britain had been granted a mandate over Mesopotamia, and at the Cairo Conference a year later Gertrude had been largely instrumental in persuading the Colonial Secretary, Winston Churchill, that Faisal ibn Husain, son of the Sharif of Mecca and Lawrence's wartime comrade in the Arab Revolt, should be made king of the territory under its new name – Iraq. A provisional government was formed and she was made Director of Archaeology, among other official duties in the British-dominated administration. 'Mr Woolley arrived on Sunday' she wrote on 1 November 1922. 'He is a first-class digger and an archaeologist after my own heart – ie, he entirely backs me up in the way I'm conducting the department ... and they are going to dig at Ur, no less, and are prepared to put in two years 'work ...' The Lady's 'two years' would become twelve in the event.

Miss Bell had just drafted a new Law of Excavations which was designed to ensure that while the countries doing the work received a fair share of the finds, the new Iraq should also enjoy the fruits of its heritage. Within two years of Woolley's arrival she created a national museum in Baghdad which had a statutory right of 'first choice' of any finds. Her determined and sometimes arbitrary manner of dividing up the treasures of a land honeycombed with the remains of successive civilizations, did not always win approval, but few of the men who led early post-war excavations in Iraq dared to dispute her judgement.

Like others before him, Woolley embarked on his chosen task with a passion born of literary preconception. His guiding light was *Genesis*. As a junior member of his team explained, he chose to 'bring to life the Old Testament'. Perhaps the thought was invested with a certain worldliness, for the same assistant remarked that 'There was still a wide Bible-reading public'. A very similar thought was in the mind of the American biblical scholar Dr Edward J. Banks when he tried unsuccessfully to obtain a permit to dig at Ur twenty years earlier. Woolley set out to find the place of Abraham's birth and to 'reconstitute the vanished picture of Sumerian civilisation'. He was to fail in the first aim and to succeed magnificently in the second, yet almost inevitably to blur the edges of discovery with conjecture.

Early excavations had been extended by Campbell Thompson's team of

Turkish PoWs, and Hall's Arab diggers, and the outlines of Ur were already revealed when Woolley arrived. It had been a fortified city, about four square miles in extent, with marine quays running far into the built-up area. It had been a substantial port in its day, and was obviously among the most important cities of an urban society with extensive trade links made possible by a complex network of waterways. Streets and houses were remarkably like those of the Iraqi villagers living round and about the excavation sites of the Euphrates. Only the great temple area at the centre markedly distinguished the city of more than four-thousand years ago with the townships of the present. The first evidence to emerge from Woolley's exploratory digging showed that custom as well as building methods die hard. The Sumerians kept the same kinds of domestic animals as their successors in the twentieth century AD, cooked and ate their food in much the same way, slept on similar beds and shopped in the market places which remained more or less unchanged. But dramatic differences soon came to light. As the houses were excavated more and more bodies were found beneath the floors. In some cases it was evident that residents had been forced to move home when basements became overcrowded with the bodies of generations of their families.

Such insights into the lives of ordinary people in the third millennium BC were fascinating enough. It was, however, the great walled structure at the centre of Ur, the ziggurat, with its associated temple buildings and its triple staircase leading up to the high chambers of gods and priests, which Woolley and his assistants were most anxious to probe. In fact, they decided at an early stage of the excavations to restore it, for it was in a good state of preservation, having been rebuilt and renovated many times over the forty or more centuries since it first overlooked the Sumerian plain. Almost as soon as they had started work on the ziggurat, Woolley discovered another important feature, the neighbouring cemetery, burial place of kings and priests who had occupied the ziggurat, and of their predecessors. There were suspicious signs that the rituals of one were closely connected with the other. But Woolley was a scrupulous excavator. He decided that his team lacked the practical experience needed for the careful work of digging the royal necropolis. He put it from his mind and waited for four years before allowing its excavation. The entire enterprise at Ur was to occupy him and his team, and a workforce of hundreds, until 1934.

Gertrude Bell's newly drafted laws forbade any foreign expedition from working in Iraq unless properly constituted and containing recognized experts in specialist fields such as epigraphy, architecture and photography. Only one expedition could excavate at any given site, and she as Director of Archaeology was the sole arbiter in deciding the limits of the dig. Work must comply with 'up-to-date methods' of excavation, all finds must be numbered and registered. All antiquities were the property of the State. Finds would, however, be divided at the end of each season's work and 'a representative selection' of objects assigned to the excavator. Such were the constraints under which Woolley began his work at Ur.

Much of the effort in the first season consisted of building houses for the excavation team out of burnt bricks found among the debris. In the first two seasons they began to disclose the streets, homes and workplaces of the Neo-Babylonian outskirts, the pavements which led from the palaces of Nebuchadnez-zar and Nabonidus, one built directly over the other, to the entrance of the temple shrine. Terracotta pipes revealed extensive systems of drainage and domestic plumbing. Ivory ritual pieces and alabaster mace-heads, and a white marble human head were uncovered. There was one notable hoard of jewelry, with a fine lapis and gold necklace and a gold pendant. But tracing the early mud-brick walls of the original buildings and the succeeding burnt-brick courses was the principal achievement of Woolley's first two years at Ur. Work was begun on the temples of E-Nun-Mah and Nin-Gal, on the ziggurat and the northern gateway of the palace of the third king of the Third Dynasty of Ur, Bur-Sin. As ancient roads were cleared, Woolley gave them the names of byways in his home town of Bath in England. With unique anachronism, signs reading *New Street*, *Gay Street* and *Quiet Street*, appeared where the first scribes had plied their trade, composing the letters of the illiterate in the pictographic language of Sumer, some five thousand years before; where for two millennia kings, priests and laity had wound their way in procession to and from the great ziggurat of Ur, earliest of all the stepped temple-towers of the ancient world, constructed in about 2100 BC.

Woolley brought his old foreman, Hamoudi, from Carchemish. Too old any longer to control the workforce single-handed, he brought his three sons with him as helpers, but the venerable Hamoudi still presided over the digging with eagle-like authority, exhorting his men with a mixture of invective and praise. By the start of the third season, excavations and excavators began to take on a new appearance. One of Woolley's chief academic assistants early on was the epigraphist Father Legrain, a nominee of the University of Pennsylvania. He was followed by A.S. Whitburn, a penurious young architect and Max Mallowan, a graduate of New College, Oxford. Mallowan had been led to a career in archaeology by the lectures of Percy Gardner who eventually filled the Wykeham Professorship of Greek Art and Archaeology at Oxford which Evans had disdained in 1881 as just another example of the university's limited 'classical' outlook, comparable with the creation of a chair of 'Insular Geography' or 'Mesozoic Geology'.

Woolley, like any expedition leader, needed strength of character and adroitness to keep order and discipline among clever and often opinionated assistants, and a workforce of between two and three hundred men of differing religious complexions for whom civil strife had much the same sporting appeal as had cricket for Englishmen or baseball for Americans. In such proximity, leader and assistants reveal all too readily their strengths and weaknesses. Woolley was a man of much wit, a brilliant lecturer, story-teller and after-dinner speaker; and, as such men often are, a private and somewhat enigmatic personality. The unfortunate Legrain, friendly and yet cynical of life and inclined to ribaldry, offended Woolley's sense of propriety with his ogling of Badu women and indelicate exchanges with servants, and was shortly replaced by the Jesuit Father Burrows, a man of wide Oriental learning who had the greatest difficulty in ordering a jug of water in the vernacular. Mallowan, the youngest member of the expedition was usually given the task of showing visitors round the dig, and it is to his recollections that we owe much of our knowledge of the personalities involved. Gertrude Bell and her many companions from the Civil Administration were frequently at the site. So was the learned American missionary of the Dutch Reformed Church at Basra, John Van Ess, whose *Arabic Grammar* was mandatory reading since all members of the expedition were expected to learn the language.

Within two years of the arrival of Mallowan and Whitburn, Woolley married Katharine Keeling, the widow of an army officer who shot himself at the foot of the Great Pyramid soon after their honeymoon. Katharine Woolley did not consult, discuss or argue. She simply issued orders. She was quick witted, prejudiced and insidious; an unashamed snob with all the wiles associated with her sex and few of its charms, except good looks. From the moment of her arrival at Muqayyar, the atmosphere was charged with intrigue. She filled strong men with terror and even the Arab workmen, to whom all women were necessarily subject creatures before the arrival Mrs Woolley, were afraid of her. From the outset she insisted on the undivided attention of the people around her. Expedition resources were diverted time and again to cope with building work on the Woolley residence, with her own separate bedroom. She was the victim of every kind of imaginary illness and a doctor had to be called in regularly from Nasiriya, about twelve miles away, to administer the standard treatment of the time for almost all ailments, blood letting. The long-suffering and hard-working Woolley seldom went to bed before two o'clock in the morning. When he had finished his labour of recording the day's work and finds, he retired with a string leading from his toe to Katharine's bed, so that in the almost inevitable nocturnal emergency she could summon attention by tugging it with a loud cry of 'Leonard!'. Since she suffered constantly from migraine, members of the expedition were summoned to administer remedial massage. Her undoubted talent as an artist was put to use in drawing artefacts as they were recovered, so that she was ever present on the site, giving instructions and counter instructions to everyone within earshot, and always posed at the centre of photographic groups as though for *Vogue* magazine rather than the excavation record books. Gertrude Bell, not it must be said a 'woman's woman', described her as 'dangerous'. The feelings of most of the expedition members were often unprintable. An overbearing manner was joined by inner doubt. She had little confidence in her real if unchannelled ability as an artist.

Mallowan suffered as much as anyone from her vigorous presence, but she did him an unsuspecting favour when she ordered him one day to take a rather retiring and apologetic lady visitor to Baghdad. Her name was Agatha Christie and she had gone to Iraq after the breakup of her first marriage. Mallowan married her in the following year.

At the beginning of the 1925 season Woolley was able to give the world a detailed description of the ziggurat of Ur, which he likened to 'Babel and the confusion of tongues'. Two hundred workers had removed thousand of tons of broken brick and sand to reveal 'the most imposing monument in the land'. Woolley saw it as an artificial mountain, a pious work dedicated to the gods, of whom the chief in the Ur pantheon was the moon god, Nannar. Evidence of large trees having adorned the upper terraces seemed to confirm the theory that its builders in the days of Ur-Nammu, looked longingly towards the mountainous regions from which they had migrated and determined to erect a man-made mountain on the plain they had inhabited. They succeeded impressively. The rich red brick with which they replaced the old sun-dried mud of the predynastic city, reached up for seventy feet or more, terminating in the little shrine of the moon god. The upper stages were reached by a magnificent triple stairway, a hundred steps to each flight.

As the excavation of the ziggurat site proceeded, tablets, cylinder seals and reliefs – found in many parts of the city, even in private homes – began to indicate in words and pictures some of the temple ritual which had been hinted at, but never openly declared, in the Babylonian and Assyrian tablets; rites which were amplified by the newly deciphered religious texts found at Nippur, Uruk and elsewhere by the pre-war expeditions.

Herodotus believed that the famous tower of Babylon was the scene of indelicate royal antics in which the king, impersonating Bel, performed a vigorous sexual act with a substitute for the goddess Ishtar, while the congregation sang hymns and uttered prayers, appropriately in the cause of fertility. Neither the German excavations at Babylon nor the earlier expeditions at the southern sites had thrown any clear light on the precise nature of the rites performed in the ancient shrines, however. Woolley's work at Ur soon began to unmask the mystery that had intrigued classical and modern historians. Among

A two-dimensional reconstruction of the Ziggurat of Ur.

its ritual functions, the shrine at the summit of the Ur temple-tower was the scene of a sacred wedding ceremony. On the appointed date each year, the king would lead the priests and choirs in a solemn ceremony, winding its way up the steep stairways to the various stages of the tower. Prayer and ritual hymn-singing were followed by a banquet. Then the king and chief priests made their way to the topmost shrine where a substitute goddess, the en-priestess, waited. Sometimes the king's own daughter filled the role; sometimes his sister. Copulation was accompanied by the crudest hymns exhorting the performers and exalting their vital parts. Thus were the gods of fertility appeased.

Increasingly spectacular finds were made in the temple complex of Ur. A limestone slab, beautifully carved in relief, showed the king receiving from the moon-god the order to build the tower, the god holding out to him the rod and line of the architect, 'the measuring reed and the flaxen line with which Ezekiel, an exile by the waters of Babylon, saw the city planned out. In another scene, the king portrays his obedience by carrying before the god the mason's tools, ready to lay the first brick of the ziggurat. Animal sacrifice and prayer are depicted, the king surrounded by the women of the harem and priests. Lists of functionaries were found: priests, ministers of state, choirmaster, controller of the household, master of the harem, directors of livestock, fisheries, dairy and donkey-transport.

That kingly enterprise, the building of the temple-tower, Woolley hastened to explain, was only a repetition of even earlier works. He dated it at 2300 BC, two hundred years earlier than the reign of Ur-Nammu. By that time, 'the temple had been completely rebuilt several times, and the building with which Abraham was familiar was perhaps the fifth to occupy the site'.

The expedition was already digging among the houses 'where the Patriarch and his family had lived'. Their sense of anticipation was shared by Woolley himself. Preconception had begun to creep into the excavator's vision of Ur of the Chaldees. The crux of Ur's social and religious life was at the great central mound, however, the area of the ziggurat and the royal palaces.

It became increasingly evident that there was more to the ritual of the temple than Woolley's team at first imagined. For four years they had looked down from the ziggurat mound and the E-Khursag palace of Ur-Nammu to the royal graveyard beyond. By 1926 they were ready to excavate it.

Just outside the area of the inner city, the *temenos*, a few simple graves were found among the accumulated rubbish of generations which had preceded the Third Dynasty, going back perhaps to the time of Gilgamesh and his contemporary Mesannepadda, the founder of the First Dynasty. Other burials were more elaborate. Tombs took the form of rectangular chambers built of stone rubble, some vaulted, others domed. Few had escaped the attention of tomb robbers in the ensuing four to five millennia. The first undisturbed grave was that of a lady of obvious distinction. A rectangular shaft led from the surface to the chamber, and had been filled in after the entombment. Half way down the shaft a magnificent gold dagger was found with a cylinder seal which bore the name of the prince Mes-kalam-dug. The keepsakes had been flung into the shaft as it was being filled. In that part of his official report on the excavations devoted to the Royal Cemetery, Woolley wrote: 'Among the 1,850 graves unearthed in the cemetery there are sixteen which stand out from all the rest not simply because of their richness – indeed, most of them had been plundered and their wealth must be taken on credit, and few have produced such treasures as marked the grave of Mes-kalam-dug, itself not one of the sixteen – but for peculiarities of structure and ritual'. In the more popular context of his book *Ur of the Chaldees* he described the next stage of investigation.

> The vault had been built over a centering of stout wooden beams which ran right through the stonework, and their decay had left half a dozen holes, through which one could glimpse parts of the dim interior and by the light of electric torches, could even see on the floor below the shapes of green copper vessels and catch an occasional glimpse of gold.

The 'Standard of Ur', from a hollow receptacle originally of wood with scenes on four sides in coloured mosaic. Two main sides depict War and Peace in about 2500 BC.

Further search by torchlight revealed more wonderful sights than artefacts of copper and gold. There were five bodies, side by side. One, judged by his raiment, was an important person, perhaps a high official. The others were servants. At the centre of the bizarre burial scene, a richly-adorned lady came into view with golden headdress, holding a fluted gold tumbler to her lips. The excavators moved on to two adjoining tombs. The true nature of the temple rituals, vaguely perceived by the excavators when they examined the sanctuary of the ziggurat, began to dawn. The occupant of one of the tombs was identified from an inscribed seal as Pu-abi, a woman and, it was presumed, queen, since she bore the title *Nin*. In the other tomb, a man had been buried in a single vault. Just by its entrance was a shaft with a ramp leading down to it, and this was filled with bodies of lesser folk, later identified as guards and attendants. Soldiers wore copper helmets and carried spears or daggers, and some of the spears were tipped with gold, others with silver. Among the attendants were women, nine of them with elaborate headdresses of lapis lazuli and cornelian. Silver and gold necklaces and bracelets still adorned them. Then came the bodies of oxen, still between the shafts of four-wheeled wagons that had brought the assembly to its grim resting place. Among the human and animal remains there were magnificent objects of Sumerian craftsmanship – including two lyres inlaid with gold and decorated with bulls' heads. The tomb of Pu-abi next door had its own 'death-pit', situated above the lady's vault and extending over the man's tomb. Five soldiers, ten court ladies and a sledge were in this tomb. A harness and silver rein-ring were found. A little figure of an onager or wild ass, made of gold-alloy, surmounted the rein-ring. Gaming boards, tools, a golden drinking 'straw', chalices of gold, copper and silver, lay around. This tomb, unlike the king's, had been missed by robbers, and gradually a veritable gallery of precious finds was rescued: a nest of silver tumblers and other vessels; a gold tumbler, fluted and chased; silver lions' heads of staggering quality, silver table offerings, imitation cockle shells in gold with cosmetics inside. Beside the bier on which lay the fully dressed queen, holding a golden cup to her lips, two ladies of the court stood in attendance. A spare diadem of white leather, covered with beads and supporting a row of gold animals – gazelles, bulls, goats and other creatures, was beside the central figure. A third and even larger tomb was nearby. Six manservants and sixty-eight female servants lay in regular rows on the floor, head to feet. A maid, late for the ceremony, had quickly pushed her silver hair-ribbon into her pocket, still rolled up.

Nothing in the tablets of Babylon or the reminiscences of the Assyrian kings who liked to pay tribute to their southern ancestors, suggested human sacrifice as part of the temple ritual. Even the Sumerian inscriptions discovered by the French and Americans at Kish, Nippur and elsewhere, divulged nothing of such matters. There was Herodotus's well-known description of the 'magnificent funerals' and 'splendid tombs' of the Scythian kings, confirmed by Wesselowsky and Bobrinskoy in 1913 near the cataracts of the river Dnieper, but their burial chambers were comparable only in the wealth of artefacts found within them, and they were almost contemporary with the 'father of history'. Indeed, despite the accumulated evidence of some eighty years of digging from Layard to Woolley, one Assyriologist, A.L. Oppenheim, felt compelled in 1964 to publish a warning about the dangers of trying to assess Mesopotamian religion on the basis of the incomplete evidence available, and the coexistence of very different religious manifestations in ancient Iraq. One chapter was headed 'Why a "Mesopotamian Religion" should not be written'. Nevertheless, one of Oppenheim's colleagues. Thorkild Jacobsen, took the bit between his teeth and wrote a perceptive book entitled *A History of Mesopotamian Religion*.

Nothing which came out of that academic dispute, nor any other investigation of the 'Babylonian' mounds, helps to explain the unique nature of Woolley's spectacular discovery at Ur. Perhaps it illustrated an isolated practice, confined for some reason to one city-state. Yet that is hard to imagine. It is surely more likely that priestly-scribes of the time, and later chroniclers who abhorred the idea of human sacrifice, remained silent; and that here, by virtue of the fortunate preservation of its necropolis, the true nature of the temple rites of early dynastic Sumer were revealed – the temple processions of kings and priests and their retinues of servants, the smoke clouds wafted between the great rivers of Mesopotamia as sacrificed creatures were burned in daily ritual ceremonies, the annual fertility rites and finally the sacrifice of the humans who had served their various purposes on earth and perhaps looked to another life through death. Here, at any rate, was incontrovertible evidence of the ritual death-march of kings, princes, priests and servants. There is, in fact, one small but significant pointer to the supposition that the sacrificial practice may not have been restricted. A tablet at the University of Pennsylvania containing part of a Gilgamesh epic, tells of the hero presenting gifts to the deities of the nether world and for 'all who lay with him' in his 'purified palace' at Uruk. The retainers cited are almost the same as those found with their sovereigns in Woolley's tombs.

Woolley, in his first official report, had suggested that the killing of the humans in the death pits might have been done elsewhere, and the corpses brought and laid in position, or that they were killed on the spot and their bodies neatly arranged afterwards. It seemed almost inconceivable that they had arranged themselves in life while they waited for death, by whatever means it was effected. Bones found by the excavators were always so broken and decayed that they revealed nothing of the manner of death. But the evidence of ornaments seemed to be conclusive. None but princes of the ruling house would be so richly adorned. The evidence of ornaments led him to accept the view 'first put forward by my wife', that 'the victims quietly drank some deadly or soporific drug'. Certainly a cup or chalice was present in each of the graves denoted as 'royal'. But equally, cups were present in the common graves nearby, usually accompanied by a water jug, and vessels for food, reminiscent of the Egyptian *ka* tombs. There was little doubt that death came peacefully, and Woolley suspected hashish. Covering the dead bodies with earth was not the last act in this ritual. When the filling of the shaft had reached a certain level, a clay floor was laid and trodden in. New rites took place on this clay platform. Drink offerings were poured to the dead, and drains in the floor carried the libation to the bodies below. Then fires were lit and a funeral feast prepared. On a matting table were set out plates and cups with sweetmeats and drink in them, and a protective clay bowl was laid over them as the filling of the shaft proceeded. Another pause higher up permitted a layer of loose plaster and clay to be laid as the foundation for the mud-brick walls of the chamber. The various layers of in-fill were applied by degrees in an ingenious ritual – a layer of earth followed by a smooth clay floor, more earth and another clay floor, each layer supplied with food and drink, and now and again a sacrificial body of animal or human. Woolley believed that when the entire process was completed, an altar or chapel was placed at the entrance to the shaft, but no trace of such a structure remained.

Some of the earliest graves had been plundered during the Third Dynasty of Ur. Pottery, cylinder seals and the graves themselves enabled Woolley to build up a detailed time-picture of events, but he usually erred by a few hundred years in favour of longevity. He dated the terminal stratum above the royal cemetery at c.3100 BC, several centuries too early. Some of the seal impressions found were, indeed, Sargonid, that is belonging to the Akkadian dynasty which was inaugurated in about 2350 BC and united the conflicting communities of Sumer. Equally, Woolley gave the stratum below the bottom level of the royal cemetery an earlier date than it deserved. Seal impressions again showed that the lower level represented the period Early Dynastic I. The royal graves are dated Early Dynastic III, 2650 to 2500 BC. Many of the common graves are later, touching on the Third Dynasty of Ur, c.2100 BC.

Mallowan described one of the royal tombs, with no less than seventy-four bodies which had been buried at the bottom of the deep shaft. It was, he said, 'like a golden carpet ornamented with beech leaf head-dresses of the ladies of the court, and overlaid by gold and silver harps and lyres which had played the funeral dirge to the end'. The royal cemetery, like the great ziggurat, was a remarkable discovery indeed. A delightful epigraphic aside to underground scenes of unrelieved gloom was provided by an inscription which told of Shulgi, the son of the royal builder of the ziggurat. Shulgi was an accomplished musician and of the forty-eight years of his reign he spent twenty-eight years as an instrumentalist, playing eight instruments, including the 30-stringed lyre, before he settled down to become an effective ruler whose power and influence extended far beyond Sumer. Shulgi also introduced royal weights and measures, embellished the temples of Ur, and 'greatly cared for Eridu which is on the shore of the sea'. His father Ur-Nammu had already made his city the centre of extensive maritime trade, by way of the rivers and canals which connected the inland cities of Sumer with the Persian Gulf, one hundred and fifty miles away.

Woolley's personal interest, despite all the remarkable discoveries of the first four years, still centred on the ordinary Ur of the Chaldees, the streets and homes of the city. As he supervised the gradual clearing of the ancient housing estates, there was an ever-present awareness that it was among these tidy suburban terraces and their moon-worshipping occupants that the family of Abraham would have lived before moving off, to another centre of the moon cult, Harran in the far north. The houses of the period from the Third dynasty onward, when kiln-baked bricks came into use, were substantial, though private homes, shops and wayside places of prayer were rebuilt many times in the fifty or so generations which followed the accession of Ur-Nammu. Woolley the informed, urbane showman, made a suberb guide. Abetted by the evidence of tablets and seals, he would tell visitors 'This was the Headmaster's house', or 'here lived a merchant' or a 'jeweller' or 'cloth-dealer', as the fancy took him. And he was convinced that he knew the quarter where the family of Abraham lived. But truth to tell, no tangible evidence was found of the Patriarch's residence in Ur.

In 1925, before returning to the ziggurat at Ur, Woolley had proceeded to the nearby mound of Al Ubaid, hoping to find there traces of predynastic occupation such as existed in the land of Sumer at the time of the great flood recounted in the epic of Gilgamesh. His incentive was the discovery of several graves in the alluvial bank close to the boundary wall which Nebuchadnezzar had erected in the sixth century BC with bricks stamped with his name and title. As he dug through the deepest levels of occupation from the end of the Early Dynastic period, about 2500 BC, and came eventually to the alluvial deposits, he was reminded of the deluge of the Old Testament. He asked his wife, always at his side during the excavations, what the sandy alluvial clay signified. She said spontaneously 'the Flood'. At Ubaid he found some reliefs and four copper bulls in the round, as well as several mosaic friezes which supplemented the finds of Hall in 1919 – the most important of which were architectural features which included four magnificent copper lions with inlaid eyes, teeth and tongues from a temple staircase. But he went to Ubaid in search of prehistoric remains, and he reconstructed a picturesque phase of 'reed huts in the primitive marshes' which fitted nicely his image of the beginnings of Ur. In fact, he had found only the last sub-phase of Ubaid. Had he dug deeper, he would have recognized pottery and other signs of habitation much earlier than the flood associated with Ut-napishtim, king of Suruppak, and the biblical flood of which it was almost certainly the literary precursor. The true Ubaid phase would, from later excavation, take the history of the region beyond 4000 BC, but that was by no means the beginning.

'Egypt was his bugbear', wrote Mallowan, citing Woolley's remark that Egypt derived its models and ideas 'from an older civilization which, as we know, had long been developing and flourishing in the Euphrates Valley'. Mallowan was impatient of the war of longevity which had been waged for nearly a century between the advocates of Egypt, Mesopotamia and Ancient Greece. 'The fact is that both civilizations, Egyptian and Sumerian, developed more or less *pari pasu*', he wrote. Still, there was overwhelming praise for Woolley's work, for his feverish energy, and his imaginative reconstruction of Sumerian life. In his excavation of the cemetery not one of two thousand or so graves went unplotted, though he and his assistants were aided by nothing more sophisticated than a measuring tape and a prismatic compass. A young architect who arrived in Iraq at the critical juncture of 1926, Seton Lloyd, was to join Mallowan in subsequent researches among the Mesopotamian mounds. At the end of his own active career

Left: Onager or wild ass, mounted on silver rein ring; and, *opposite*, Queen Pu-abi's gold cup, from entrance to grave at Ur.

as excavator and teacher he summarized Woolley's immense achievement, and the folly of the great man's haughty independence and preconceptions.' 'The fact is, that Woolley's progressive interpretation of his finds and the periodical conclusions to which it led, were very much a one-man affair. Consultations with his staff were on the whole minimal; so that at times they would even remain in ignorance of some major decision until reading of it in his seasonal report.'

As for biblical allusion and imagery, Lloyd wrote: 'Contrary to the view consistently argued by Woolley, there is no actual proof that Tell-el Muqayyar ... was identical with Ur of the Chaldees in Genesis 1:29–32. Nor is there any agreed opinion on the existence of Abraham himself, on his social and ethnic origins, on his history and chronology, above all on his connection with the enigmatic Chapter 14 of Genesis'.

Even on the question of the 'Royal Graves' as defined by Woolley, there is disagreement. When the official accounts of the excavations were published by the British Museum in the 1930s, the Assyriologist Sidney Smith put forward the suggestion that the tombs were connected with mysterious structures mentioned in the texts and called *gigunus*. These were apparently situated near the sacred

quarters of the cities, and were occupied not by royalty but by priests and priestesses, who participated in a mystery play celebrating the marriage of a god. He considered that the idea of human sacrifice at a king's funeral, and even more a queen's, was unthinkable. But Smith was working on the evidence of only two graves. Of the 'royal' status of the occupants of most of the sixteen graves with their dark evidence of ritual sacrifice, there can be little doubt though arguments for priestly occupation persist.

Beyond any argument are the creative achievements of the third millennium uncovered at Ur. The art rescued from the tombs of the Early Dynastic periods throws a penetrating light on the work of craftsmen at the very beginning of civilization. The tombs of the Third Dynasty had been raided and deprived of much of their magnificence. But the earlier graves were virtually untouched. Such works represent art at its most vigorous and unaffected, before convention had embraced the creative skills of man with a grip that would never again be released. The head-dress of Pu-abi (Queen Shubad as she was also designated) and the golden helmet of Mes-kalam-dug, the first of the grave artefacts to emerge, were restored by Woolley, the former with the support of a dummy head modelled by his wife (incorrectly as it transpires); but they show something of the magnificence of dress and the jeweller's craft around 2500 BC. The famous harp found alongside Pu-abi, with its oblique strings running from a sounding box to a vertical arm with gold tuning pins, and the lyre ornamented with an opulent bull's head of sheet gold hammered over a wooden core, its beard and mane boldly carved in lapis lazuli, are not easily compared or categorized. They are eternal, like the goat rearing on its hind legs to sniff the flowers of a tree, breathtaking in its confidence.

'The Ram in the Thicket' as it is otherwise called, with reference to another biblical analogue, is part of a pair of standing goats, and has a tube running from its shoulder which suggests that it once supported an article of furniture. It was found in the death pit by the royal tomb with seventy-four servants buried within. And then there is the famous 'Standard of Ur', depicting war and peace in three registers on either of the main sides, and rustic scenes on its end panels. It was one of Woolley's, and the world's favourite examples of ancient craftsmanship, found by the shoulder of a man in grave-pit 779. But it is in their three-dimensional stone and clay modelling, and their metal work, already using copper-casting techniques for heads, often in conjunction with hammered metalwork for bodies, that these early craftsmen show a confidence and freshness, and their work a dynamic inner force, that is peculiarly of the Sumerian age. The first part of the Sumerian Flood saga says that after the gods An, Enki and Ninhursag had fashioned the 'black-headed people', the Sumerians, all the plants and creatures were brought 'artfully' into existence, and the first five royal cities were founded in Sumer. Ziusudra, king of Shuruppak, was revered as the preserver of the 'seed of mankind'. They saw themselves as the chosen people. The arts and crafts of Sumer mirror the self-confidence of a people who saw their neighbours, the Elamites and Asiatic societies to the north and west such as the Hurrians, as at worst barbarians, at best 'fools', 'boors' and 'cry-babies'. Places still hidden beneath the mounds of present-day Syria on the other side of the Euphrates would reveal that such arts and attitudes were not confined to the southern culture of Mesopotamia.

Before leaving for the Euphrates Valley in 1922, Woolley wrote an account of his season's dig in Egypt, in the workers' compound two miles from Akhenaten's city of Amarna. The tomb-quarriers were he said 'a rough lot, given to riots and strikes'. They were housed in a walled estate where they could live in some comfort, watched over by sentries, and marched each day to the site where the young king's unitary god, symbolized by the disc of the sun, might be worshipped.

Only for about twenty years did the dreamer enjoy his retreat; then he died or was killed; his mushroom city was laid under a curse by the priest of the orthodox faith; the Court returned to Thebes; the merchants and artisans drifted away; and soon over the deserted and plundered houses the wind heaped up the sand which was to preserve them for the spade and camera of the modern archaeologist.

Its was the fate of many an Egyptian city in the course of three thousand years of dynastic rule.

George Edward Stanhope Molyneux Herbert, Lord Porchester, 5th Earl of Carnarvon, 'Porchy' to his friends, first went to Egypt in 1903. He came of a long and noble line of Turcophiles in the political mould of Disraeli. He was thirty-six years old when he arrived in the Nile Valley, and for fifteen of those years he had nursed a desire to try his hand at 'digging'. In 1906, like the true-blue amateur he was, he began to dig at Thebes with only his own enthusiasm to guide him. Fortunately, he turned to Sir Gaston Maspéro, the great Frenchman whom Britain had honoured with a knighthood. Maspéro advised him to seek out a young excavator who had come to his notice by the name of Howard Carter.

The ensuing friendship and collaboration, which was to last for the remaining sixteen years of the Earl's life, was founded on an almost total disparity of background and personality. 'Porchy', one of the wealthiest landowners in Britain, connected by blood and marriage to a dozen lines of aristocracy and by patronage to every branch of the English establishment, has been described as a cross between Beerbohm's Duke of Dorset and Wodehouse's Bertie Wooster. Carter, born in 1873 and therefore seven years Carnarvon's junior, was one of nine children of a poorly rewarded animal painter. Carnarvon was an 'amiable nobleman', Carter a moody, ill-tempered and occasionally violent artist who deferred to nobody. At the age of seventeen he had been introduced to the distinguished Egyptologist P.E. Newberry, for whom he executed some tracings of tomb scenes. His youthful apprenticeship with Petrie and Pitt-Rivers was followed by six years with Naville as draughtsman and illustrator at the temple of Queen Hatshepsut.

In 1900, at twenty-seven, he was made Inspector-General of the Monuments of Upper Egypt and Nubia, under the direction of Maspéro. Thus, at the high-point of Egyptian discovery, he arrived at Thebes. He excavated the tombs of Hatshepsut and Tuthmosis IV of the eighteenth Dynasty, discovered the cenotaph tomb of Mentuhotep I of the Eleventh Dynasty, and installed electric lighting and iron doorways at some of the tombs in the Valley of the Kings, and at the temple of Abu Simbel. He had worked at Tel al-Amarna. He spoke Arabic

Howard Carter, from a gravure.

fluently, and was admired as an excavator of the highest calibre by the great archaeologists of his day. In 1903, his hot temper brought him into conflict with his chief, Maspéro. He was involved in a brawl with drunken French tourists who demanded entry to the Serapaeum at Saqqara. A fight ensued in which Carter incited the guards to attack the French visitors. Maspéro suggested a tactful apology. Carter refused. The matter was referred to Lord Cromer, the British Resident, who ordered Carter to apologize. Again he refused. Maspéro pleaded with him to relent. But the stubborn Carter was unmoved and his unfortunate superior was forced to dismiss him.

He remained in the wilderness for four years, until Lord Carnarvon appeared on the scene. They went off together to Thebes where, in the next four years, they made important but by no means exceptional discoveries among the plundered tombs of the Valley of the Kings. In 1907 the American Theodore Davis relinquished his concession, considering the Valley 'exhausted'. Carter had worked for Davis several years earlier, clearing two tombs for him. He did not share the American's belief, or indeed Maspéro's, that further work would be wasteful of time and resources. He decided intuitively that he and his patron should dig between the tombs of Ramesses VI and Ramesses IX. The burial places of most of the rulers of the Eighteenth and Nineteenth Dynasties had been accounted for in the network of tunnels which archaeologists had dug for a hundred years, since the giant Belzoni bestrode the region. One king, however, remained an enigma in death, as he had been in life – the boy Tutankhamen, successor and reputed son-in-law of Akhenaten.

When Carter's wartime work at GHQ Cairo was summarily terminated by the military authorities, he returned to the Valley and by 1917 was ready to begin a task which would make him, even at the moment of Woolley's great discoveries in Mesopotamia, and the magnificent accomplishments of Evans and Halbherr in Crete, the most famous of archaeologists and, for a time at least, the most famous of men.

Carter's own account of what followed in *The Tomb of Tut.ankh.Amen*, the first part of which was published in 1923, is a literary masterpiece. In plotting the excavations, so often barren that he many times considered abandoning them, and in portaying the historical background of the royal family whose 'missing' king he sought, his prose is lucid and sustained in its power. 'Let me try and tell the story of it all. It will not be easy, for the dramatic suddenness of the initial discovery left me in a dazed condition, and the months that have followed have been so crowded with incident that I have hardly had time to think.'

Only two years before those words were written he had been digging in 'a small lateral valley' at Luxor. High up in the cliff side was the tomb of Tothmes (Tuthmosis) III which the Frenchman Loret had found in 1898. In the valley below was an empty, unfinished tomb which Carter thought the king must have abandoned because of the danger of flooding and so sent his workmen to the eyrie in the cliff above to make a resting place for his mummy. Nearby, at the lower level was the tomb of Ramesses VI. As he began to investigate the boulders and ancient workmen's huts at the foot of the tomb he noted 'a kind of superstitious feeling that in that particular corner of the Valley one of the missing kings, possibly Tut.ankh.Amen [he always divided Egyptian proper names into their constituent parts], might be found'.

He arrived at Luxor on 28 October 1922 to resume the work he left in the previous season. By 1 November he had taken on his workforce and was ready to begin. Carnarvon was at home in England. Carter had stopped work at the north-east corner of the Ramesses tomb, and from that point he started to trench southwards.

At the back of his mind was the evidence of conflict between Khamwase, Vizier of Upper Egypt, and Peser and Pewero, senior officials of the effete Twentieth Dynasty of Egypt, during which tomb robbery was rife. 'To people of our class what do the tombs of private individuals matter?', one was reported as saying to another in a papyrus found at Thebes. From the translations of the

American scholar Breasted, he recalled the confessions of prisoners: 'There was a numerous list of amulets and ornaments at its throat; its head had a mask of gold upon it; the august mummy of this king was overlaid with gold throughout. Its coverings were wrought with gold and silver, within and without; inlaid with every costly stone. We stripped off the gold . . . We found a king's wife likewise . . . We set fire to the coverings . . . We divided the gold which we found on these two gods . . .'. Such riches would surely not survive the avarice of thirty centuries.

The way was blocked by the workmen's huts which covered the ground in front of the entrance to the tomb of Ramesses VI and joined up with a similar crop of buildings where Davis had been working. By 4 November the huts had been documented and removed, so that Carter could dig through the three-feet of earth beneath them. Underneath the first hut there were steps cut into the rock. He had found the steep sixteen-step route to a tomb just a few feet below the entrance to the Ramesside tomb. 'There was always the horrible possibility . . . that the tomb was an unfinished one . . . On the other hand there was just the chance of an untouched or only partially plundered tomb . . .' At the foot of the stairs he came to a sealed doorway. 'With excitement growing to fever heat I searched the seal impressions on the door for evidence of the identity of the owner, but could find no name.' He was seized by a desire to tear down the door there and then, but he recalled Petrie's words, always to exercise patience and care, never to act hastily. There was a space under the wooden lintel over the door large enough to admit a torch. He could see that the passage beyond was filled with rubble. 'It needed all my self control to keep from breaking down the doorway'. But he waited for three weeks, while he contacted his patron in England, examined the seal impressions on the door, and concealed his discovery from prying eyes. Carnarvon arrived at Luxor on 23 November with his daughter Lady Evelyn Herbert, 'his devoted companion in all his Egyptian work'.

With A.R. Callender, his chief assistant, at his side and his photographer Harry Burton waiting behind to take the first photographs of the interior of the tomb, he began next day to clear the sixteen steps and to re-examine the door seals. Dust and grime had been removed and now he could read the name *Tut.ankh.Amen* on several of them. In the next week or two the world's leading Egyptologists had joined the Carnarvon party at the Valley of the Kings. From the Cairo Museum, the Metropolitan Museum in New York, Pennsylvania and Yale, the British Museum and the Louvre, the most distinguished Orientalists of the world gathered in expectation. Hopes were dashed early on. When the door was exposed fully to the light it was apparent that there had been two successive openings and re-closings. The seal that was first noticed, with the jackal, sacred to the god Anubis who conducted the dead to the Celestial Field, had been applied to the reclosed portions of the entrance. The sealings of Tutankhamen covered the untouched part of the doorway. The tomb had been entered after it was originally sealed. There was another cause for concern. The rubbish that had filled the stairway had contained potsherds and presentation boxes, the latter bearing the names of the despised Akhenaten and Smenkhare, as well as Tutankhamen who had returned to the true faith. And there was a scarab of Tothmes III, and a fragment with the name of Amenhotep (Amenophis) III. Was all the heightened expectation to lead merely to a cache of items representative of the 'cursed' Eighteenth-Dynasty kings, brought from Amarna by Tutankhamen as keepsakes and locked away for safety?

On 25 November, the seal impressions noted and photographed, the door was opened by the removal of blocking stones, in the presence of the Chief Inspector of the antiquities department. The passage was cleared of its thousands of broken and fragmented pottery and alabster fillings. 'The day following (November 26th) was the day of days, the most wonderful that I have ever lived through, and certainly the one whose like I can never hope to see again.'

Thirty feet down from the first door another locked doorway was found. Again seal impressions were those of Tutankhamen and of the royal necropolis. Again there were signs of opening and re-closing. Davis had found a similar tomb layout nearby where he uncovered a cache of Akhenaten material, but no kingly remains. Beyond the second doorway lay the answers to all the questions that had been in Carter's mind for years and which had tormented him for the past month. Debris was cleared from the passage and with trembling hand he made a small breach in the upper corner of the doorway. An iron rod was pushed through. Beyond the space was clear, uncluttered with the filling of the other passages. With Callender, Carnarvon and Lady Herbert at his side, Carter peered through the hole.

'... presently, as my eyes grew accustomed to the light, details of the room within emerged slowly from the mist, strange animals, statues and gold. For the moment – an eternity it must have seemed to the others standing by – I was struck dumb with amazement, and when Lord Carnarvon, unable to stand the suspense any longer, inquired anxiously, "Can you see anything?" it was all I could do to get out the words, "Yes, wonderful things".' '

The Times reported the news on 30 November 1922: 'At last the dogged perseverance of Mr Carter, his thoroughness, above all, his *flair* were rewarded by the discovery, where the royal necropolis of the Theban Empire was situated, directly below the tomb of Ramesses VI, of what looked like a *cache*.' Woolley, before leaving for Ur of the Chaldees, had been asked by the *Illustrated London News* to provide its readers with the historical background to the Eighteenth Dynasty and the House of Akhenaten, of which the young Tutankhamen was part, in continuation of his description of the workmen's houses at Tel-al-

Amarna. He described how, towards the end of Akhenaten's life, Nekht, the Overseer of Public Works, and the Grand Vizier had vied for favour in the service of Aten, and the Overseer stepped into the Chief Minister's shoes, changed his name to Nekht-pa-Aten, and started to build a tomb alongside those of other courtiers in the cliffs of the sacred valley, where the soul of the sun-disc worshipper might find peace. 'But soon Akhenaten died, his new monotheism went out of favour, and his new capital was accursed.' The usurper Chief Minister ordered work on his tomb to cease and went back with the court, whence it came, to Thebes. '. . . and, as there was plenty of work to be done restoring the temples of the old religion, we may imagine him, with his name changed again, back at his old business and doing very well!'

Woolley understood the art of popular journalism, and he set the scene well for the saturation coverage that was to follow of events in Egypt in the fourteenth century BC. Carter was still hard at work, making preliminary investigations of the chambers 'closed and sealed by pious hands so many centuries ago'. It would take Carter ten years from the time he started digging in 1921 to the completion of his labours, almost exactly the span of time taken by Woolley to finish his work at Ur. It was the latter's tragedy that his remarkable discoveries went in tandem with Carter's, for nothing could ever attain the same force in the popular imagination as the resplendent golden-masked figure of Tutankhamen and the rich adornments of his tomb.

Carter worked on under an avalanche of tourists. Requests to visit the site came in their tens of thousands in the first week of the discovery. Writers, photographers and important people appeared as if descending from Egypt's translucent sky. Carter, never the best-tempered of men, was not always polite to his visitors, but nothing could dampen the new-found enthusiasm for Egyptology drummed up by the Press. The excavator was lost in his own world. He described his finds as they came into view. First, three great gilt couches, their end supports carved in the form of fabulous beasts, 'uncanny at any time: seen as we saw them, their brilliant gold surfaces picked out of the darkness by our electric torch . . . their heads throwing grotesque distorted shadows on the wall behind them, they were almost terrifying'. Two statues came into view, black, life-size figures of a king, 'gold kilted, gold sandalled, armed with mace and staff, the protective sacred cobra upon their foreheads'. And between and around those objects: 'exquisitely painted and inlaid caskets; alabaster vases, some beautifully carved in openwork designs; strange black shrines, from the open door of one a great gilt snake peeping out; bouquets of flowers or leaves; beds; chairs, beautifully carved; a golden inlaid throne . . . beneath our eyes, on the very threshold of the chamber, a beautiful lotiform cup of translucent alabaster; on the left a confused pile of overturned chariots, glistening with gold and inlay; and peeping from behind

[320]

them another portrait of a king'.

Carter was joined by Sir Alan Gardiner, Arthur C. Mace of the Metropolitan Museum of Art, Sir William Garstin, the chemist A. Lucas, draughtsmen Hall and Hauser, and a host of other experts. Princes and politicians, the famous of Europe and America, looked on, while the press reported every new development. In 1923, details of the Pharaoh's burial and the coronation throne were revealed. There was a hiatus in 1924 when Carter had a violent disagreement with the Egyptian authorities and closed the site. By then he had opened the door to the three remaining shrines, nested together, and containing the sarcophagus of the king, though it was not opened until more than a year hence. Carter could not stay away for long, however, and he returned to produce the gold state chariot, the gold coffin of the king, the mummified body revealing the shrivelled face that had been preserved for three thousand years, and the solid-gold image of Tutankhamen as Osiris, inlaid with precious stones, which quickly became the most familiar of all the artefacts of ancient civilization. That Woolley's finds at Ur were mostly a thousand years older than those of the Valley of the Kings was true enough. But the public was besotted with the young Pharaoh. Not to be outdone entirely, Alan Wace at Mycenae (engaged in the British School's third campaign) announced the reconstruction of the palace at the summit of the citadel, with its private apartments, 'among which a tank-bath, lined with red stucco, was discovered'. He wrote: 'Local rumour declares this to be the scene of the murder of Agamemnon.' The article appeared under the heading 'Mycenae in Tutankhamen's Time'.

It was a hundred years and two months after Champollion's announcement of his decipherment of the Egyptian script that Carter opened the tomb of Tutankhamen and made the young Pharaoh the most illustrious monarch in history. It was the climax of a remarkable story of archaeological endeavour.

As the work of clearing the tomb went on, Howard Carter began, with the aid of assistants and collaborators, to tell the story of Tutankhamen as it unfolded; and the excavator was modest in his claim to knowledge. Putting aside, as he wrote, the 'might have beens' and the 'probablys', little more was known after the event than was known, or guessed at, before. 'In the present state of our knowledge we might say with truth that the one outstanding feature of his life was the fact that he died and was buried'. But there were indications of more substantial facts. 'He was the son-in-law, as everyone knows, of that most written-about, and probably most overrated, of all the Egyptian Pharaohs, the heretic king Akh.en.Aten. Of his parentage we know nothing. He may have been of the blood royal and had some indirect claim to the throne on his own account. He may on the other hand have been a mere commoner. The point is immaterial, for, by his marriage to a king's daughter, he at once, by Egyptian law

of succession, became a potential heir to the throne.'

Carter traced the decline of the great empire built up in the fifteenth century BC by Tothmes III and brought close to ruin by the events of the following century. The priests of the ancient faith saw their gods flouted and their own status compromised. The soldier class, reduced to passivity, seethed with discontent. Foreign women brought to the harem became the focus of intrigue. 'And through it all, Akh.en.Aten, Gallio of Gallios, dreamt his life away at Tell al Amarna.' The question of succession was vital. Interest centred on the eldest princess, Mertaten, whose husband, Smenkhkare, became Akhenaten's co-regent, at the end of his reign. But Smenkhkare died soon after Akhenaten, if indeed he did not predecease him. No more is heard of Mertaten. The second princess in line died unmarried. The third Ankhesenpa-Aten married Tutankhamen, when both were minors; she cannot have been more than ten years old. Ay, the Court Chamberlain, took over the affairs of state and of the royal family. He was close to Akhenaten and his wife, Ti, was nurse to Akhenaten's queen, Nefertiti. Ay would marry into kingship after Tutankhamen's death, by taking the hand of his widow, and with unprecedented temerity inscribe his own name in the sepulchral chamber in the Valley of the Kings which he had almost certainly built for his predecessor; an inscription which would remain for Carter to discover three millennia later. Ay's own succession by a commoner, General Horemheb, set the stage in 'this little by-way of history', between the years 1375 to 1350 BC, 'for dramatic happenings', Carter wrote.

Was the picture anything like complete, even after the clearing of the tomb? When did Tutankhamen change his name from the heretical Tutankhaten and lead the way back to the old faith, and to the old capital at Thebes? A stela found a Karnak speaks of his concern at the dereliction of the old temples, but there is no indication of when or why his change of faith took place. And was he a delicate, perhaps effete ruler? Carter wrote: 'We know from the tomb of one of his officials that certain tribes in Syria and the Sudan were subject to him and brought him tribute, and on many of the objects on his own tomb we see him trampling with great gusto on prisoners of war, and shooting them by hundreds from his chariot, but we must by no means take for granted that he ever in actual fact took the field himself'.

And what of the wife who changed her name with him, from Ankhesenpa-Aten to Ankhesen-Amen? Graceful and, by all accounts loyal, left a widow at seventeen or perhaps eighteen years of age, she claims the popular attention almost as much as her husband. A sequel to the young king's death was found by

Opposite: Tutankhamen in gold mask.

the German excavators of the Hittite capital at Boghozkoi. In the crisis which followed her husband's death, with no legitimate heir at hand, she wrote to Suppiluliuma the Hittite king, begging him to send her a husband, that by marriage he might become the legitimate Pharaoh. 'Did the Hittite prince ever start for Egypt?' asked Carter. He added, 'We shall probably never know'. The Hittite tablets, just being translated in Berlin when Carter penetrated the tomb of Tutankhamen, revealed that Suppiluliuma despatched a prospective bride-groom, but that on the way he was ambushed by Egyptian cavalry sent by Horemheb. The well-set stage of which Carter wrote was not for heroic drama, but for 'a fascinating little tale'. Had the young queen's plot succeeded, the course of history might have changed, and as Carter asserts, 'there would never have been a Ramases the Great'. As it was, the Queen ruled shortly with Ay, the Chamberlain who claimed recognition in her husband's tomb, and then the aggressive Horemheb took over, until the throne of Egypt returned to a true line of kings.

Lord Carnarvon did not live to see more than the first fruits of the discovery which he, by money and perseverance, had made possible. As the tomb was closed at the end of the first season of clearing work, he was bitten by a mosquito. The wound became infected and he died on 6 April 1923. At almost the same time, Georges Bénédite, head of the Egyptian Department of the Louvre, was attacked by sunstroke in the Valley of the Kings and died suddenly. Arthur C. Mace, Carter's friend, adviser and literary collaborator went soon after. The kind of dark mystery which hangs so easily over Egypt and which so angered Petrie and the other pioneers of scientific archaeology, emerged once more. The curse of the house of Akhenaten, the 'angry shade' and the invocations of the gods, added the appeal of mumbo-jumbo to the majestic discoveries of Carter and his team in the public imagination. The 'Curse of Tutankhamen' entered the vocabulary of the twentieth century, and a flimsy literary edifice was built up from it.

In the between-the-wars period, when archaeology reached the zenith of discovery and its practitioners bestrode the stage like film stars or the physicians of Medici Florence, honours were freely given. In Britain, governments, universities and institutions thrust knighthoods and honorary degrees, official banquets and 'freedoms' on Petrie, Evans, Woolley, and a host of others, even on the Frenchman Maspéro. All richly deserved the rewards and the recognition. But for Carter there was tardy official response. He died in 1939 without a single prize, only the gratifying knowledge, as one writer put it, that he was 'not the least of the Pharaoh's servants'. An unrelenting professional in everything he ever attempted, with a 'characteristic belief in his own infallibility', he was not the kind of man with whom the English establishment easily comes to terms. He died, to quote again, 'denied the petty satisfaction of scrolls and ribands', but he had enjoyed a more glorious reward. He had turned back time, more dramatically than anyone before or since.

A last word on the discovery of Tutankhamen deserves to be said by the man who introduced Carter to Egypt, Percy E. Newberry, who was in charge of the Archaeological Survey of Egypt when Carter was an apprentice to the great men of the profession. In February 1923 he wrote:

> The contents of the tomb make us realise the vast amount of wealth that at one period was buried in the subterranean chambers of the desolate Valley of the Tombs of the Kings. Certainly twenty-five monarchs were interred here, and Tutankhamen was one of the least important of them. His funeral furnishings, wonderful as they really are, probably could not have compared with the funeral outfits of such mighty kings as Thotmes III, Amenhotep III, the 'Magnificent', or Rameses 'the Great'. What a wealth of treasure the huge tomb of Seti I must have contained ...

As at the start, archaeology could only contemplate wistfully what might have been, were it not for the greed and acquisitiveness of mankind.

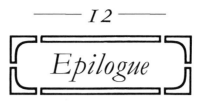

12

Epilogue

While the sagas of the Woolley and Carter camps occupied the academic world and fed the public yearning for antiquarian riches, Crete and Greece were not to be denied. Döerpfeld's work at Pylos in south-west Morea, begun in 1907, gave rise to the discovery of a prehistoric acropolis and three beehive tombs similar to those at Mycenae. By 1925, Evans had become interested in the sacked tombs. In the Homeric tradition of Aegean archaeology, the largest vault was named the 'Tomb of Nestor' and Evans, following up the depredations of the war years, traced a solid gold ring that had been 'stolen' from it. The ring's intaglio design included the tree of life and the familiar Minoan goddess and a companion, with two butterflies fluttering over them, illustrating a common theme of the ancient world – the butterfly and the *psyche*, the departed spirit. A youth with shoulder-length locks and loin-skirt, otherwise naked, emphasized the Minoan connection. Evans called it the 'Ring of Nestor ... the echo of a Minoan masterpiece'.

It transpired that the 'Ring of Nestor' was a clever fake. A leading scholar in the field, Martin P. Nilsson, wrote that in interpreting the features of the ring 'Sir A. Evans has drawn a colourful picture of Minoan mystery cult and conceptions of the after-life. It differs most markedly from other Mycenaean rings ...'. He found characteristics in the design of the ring 'which cannot be imputed to a Minoan artist or to the Minoan age'. But the decisive argument, he says, is that the engraver has misunderstood the ritual slaughtering-table, making it the pedestal of the cult image of the Lion ...'. Nilsson examined several of the most famous cultic artefacts from the Aegean and found them wanting in authenticity. He included in his list of doubtful objects a number of rings, including the Rings of 'Nestor' and 'Minos' published by Evans, a famous goddess figure at the Fitzwilliam museum in Cambridge, and three statuettes, two female and one of a boy, published by Evans, and a statuette in Philadelphia. He also reinterpreted some of the lore based on scenes at Evans's 'Griffin's Court' with its ceremony of initiation. Nilsson found *prima facie* evidence of a cult not of the long-skirted, bare-breasted goddess but of the Griffin, 'which is evidently a form of the epiphany of the goddess'.

In 1926, a Swedish expedition led by Professor Persson found an unplundered beehive tomb at Dendra, close to the great citadel of Midea in the Argolid. The royal burial ritual became clear as never before. A princess with gold rosette necklace was buried first. Then the king and queen, at opposite ends of the long grave, feet towards each other. Weapons, gold and silver bowls and signets lay beside the king. The queen wore an 'ivy-leaf' gold necklace and beside her were a lamp and an ostrich egg with gold, silver and ceramic ornamentation. An octopus cup laid on the king's breast contained a signet of exceptional size with scenes of recumbent oxen and lions tearing at bulls, the competing symbols of Mycenae and Crete. More marvellous craftsmanship and fine art came from surrounding tombs. Archaeologists found one of the richest collections of bronze vessels ever recovered from the soil of Greece, decorated with superbly incised floral, marine and geometrical themes. Another empty tomb was thought to be a cenotaph of about the time of the Trojan War, calling to mind the Homeric reference to the mounds which Achilles built for Patroclus at Troy and Menelaus for Agamemnon in Egypt; perhaps too, of Odysseus in the Underworld, when he enticed the shades of lost heroes with the blood of his sacrificial victims. A place for the lost soul to come home to and rest in peace.

Just before the outbreak of the Second World War, Carl Blegen began work at Pylos, where in the nick of time he found outside the courtyard wall an archive chamber with some six hundred tablets inscribed in the Linear-B. He returned in 1952 under the auspices of the University of Cincinnati to reveal the Palace of Nestor, and to unearth hundreds of fragments of gaily painted wall frescoes. A second archive room contained a further three-hundred tablets, mostly book-keeping and accountancy documents, in the script that was now recognized as primitive Greek.

While Blegen continued his Pylos excavations, Papadimitriou at Mycenae returned to the grave circles which revealed among the tombs of pre-Homeric Greece art works which included a unique rock-crystal bowl in the shape of a duck, and magnificent jewels lying alongside the skeletal remains of their owners.

Yet Greece, despite two centuries of intensive excavation and remarkable feats of scholarship, remains as mysterious at the present day as at the start of the great classical onslaught. The riddle which has been at the heart of European research into the past, refuses still to yield to the investigator more than buildings and grave circles, enigmatic goddesses, fragmentary works of art, and nameless bodies. Whereas the pantheons and king lists of Egypt and Western Asia are full to overflowing, documented by contemporary records, checked and cross checked by diplomatic and cultural exchange, we have only the evidence of palaces and citadels, a few translatable inscriptions which archaeologists themselves dismiss as mere 'shopping lists', and the poets with whom we set out, to attest the existence of an ancient Aegean civilisation. Perhaps we shall discover some day who were the occupants of the Mycenaean tombs, which the kings and governors who ruled Crete and Argos, Orchomenos and Pylos, Mycenae and the Troad. For the time being, as when Grote wrote his History, we can accept the traditions of the poets or dismiss them, as we please. There is not a jot of written evidence to confirm or deny their cast or the events they portrayed.

Renewed excavations between the great wars in Egypt, Asia Minor and Syria, were destined to throw into the melting pot many accepted ideas and hardy conclusions about peoples, places, and languages.

The last small room of Tutankhamen's tomb had concealed some of the most spectacular treasures of this 'modest' pharaonic burial site, including the canopic shrine and chest, which contained the king's viscera. By 1931, a public sated with the royal hatboxes, the young monarch's toys and ceremonial robes, the jackal god and the goddesses who stood sentinel outside the doors of the gilded shrine which housed the alabaster canopic chest, turned to other matters.

Pierre Montet of Strasburg University reopened the vast mound of Tanis in the Egyptian Delta, abandoned since the excavations of Mariette and Petrie. In eleven seasons, which took him to 1939, he unearthed many statues and sacrificial remains which showed how decisively this northern *nome* was exposed to Asian influence. Montet eventually revealed the tombs of the Twenty-first and Twenty-second Dynasty Pharaohs Psusennes and Orsokon. Their burials were very different from those of the Theban monarchs in their rock-cut chambers in the Valley of the Kings. The tombs of Tanis consisted of small rooms, built into layers of silt, and the Delta pharaohs were buried in the temple precincts of their gods.

Sais, on the other side of the Delta from Tanis, has never been properly investigated, though Herodotus asserted that the kings of the Twenty-sixth Dynasty were buried there. It is to their predecessors, the Sudanese and Ethiopian princes such as Shabaqa and Taharqa of biblical renown, that modern attention has turned. While northern Egypt was locked in battle with the Assyrians in the seventh century BC, these dark and formidable warrior kings ruled the dual monarchy of Egypt and the Sudan from Thebes. There they worshipped the ram-god Amon, built shrines to Osiris, 'Lord of Life and Eternity', erected fine monuments and buildings with lotus-papyrus columns and round-topped walls decorated with scenes of royal jubilees. They sometimes left their kingdom in the care of the sacred virgins while they retired to their homes in the land of Kush beyond the fourth cataract of the Nile. Their rule marked the last great resurgence of Egyptian art, and many scholars would rather call their period 'Ethiopian' than perpetuate the name 'Saite', implying the influence of the Greeks who came in the second half of the first millennium and assimilated into

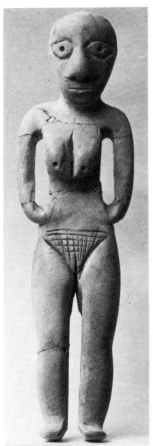

Pre-dynastic Egyptian ivory of woman, Badarian culture of 5th millennium BC.

their own pantheon the gods of the Nile. 'Osiris is he who is called Dionysus in the Greek tongue', said Herodotus.

After the Second World War, archaeology and the demands of the modern world came into head-on conflict in the lands of the dark-skinned Pharaohs of Upper Egypt and Sudanese Nubia. The search for the ancient past does not have universal sanction. It is looked on by some as a waste of resources; a reactionary activity opposed to the overt purpose of nature, which is to absorb dead matter and use it in the renewal of life, to throw a veil of dust and earth over defunct inanimate objects and thereby provide the foundations of new homes and communities. In Egypt, twentieth century reasoning was even more down to earth. The Aswan dam scheme, originally devised by the quixotic English engineer William Willcocks, was carried into effect in 1955. This political and technical miracle, enabling the cultivation of enough arable land to raise the country's agricultural production by twenty per cent, was an economist's delight and an archaeologist's nightmare. As the waters gradually rose, spreading to the heart of ancient Nubia, teams from twenty-two countries rushed to the scene to carry out hurried surveys of neglected areas and photograph every accessible building and inscription. Largely at the instigation of the French and Germans, entire temples were dismantled and rebuilt on safe ground on the banks of the new artificial lakes or on high ground.

The most famous exploit of the rescue operation was the removal of the temples and colossi of Ramesses II and his wife Nefertari cut into the rock face at Abu Simbel. The monuments and ceiling and wall reliefs were cut into sections and reassembled at the top of the cliff, attached to a concrete frame. The marvellous impression of the original rock sculpture was lost, but some of the finest feats of ancient art and workmanship were preserved.

The dam project with its great reservoirs and artificial lakes has concealed incomparable treasures for ever. Yet this immense archaeological disaster has a positive aspect. Whole regions which might otherwise have been ignored for generations have been surveyed by the most advanced photographic and scientific techniques. Geologists and anthropologists, chiefly from the United States, joined in the search. In just thirteen years prior to the completion of the scheme, hundreds of new sites were discovered. Neolithic remains and later burial sites revealed a great deal more than was known hitherto about the transition from nomadic to settled life beyond the fourth millennium BC. Nubia is now seen as a transitional culture, with distinct African attributes. At Tomas, above Abu Simbel, rock engravings show vast numbers of subtropical animals, many of them unknown in later Egyptian history. Other drawings show domesticated animals, often with pendants round their necks and with decorated hides, suggesting pastoral communities which existed in the fourth millennium.

It was an accident of the academic world rather than field discovery which gave rise to perhaps the most important advance in Egyptology at the time of the Aswan drama. The report which Petrie and Quibell had published jointly on the predynastic graves of Upper Egypt in 1896, was scanty in its detail. It seemed almost to minimise the importance and size of some of the tombs. The same could be said of Petrie's later treatise, his *Prehistoric Egypt*, published in 1920. Unfortunately, Petrie's notes and other papers were so voluminous that they presented a storage problem for his successors at University College. Margaret Murray, the student-disciple who followed him in his professorial post and lived on to the ripe age of a hundred-and-one, decided in 1932 that the Petrie papers must be disposed of in order to provide much needed space. Most, after all, had been published in the great man's lifetime. By a happy chance, the so-called 'London Box' which contained his Naqada notes survived this archaeological holocaust. They remained concealed beneath a telepone box and were re-discovered in 1969. Elise Baumgartel, a student of prehistoric Egypt, made good use of them. She analysed much of the unpublished material from both Petrie's and Quibell's excavation notes. She, like the academic world at large, realised that the 1896 report did scant justice to the master's immense labours. All the same, Miss Baumgartel pointed to 'serious defects' in Petrie's sequence dating. Classes of pottery used as the foundation of his system are 'now known to have ranges different from those originally assigned to them', she wrote in 1970. Baumgartel's own assessment came under critical scrutiny within a short time, and she was accused of 'the same shortsightedness as Petrie' in ignoring the Palaeolithic cultures, and of making 'short shrift' of co-existent but differing predynastic cultures in the Delta and the Fayum. According to the American archaeologist and writer Michael A. Hoffman, she had compounded the error of prehistorians before and after her who 'saw the uniqueness of the culture that arose in the Nile Valley after the coming of the Neolithic Subpluvial', but failed to understand 'how such an artistically precocious people could be tied to their neighbours in the Delta and the peoples of the desert frontiers'. Nevertheless, her work on the posthumous papers vindicated the general lines of Petrie's prodigious work among the mass graves of Naqada which preceded the building of Memphis and Thebes, and enabled the sequences of late Neolithic and Chalcolithic societies to be placed in order and dated with at least approximate accuracy. It was, after all, Petrie's persistent work which made possible an understanding of the slow evolutionary progress from the first Badarian farming communities of the sixth millennium, through the Amratian and Gerzean periods, to the distinctive, unalterable, immensely conservative and bureaucratic tradition of dynastic civilization in the Nile Valley. The true significance of Naqada was finally appreciated seventy-five years after the discovery of the graves with their evidence of sacrificial practices which, it now seems, occurred in predynastic and early dynastic Egypt on something like the same scale as those of Woolley's Ur. Human sacrifice, as part of the ritual of royal burial, must have occurred at the extremes of the fertile crescent over a time-span of some two thousand years.

The Germans under Hermann Junker extended Petrie's work in the realm of prehistory, searching for remains beyond the Naqada period in an atmosphere of increasing rivalry between the Egyptians and their guest excavators. The new nationalism was not inimical to Junker, however. His predecessor, the great Ludwig Borchardt from whom he took over in 1929, was implacably opposed to the National Socialist regime, but Junker accommodated himself to both Berlin and Cairo. In the chauvinistic rivalry of the 1920s, there had been fierce debate about the rightful ownership of one of the finest of all Egyptian artefacts, the Nefertiti head which Borchardt found in the artist's studio at Amarna. It remained in Berlin.

The American George Reisner, who excavated the Kushite sites of Meroe and Napata from 1916 to 1923, and the British pioneers of Sudanese archaeology John Garstang and Frank Griffith (assisted briefly by Woolley), showed that these Nubian sites were not only the southernmost centres of Nile civilisation, but also pivots of industry in the last centuries of the first millennium BC. Immense metal deposits show that Meroe was, in Garstang's words, 'the Birmingham of Africa'. The pyramids of Meroe and Napata have much in common with their Egyptian counterparts. So have the burial sites. Towards the beginning of the fourth century BC, when the new Abyssinian dynasty of Axum came to deliver a death blow to the declining Meroitic Empire, Roman influence was apparent in the dominance of Isis over Osiris, the pre-eminence of goddess over god characteristic of the Mediterranean devotion to Isaic cults.

There is a leap of some nine centuries from the brief, creative despotism of the Ethiopian pharaohs to the builders of the astonishing structures of early Christianity discovered in the Nubian desert by the Polish expedition led by Michalowsky in 1960. Buried beneath the sand of Faras, on the present-day Egypt-Sudan border, was the entire cathedral of Pachoras. Another church was revealed nearby. A vast basilica, magnificently covered in murals portraying the virgin and the archangels, the three Israelites in the fiery furnace, three kings dressed in the Parthian manner, and many other subjects, was uncovered. The Christian era is outside the boundary of this essay, yet Michalowsky's must be accounted one of the most remarkable of the archaeological discoveries which came in the wake of the Aswan project and the rush to the cataracts of the Nile. Even more recent work in the region of ancient Ethiopia has brought to light a Sabaeo-Ethiopian period. Close to Axum, the mound of Gobochela contained a sanctuary dated provisionally fifth century BC, dedicated to the South Arabian moon-god Almaqah. Inscriptions in the finely carved writing of the Sabaeans, and the magnificent craftsmanship of the Ethiopians, exemplified by some beautifully carved bull-figures, show how powerful were the cross currents of trade and cultural exchange in these remote reaches of the Nile from the eighth to the fifth centuries BC.

By the close of the Second World War, French archaeology had been officially represented in Egypt for almost a century and a half. The Palestine exploration societies of America, Britain, Germany and France had been prospecting and digging for the best part of a hundred years, and the major European powers had supported well established schools in Greece since the 1840s. Iraq, though

Ivory from Nimrud in the 'Syrian' style'; Mallowan, who found it, dubbed it 'Mona Lisa' This lady with the enigmatic smile could be the goddess Astarte, the Phoenician Ishtar.

organized excavation had gone on there for almost exactly a hundred years, was not represented by an organized professional body until 1932.

Gertrude Bell, who died in Baghdad in the summer of 1926, between Woolley's fourth and fifth seasons at Ur, left to the Trustees of the British Museum six thousand pounds for the creation of a British School of Archaeology in Iraq. Six years later, the School was formed as the 'Gertrude Bell Memorial'. Its accomplishments in the fifty years which followed were considerable. Max Mallowan, its director in the last seven years of his life, said at the 'Silver Jubilee' exhibition opened by Sir Leonard Woolley in 1956, that 'only a moron could fail to be roused' by its achievements. The fiftieth anniversary celebrations in 1982 marked some of the most important archaeological discoveries of the twentieth century. Iraq was not by any means a British pasture, however.

In 1929, Chicago's Oriental institute under James Breasted extended its activities from Egypt to Iraq, financed by the Rockefeller Foundation. It completed the work which Botta had started almost a hundred years before at Khorsabad, and then moved on to new sites in the Diyala region, east of Baghdad. There, under the direction of Henri Frankfort, Sumerian shrines were unearthed at the mounds of Asmar, Khafajah and Agrab. Great quantities of sculpture from the third millennium BC were recovered. Such finds were reinforced by the work of the Germans at Warka (Uruk), and Stephen Langdon's Oxford team at Kish. The Germans devised a probing method which gave a new thoroughness to field enquiry and was quickly adopted by the other Iraq teams. When they had excavated to what was thought to be the lowest level of occupation, they sank a shaft which penetrated even deeper, through all the levels of habitation as revealed by pottery typical of each sequence, until they reached clean soil of the pre-pottery Neolithic period. Thus they gradually pushed back the known levels of occupation to the seventh millennium BC.

A striking similarity was noted between the pre-Sumerian pottery finds at all the most ancient sites — Ur, Warka, Kish; extending eventually to the Assyrian sites to the north. In every case, three pre-Sumerian phases were evident, suggesting an almost uninterrupted social evolution. The first of these phases, the 'Ubaid' (4000–3500 BC), was represented by pottery with a greenish body and black-painted abstract designs of fine quality on the unglazed surface. The earliest inhabitants, probably from the Iranian highlands, had built themselves reed huts on fertile 'islands' among the marshes where the Tigris and Euphrates came together. The second phase, given the name 'Uruk' from the site where it was first recognised (3500–3000 BC), was typified by undecorated pottery. It represented a culture typical of Woolley's Phase I at Ur. Already, temples were being built of mud-brick and decorated with a primitive mosaic. The first pictographic writing was evident on inscribed tablets signed with cylinder seal impressions. The first relief sculptures appeared. Then, named from Langdon's site of Jamdat Nasr near Kish, a painted pottery with applied decoration in two colours, with elaborate geometrical patterns appeared in temples and graves. This phase (3000–2800 BC), suggested a new immigration wave from the Iranian region.

These pottery phases, representing the so-called 'Chalcolithic', were soon in need of revision. Von Oppenheim's site at Tel Halaf, produced its brilliantly painted polychromatic pots, which took the sequence of habitation, covering the vast area from the lower Tigris westward to the Mediterranean, back beyond 4000 BC. Thus, Phase I became the 'Halaf', and the other sequences were renumbered.

In 1931, Mallowan had left the Ur excavations to resume work at Nineveh for the British Museum. Beneath the foundations of an Assyrian temple he sank a shaft to virgin soil some seventy feet below. In a dark and narrow pit just before he reached clean soil, eleven potsherds with primitive scratched design were found. He had reached the very earliest, unnamed level of civilized habitation. In 1928, Dorothy Garrod of Cambridge University had found traces of Palaeolithic man in the Kurdish mountains. From there, sometime during the five thousand years which preceded the first civilized habitations, people had wandered in the Tigris valley. After seven thousand years or more the remnants of their camp fires and household articles remained.

In the 1940s when the rest of the world was at war, a new-generation team of Iraqi archaeologists went to Tel Uqair, south of Baghdad, where they found the well-preserved remains of a temple of the proto-literate period, its walls covered with painted frescoes. They went on to Hassuna on the Tigris. The surface was littered with pottery such as Mallowan had found at the lowest occupied level of Kuyunjik. The 'Hassuna', for the moment at least, marked the earliest chapter of communal life, taking the record back to 5000–4500 BC.

Soon after the end of the Second World War, Max Mallowan as field director of the British School in Iraq, led the procession back to the great sites of Assyria, most of which were thought to have been exhausted by the pioneer excavators, but which were yet to divulge many treasures and much information. By that time, antiquarian research was about to pass from royal to republican stewardship, and to face the hazards of a series of violent revolutions and wars. For the next thirty years, under the direction of stalwart Iraqi directors, who succeeded to the role of Gertrude Bell, field research and the enrichment of the great Baghdad Musuem proceeded in defiance of political upset, bombs and rockets. Led by the British school, Europeans returned to the scene as guest excavators, and soon literally hundreds of sites were being investigated, some as a matter of urgency. In the Hamrin basin, for example, a dam project threatened a repetition of the Aswan catastrophe, and hurried digging at Suliemeh produced some unique cylinder seals of the Early Dynastic period (2500–2300 BC), one showing what was probably the first ever scene of a ploughing formation – four people and two quadrupeds; others illustrated ritual scenes, including a goddess whose throne seemed to consist of a human figure bending over a heap of hay.

Nimrud, where Mallowan went first, proved a rewarding site. Between 1949 and 1963 the British expedition there produced some of the most remarkable finds of twentieth century archaeology. There was the yellow-stone stela from Ashurnasirpal's throne room, which Layard had missed by a few feet, recording the astonishing bean feast which marked the inauguration of the new Palace; and telling of the king's conquests and achievements in the ninth century, and of the manner in which the new city was populated with deportees from eight tributary lands. A cache of tablets forming part of the voluminous correspondence of Assyrian kings was found at Layard's North-West Palace, valuable for their accounts of subject territories in the seventh century, when the Assyrian Empire ruled a stretch of the world from Egypt to Persia. The same palace, built on a massive platform within the citadel, divulged magnificent bronzes, jewelry and sculpture, and a collection of ivories which were manifest wonders of ancient craftsmanship. Many of these fragmentary masterpieces came from furnishings. Among them was the lady nicknamed 'Mona Lisa', with stained black hair, eyes and brows, and her companion, dubbed the 'Ugly Sister'. And there was a more elaborate and exceptionally beautiful pair of ivory plaques showing a lion killing an African under a floral canopy. Gold, lapis and carnelian inlays, partly worn away, decorated these sumptuous works, typical of the many masterpieces that came from wells into which they were probably thrown in those final moments of panic when Kalhu-Nimrud was sacked by the Medes in 614 and 612 BC.

In 1852, Commander Felix Jones, Rawlinson's companion at Behistun, had surveyed Nimrud and its surroundings, and he showed in the south-east corner of the city a fortified area which was the arsenal of Shalmaneser III; Fort Shalmaneser. There, Mallowan found a throne dais carved on its sides with scenes of tribute and at its front with the friendly meeting of the kings of Assyria and Babylon, presented to the King by the city's governor. At the fortress they found the largest number of carved ivories (exemplifying a distinct native style and also Egyptian, Syrian and Phoenician-Palestinian influences), beautifully coloured glazed-brick panels and many more documents containing new versions of ancient classical tales, details of temple functions, and the arrangments for succession to the doomed throne of the Empire.

In the 1970s the republican government of Iraq began to turn Nimrud into a major tourist attraction, and a decade later it decided to restore Babylon to its ancient glory. The first scheme was well advanced by the outbreak of the protracted war with the old enemy, Iran. There is irony of an unusually poignant kind in the contemporary battles which rage over deserts, marshes and mountains which Elamites and Sumerians, Medes, Babylonians and Assyrians, Achemenians, Seleucids and Parthians contested, on and off, for three thousand years before the beginning of our own era. Those battles have delayed the intended restoration of Babylon, but if the Iraqis ever succeed in their ambitious plan, they will give back to the world two of the seven ancient wonders adumbrated by the Greeks: the great double walls of the city and the Hanging Gardens whose miracle of suspension Koldewey had envisaged in his reconstruction plan. They will have to rebuild the great ziggurat and many splendid temples, and the immense forts at the north of the city where the quay wall, designed to prevent a river-borne invasion, was measured by Gertrude Bell in 1911; she

Urartian bronze bull, found near Lake Van. c.700 BC.

found it to be twenty-two metres thick. With all its resources, the modern world will not find such a task easy.

In 1956 Mallowan moved on to Balawat, scene of Rassam's controversial dig in 1878. Further excavation made possible the identification of the temple of Mamu, where Rassam had found a stone coffer and tablets of Ashurnasirpal II. A third pair of gates overlaid with bronze was found and an Ashurnasirpal tablet told of their construction of cedar in the Mamu temple, fastened 'with bronze bands and hung in its doorways'. The present-day archaeologist Dr David Oates, whose wife Joan assisted Mallowan at Balawat, suggests that the two pairs of gates found by Rassam were incorporated in a palace, and were part of the courtyard entrance to two reception rooms built by Ashurnasirpal II and Shalmaneser III respectively.

But some of the most significant digs of the post-Second-World-War period have been on the other side of the Euphrates, in present day Syria, and the stretch of territory which sweeps north-west through ancient Canaan, Phoenicia and Palestine; giving substance as it were to the belly of the fertile crescent. Excavation had been spasmodic in Syria since 1888 when Felix von Luschan discovered the Iron Age settlement of Sam'al at the mound of Zenjirli, one of the 'cities of the plain' of Joshua. There had been earlier soundings at Byblos, Sidon, Tyre and Arwad by a French expedition of 1860 under Ernest Renan, and there were the Henderson-Hogarth expeditions at Carchemish. These enterprises gave rise to valuable artistic finds but to few useful written records. It was texts from other sites, particularly the Middle Hittite documentation of Hattusa (Boghazkoi), that eventually revealed the true importance of Carchemish in the imperial Hittite period from the fourteenth century, and the time of the Amorite dynasties in the early eighteenth century BC.

Tel Halaf, situated between the two rivers and essentially Mesopotamian in geographical terms, was shown eventually to have been a capital city of the Aramaean period. But dating – based on comparative architectural methods in which Koldewey's assistants lent a helping hand – was misleading. Von Oppenheim insisted on dating some of the reliefs found there to the fourth millennium BC. Aesthetic prejudice gave rise to a discrepancy of two millennia. The ancient architectural works of Tel Halaf were shown to be no earlier than the tenth century BC (though pottery finds at the site were indeed of the fourth to fifth millennia).

At the end of the nineteenth century, Petrie, assisted by the American J.F. Bliss, had laid the foundations of stratigraphic archaeology at Tel al-Hesi in southern Palestine, a technique of architectural disclosure and artefact dating that Kathleen Kenyon would carry to near perfection at Jericho. Between those excavations, discoveries of monumental importance awaited the diggers' spades and trowels.

The discovery at Ras Shamra on the Mediterranean coast of ancient Ugarit by a French team under C.F.A. Schaeffer, led to the finding of cuneiform texts in an alphabetic north-west Semitic language similar to Phoenician. Schaeffer's work followed the accidental discovery of the site in 1928 when a Syrian peasant woman ploughed into a Mycenaean tomb there. Schaeffer's exploration began within a year of that discovery. Not only had people of the Aegean and Canaan mingled hereabouts; the languages and dialects of distant Semitic cultures had come into contact. Babylonian, Hittite and Hurrian texts emerged, along with sculptures, ivories and stelae, to strengthen the notion of an important late

Terracotta of woman from Habu Kabira; c.2500 BC.

Bronze Age culture – a Syrian culture – standing between the civilizations of Egypt and Asia Minor, and sharing artistic, commercial and linguistic ties of the first importance.

Even Ugarit was overshadowed by the announcement in 1935 of the finding of hundreds of charred inscribed potsherds at Tel al Duweir, or ancient Lachish, the Canaanite site which Petrie believed he had found in 1890 at Tel al Hesi. Excavations carried out by the Wellcome Archaeological Research Foundation beneath the Persian level of the township revealed the first personal documents in pre-exilic Hebrew writing. Because the letters were written on pottery they survived the flames which eventually destroyed Lachish, when Nebuchadnezzar brought the Judaean kingdom to its end in 586 BC. Here was a city close enough to biblical legend to invest the discovery with public appeal. 'We now know how the ancient books of Kings and Prophets were written,' said Professor Harry Torczyner of Jerusalem University. The 'loving penmanship' of the Hebrew scribes in the Phoenician-Hebrew language, the original language of the Pentateuch, was another milestone of twentieth century archaeology.

The excavation of related sites in the Jewish and Christian holy lands, such as Hazor and Megiddo, was resumed by Israeli archaeologists after 1948. It was another Mycenaean connection – pottery on this occasion – which made it possible to date destruction levels consistent with an Israeli conquest in the thirteenth century, about the time of the Trojan war.

In 1933, a French team under Parrot moved from Larsa to Tel Hariri on the Euphrates, which the American W.F. Albright had nominated some years before as the probable site of ancient Mari. Sure enough, they found Mari. And they made more discoveries that indicated a fundamental stage in the development of the ancient Near East. In the course of excavations that have gone on until the present day they have laid bare one of the principal Mesopotamian settlements of the period of Hammurabi of Babylon, who eventually conquered and destroyed Mari in about 1760 BC. The official archives have provided correspondence dating from the reigns of Yasmah-Addu, son of the Assyrian king Shamshi-Adad I (1813–1781 BC), and of the last King of the city, Zimri-Lim. These documents prove a close contact with the north Syrian and Anatolian states, but little communion with powerful southern Mesopotamian neighbours whose culture Mari shared.

The revelations of the French at Mari, which continues to emerge after fifty years of digging, were complemented by those of Mallowan and the British School in the Khabur and Balikh river basins of Upper Mesopotamia from 1933 onwards. The region they excavated had established contacts with the important centres of north-west Iran, the Tigris valley and northern Syria from about 3500 to 2100 BC. During the second millennium, it was on the cross roads of Assyria and Cappadocia, where Old Assyrian trading posts were established. At Chagar Bazar in the Khabur basin there was evidence of an important predynastic settlement which developed during the proto-historic or (Jamdat Nasr) period into a major centre of Bronze Age culture, typified by monochrome painted pottery with geometrical patterns. At Tel Brak nearby, red pottery, locally produced, was similar to wares made at Sumer and Elam. Here was a flourishing township of the Uruk period. A sacred building, the 'Eye Temple' had much in common with the temples of Sumerian Uruk, but it had been rebuilt in the proto-historic period. Even more importantly, a great palace was unearthed, built by Naram-Sin, king of Akkad. The palace had been destroyed soon after it was built and reconstructed in the time of Ur-Nammu, founder of the Third Dynasty of Ur.

While Mallowan's work progressed, Woolley was excavating Tel Atchana in the Orontes valley. Here was ancient Alalakh, once a vassal city of the Amorite rulers of Aleppo, a middle-late Bronze Age centre. Woolley gave it a much earlier date than could possibly be substantiated. But its significance was considerable. All administrative documents were written in Akkadian, confirming the international currency of this language throughout the Amorite kingdoms of the second millennium, from southern Mesopotamia to northern Syria.

By the 1960s, the rediscovery of ancient Syrian civilization was in full flood. The fertile crescent, once seen more as a pair of horns dipping, as it were, into the Nile at one end and the Persian Gulf at the other, began to assume the look and shape of a luminescent half-moon.

Moortgat at Tel Khuera and Italians under Paolo Matthiae at Tel Mardikh revealed cultures of the third and second millennia respectively, with signs of Hurrian and Amorite occupation. The work of the Italians at Mardikh, identified as ancient Ebla, abut forty miles south of Aleppo, was a linchpin of Near Eastern archaeology. Excavations began there in 1964 under the auspices of the University of Rome. The name Ebla, familiar from the records of Sumer-Akkad, was found on a statue which was discovered in 1968. Not until 1973 did they reach the level of the ancient city itself, burned down in about 2000 BC. A year later they found forty cuneiform tablets, and in 1975 the royal archive was discovered. Ebla was a thriving centre of trade and industry whose foundations were contemporary with Ur and the other great cities of Sumer, going back to the fourth millennium. Fine architecture, ornaments and seals came from the Early Bronze Age level, along with some 15,000 clay tablets in an archaic Semitic language. The discovery of Ebla, close enough to the axis of biblical history to rekindle the flames of nineteenth-century enquiry, caused the biggest stir since Arab tribesmen produced the Dead Sea Scrolls from the caves of Qumran in 1947. An archaeologist working at Abu Salabikh in Iraq, had found Sumerian tablets which closely parallelled those of Ebla. Indeed, about a hundred of the Ebla texts were already known from both Fara and Abu Salabikh. All three sites gave up lexical texts of the third millennium which both illuminated and confounded existing ideas as to the development of language from its early logo-syllabic forms to alphabetic systems. The Abu Salabikh texts had also revealed another Sumerian myth concerning Lugalbanda and Nin-sun, parents of Gilgamesh, though in tantalizingly broken form.

Almost inevitably, academic controversy accompanied these spectacular discoveries. While journalists, particularly in America, drew vivid parallels between names in the new-found 'Eblaite' language and the Old Testament, experts in the cuneiform scripts were at pains to point out that the records of early Ebla were a thousand years older than Abraham. Matthiae and his epigraphist,

Giovanni Pettinato, disputed the history and chronology of the ancient Near East. They were admittedly at odds over a mere century or two in several thousand years, but differences of opinion were to break out into open hostility of a kind familiar to students of archaeology. The usual gladiatorial roles were reversed this time, the field archaeologist insisting on a later date than the philologist.

Pettinato preferred to date the archive to about 2500 BC, Matthiae the Akkad Period, a century or two later. In 1977, an Egyptian vase was discovered at the Royal Palace of Ebla, inscribed with the name of Pharaoh Pepi I, whose reign is thought to have straddled the kingships of Sargon of Akkad and the latter's grandson Naram-Sin, between the years 2334 and 2218 BC. It is quite probable that Naram-Sim destroyed the palace, since he boasted in an Akkadian document that no king had conquered Ebla since the creation of man. Pettinato, however, denies that Naram-Sin was the destroyer. The dispute was still in the air when, in 1982, the Instituto Universitario Orientale met in Naples to hear the momentous news of the first bilingual dictionary in human history, a compilation of 1500 cuneiform signs and symbols indicating the same words in Sumerian, the pre-Semitic language of Mesopotamia which Rawlinson, Hincks and Grotefend had pondered over a century before, and the Semitic Eblaite. The relationship of Eblaite to other Semitic languages, and implicit biblical synonyms, will occupy cuneiform scholars and a much larger public for many a year to come.

The directorate of antiquities at Damascus, successor to the inter-war authority of France, launched an appeal in 1967 for the rescue of sites threatened by the dam project in the Euphrates Valley. Several teams moved into an area at the centre of which was present-day Tabqa. In 1970 UNESCO took over responsibility for the operation. At Meskene nearby, a French expedition under J.C. Marguèron's direction discovered ancient Emar, a centre of great importance under the Hittites in the thirteenth century BC, rebuilt in the fourteenth century (some way from its original site) on a bend of the Euphrates. Its chief yield was its architecture; temples of unusual construction, three-roomed houses with stepped terraces. Tel Mumbaqat, higher up on the other side of the river, showed clear links with Emar. There, the Deutsche-Orient Gesellschaft under Heinrich, and later under Orthmann, found a large temple similar to those at Emar, and providing information which traversed the whole of the Late Bronze Age. At Tel Fray, some twenty miles below Meskene, only a single season's digging was possible, but in that time Matthiae and the Syrian Bounni were able to reach a level at which a Bronze Age city was destroyed around the year 1250, probably by Hattusilis III during struggles between Hittites and Assyrians for control of the region. Another temple linked this city with Emar and Mumbaqat.

'Treasure of Ur', gold and lapis lion-headed eagle from Mari, c.2300–2100.

By far the most important site of this region, however, was the mound of Habuba Kabira on the opposite bank of the Euphrates from Mumbaqat. In the autumn of 1968, a German team under Ernst Heinrich began work there. An adjacent mound, Kannas, had already been investigated by a Belgian expedition

[343]

under Finet. A year later, Heinrich was able to say that, 'Habuba contained strata representing phases of habitation from the first half of the second millennium to the fourth millennium.' Excavations over the next five years gradually revealed one of the largest and most important centres of the Protodynastic Period at the end of the fourth millennium.

In 1973 Eva Strommenger-Nagel of the Deutsche Orient-Gesellschaft took charge of perhaps the most important dig undertaken by that institution since the great days of Babylon and Assur. Heinrich and she between them unearthed pottery and artefacts which corresponded to an advanced stage of the Uruk period. A rectilinear mud-brick wall with quadrangular towers suggested an Uruk III date. Temple buildings, both at Habuba Kabira and Kannas recall a three-part structure characteristic of temples found at level IV of Uruk, with the distinctive architectural feature of a nave cut by a transept. Similar design features were discovered by Dutch excavators at another Euphrates site, Jabal Aruda. Perhaps more than any other Syrian site, Habuba Kabira produced through its pottery and furnishings, even its playthings, and in particular its cylinder seals, a composite picture of the lives of ordinary people in the world of four to five thousand years ago. The potter and silversmith at work, the musician playing the lyre; the wild-boar hunt; carved stonework; terracotta figures; red and white stone 'sparklers' for the 'woman in the street'; gorgeously imperfect plaster reliefs. The city has been magnificently recreated in a model at the Museum of Pre- and Early History in Berlin.

The completion of the Tabqa Dam project by Syrian and Soviet engineers in 1974 left some sites intact on the boundaries of a great new lake. Others were submerged for ever. But by then, the map of the ancient Near East had been filled in at its centre. The progress of civilization, once seen essentially as the projection of Egyptian and Sumero-Akkadian cultures from the tips of the cresent towards its centre, was now visible in another light. Kathleen Kenyon, taking up the earlier work of Garstang at Jericho, had traced the occupation of the Palestine region back beyond 8000 BC.

Nomad hunters had settled during the late Neolithic and had become an established urban society by the period of transition from copper to bronze usage, the Chalcolithic. By about 3000 BC urban habitations had spread across the vast area between the mountains of central Asia and the Red Sea, between the Mediterranean and the Persian Gulf. The land became a golden ocean of wheat and barley, watered by a network of canals. Animals were domesticated and the land husbanded, and men milked their cattle in the open field. Lion and antelope wandered in the wild, birds of prey stalked the air, water-buffalo swam in the rivers. The bow had long been in use, to assist the hunter in the pursuit of game and precious ivory. Science and medicine thrived and social life was sustained and

Sphinx from Etruscan tomb painting.

improved by untold thousands of workshops using eternal techniques of metalwork, pottery, carving and painting, communicating at first by pictographic scripts, then by consonant-representation of the sounds of the human voice, and finally by flexible alphabetic patterns of writing.

The tide of that life may have ebbed and flowed across the land masses of Asia Minor, the eastern Mediterranean and north-west Africa. City may have succeeded to city and empire to empire. But for much of three thousand years the first civilizations were no less stable than those that followed, and their creative achievements were, by any standard, astonishing.

What we now know of early civilizations in these fertile lands derives from many sources: from the 'official' record, as it were, written by priests and paid scribes on hundreds of thousands of clay tablets and the glyptic works of skilled craftsmen, and from visual arts and literature, telling in allegory, myth and legend of fears and aspirations, religious and social customs, alliances and enmities. Many of those sources had long suggested that the story of urban life did not necessarily begin or end in a compact region of the world, nicely defined by ocean and river boundaries.

In 1925 Sir John Marshall, director of archaeology to the government of India, began to excavate sites in the Indus Valley and the westward region of Baluchistan. Within a few months he announced the discovery of what he called, provisionally, an 'Indo-Sumerian' culture. He did not expect to find anything 'as magnificent as the royal tombs or temples of early Egypt', but he doubted that either Egypt or Sumer had anything to offer comparable with the 'average type of citizen's houses' which he and his eight hundred workmen were uncovering in great numbers at Mohenjo-daro and Harappa.

Among the most interesting finds were engraved stamp-seals, some rectangular and others rounded in shape and engraved with beautifully drawn images, many representing the Brahmani bull, others elephants, tigers, rhinoceros, and fabulous creatures. These miniature works of art, said Marshall, recalled 'the best glyptic efforts of Mycenaean Greece'. Nearly thirty years later, after Sir Mortimer Wheeler had taken over the excavations of the Indus Valley, a Danish team under Peter Vilhelm Glob went to the Persian Gulf to search for that place which Sumerian legend had spoken of so often: Dilmun, whose ships took wood 'as tribute from foreign lands' to Ur-nanshe, king of Lagash in about the middle of the third millennium.

Dilmun, of which the Nippur tablets in their rhapsody of Enki and Ninhursag, say:

> The holy cities – present
> them to him,

> The land of Dilmun is holy.
> Holy Sumer – present it to
> him,
> The land of Dilmun is holy.

It was known as the 'Land of the Crossing', 'The Land where the Sun Rises', 'The Land of the Living'. Other references in the legends of Sumer refer to Magan, to the sinking of 'the Magan-boat', and Sargon the Great recorded that the boats of Magan, Meluhha and Dilmun rode at anchor in the harbour of his capital, Agade (or Akkad). The myth *Enki and the World Order* links Dilmun and Magan, whose ships brought silver and gold to Nippur for Enlil, 'the king of all the lands'.

The Danish archaeologists found Dilmun in the Persian Gulf, at Bahrain, where they uncovered temples and ceremonial remains at Barbar, a site which Captain E.L. Durand had visited in 1878 and where he found an inscribed stone bearing the pious words of the man Rimum, describing himself as the 'servant' of Inzak, Dilmun's tutelary divinity. Sir Henry Rawlinson had translated the inscription. The Danes also found an outpost of this ancient and holy centre on Failaka island off Kuwait. At both places, numerous seals of the Indus Valley variety were discovered. Occasionally, such seals were found in the Iraq cities, and even in northern Syria and the Aegean. So too, cylinder seals characteristic of Mesopotamia were found in the Indus cities and at Bahrain and Failaka. It is certain that those Gulf islands were part of the land of Dilmun, whose ships voyaged so far afield, whence Ziusudra in the Sumerian version of the Flood story was transplanted by the gods. But did they constitute Dilmun in its entirety?

Kramer, the foremost of Sumerologists, is sceptical. He has argued that 'Dilmun may turn out to include the region in Pakistan and India where a remarkable urban, literate culture flourished towards the end of the third millennium BC, the so-called Harappan, or Indus Valley culture.' Unfortunately, the language of the Indus Valley civilization has so far resisted all attempts at translation. It has no convenient bi-lingual inscriptions. We know only that its contacts with Sumer and Akkad were close. Kramer has also pointed to 'southwest Iran' as a possible geographical location of Dilmun proper. Another American scholar, Peter B. Cornwall, has argued forcibly that there can be no reasonable doubt 'that Dilmun was the island of Bahrain', the land of the two Seas as its name literally implies, the 'place where the sun rises'. Cornwall also believes that at some periods a stretch of territory on the Arabian mainland was part of Dilmun. Geoffrey Bibby, an English archaeologist who wrote the definitive account of the Danish expedition, is in no doubt that Bahrain and its Barbar culture were at the heart of Dilmun. But where was Magan, the 'place of copper'? And where Meluhha? Oman in the Gulf is a much favoured location for the former, but Kramer prefers Egypt. There is, according to Kramer, general agreement that Ethiopia is the likely site of Meluhha. Other academics, however, insist that Magan straddles the Straits of Hormuz, while Meluhha lies somewhere near the Indus Valley. And where is the 'Cedar Land' of Lugalannemendu, 'king of the four quarters of the universe'? Some say the Lebanon. Kramer says 'a land to the east of Elam', perhaps Makran, not improbably Dilmun.

The search for the urban world of the fourth millennium ends, as it began, with disagreement. Perhaps the vital facts are concealed somewhere beneath sea or river waters, or embedded in silt. The locations of lost empires, like the conundrums that gave impetus to the unveiling of the ancient world in the nineteenth century, cannot all be resolved. Carbon-14 dating (reliable within a century or two beyond the fourth millennium BC), to say nothing of the computer and the international cross-checking it makes possible, bring us ever closer to the historical marrow.

In October 1984 one of hundreds of man-made satellites orbiting the earth completed a three-day programme in which all the world's deserts were surveyed by X-ray photography in a search for lost cities. At about the same time, a computer study at the California Institute of Technology set out to determine the exact dates of planetary alignments on a Parthian limestone slab (known as the Cerberus Slab) from the temple shrine a Hatra, where Ainsworth, Layard and Rassam had reconnoitred in 1841. Scientists working with Vladimir S. Tuman and his Assyriologist wife in California were able to determine a precise date for the inscription of the slab, the middle of the first century AD, and to deduce clear astronomical meanings from symbols which had hitherto been interpreted as pure religious iconography. Babylonian, Assyrian, Persian and Greek mythological influences are brought into focus. Research such as this, applied to the records of Babylon and Assyria – many of the tablets of Ashurbanipal's vast library contain astronomical data garnered from every part of the neo-Assyrian Empire – would almost certainly throw a great deal of light on natural phenomena of the ancient world and on the development of religious and mythological beliefs.

Technology, psychology and creative literature have pushed the biblical scholar and classicist from the centre of the stage in recent times. The cultic practices and legends of Mesopotamian, Nilitic and Aegean civilizations have opened up new avenues of analytical study and literary invention. Together with modern technology, such studies bring us closer in spirit if not in hard fact to that Socratic vision of a state of instictive unity with the universe; to that notion of the 'breath of life' so poignantly expressed by Bertrand Russell, 'fierce and coming from far away, bringing into human life the vastness and fearful passionless force of non-human things'. But in the end, modern resourcefulness is unlikely to do more than reinforce the humanist view of homo sapiens as the 'clever dwarf' of the animal kingdom, uniquely capable of mighty achievement and wanton destruction. As the devout cynic Chesterton put it, 'the most terrible of the beasts'.

Few statements of modern times have had quite such a shocking impact as Sigmund Freud's assertion that Moses was not a Jew at all, but an Egyptian noble of the house of Akhenaten, and that he had made the journey through the wilderness in the years immediately following the pharaoh's death, c.1358 BC, armed with the monotheism of sun-disc worship as the rudiment of the one God of Israel. Such a revolutionary view of a bedrock of Old Testament history was as unacceptable fifty years after Darwin had turned western thought on its head as it would have been in the eighteenth century. Even his proposed date was 'ridiculous'. The best-informed archaeological guess, after all, was that the tribes of Israel made their troubled journey a century or so after Akhenaten's death. Freud's theory caused the roof of academic criticism to fall about his ears, but his theory at least attempts to explain an otherwise hopelessly tenuous chapter of biblical history. Thomas Mann, traversing with most intellectuals of his day the philosophical paths of 'being' and 'existence', suggested in his novel *Joseph in Egypt* that the Patriarchs arrived at precisely the time Freud said they left, the Amarna period when Palestine and Egypt were disrupted by the incursions of the Habiru. If the Habiru were Hebrews, as most scholars believe they were, Freud's Exodus led by the Egyptian Moses must have crossed the path of the prototypical Israelites. Mann's Patriarchal force would at least have been travelling the same route. Such matters will almost certainly remain for ever in the realms of supposition and make believe. Those who follow in the tracks of archaeological discovery and seek the answers to deep questions through a knowledge of the past, like those who probe the universe itself in our own age, will always address themselves to the imponderable and the unknowable. Discovery, in terms of detail, has been immense in the two centuries of archaeological investigation which came as the response and the reaction to the Enlightenment, but many an intriguing question remains unanswered.

'Most people despise everything B.C. that isn't Greek, for the good reason that it ought to be Greek if it isn't', wrote D.H. Lawrence in 1932 of his first visit to the tombs in middle Italy of those enigmatic people the Etruscans, who bestrode east and west and whose language, though it uses the Greek alphabet, remains unintelligible to the present day. And the novelist conveyed in a single paragraph, descriptive of the Tarquinian tombs, the new dimension of aesthetic appreciation which early twentieth literature brought to archaeology: 'There is a mystery and a portentousness in the simple scenes which go deeper than commonplace life. It seems all so gay and light. Yet there is a certain weight, or depth of significance that goes beyond aesthetic beauty'. And then

> And how lovely these things have been, and still are! The band of dancing figures that go round the room still is bright in colour, fresh, the women in spotted dresses of linen muslin and coloured mantles with fine borders, the men merely in a scarf. Wildly the bacchic woman throws back her head and curves out her long, strong fingers, wild and yet contained within herself, while the broad-bodied young man turns round to her, lifting his dancing hand to hers till the thumbs all but touch.

Without a geographical anchorage, the reader could as well believe that the description was of an Egyptian or Aegean wall painting. Lawrence noted how maladroit were most European copies of Etruscan art . . . 'so Flaxmanized and Greekified'. The twentieth century critical view remains largely unimpressed by such literary outbursts.

Yet, in the labyrinth of revelation and disappointment which archaeology has opened up in the past 150 years, one overriding generality stands out; that the European heritage which came by way of classical Greece and Rome, along with the spiritual torch of Juda, had essentially eastern origins. That thought had occurred to Gertrude Bell when as a young woman she wandered in Anatolia with the great archaeologist and historian Sir William Ramsay: 'Race, culture, art, religion, pick them up at any point you please in the long course of history, and you shall find them to be essentially asiatic', she wrote in 1909. It was, in its implications, a more drastic contention than Freud's, and it appeared in a book which was written jointly with Ramsay, the most distinguished scholar of early Christian history of his time. The contention has remained largely the private property of a few Orientalists to the present day, and even they in the view of some scholars are so wrapped up in their restricted areas of specialisation that they can't see the Asiatic wood for the Aegean trees. There have, of course, been rumblings of dissent from those – and they are still in the overwhelming majority – who see the European cultural heritage as the undisputed gift of the classical world and of Judaism. But in general, each side keeps a disdainful distance. Kenneth Clark, for example, in his literary and television saga 'Civilization', made only the most perfunctory reference to Egypt and Mesopotamia before moving on to 'the miracle of Ionia and Greece'. Most modern works on the history of art bask in a warm sense of generosity when they devote a single chapter to the ancient societies. The academic world as much as the critical coterie of the visual arts seems to have become bored by arguments which, not so many years ago, caused men to disown their children and the keepers of the European conscience to send doubters to penal colonies for the good of their souls. Less radical theories than those of the cultural 'Easterners' were condemned with all the force of ecclesiastical, political and academic authority in the century or so of the Great Debate which followed Voltaire and the deist heresies.

Even in the late eighteenth century, when modern archaeology stood at the starting blocks, there was no lack of criticism of the European inheritance, or at any rate of what Europeans had made of it. Gibbon, in his testament to the fall of the Roman Empire, attracted the most famous of admonitions for his reference to that 'inevitable mixture of error and corruption' to which Christianity had been reduced by its 'long residence on earth among a weak and degenerate race of beings'. Perhaps the response of the theologian Paley – 'Who can refute a sneer?' – was merely an echo of words that had been uttered in the temples of Sumer and Akkad, Egypt and Assyria, Elam and Greece, and many another nation, in five millennia past.

Chapter Notes

Layard XII, 102; Baron C.A. de Bode XIII, 75 and 86; Layard XVI, 1; W.K. Loftus, XXVII, 120
Commander Jones. East India Company Report, Bombay 1849
Rawlinson at Behistun. Ibid; and *Transactions* of the Royal Asiatic Society: IX, v (old series), 'Extraordinary Discoveries'; XII, i (os), Persian Inscriptions at Behistun

51 Remaining language. Ibid, XII, i (os)
Cuneiform inscriptions. See Pallis, *The Antiquity of Iraq*, p. 120ff, in which the 'second' version of the texts is examined under the headings 'Median', 'Scythian', 'Elamite', 'Sakian', 'Medo-Scythic', 'Susian', 'Amardian' and 'Anzanian'

52 Hincks. Ibid, p. 121, epoch-making lecture of 9th June 1846
Hincks' background. E.F. Davidson's *Edward Hincks*, Oxford, 1933. Relations with Layard and Rawlinson, correspondence in British Museum Add Ms. 38977

54 Fox Talbot's challenge. Transactions of Royal Asiatic Society XVIII, 1 (os), Transl. of Tiglath-Pileser. Also, correspondence with Edwin Norris, Secretary of RAS, in Society's library. And Budge, *The Rise and Progress of Assyriology*, p. 92ff

55 Oppert, German by birth but French by adoption. See Pallis, ibid, p. 121–2
On translation of the cuneiform texts generally, and Sumerian, see Kramer, *The Sumerians*, Chapter 1
Oppert quoted: Cordier, *Éloge*, Paris, 1895

3 Nineveh Revealed

56 Layard's career. See Waterfield, *Layard of Nineveh*

57 Layard's attitude to Assyrian art, ibid, p. 124; and Letter to Canning, 21 April 1846, BM Add Ms. 40637. Also *Nineveh and its Remains*, II, p. 280

59 Coste, quoted. *Larousse* Encyclopedia of Archaeology, p. 163–4

61 Baron de Bode. *Geographical Journal*, Vol. XIII, p. 75

65 Layard, 'mere duplicates'. Letter of 12 September 1851 in British Museum Central Archive, Vol. XLVI of *Original Letters and papers*
Assyrian Reliefs. See Reade, *Assyrian Sculpture* (1983); and Barnett, *Illustrations of Old Testament History* (1977), and *The Sculptures of Ashurbanipal* (1976)

81 Ophir. 2 *Chron*. viii, 17
Ships of Tarshish. 1 Kings x. 22–24, 2 Chron ix. 10–11

82 Tiglath-Pileser III. Barnett and Falkner, *Sculptures of*, (1962); and *Illustrations of Old Testament History*, p. 39–52
Sargon's inscriptions. See Luckenbill's *Ancient Records of Assyria and Babylonia*; Vol. I, Assyria

90 Budge and Layard. R.D. Barnett in *Reallexikon der Assyriologie und Vorderasiatischen Archäologie* (1983, Berlin and New York)

4 The Riddle of Greece

93 Pelasgi. Herodotus, v, 68
Grote. *History of Greece,* quoted in How and Wells, *A Commentary on Herodotus,* Appendix XV

94 Thucydides, i, 22.4
Darius inscription. Herzfeld, *The Persian Empire*, p. 288–9. *Daniel* vi, 1, 120 satraps; *Esther*, i, 1, '127 provinces' Zoroaster. E. Herzfeld, *Zoroaster and His World* (Princeton, 1947)
Herodotus and Assyria. How and Wells, op. cit., Append. V-VIII. 'used Assyria and Babylon indifferently'

97 Schliemann. General refs. *His Troy and its Remains* (1875); *Ilios* (1880); *Mycenae* (1878); and, with Doerpfeld, *Bericht ueber die Ausgrabungen in Troja im Jahre 1890* (1891); Carl Schuchhardt's *Schliemann's Excavations*, trnsl. (1891); and Deuel's *Memoirs of Heinrich Schliemann*
Ekaterina. Deuel, op. cit., p. 21

99 Hissarlik. Calvert, Maclaren etc. Deuel, op. cit., p. 131

100 Consigned to rubbish heap. Cottrell, *The Bull of Minos*, p. 53

102 Omitted fom English version. Deuel, op. cit., p. 193

110 Lecture at Burlington House. *Illustrated London News*, March 31, 1877

111 Gladstone. Schliemann had dedicated the American edition of *Mycenae* to the British Prime Minister

5 Egypt and the Pharaohs

114 Savants. W.V. Davies in James, *Excavating in Egypt*, p. 51ff; and Marlowe, *Spoiling the Egyptians*, Chapter 1; J.C. Herold, *Bonaparte in Egypt*, London, 1963, p. 165ff; F. Charles-Roux, *Bonaparte Gouverneur d'Egypte*, Paris, 1910, p. 152; Johnson, *The Civilization of Ancient Egypt*, ch. 9

115 Belzoni. See his *Narrative*
Salt and Belzoni. Greener, *The Discovery of Egypt*, p. 119ff
Burckhardt and Bankes. Ibid
Drovetti. Ibid, and Marlowe, op. cit

116 Mariette. Greener, op. cit. p. 176ff; and James, op. cit., p. 51ff

117 Mariette quoted. Greener op. cit

119 Quote. ibid

121 Quote. ibid
Spiegelberg on Herodotus. Lecture 1921, see How and Wells, op. cit., p. 453

122 Memphis excavation. Greener, op. cit., p. 162ff

124 Tomb or Ka figures. See Amelia Edwards' *Pharaohs, Fellahs and Explorers*, p. 113ff; and Budge, *From Fetish to God*, p. 33 et al

125 Valery. Quoted in Philip Rawson's *Ceramics*, Oxford, 1971

126 Appraisal of arts. See Amelia Edwards, *Pharaohs etc*, and Heinrich Shaefer, *Principles of Egyptian Art*, Oxford, 1974. Also, Johnson, *op. cit.*, p. 177, 'obsequious subservience to royalty' Egyptian arithmetic. Rhind papyrus, British Museum; see Kees, *Ancient Egypt, a Cultural Topography* and

Johnson op. cit
Mariette, de Vogüe, Brugsch, Maspéro. Greener, op. cit

128 Petrie. His *Ten Years' Digging in Egypt*, and *Seventy Years in Archaeology*

129 Stillborn. His was one of the first births under anaesthesis. Mrs Drower to author
Charles Piazzi Smyth. See I.E.S. Edwards, *The Pyramids of Egypt*, p. 225

130 Early work and disputes. Correspondence in Petrie Museum, University College, London

131 Petrie and Pyramids. See his entry under 'Pyramids' in Encyclopaedia Britannica, 11th Edition. Also, his *On the Mechanical Methods of the Ancient Egyptians*, and Edwards op. cit

132 Quote, Edwards, ibid.

134 Egypt Exploration Fund (later Society). See James, op. cit
Naville. Annual Report of Fund, 3 July 1883
Petrie on Fund and Naville. Petrie Museum corresp. 11. ii. 1881 — 30. v. 1892. And his *Ten Years*

135 Embalmed corpses. Amelia Edwards, *Pharaohs* etc., p. 5

137 Chronology. Petrie, *Seventy Years*. But see account of expert divergences in Emery, *Archaic Egypt*, Introduction Pottery, Mariette and others. *Seventy Years*, p. 35

138 Herodotus. ii. See How and Wells, i, 252

140 Lydians (Ludim). *Jeremiah* 46.9
Captivity. *Jeremiah* 50.2
Naucatis and Daphnae. Cecil Smith ILN, 11 Sept, 1886

141 Linguistic interaction. See Gordon, *Before the Bible*

142 Petrie's return to Egypt. See his *A Season in Egypt*, London, 1888
Petrie and Naville. See James, op. cit., p. 18ff. 'In many ways the two men were diametrically opposed . . .'
Pithom-Succoth. ILN, August 4, 1883

143 Amelia Edwards and Old Testament.

Letter dated 21 July 1889 to Mr Thayer, Petrie Museum

144 Sothic calendar. Hall, *Ancient History*, p. 23, 'pushed back whole Sothic period of 1461 years . . . curious'; and Petrie, *A History of Egypt*, Vol. 1, p. 248ff
Edwards Professorship. Murray, *My First Hundred Years*

6 The Promised Land

146 Merenptah stela. Translation from Keller, *The Bible as History*, p. 161

147 Kean. See his *Among ther Holy Places*, London, undated

148 P.E.F. Articles of Association. First meeting held at Jerusalem Chambers, London, May 12th 1865
Warren. Annual Statement of P.E.F., 1867–69. See also his *Underground Jerusalem*, and Williams, *The Life of General Sir Charles Warren*

150 Warren to Grove. P.E.F. Report No. 1
Wilson. See Watson, *The Life of Major-General Sir Charles Wilson*
Kitchener. See Sir Philip Magnus's, *Kitchener*, London, 1958

151 Clarke and others. See H.V. Hilprecht, *Explorations in the Bible Lands During the 19th Century*, Philadelphia, 1903; R.A.S. Macalister, *A Century of Excavation in Palestine*, London, 1925; and Silberman, *Digging for God and Country*, New York, 1982
Robinson. See King, *American Archaeology in the Mid East*; and Silberman, op. cit. Chapter 5

152 Church of Holy Sepulchre. Macalister, op. cit. p. 24
Smith. Silberman, op. cit

153 Codex Sinaiticus. Keller op. cit. p. 138
Robinson's Arch. Ibid
Robinson's biographer., Roswell D. Hitchcock, *The Life, Writings and Character of Edward Robinson*, New York, 1863. And Macalister, op. cit., p. 20ff

154 Tobler and Guerin. King, op. cit., Chapter I
Jerusalem excavations. P.E.F. Quarterly

Statements
Conder. Ibid
American P.E.S. Silberman, op. cit., p. 115ff
Saulcy. Ibid, p. 66ff

156 Queen Sadan. Macalister, op. cit., p. 27

157 Moab stone. F.A. Klein, 'The Original Discovery of the Moabite Stone' in P.E.F. Quarterly Statement (1870), p. 281ff; and Silberman, op. cit., Chapter 11
House of Omri. Barnett, *Illustrations of Old Testament History*, p. 37ff
Clermont-Ganneau. See his *Archaeological Research in Palestine 1873–9*

159 Text of Moab stone. Keller, op. cit., 233
Press reports. Quoted in Silberman, op. cit., p. 108–9

161 Tyrwhitt-Drake and Palmer. See their *The Desert and the Exodus*, New York, 1872; and Walter Besant's *The Life and Achievements of Edward Henry Palmer* London, 1883
Shaikh Ahmed, quoted. Silberman, op. cit., p. 110ff
Death of APES. King, op. cit.
Merrill. Silberman, p.119; and King, op. cit., Chapter 1
Deutsche Palaestina-Verein. King, op. cit.
Petrie. King, op. cit., p. 19ff
Albright. Quoted, ibid

162 Petrie at Amarna. Petrie, Sayce, Griffith and Spurrell, *Tell el Amarna*, and *Syria and Egypt from the Tell el Amarna Letters*. And Petrie's notes to E.E.S. Exhibition of Antiquities from Tell el Amarna, July, 1921, Amarna 'name wrongly given . . .'
Akhenaten. Aldred, *Akhenaten, A New Study*

163 Letters. Giles, *Ikhnaton, Legend and History*, Intro
Royal archive. Giles, op. cit., 148–9, 'questionable' whether large number perished

164 Correspondents. Ibid, p. 158. And see Keller, op. cit, p. 111

166 Dates. See Professor Brinkman's chronology of Mesopotamian reigns in Oppenheim's *Ancient Mesopotamia*, and Giles' on period of co-regencies. occupation of A (I) khetaten etc, p. 153ff
Years of 'heresy'. Dame Kathleen Kenyon, Royal Cities of the Old Testament p. 6, gives '1390–1360', but this would not allow for kingship of Burnaburyash (1359–1333, Brinkman) Hapiru. Quotes from Keller, op. cit., p. 144–5
Suwardata. Ibid
Jew and Egyptian. Quote, Gordon, *Before the Bible*, p. 104
Apiru, See Gordon, op. cit., 104 footnote

169 Quote. 1 *Kings* 12.20
170 Josiah 2 Kings 23–24
172 David. Keller, op. cit., p. 192
Jericho. Quote, *Joshua 6*, 20.14
Garstang. See his *The Story of Jericho*
Kenyon and Jericho sculpture. See her *Archaeology in the Holy Land*, and account of the work of the British School's excavations 1952/1958 by Kenyon and J.C. Payne, 'Jericho: c.8000–3000' in *World of the Bible*, Victoria and Albert Museum and P.E.F. (1965), marking centenary of the P.E.F. Palestine Exploration Fund. Skulls from Garstang's excavations

173 Sealed *karu*. Ronny Reich, *Israel Exploration Journal*, 34.1, 1984, p. 32ff

174 Shapira. Silberman, op. cit., Chapter 13 Dead Sea Scrolls. See monograph by Menahem Mansoor, *The Case of Shapira's Dead Sea (Deuteronomy) Scroll of 1883*, New York, 1956, cf. Silberman p. 213; and J.A. Sanders *The Dead Sea Psalms Scroll* (1966)

7 Lands of the Twin Rivers

176 Layard quoted. *Journal Asiatique*, Vol. VI, P. 584

177 Mrs Christian Rassam on Rawlinson. See John Curtis, 'Parthian Gold from Nineveh', in *The Classical Tradition*, British Museum Year Book I 1976, p. 47ff
Loftus in Chaldaea. *Journal of the Royal Geog. Soc.* 26, 1856, Notes on a Journey, 1849, Communicated by Lord Clarendon, read 10 March 1856

178 Nebuchadnezzar. *Daniel*, 4.30

179 Muqayyar. JRES, 26, p. 148–50, Loftus disagreements with findings of earlier visitor, Baillie Fraser

181 Death of Loftus. JRGS, 29 (1859) Taylor. See *Journal of the Royal Asiatic Society*, XV (1854), 'Notes on the Ruins of Mugeyer'. And H.R. Hall, *A Season's Work at Ur*, London, 1930
Nabonidus cylinder. JRGS, 35 (1865), p. 21–25 and map

182 Harran and Ur of the Persians. JRGS, 11 (1841), p. 1–19 'Notes of an Excursion to Kal'ah Sherkat, the U'r of the Persians, and to the Ruins of Al Hadhr, the Hutra of the Chaldees, and Hatra of the Romans', by Wm Ainsworth

182 Mignon, Taylors and others. See Lloyd, *Foundations in the Dust*

183 Rassam. See his *Asshur and the Land of Nimrod*, New York, 1971 (new edtn.). And DNB (1910) entry by T.G.P. (Pinches)

184 Rawlinson. S. Lane-Poole in DNB, 'a fine specimen of the old school of Anglo-Indian officials'. And Sir Frederic J. Goldsmid. obit, in *Geographical Journal* V, 1895

185 Smith. See Sollberger, *The Babylonian Legend of the Flood*. And *Encycl. Brit.* 11th editn
Tablet of Shalmaneser. *Gordon, Before the Bible*, p. 42

186 Assyrian tablets and texts. Summarised and illustrated in Reade's *Assyrian Sculpture*
Translation of texts. Luckenbill, *Ancient Records*, corrected for personal names and dates according to Oppenheim, *Ancient Mesopotamia*, and Brinkman's Chronology within that work

187 Smith's findings. *Transactions* of Society of Biblical Archaeology, July 1873

192 Thompson. *A Pilgrim's Scrip*

193 Balawat Gates. See Rassam, op. cit., R.D. Barnett, 'More Balawat Gates' in *Studies Dedicated to F.M.T. de L. Böhl*, Leiden, 1973; and Lloyd, *The Archaeology of Mesopotamia*
Pinches. ILN, 16 November, 1878

194 Kings of Israel. 1 *Kings* 22.39
Syrians, Assyrians and Israelites. See Barnett, *Illustrations of Old Testament History*, p. 24ff

195 Discovery of Gates and aftermath. See John Curtis, 'Balawat', in *Fifty Years of Mesopotamian Discovery*, Ed. Curtis, British School of Archaeology in Iraq, 1982
King, quoted. Ibid, p. 113
Budge. Lloyd, *Foundations in the Dust*, and Curtis, op. cit

196 Jirjib. Julian Reade, 'Rassam's Jirjib Sounding, 1882', in *Iraq* XLV, Spring 1983, p. 97ff
Sippar and gods. Oppenheim. op. cit., p. 195ff. And Kramer, op. cit., p. 130ff

198 Budge in Mesopotamia. Curtis, op. cit., and Lloyd, op. cit
High Court action. T.G. Pinches in DNB, and *The Times*, obit, 17 September 1910

199 Lloyd at Balawat. *Foundations*, and Curtis, op. cit
Mallowan at Balawat. Curtis, op. cit., work 'sufficient fully to vindicate Rassam's integrity'

201 de Sarzec. Lloyd, *The Archaeology of Mesopotamia*, p. 148ff

202 Telloh and Lagash. Oppenheim, op. cit., and Kramer, *The Sumerians*
Cylinder seals. H. Frankfort, *Cylinder Seals* (London, 1939)
Social life in Mesopotamia. As portrayed by seal impressions, cf. above; and Postgate and Reade, 'The Ordinary Folk of Mesopotamia' in UR 1, 1983; and other authoritative articles in same journal

203 H.G. Wells. *Phoenix*, 1942, cf. Lloyd, *Foundations*
American expedition. King, *American Archaeology in Mid East*, Chapter 1. And Wellard, *By the waters of Babylon*

204 Pennsylvania expedition and Nippur. See Kramer. *The Sumerians*, p. 22ff, and P.J. King, op. cit

8 Egypt and the Israelites

205 Kenyon. *The Bible and Recent Archaeology*, p. 25ff
Children of Israel. *Exod.* 1.20, et seq

206 Naville. ILN, Sept. 17, 1887

207 'Slipper' graves. Griffith thought graves Ramesside, Naville disagreed. Nowadays thought to be Phoenician

208 Zerakh. II *Chron.* 14

209 Tel Bast. ILN, loc. cit

210 Manchester businessmen. Mrs Drower to author
Donation. E.E.S. Annual Report, 1900
Edfu. Emery, *Archaic Egypt*, p. 24ff
Petrie and de Morgan. Hoffman, *Egypt Before the Pharaohs*, p. 29ff
Amélineau. Ibid

211 Prehistoric sites. Ibid, p. 25ff
Tombs. Ibid, p. 107

212 Quote, 'The rich . .'. Ibid, 117
Tomb of Nit-hotep. Emery, op. cit., p. 25
Emery quoted. Ibid, 21
Champfleury. *Histoire des faïences patriotiques sous la Révolution*, Paris, 1867

213 Manetho and dynastic reigns. Petrie, *History of Egypt*, chapter 2. And James, *The British Museum and Ancient Egypt* (1983)

215 Work in Sinai. Petrie, *Researches in Sinai*, Chapter 12
Reliefs at Wadi Maghara. Edwards, *Pyramids of Egypt*, p. 57
Serabit. ILN, 29 July 1905

218 *Book of the Dead or Going Forth by Day.* Studies in Ancient Oriental Civilization (No. 37), E.B. Hauser, trnsl. Thomas George Allen, Oriental Institute, University of Chicago

De Rougé. Budge, *From Fetish to God,*
p. 3–4, and 52–3
Newton. Ibid, p. 3
219 One God. *Deut.* 6.4
Moses. Budge, op. cit., p. 40n, quotes
Sir Gardner Wilkinson, 'striking
resemblance' of Jewish and Egyptian
religious rites
Egyptian myths and legends. Breasted,
*Development of Religious Thought in Ancient
Egypt* (NY, 1912), p. 76ff
223 Un-Nefer. Budge, op. cit., p. 26
Osiris in casket (Plutarch), Byblos. Ibid,
p. 182, 'papyrus plant, confused by
scribe' with place in Lebanon
224 Cooke. Ibid, p.9
Lahun jewels. Now in Metropolitan
Museum, NY
Solar-disc worship. A. Erman, *Die
Religion der Aegypte,* Berlin, 1934; and
Breasted, op. cit., 'a rationalist
enterprise'
Egyptian legends. James B. Prichard,
Ancient Near Eastern Texts, p. 3ff,
translations by John A. Wilson
226 Khyan pot-lid. How and Wells,
Commentary, p. 418
Hyksos, Petrie, *Hyksos and Israelite Cities,*
London, 1904
Origins of Hyksos. Meyer, *Geschichte des
Altertums,* i, p. 304; How and Wells,
Appendix X; Breasted, op. cit., p. 214ff
227 Kamose. Johnson, op. cit., p. 79–82
228 Tuthmosis III. Pritchard, op. cit., p. 243

9 Mycenae, Troy and Knossos
229 Thucydides. *Larousse,* p. 267
230 Schliemann at Mycenae. Alan J.B. Wace
Mycenae, Princeton, 1949
231 Doerpfeld on Schliemann. Quoted in
Cottrell, *The Bull of Minos,* p. 93
232 Shaft graves. Carl Schuchardt,
Schliemann's Excavations, London, 1891
234 Papadimitriou, ILN, 27 Sept, 1952
Evans and Schliemann. Cottrell, op. cit.,
p. 96
237 Work of British School. *Journal of
Hellenic Studies,* vol xiv, 1894, xvii, 1897,

xxi 1901; *Proceedings* of Brit. Association,
1896
Excavations in Crete. Ann Brown,
Arthur Evans and the Palace of Minos
238 Sensational discoveries. Cottrell, op. cit.,
p. 129
240 Visitors. Pernier and Mosso, an
anthropologist, digging at Phaestos;
Ernest Gardner followed Petrie at Greek
necropolis of Naucratis (1885–6),
director of British School Athens
1887–95
Manolakis (Emmanouel Akoumianakis).
See Dilys Powell's *The Villa Ariadne*
(1973)
241 Philological jigsaw. See Gordon, *Before
the Bible,* Chapter 6
Ventris and the Linear-B. See M.
Ventris and J. Chadwick, *Documents in
Mycenaean Greek,* Cambridge, 1956
Content of tablets. Gordon, op. cit.,
p. 32 and 36n
Corslet. Brown, op. cit., p. 54
242 Harriet Boyd. Later Harriet Boyd
Hawes. ILN, August 13, 1910
Evans. Quoted in Cottrell, op. cit.,
p. 132
243 Classical historians. How and Wells,
Commentary, Appendix; and Hall, *Ancient
History*
Egyptian records. Inscriptions at Karnak
and Madinat Habu in Breasted, *Ancient
Records*
244 Manolakis. Cottrell, op. cit., p. 132
'Palace' chronology, Brown, op. cit.,
p.10
246 Evans' own concept. Brown, op. cit.,
p. 41–2
Imported vase. Ibid, p. 56
Hogarth. ILN, Sept. 22, 1906
250 Hogarth at Ephesus. Correspondence,
Archive of Greek and Roman
Department, British Museum
252 Halbherr and others in Crete, ILN,
Sept, 1906–March 1922
Lawrence Durrell. See his *The Greek
Islands,* London, 1978
253 Ariadne's Web. Cottrell, op. cit., p. 176

Blegen. His *Troy*, in 'Ancient Peoples and Places' (1963)
Pendlebury. *The Archaeology of Crete*
254 De Jong and Doll. Brown, op. cit
Schliemann, comments. Deuel, op. cit., p. 352–3
255 Calder. *Greek, Roman and Byzantine Studies*, 13, p. 335–53
Easton. *Antiquity*, LV, 1981. See also 'The Schliemann Papers' in *Annual* of the British School at Athens, 77, 1982; and *Anatolian Studies* (annual), 1984
256 Traill. *Antiquity*, LVII, 1983, p. 181ff. See also 'Schliemann's Mendacity' in *Classical Journal*, 74, 1979, p. 384ff; and *Journal of Hellenic Studies*, 104, 1984

10 The Gates of Ishtar

260 French in Persia. Huot, *Persia*, in 'Archaeologia Mundi'
French permit. May 1897, Shah grants monopoly to France. Lorimer, *Gazetteer of Persian Gulf*, India Office Records
Deutsche Orient-Gesellschaft. *Seit 1898 im Dienste der Forschung*, Museum fuer Vor- und Fruehgeschichte, Berlin
Koldewey. *The Excavations at Babylon*
261 Herodotus. How and Wells, *Commentary*, i, p. 136ff
262 History and layout. L.W. King, *History of Babylonia*, Vol. 2; and Lloyd, *The Archaeology of Mesopotamia*, Chapter 10
Nebuchadnezzar. 'Augustus', Canon G. Rawlinson, in *Memoir*
'Sudden shock'. E. Meyer, *Mitteilungen der Deutschen Orient-Gesellschaft*, 62 (1923) p. 8ff
263 Temple at Cythera. 'Oldest in Greece', How and Wells, op. cit., I, 113
18th Century. Kramer, *The Sumerians*, p.8
264 Art of Babylon. Frankfort, *The Art and Architecture of the Ancient Orient*. See Lloyd, op. cit., p. 231
265 Code of Hammurabi. See Oppenheim, *Ancient Mesopotamia*, 'Codex Hammurabi'; Trnsl. of text. Theophile J. Meek, in Luckenbill, *Ancient Records*, p. 163–179

267 Urakagina text. A. Parrot, *Tello*, Paris, 1948. And see Kramer, op. cit., Chapter 3
Ur-nammu. I.M. Diakanoff, *Sumer: Society and State in Mesopotamia*, Moscow, 1950
269 Pre-Sargonic Sumer. Ibid
270 Geologists. Kramer, op. cit., p. 39
271 Climatic cycles. Museums Department, Kingdom of Saudi Arabia
272 Urban communities. Bray in Needham, *Science and Civilisation*, p. 27–37
273 Germans in Egypt. Borchardt in *Mitteilungen*, 55 (1914)
Andrae at Assur. See his *Das wiedererstandene Assur* (Berlin, 1938)
Hittites. Bittel, *Die Hethiter*, and *Hattusha, The Capital of the Hittites*
274 Mursil. Hall, *Ancient History*, p. 335
Trojans and Hittites. How and Wells, op. cit., i, 56
Art and language. Hall, op. cit., 334ff; Kretschmer, *Einleitung*, p. 337; and Gordon, *Before the Bible*
Languages and dialects. *Larousse*, p. 170–1
275 Babylonian rituals and customs. Trnsl. texts by A. Sachs in Pritchard, *Ancient Near Eastern Texts*, p. 341ff 'Akkadian Rituals'
277 Uruk. Pritchard. op. cit., p. 342
279 Pieces of silver. Oppenheim. op. cit., p. 106
280 Demonology. Thompson, *Semitic Magic*, p. 219ff
280 'Sanctify unto me'. *Exod.* 13.2
Frazer, *Golden Bough*, i, xix
281 Amosis. Thompson, op. cit., 220–22
First born and Unclean beasts. *Exod.* 13. And Frazer, loc. cit
Hittite ritual. Pritchard, op. cit., p. 348ff
Leviticus/ 11.13–20
283 Virginity in sacrifice. Thompson, *Devils and Evil Spirits*, Introd
284 Spittle. Ibid
285 Musil and Bell. See author's *Illicit Adventure*, Chapter 2

286 Halaf. Oppenheim, Baron Max von, *Von Mittelmeer zum Persischen Golf*, Berlin, 1900. See Lloyd, op. cit., p. 66–7 Thompson, King, and Lawrence. Thompson, *Pilgrim's Scrip*. And the *Letters of T.E. Lawrence* (1938), and the *Letters of Gertrude Bell* (1927)

287 Hogarth. BM Correspondence and papers in Greek and Roman Department; and Brown, *Arthur Evans* Carchemish excavations. Hogarth, Woolley and Barnett, *Carchemish Report*, (BM) 1914–1952

290 Woolley, *Dead Towns and Living Men* (1920), *As I Seem to Remember* (1962) Sinai, Ibid. And C.L. Woolley and T.E. Lawrence, *The Wilderness of Zin* (1915)

11 Gods, Kings and Legends

292 Pagan critics. Franz Dornseiff. See Gordon, *Before the Bible*, p. 11 Traditions. W. Baumgartner, *Zum alten Testament und seiner Umwelt* (Leiden, 1959) Linguistic alliance. Gordon, op. cit., p. 53ff Hattusili. Ibid, p. 59

293 Gilgamesh. cf. Pritchard *Ancient Near Eastern Texts*, p. 73, 'utilises certain motifs from Sumerian poems'

294 Sumerian contributions. JAOS, LXIV (1944), p. 7ff Trnsl. Pritchard, op. cit., p. 75

295 Amanus. Generally Lebanon. Hall, *Ancient History*, p. 178, 'Elam' Women of Israel. I Samuel, 18.6–9

297 Scheill and King Lists, Kramer, op. cit., Append. E., and Oppenheim, op. cit., p. 370–4

298 Tummal text. Hilprecht Collection, Fr. Schiller University. See Kramer, *The Sumerians*, p. 48ff 'King of Kish;. Title used universally in early dynastic period Carter. Carter and Mace, *The Discovery of the Tomb of Tutankhamen*, Intro. to Dover Edition by Jon Manchip White Cairo in wartime. *Illicit Adventure*, 'The Intrusives', Chapter 9

299 Muqayyar excavations. Hall, *A Season's Work at Ur* (London, 1930) Taylor's sites. JRAS, XV a91854) Al Ubaid. Lloyd, *Foundations*, p. 178ff (revised edtn)

300 Woolley at Ur. Hall, op. cit., and Lloyd op. cit Gertrude Bell. Quote from *Letters,* p. 528 Guiding light. Mallowan, *Memoirs,* p. 34ff

301 New laws. See author's *Gertrude Bell,* p. 253

302 Early evidence. Ibid, p. 35; and Lloyd, op. cit., p. 183ff Street names. BM photographic record of expedition Personnel. Mallowan, op. cit Hamoudi. Portrait bust in Horniman Museum, South London Evans disdained. Cottrell, *Bull of Minos,* p. 110

303 Marriage. Mallowan, op. cit

304 Agatha Christie. Mallowan, op. cit., p. 45 Detailed description. ILN, 23 October 1924

305 Religious texts. Lloyd, op. cit., p. 184 Excavation of Ur. Woolley, *Ur of the Chaldees* Ritual. See Oppenheim, *Ancient Mesopotamia*, Chapter IV; and Kramer, *Sumerians*, Chapter Four

306 Royal graves. Woolley, Burrows, Keith, Legrain and Plenderleith, *Ur Excavations*, Vol. II (1934), 'The Royal Cemetery'

308 Herodotus. Bobrinskoy, ILN, January 3, 1914; and Woolley, 'Royal Cemetery', p. 38 Jacobsen. W.G. Lambert in UR, 1–1983, Review, p. 60

309 Isolated practice? Kramer, op. cit., p. 130

310 Mallowan. Op. cit., p. 48ff Maritime trade. Mallowan, op. cit., p. 57, quotes Oppenheim paper, ' The Seafaring Merchants of Ur'

Ur of the Chaldees and Abraham.
Anachronistic. Chaldaeans arrive c.1300
BC; could not have been Chaldaean in
Abraham's time
Third-dynasty Ur. David Oates in UR,
Sept-Oct, 1978

311 Deluge. Mallowan, op. cit., p. 46
Ubaid finds. Woolley, ILN, April 25th,
1925
Much earlier. Lloyd, UR, 2/3, 1982,
review 'The Accomplishments of
Woolley'
'Bugbear'. Mallowan, op. cit., p. 49

312 Lloyd, quoted. Op. cit
Smith. JRAS Oct 1928. But cf. Moorey,
Iraq 1984, argues for priestly status

313 Creative achievements. T.C. Mitchell,
*Sumerian Art Illustrated by Objects from
Ur and Al 'Ubaid* (1969). And Barnett
and Wiseman, *Fifty Masterpieces*

314 Woolley at Amarna. ILN, 6 May 1922

315 Carnarvon and Carter. Carter and Mace,
op. cit., Introd. viii

318 Breasted. *Ancient Records*, vol. IV, p. 538

319 Woolley. ILN, December 16, 1922
Tutankhamen's sepulchre. Percy E.
Newberry, ILN, February 24, 1923

320 Coronation throne. ILN, November 10,
1923

321 Wace. ILN, March 31, 1923; and ibid,
'Stained with Agememnon's Blood?'
Tutankhamen's family, relationships,
and co-regencies. cf. Desroches-
Noblecourt, *Tutankhamen*, Chapter 4,
and Genealogical tree, p. 120–1

324 Carter's rewards. Guy Brunton, obit, in
Annales du Service des Antiquités de'l'Egypte

325 Newberry. Loc. cit

12 Epilogue

326 Ring of Nestor. Ibid
Fake. Nilsson, *The Minoan-Mycenaean
Religion*, Appendix 2, 'Suspect Objects'

327 Dendra. Wace, ILN, June 9, 1928
Blegen Cottrell, *The Bull of Minos*. And
Larousse, p. 245, 'seven meticulous
campaigns from, 1932 to 1938'
Papadimitriou. ILN, Sept 27, 1952

329 Herodotus. Johnson, *Ancient Egypt*,
p. 148
Nubia and Aswan scheme. *Larousse*,
p. 211ff

330 Willcocks. 'Don Quixote', Gertrude
Bell, *Letters*, Baghdad, 21 March, 1911

331 Baumgartel. *Petrie's Naqada Excavation:
A Supplement* (London, 1970)
Hoffman. *Egypt Before the Pharaohs*,
p. 122

332 Reisner. Joint Expedition of Harvard
and Boston Museum of Fine Arts. Later
(1927) discovered tomb of Hetepheres,
wife of Sneferu and mother of Cheops,
at Giza. ILN, March 12, 1927
Garstang, quoted. *Larousse*, p. 237
Michalowsky. Ibid, p. 234

330 British School. *Fifty Years*

334 Sumerian shrines. Frankfort in ILN,
May 19, 1934
Pottery and sequence dating. Lloyd, *The
Archaeology of Mesopotamia*, Chapter
Three

335 Garrod. Ibid, p. 23ff
Mallowan. ILN, July 28, Aug 4, 1951
Hamrin. Roaf in *Fifty Years*, p. 40ff; and
al-Gailani Werr, UR 1–1983
Nimrud. Mallowan, ILN, Aug 16, 1952.
And *Nimrud Ivories* (1978)

336 Ivories. Reade in *Fifty Years*, p. 99ff
Babylon's features. Wellard, *By the
Waters of Babylon*, p. 154ff. Quay walls,
Gertrude Bell's notebook, 1911 (RGS)

337 Balawat. Curtis, 'Balawat' in *Fifty Years*,
p. 113ff. Suggested reconstruction of
citadel by Oates

338 Zenjirli. Oppenheim, op. cit., p. 131.
And Matthiae, *Ebla*, p. 16 (dates to
c.1200–535 BC)
Misleading. Matthiae, op. cit., p. 18
Petrie and Bliss at Tel al-Hesi. Amiran
and Worrell in *Encycl. of Archaeological
Excavations in the Holy Land*, Ed. Avi-
Yonah (Oxford 1976)
Ras Shamra. Claude F.A. Schaeffer,
ILN, March 3, 1934
Ugarit in Amarna letters. Gordon, *Before
the Bible*, p. 128ff

339 Syrian culture. Matthiae, op. cit., p. 27
Lachish. Torczyner and Others, *The Lachish Letters*

340 Parrot. *Larousse*, p. 187
Albright. King, *American Archaeology in the Mid East*, p. 196ff
Chagar Bazar. Curtis in *Fifty Years*, p. 79ff
Hazor and Megiddo. Bermant and Weitzman, *Ebla*, p. 3 et seq

341 Atchana/Alalakh. Matthiae, op. cit., p. 29 et seq
Moortgat. Matthiae, op. cit., p. 32ff
Mardikh/Ebla. Matthiae, op. cit
Texts. Ibid. See also Biggs 'The Ebla Tablets' in *Biblical Archaeologist*, Spring 1980; and Bermant and Weitzman, op. cit
Old Testament. Bermant and Weitzman
Word lists. W.G. Lambert in *Il Bilinguismo A*

342 *Ebla*, Summary of International Convention at Naples, April 19–22, 1982, Instituto Universitario Orientale, Naples, 1984
Bilingual dictionary. Lambert in UR 1–1983, p. 44ff
Margueron. Matthiae, op. cit., p. 25 et seq

343 Habuba Kabira. Eva Strommenger-Nagel, *Habuba Kabira, Ein Stadt vor 5000 Jahren*

Heinrich. *Mitteilungen*, 101 (1969)
Temple of Uruk. Matthiae, op. cit., p. 37
Reconstruction. Strommemger-Nagel
Creatures of 4th–3rd Mill. Elephant and water-buffalo are shown in early seal impressions, but there is a lapse of evidence between 3rd millennium and the Christian Era. Collon, *Anatolian Studies* III (1983), *Iraq* XXXIX (Autumn 1977), and UR 2/3 (1982) suggests probably imported, perhaps from Indus

346 Indus Valley. Sir John Marshall, ILN, Feb 27, 1926, and Jan 7, 1928. Sir Mortimer Wheeler, May 27, 1950. And Wheeler, *Early India and Pakistan*
Dilmun. Bibby, *Looking for Dilmun*, and Rice, *Dilmun Discovered*

347 Kramer. *The Sumerians*, p. 286ff
Cornwall. *Bulletin* of the American Schools of Oriental Research 103, October 1964

349 Freud. *Moses and Monotheism*, Trnsl. Katherine Jones (New York 1939)
Habiru. Mann and Freud on Exodus. See Joseph Campbell, *The Masks of God*, Chapter 3, 'Gods and Heroes of the Levant'

350 Gertrude Bell, quoted. Ramsay and Bell, *Thousand and One Churches*, London, 1909

351 Gibbon, *The History of the Decline and Fall of the Roman Empire*, Boston, 1852
Paley, quoted. Milman's Preface, xvii

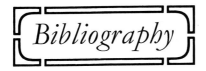

Bibliography

INSTITUTIONAL

British Museum, Egyptian Antiquities:

ANDERSON, R., *Catalogue of Egyptian Antiquities, III Musical Instruments,* 1976
ANDREWS, CAROL, *Egyptian Mummies,* 1984
— *The Rosetta Stone,* 1981
— *Near Eastern Art,* 1969
ANDREWS, C.A.R., *Catalogue of Egyptian Antiquities, VI Jewellery from the Earliest Times to the End of the Seventeenth Century,* London, 1981
ANON., *Jewellery through 7000 Years,* 1976
BIERBRIER, M.I., *Hieroglyphic Texts from Egyptian Stelae etc, Part X,* 1982
— *The Tomb-Builders of the Pharaohs,* 1982
BUDGE, E.A. WALLIS, *Der Stein von Rosette,* 1978
EDWARDS, I.E.S., *Hieratic Papyri in the British Museum: Oracular Amuletic Decrees of the Late New Kingdom,* 2 vols., 1960
JAMES, T.G.H., *The British Museum and Ancient Egypt,* 1983
— *Excavating in Egypt: The Egypt Exploration Society 1882–1982,* 1982
— *Hieroglyphic Texts from Egyptian Stelae etc., Part IX,* 1970
— Ed., *An Introduction to Ancient Egypt,* 1979
— and W.V. DAVIES, *Egyptian Sculpture,* 1983
KATAN, NORMA JEAN, *Hieroglyphs: The Writing of Ancient Egypt,* 1985
POSENER-KRIEGER, P., and CENIVAL, J.L., *Hieratic Papyri in the British Museum: Abu Sir Papyri,* 1968
SMITH, SIDNEY, *Sir Flinders Petrie,* 1943
SPENCER, A.J., *Excavations at El-Ashmunein,* 1983

British Museum, Western Asiatic Antiquities

BARNETT, R.D., *Illustrations of Old Testament History,* 1977
— *The Sculptures of Ashurbanipal,* 1976

BARNETT, R.D., and WISEMAN, D.J., *Fifty Masterpieces of Ancient Near Eastern Art*, 1969

BARNETT, R.D., and FALKNER, M., *Sculptures of Tiglath-Pileser III (745–727 BC)*, 1962

BIVAR, A.D.H., *Catalogue of the Western Asiatic Seals in the British Museum: Stamp Seals II, The Sassanian Dynasty*, 1969

COLLON, DOMINIQUE, *Catalogue of the Western Asiatic Seals in the British Museum: Cylinder Seals II, Akkadian – Post Akkadian II – Ur III*, 1982

FIGULLA, H.H., *Catalogue of the Babylonian Tablets in the British Museum, Vol. I*, 1961

FRANKEL, DAVID, *The Ancient Kingdom of Urartu*, 1979

— *Archaeologists at Work: Studies in Halaf Pottery*, 1979

GARELLI, P. and COLLON, D., (Sealings), *Cuneiform Texts from Cappadocian Tablets in the British Museum*, Part VI, 1975

GURNEY, OLIVER R., *Ur Excavations, Text Series Vol. VII, Middle Babylonian Legal Documents and other texts*, 1974

HOGARTH, D.G., WOOLLEY, C.L., and BARNETT, R.D., *Carchemish Report on the excavations at Jerablus on behalf of the British Museum: Part I, Introductory*, 1914; *Part II, The Town Defences*, 1921; *Part III, The Excavations in the Inner Town, and The Hittite Inscriptions*, 1952

KENYON, KATHLEEN M, *The Bible and Recent Archaeology*, 1978

LAMBERT, W.G., and MILLARD, A.R., *Catalogue of the Cuneiform Tablets in the Kuyunjik Collection of the British Museum*, 1968

LEICHTY, ERLE., *A Bibliography of the Cuneiform Tablets of the Kuyunjik Collection in the British Museum*, 1964

MALLOWAN, SIR MAX, *The Nimrud Ivories*, 1978

MOOREY, P.R.S., *Ancient Bronzes from Luristan*, 1974

READE, JULIAN, *Assyrian Sculpture*, 1983

SOLLBERGER, E, *The Babylonian Legend of the Flood*, 1971

WALKER, C.B.F., *Cuneiform Brick Inscriptions in the British Museum; the Ashmolean Museum Oxford; the City of Birmingham Museum and Art Gallery; The City of Bristol Museum and Art Gallery*, 1981

WOOLLEY, C.L., *Ur Excavations II, The Royal Cemetery, 2 vols.* London. 1934

WOOLLEY, SIR LEONARD, and MALLOWAN, SIR MAX, *Ur Excavations, Archaeological Series Vol. VII The Old Babylonian Period*, 1976

British Museum, Greek and Roman Antiquities

BAILEY, D.M., *Greek and Roman Pottery Lamps*, 1976

COOK, B.F., *The Elgin Marbles*, 1984

— *Greek and Roman Art in the British Museum*, 1976

COOK, BRIAN, *Cypriote Art in the British Museum*, 1980

DOUMAS, CHRISTOS, *Cycladic Art*, The N.P. Goulandris Collection, 1983
FINLEY, M.I., *The Idea of a Theatre: The Greek Experience*, 1980
HARDEN, DONALD B., *Catalogue of Greek and Roman Glass in the British Museum: Vol. I, Core- and rod- formed vessels*, 1981
HAYNES, D.E.L., *The Portland Vase*, 1975
HAYNES, SYBILLE, *Etruscan Bronze Utensils*, 1974
HIGGINS, R.A., *Catalogue of Terracottas, Vol. 1 Greek, 730–330 BC*, 1970; *Vol. 2 Plastic Vases of the 7th and 6th Centuries BC, Plastic Lekythoi of the 4th Century BC*, 1975
— *Greek Terracotta Figures*, 1969
HIGGINS, REYNOLD, *The Aegina Treasure: An Archaeological Mystery*, 1980
— *Jewellery from Classical Lands*, 1965
HUSKINSON, JANET, *The Roman Sculptures from Cyrenaica (Corpus Signorum Imperii Romanii LL,1)*, 1975
JOHNS, CATHERINE, *Sex or Symbol, Erotic Images of Greece and Rome*, 1982
MURRAY, A.S., SMITH, A.H., and WALTERS, H.B., *Excavations in Cyprus*, 1970
PAINTER, KENNETH, *Gold and Silver in the Late Roman World*, 1977
STRONG, D.E., *Catalogue of the Carved Amber in the Department of Greek and Roman Antiquities*, 1966
SWADDLING, JUDITH, *The Greek Theatre*, 1977
— *The Ancient Olympic Games*, 1980
WAYWELL, G.B., *The Free-standing Sculptures of the Mausoleum at Halicarnassus in the British Museum*, 1978

British Museum, Ethnography

FAGG, WILLIAM, *The Tribal Image: Wooden Figure Sculpture of the World*, 1978

IRAQ CULTURAL CENTRE, LONDON

Catalogues of exhibitions:
Sumerian Civilization, December 1979–January 1980
The Epic of Gilgamesh, January–March 1982

Ur Magazine

Sept.–Oct. 1978:
OATES, DAVID, 'Ur and Sumer'
RASHID, FAWZI, 'Sumerian Singing'

Nov.–Dec. 1978:
HAWKES, HOWARD A., 'The Assyrian City of Nimrud'
SARKHOSH, VESTA, 'Hatra – City of the Sun'
WISEMAN, DONALD J., 'London's Assyrian Treasures'

March–April 1979:
KISHTAINY, KHALID, 'The Epic of Gilgamesh'

May–July 1979:
KUBBA, SHAMIL, 'Furniture in the Assyrian Style'

Autumn 1979
ABU-HAIDAR, FARIDA, 'Sumerian Schools'
GAILANI WERR, LAMIA AL, 'Cylinder Seals of Mesopotamia'
RASHID, SUBHI ANWAR, 'Musical Instruments Ancient and Modern'

1 – 1980:
HAWKES, HOWARD, 'Ivory Carvings from Assyrian Nimrud'

3 – 1981:
FERENS, ALEXANDER, 'The Question of Ancient Ebla'
MAXWELL-HISLOP, RACHEL, 'The Goldsmiths and Jewellers of Ur'

1 – 1982:
HADDAWY, HUSAIN, 'English Arabesque: Orientalism and the Oriental Mode in 18th
    Century English Literature' Pt 1

2/3 – 1982:
COLLON, DOMINIQUE, 'Water-buffaloes in Ancient Mesopotamia'
LLOYD, SETON, 'The accomplishment of Woolley'
REINHOLD, ROBERT, 'Uncovering Arabia's Past'

1 – 1983:
GAILANI WERR, LAMIA AL, 'Cylinder Seal Discoveries in the Hamrin Basin'
HADDAWY, HUSAIN, 'English Arabesque', Pt 2
LAMBERT, W.G., 'The Earliest Bi-lingual Dictionary'
— 'Mesopotamian Religion' Review

1 – 1984:
HADDAWY, HUSAIN, 'English Arabesque', Pt 3
MATVEYEV, K., 'Medicine in Babylonia'

AMERICAN ORIENTAL SOCIETY, YALE
Journal, Vol.37 (1917) – Vol.102 (1982)

AMERICAN SCHOOLS OF ORIENTAL RESEARCH
Annual: Vol.1 (1919–29) – Vols.47–48 (1980–81)
Bulletin, December 1944, Dr S.N. Kramer October 1946, P.B. Cornwall; 'On the Location
  of Dilmun'

ANNALES ARCHEOLOGIQUE DE SYRIE
Tome I (1951) – XXXI (1981)

ANNALS OF ARCHAEOLOGY AND ANTHROPOLOGY
Vols I–28, 1908–, University Press, Liverpool

Antiquity, Vol.1 (1927) – Vol. LVIII (1984)

Archiv Fuer Orient-Forschung
Annual: Vols. 5–16, Berlin and Graz, 1928–53

BAHRAIN DEPARTMENT OF ANTIQUITIES AND MUSEUMS
Dilmun Discovered, Edited and introduced by Michael Rice, 1983; *The Temple Complex at
  Barbar, Bahrain*, a guide (published by Ministry of Information)

BRITISH BROADCASTING CORPORATION
ALDRED, C., *Tutankhamun's Egypt*, 1972
DAVIES, ROY, *The Man Behind the Mask*, Chronicle, 20 Jan 1982 (Script)

BRITISH INSTITUTE OF ARCHAEOLOGY AT ANKARA
Anatolian Studies: Annual, London

BRITISH INSTITUTE OF PERSIAN STUDIES
Iran: Annual

BRITISH SCHOOL OF ARCHAEOLOGY IN IRAQ (Gertrude Bell Memorial)
*Fifty Years of Mesopotamian Discovery: The Work of the British School of Archaeology in Iraq,
  1932–1982*, Intro by Seton Lloyd, Ed. John Curtis
Iraq: Annual

BRITISH SCHOOL AT ATHENS
Annual

BRITISH SCHOOL AT ROME
Annual

DEUTSCHE ORIENT-GESELLSCHAFT, BERLIN
History; *Seit 1898 im Dienste der Forschung*, Museum für Vor- und Frühgeschichte, Schloss
  Charlottenburg, Berlin

EGYPT EXPLORATION SOCIETY
Annual Report, 1883–1983
Journal of Egyptian Archaeology, 1 (1914) – 69 (1983)
Greco-Roman Memoirs (Papyri etc), I (1908) – XLVII (1980)

INSTITUTE OF ARCHAEOLOGY, UNIVERSITY OF LONDON
Bulletin, 1 (1958) – 18 (1981)

ISRAEL: DEPARTMENT OF ANTIQUITIES AND MUSEUMS
Newsletter Nos.78–81
'Atiqot (Journal of Dept), I–XV, 1955–1982
Excavations and Surveys in Israel, Vol.1, 1982

JEWISH PALESTINE EXPLORATION SOCIETY
Bulletin Vol.1 (1933–4) – Vol.31 (1967)

JORDAN: DEPARTMENT OF ANTIQUITIES
Annual, Vols.XIII (1964) – XXV (1981)

MANCHESTER UNIVERSITY
Journal of Semitic Studies, Vol.I (1956) – Vol.XXVIII (1983)

MINISTÈRE DES RELATIONS EXTERIEURES
Association Francaise d'Action Artistique: Catalogue of Exhibition, *Au pays de Baal et
  d'Astarte – 10,000 ans d'art en Syrie*, Musée du Petit Palais, October 1983 – January 1984

MUSEUM OF ARCHAEOLOGY AND ETHNOGRAPHY, RIYADH
A Handbook for Visitors, Department of Antiquities and Museums, Ministry of
  Education, Kingdom of Saudi Arabia, N/D

MUSEUM OF ARCHAEOLOGY AND ANTHROPOLOGY, UNIVERSITY OF PENNSYLVANIA
Expedition Magazine, Vol.20, No.3 (1978) – Vol.25, No.4 (1983)

NEDERLANDS INSTITUUT VOOR HET NABIJE OOSTEN
Bibliotheca Orientalis, Jaargang XXVII, Nos.5/6, Sept./Nov. 1970: Review in English by
  M.N. Van Loon, Chicago, of Ghirshman's Tchoga Zanbil

PALESTINE EXPLORATION FUND
Quarterly Statement, Vol.1 (1869–70)
PEF Annual, 1 (1911) to present
Catalogue of Centenary Exhibition, 1865–1965, *The World of the Bible*, V & A Museum,
  Oct.–Nov. 1965

PALESTINE PILGRIMS' TEXT SOCIETY
Vols I–XIII, AD326–1193

PONTIFICIO INSTITUTO BIBLICO, ROME
Biblica, Vol.1 (1920) – Vol.60 (1979)

ROEMER- UND PELIZAEUS-MUSEUM, HILDESHEIM
Catalogue: *Sumer-Assur-Babylon, 7000 Jahre Kunst und Kultur zwischen Euphrat und Tigris*,
  Exhibition June–September 1978

ROYAL ASIATIC SOCIETY
Journals and papers of Sir Henry Creswicke Rawlinson
Transactions: Vols.I–III, 1827, 1830, 1835
Journal of RAS: Vols.I–XX, 1834–63; New Series, 1865–88

ROYAL GEOGRAPHICAL SOCIETY
Add Papers: Journals and papers of Sir Henry Creswicke Rawlinson
Journal of the Society:I (1831) – L(1880)
Proceedings: Vol.1 (1855–7) to Vol.22 (1877–8); New Series Vol.1 (1879) to Vol.14 (1892)
Geographical Journal: Vol.I (Jan.–June 1893) – Vol.LXXXIV (July–Dec. 1934); Vol.85
  (Jan.–June 1935) – Vol.150 (March–July 1984)

GENERAL, A–G

ABBOTT, E., *Greek History*, London, 1892
ADAMS, ROBERT McC., *The Evolution of Urban Society, Early Mesopotamia and Prehispanic
  Mexico*, Chicago, 1966
ADAMS, W.Y., *Nubia, Corridor to Africa*. London, 1977
AKURGAL, E., *Ancient Civilizations and Ruins of Turkey*, Istanbul, 1973
— *Die Kunst Anatoliens von Homer bis Alexander*, Berlin, 1961

— and HIRMER, M., *die Kunst der Hethiter*, Munich, 1961

— *The Art of the Hittites*, London, 1962

ALBRIGHT, W.F., *The Archaeology of Palestine*, London and New York, 1949

ALDRED, CYRIL *Ancient Peoples and Places: The Egyptians*, London and New York, 1961

— *Egyptian Art*, London, 1961

— *Egypt to the End of the Old Kingdom*, London, 1965

— *Akhenaten, a New Study*, London, 1968

— *Akhenaten and Nefertiti, the Art of the Amarna Period*, London, 1973

ALKIM, U.B., *Anatolia I: Beginning to end of 2nd millennium* BC, Geneva and London, 1968

ALLEN, T.G., *The Egyptian Book of the Dead*, Chicago, 1960

— and HAUSER, ELIZABETH B., *The Book of the Dead or Going Forth by Day*, Chicago, 1974

ALLIOT, MAURICE, *Le Culte d'Horus à Edfou au temps des Ptolémées*, 20 vol., Cairo, 1949–54

AMIET, P., *La Glyptique mesopotamienne archaïque*, Paris, 1961

ANDREWS, C.A.R., and HAMILTON-PATISON, J., *Mummies*, London, 1978

ARBMAN, HOLGER, *Ancient Peoples and Places: The Vikings*, New York and London, 1961

AUBERT, J.F. and AUBERT, L., *Statuettes Egyptiennes*, Paris, 1974

AVI-YONAH, M., *The Jews under Roman and Byzantine Rule*, Hebrew University, Jerusalem, 1984

AZARPAY, G., *Urartian Art and Artifacts*, Berkeley and Los Angeles, 1968

BACON, EDWARD (Ed.), *Vanished Civilizations*, London and New York, 1963

— *The Great Archaeologists*, London, 1976

BADAWY, A., *Coptic Art and Archaeology*, Massachusetts, 1978

— *A History of Egyptian Architecture*, 3 vols., Giza, 1954; Los Angeles, 1966–68

BAIKIE, J., *Egyptian Antiquities in the Nile Valley*, London, 1932

BAINES, J., and MALEK, J., *Atlas of Ancient Egypt*, London, 1979

BAKER, H., *Furniture in the Ancient World*, London, 1966

BASHAM, A.L., *The Wonder that was India*, London, 1954

BASS, GEORGE F., *Archaeology Under Water*, New York and London, 1970

BAUMGARTEL, ELISE J., *The Cultures of Prehistoric Egypt*, 2 vols, Oxford, 1947/60

— *Petrie's Naqada Excavation*, A Supplement, London, 1970

BELL, GERTRUDE, *The Letters of*, Ed. Lady Bell, London, 1927

BELOCH, J., *Griechische Geschichte*, Strasburg, 1893

— *Die Attische Politik seit Perikles*, Leipzig, 1884

BELZONI, G., *Narrative of the Operations and Recent Discoveries within the Pyramids, Temples, Tombs, and Excavations, in Egypt and Nubia, etc.* London, 1820

BERGMAN, JAN, *Ich bin Isis*, Uppsala, 1968

BERMANT, C. and WEITZMAN, M. *Ebla: An Archaeological Enigma*, London, 1979

BEVAN, E., *A History of Egypt under the Ptolemaic Dynasty*, London, 1927

BIBBY, GEOFFREY, *Looking for Dilmun*, London, 1970

– *The Testimony of the Spade*, New York, 1956

BILLE DE MOT, E., *The Age of Akhenaten*, London, 1966

BISSING, F.W. VON, *Ein thebanischer Grabfund aus dem Anfange des neuen Reichs* (illustr. H. Carter), Berlin, 1900

BITTEL, K., *Hattusha, The Capital of the Hittites*, Oxford, 1970

— *Die Hethiter*, Munich, 1976

BLEGEN, CARL W., *Ancient Peoples and Places: Troy*, London and New York, 1963

BLISS, F.J., MACALISTER, R.A.S., and WUENSCH, R., *Excavations in Palestine, 1898–1900*, Palestine Exploration Fund, 1902

BLOCH, RAYMOND, *Ancient Peoples and Places: The Etruscans*, London and New York, 1958

— *Ancient Peoples and Places: The Origins of Rome*, London and New York, 1960

BONFANTE, G, and BONFANTE, L., *The Etruscan Language*, Manchester, 1983

BONNEAU, DANIELLE, *La Crue du Nil*, Paris, 1964

BORDES, F., *The Old Stone Age*, New York and London, 1968

BOSSERT, H.T., *Altanatolian*, Berlin, 1942

BOTHMER, B.V., *Egyptian Sculpture in the Late Period*, New York, 1960

BOYCE, M., *Zoroastrians: Their Religious Beliefs and Practices*, London, 1979

— *A History of Zorastrianism*, I, Leiden, 1975

BRACKEN, C.P., *Antiques Acquired*, Newton Abbot and New York, 1975

BRAIDWOOD, R.J., *The Near East and the Foundations of Civilisation*, Oregon, 1952

BRAMSTON, M., *The Empires of the Old World*, London, 1911

BRATTON, F. GLADSTONE, *A History of Egyptian Archaeology*, London, 1967

BREASTED, J., *Ancient Records of Egypt: Historical Documents*, Chicago, 1906

— *History of Egypt*, New York, 1910

BRENT, J.T., *Aegean Islands, The Cyclades*, Chicago, 1966

BREUIL, H., *Four Hundred Centuries of Cave Art*, London, 1952

BRIFFAULT, R., *The Mothers*, London, 1927

BROVARSKI, E., DOLL, S.K. and FREED, R.E. (Eds.), *Egypt's Golden Age*, Boston, 1982

BROWN, ANN, *Arthur Evans and the Palace of Minos*, Ashmolean Museum, Oxford, 1983

BUCHHOLZ, HANS-GUENTER, and KARAGEORGHIS, *Prehistoric Greece and Cyprus*, Trnsl. from German by Francisca Garvie, London and New York, 1973

BUCKINGHAM, J.S., *Travels in Syria and Palestine*, London, 1825

BUDGE, SIR E.A., *Amulets and Superstitions*, Oxford, 1930

— *The Mummy*, Cambridge, 1925

— *From Fetish to God in Ancient Egypt*, Oxford, 1934

BURCKHARDT, JOHN LEWIS, *Travels in Syria and the Holy Land*, London, 1822

BURFORD, A., *Craftsmen in Greek and Roman Society*, London, 1972

BURN, A.R., *Persia and the Greeks: Defence of the West 546–478 BC*, London, 1962

BURNEY, C, and LANG, D.M., *The Peoples of the Hills*, London, 1971

BURROWS, M., *The Dead Sea Scrolls*, New York and London, 1955

BURTON, A., *Diodorus Siculus, Book I: A Commentary*, London, 1934

BURY, J.B., *History of Greece*, London, 1902

BUSOLT, G., *Griechische Geschichte*, Gotha, 1873

BUTZER, KARL, *Environment and Archaeology*, London and Chicago, 1965

BUTZER, W., *Early Hydraulic Civilization in Egypt*, Chicago and London, 1976

CADOUX, C.J., *Ancient Smyrna*, Oxford, 1938

CAMERON, *History of Early Iran*, Chicago, 1936

CAMPBELL, JOSEPH, *The Masks of God: Occidental Mythology*, New York, 1964

CARTER, HOWARD and MACE, A.C., *The Tomb of Tut-Ankh-Amen Discovered by the Late Earl of Carnarvon and Howard Carter*, London, 1923–33

— *The Discovery of the Tomb of Tutankhamen*, New York, 1977

— and NEWBERRY, P.E., *Thoutmosis IV*, London, 1904

CASSON, STANLEY, *Ancient Cyprus*, London, 1937

CELORIA, FRANCIS, *Archaeology*, London, 1970

CERAM, C.W., *Gods, Graves and Scholars*, New York, 1951

CERNY, J., *Paper and Books in Ancient Egypt*, London, 1953

— *Ancient Egyptian Religion*, London, 1952

CESNOLA, GENERAL LOUIS PALMA DI, *Cyprus: Its Ancient Cities, Tombs, and Temples*, London, 1877

CHADWICK, H.M., *The Heroic Age*, Cambridge, 1912

CHALIOUNGUI, P., *Magic and Medical Sciences in Ancient Egypt*, London, 1963

CHAMPOLLION-LE-JEUNE, *Monuments de l'Égypte et de la Nubie*, 4 vols., Paris, 1835

CHANCE, A.B., *The Rhind Mathematical Papyrus*, Virginia, 1979

CHARLES-PICARD, GILBERT, *Carthage*, London, 1964

CHILDE, V. GORDON, *The Aryans*, London, 1926

— *Dawn of European Civilisation*, London, 1927

— *Man Makes Himself*, London, 1936

— *What Happened in History*, London, 1942

— *New Light on the Most Ancient East* (revised), London, 1952

— *The Prehistory of European Society*, London, 1958

CLARK, GRAHAME, *World Prehistory*, Cambridge, 1961

CLARKE, GRAHAME, *Prehistoric Societies*, London, 1965

CLARKE, S., and ENGELBACH, R., *Ancient Egyptian Masonry*, Oxford, 1930

CLARK, J.D.E., *The Prehistory of Africa*, London, 1970

CLARK, J.G.D., *World Prehistory*, Cambridge and New York, 1969

CLERMONT-GANNEAU, CHARLES, *Archaeological Research in Palestine*, 1873–4, 2 vols., Palestine Exploration Fund, London, 1899

COLE, J.M., and HIGGS, E.S., *The Archaeology of Early Man*, London, 1969

COLLEDGE, M.A.R., *The Parthians*, London, 1967

— *Parthian Art*, London, 1977

CONDER, MAJ. C.R., *Palestine*, London, 1889

— *Syrian Stone-Lore*, PEF, London, 1896

— *The Latin Kingdom of Jerusalem*, PEF, London, 1897

— *Survey of Eastern Palestine*, PEF, London, 1889

— and KITCHENER, LT.H.H., *Survey of Western Palestine*, Ed. Palmer and Besant, 3 vols. PEF, London, 1881–3

— and WARREN, COL.SIR CHARLES, *Survey of Western Palestine-Jerusalem*, PEF, London, 1884

CONTENAU, G., *Everyday Life in Babylon and Assyria*, London and New York, 1954

COOK, A.B., *Zeus*, Cambridge, 1940

COOK, J.M., *Ancient Peoples and Places: The Greeks in Ionia and the East*, London and New York, 1963

COOK, R.M., *Ancient Peoples and Places: The Greeks until Alexander*, London and New York, 1962

COON, CARLETON S., *The History of Man*, New York, 1962

CORNFELD, GAALYAHU (Ed.), *Adam to Daniel*, New York, 1961

CORNFORD, F.M., *From Religion to Philosophy*, London, 1913

COTTRELL, LEONARD, *The Lost Pharaohs*, New York, 1961

— *The Bull of Minos*, London and New York, 1953

— *The Lion Gate*, London, 1963

COULBORN, RUSHTON, *The Origins of Civilized Societies*, Princeton, 1959

CURTIUS, E., *History of Greece*, trnsl. and introd. by A.W. Ward, London, 1868

DANIEL, GLYN, *The First Civilizations*, Crowell, New York, 1968

— *A Hundred Years of Archaeology*, London and New York, 1950

— *The Origins and Growth of Archaeology*, London and New York, 1967

DAREMBERG, C., and SAGLIO, E., *Dictionnaire des antiquités grècques et romaines*, Paris, 1877–1919

DARESTE, R., HAUSSOUILLER, B., and REINACH, T., *Recueil des inscriptions juridiques grècques*, Paris 1891–8

DAVID, A. ROSALIE, *Religious Ritual at Abydos*, Warminster, 1973

DAVIES, N. DE G., and MARTIN, G.T., *The Rock Tombs of El-Amarna*, 7 vols. London, 1903–8, 1974

DAVIES, N.M., and GARDINER, A.H., *Ancient Egyptian Paintings*, 3 vols. Chicago, 1936

DAVIS, THEODORE M., *Excavations*, (illust. Howard Carter), London, 1907

— *Description and Excavation of the tomb of Hatshopsitu*, London, 1906

DEBEVOISE, N.C., *A Political History of Parthia*, Chicago, 1938

DE GAURY, GERALD, and WINSTONE, H.V.F., *The Spirit of the East*, London, 1979

— *The Road to Kabul*, London, 1981

DEUEL, LEO, *Memoirs of Heinrich Schliemann*, London, 1978

DRESDEN, M.J., *Mythology of Ancient Iran*, in Kramer, S.N. (Ed.), 'Mythologies of the Ancient World', New York, 1961

DESROCHES-NOBLECOURT. C., *Tutankhamen*, London and New York, 1963

DEUBNER, A.F., *Attische Feste*, Berlin, 1932

DIEHL, E., *Anthologia Lyrica Graeca*, Leipzig, 1925

DIETRICH, A., *Mutter Erde*, Leipzig and Berlin, 1905

DITTENBERGER, G., *Sylloge Inscriptionum Graecarum*, Leipzig, 1903–5

DOPSCH, A., *Wirtschaftliche und soziale Grundlagen der europaeischen Kulturentwicklung*, Vienna, 1923–4

— *Economic and Social Foundations of European Civilisation*, London, 1937

DUCHESNE-GUILLEMIN, J., *La réligion de l'Iran ancien*, Paris, 1962

— *The Hymns of Zarathustra: Being a Translation of the Gathas together with Introduction and Commentary*, London, 1952

DUNCKER, M., *Geschichte des Altertums*, trnsl. S. Alleyne, London, 1883

DURRELL, LAWRENCE, *The Greek Islands*, London, 1978

DURUY, V., *History of Greece*, trnsl. and introd. by J.P. Mahaffy, London, 1892

DYSON, R.H., *Problems of the Relative Chronology of Iran*, in Erich (Ed.), 'Chronologies in Old World Archaeology', Chicago, 1965

EBBELL, B., *The Papyrus Ebers*, Copenhagen, 1937

EDOUX, HENRI-PAUL, *In Search of Lost Worlds*, London and New York, 1971

EDWARDS, AMELIA B, *Pharaohs, Fellahs and Explorers*, London, 1892

EDWARDS, I.E.S., *The Pyramids of Egypt*, London and New York, 1947

— (Ed.), and others, *Cambridge Ancient History*, Vols. I and II, 1981

— *Treasures of Tutankhamun*, London, 1978

— *Tutankhamun – His Tomb and its Treasures*, London, 1979

ELEUTHEROPOULOS, A., *Wirtschaft und Philosophie*, Berlin, 1900

ELLIOT-SMITH, G. and DAWSON, W.R., *Egyptian Mummies*, London, 1924

EMERY, W.B., *Archaic Egypt*, London, 1961

ERMAN, A., *Life in Ancient Egypt*, New York, 1971

ERSKINE, MRS STEUART, *Vanished Cities of Arabia*, London, 1925

EVANS, A.J., *The Palace of Minos*, London, 1921–35

ETARK, GRAHAME, *From Savagery to Civilization*, London, 1946

FAGAN, BRIAN M., *The Rape of the Nile*, London, 1977

FAIRMAN, HERBERT W., *The Triumph of Horus, An Ancient Egyptian Sacred Drama*, London, 1974

FAKHRY, A., *The Pyramids*, Chicago and London 1969

FARNELL, L.R., *Cults of the Greek States*, Oxford, 1896–1909

FARRINGTON, B., *Diodorus Siculus*, Swansea, 1937

FAULKNER, R.O.m *The Ancient Egyptian Pyramid Texts*, Oxford, 1969

— *The Ancient Egyptian Coffin Texts*, 3 vols., Warminster, 1973–8

FINEGAN, JACK, *Light from the Ancient Past*, Princeton, 1947

FINNIE, DAVID H., *Pioneers East: The Early American Experience in the Middle East*, Harvard Middle Eastern Studies 13, Harvard UP, 1967

FISCHER, H.G., *Ancient Egyptian Calligraphy*, New York, 1979

FISHER, H.A.L., *History of Europe*, London, 1936

FLEMING, STUART, *Dating in Archaeology*, London, 1976

FORBES, R.J., *Metallurgy in Antiquity*, Leiden, 1950

FOUCART, P., *Le culte de Dionysos en Attique*, Paris, 1904

FRANKFORT, H., *The Birth of Civilisation in the Near East*, Indiana UP, 1951

— *The Art and Architecture of the Ancient Orient*, London, 1970

FRAZER, J.G., *Apollodorus*, London, 1921

— *The Golden Bough*, London, 1923–7

— *Lectures on the Early History of Kingship*, London, 1905

— *Myths of the Origin of Fire*, London, 1930

— *Pausanias's Description of Greece*, London, 1898

— *Totemism and Exogamy*, London, 1910

FRIEDRICH, J., *Die Hethitischen Gesetze*, Leiden, 1959

FRYE, R.N., *The Heritage of Persia*, London, 1963

GARDIN, J.C., *Archaeological Constructs*, Cambridge, 1940

GARDINER, ALAN, *Egypt and the Pharaohs*, Oxford and New York, 1961

GARDINER, SIR A.H., *Egyptian Grammar*, Oxford, 1969

GARDNER, E., *Ancient Athens*, London, 1892

GARRATT, G.T., *The Legacy of India*, Oxford and New York, 1937

GARSTANG, JOHN, *The Heritage of Solomon*, London, 1934

— and GARSTANG, J.B.E., *The Story of Jericho*, London, 1940

GERSHEVITCH, I., and others, *Iranistik, II, Literatur, I*, Leiden, 1968

GHIRSHMAN, R., TCHOGA ZANBIL (Dur-Untash), *Mémoires de la Délégation Archéologique en Iran*, Paris, 1966

— *Iran*, London, 1954

— *Iran: Parthians and Sassanians*, London, 1962

— *Persia: from Origins to Alexander the Great*, London, 1963

GIBBON, EDWARD, *The History of the Decline and Fall of the Roman Empire*, with notes by the Revd. H.H. Milman, 6 vols., Boston, 1852

GILBERT, G., *Beitraege zur inneren Geschichte Athens*, Leipzig, 1887

GILES, F.J., *Ikhanaton, Legend and History*, London, 1970

GILLINGS, R.J., *Mathematics in the Time of the Pharaohs*, Massachusetts, 1972

GLOTZ, G., *Aegean Civilisation*, London, 1925

— *Ancient Greece at Work*, London, 1926

GOETZE, A., *Kleinasien*, Munich, 1957

GORDON, CYRUS H., *Before the Bible*, London, 1962

GRAHAM, JAMES WALTER, *The Palaces of Crete*, Princeton UP, 1962

GRANT, MICHAEL (Ed.), *The Birth of Western Civilization*, London, 1964

— *The Roman World*, London, 1960

GREENER, LESLIE, *The Discovery of Egypt*, London, 1966
GRIFFITH, J. GWYN, *Apuleius of Madauros: The Isis Book, Metamorphoses Book XI*, Leiden, 1975
— *Plutarch: De Iside et Osiride*, Trnsl. and Commentary, Wales, 1970
— *The Conflict of Horus and Seth*, Liverpool, 1960
GROTE, GEORGE, *A History of Greece*, Condensed and edited by J.M.Mitchell and M.O.B. Caspari, London, 1907
GRUNDY, G.B., *The Great Persian War*, Oxford, 1901
GUIRAUD, P., *La propriété foncière en Grèce*, Paris, 1893
GURNEY, O.R., *The Hittites*, London and New York, 1953
GUTHRIE, W.K.C., *Orpheus and Greek Religion*, London, 1935

H–O

HABACHI, L., *The Obelisks of Egypt: Skyscrapers of the Past*, London, 1977
HALL, H.R., *The Ancient History of the Near East*, London
— *The Oldest Civilization of Greece*, London, 1901
— *Aegean Archaeology*, London, 1915
— *The Civilization of Greece in the Bronze Age*, London, 1928
HARDEN, D.B., *Sir Arthur Evans: A Memoir*, Oxford, 1983
HARPER, P.O., *The Royal Hunter: Art of the Sasanian Empire*, New York, 1978
HARRIS, J. and WENTE, E.F., *An X-Ray Atlas of the Royal Mummies*, Chicago and London, 1980
HARRIS, J.R., *The Legacy of Egypt*, Oxford, 1971
HARRISON, J.E., *Prolegomena to the Study of Greek Religion*, Cambridge, 1922
HASEBROEK, J., *Staat und Handel im alten Griechenland*, Tuebingen, 1928
HASTINGS, J., *Encyclopaedia of Ethics and Religion*, Edinburgh, 1908–18
HAUVETTE-BESNAULT, A., *Herodote Historien des Guerres Mediques*, Paris, 1894
HAWKES, JACQUETTA, AND WOOLLEY, LEONARD, *Prehistory and the Beginnings of Civilisation*, New York, 1962; London, 1963
HAYES, W.C., *The Scepter of Egypt*, 2 vols., New York, 1953–59
— *Most Ancient Egypt*, Chicago, 1965
HEAD, B.V., *Historia Numorum*, Oxford, 1911
HEICHELHEIM, F., *Wirtschaftsgeschichte des Altertums*, Leiden, 1939
HEINEMANN, K., *Die tragischen Gestalten der Griechen in der Weltliteratur*, Leipzig, 1920
HELCK, W. and OTTO, E., *Lexicon der Aegyptologie*, Wiesbaden, 1972
HENNING, W.B., *Zoroaster, Politician or Witch-Doctor?*, Oxford, 1951
HERBERT, GEORGE E.S.M., (5th Earl of Carnarvon), and CARTER, H., *Five Years Exploration at Thebes*, London, 1912

HERRMANN, G., *The Iranian Revival*, London, 1977

HERZFELD, ERNST, *The Persian Empire*, in Studies in Geography and Ethnography in the Near East, (Ed.), Wiesbaden, 1968

HIGGINS, REYNOLD, *Minoan and Mycenaean Art*, London, 1967

HILL, D.K., *Catalogue of Classical Bronze Sculpture in the Walters Art Gallery*, Baltimore, 1949

HILLIER, BEVIS, *Pottery and Porcelain 1700–1914*, London, 1968

HINZ, W., *The Lost World of Elam: Re-creation of a Vanished Civilization*, London, 1972

HOCART, A.M., *Kingship*, Oxford, 1927

HOBHOUSE, L.T., WHEELER, G.C., and GINSBERG, T., *Material Culture and Social Institutions of the Simpler Peoples*, London, 1930

HOFFMAN, M.A., *Egypt Before the Pharaohs*, London, 1980

HOGARTH, D.G., *Philip and Alexander*, London, 1897

— (Ed.) *Authority and Archaeology, Sacred and Profane*, London, 1899

— *The Penetration of Arabia*, London, 1904, Oxford, 1922

— and others, *Excavations at Ephesus*, London, 1908

HOLM, A., *History of Greece*, trnsl., London, 1894

HOOD, M.S.F., *The Minoans, Crete in the Bronze Age*, London, 1971

HOOKE, S.H., *Myth and Ritual*, Oxford, 1933

HOPPER, R.J., *The Acropolis*, London, 1971

HORNUNG, E., *Skarabaen und Andere Siegelamulette aus Basler Sammlungen*, Mainz, 1976

— *Der Eine und die Vielen*, Darmstadt, 1971

— *Das Totenbuch der Aegypter*, Zurich and Munich, 1979

HOUSTON, M.G., *Ancient Egyptian, Mesopotamian and Persian Costume*, London, 1954

HOW, W.W, and WELLS, J., *A Commentary on Herodotus*, 2 vols., Oxford, 1912

HROUDA, B., *Vorderasien, Vol.1 Mesopotamien, Babylonien, Iran und Anatolien*, Munich, 1971

HUOT, JEAN-LOUIS, *Persia, I* (Archaeologia Mundi), London, 1965

HUTCHINSON, R.W., *Prehistoric Crete*, London, and New York, 1962

IRWIN, C.H., *The Bible, The Scholar and the Spade*, Religious Tract Society, 1832

IVERSON, E., *Obelisks in Exile*, 2 vols., Copenhagen, 1968–72

JACOBSEN, THORKILD, *The Treasures of Darkness: A History of Mesopotamian Religion*, Yale UP, 1976

JAMES, T.G.H., *An Introduction to Ancient Egypt*, London, 1979

— *The Archaeology of Ancient Egypt*, London, 1972

— (Ed.), *Excavating in Egypt*, London, 1982

JENKINS, N., *The Boat Beneath the Pyramid*, London, 1980

JOHNSON, PAUL, *The Civilization of Ancient Egypt*, London, 1978

KAMIL, J., *Luxor*, London, 1979

— *Saqqara*, London, 1978

KEES, H., *Ancient Egypt, A Cultural Topography*, Chicago, 1977

KELLER, WERNER, *The Bible as History*, Trnsl. Wm. Neil, London, 1956

KENT, *Old Persian Grammar Texts*, New Haven, 1953

KENYON, SIR FREDERICK, *The Bible and Archaeology*, London, 1940

KENYON, KATHLEEN M., *Archaeology in the Holy Land*, London, 1960
— *Royal Cities of the Old Testament*, London, 1971

KERN, O., *Orphicorum Fragmenta*, Berlin, 1922

KILLEN, G., *Ancient Egyptian Furniture, I, 4000–1300 BC*, Warminster, 1980

KING, PHILIP J., *American Archaeology in the Mid East*, Philadelphia, 1983

KINKEL, G., *Epicorum Graecorum Fragmenta*, Leipzig, 1877

KITCHEN, K.A., *The Third Intermediate Period in Egypt*, Warminster, 1973

KITTO, H.D.F., *Greek Tragedy*, London, 1939

KLUGE, K, and LEHMANN-HARTLEBEN, L., *Die Antiken Grossbronzen*, 2 vols., Berlin and Leipzig, 1927

KOCK, T., *Comicorum Graecorum Fragmenta*, Leipzig, 1880–8

KOLDEWEY, R., *The Excavations at Babylon*, London, 1914

KRAMER, SAMUEL NOAH, *From the Tablets of Sumer*, Colorado, 1956
— *The Sumerians*, Chicago UP, 1963
— (Ed.) *Mythologies of the Ancient World*, New York, 1961

~~KRAUSS, SAMUEL, *Talmudische Archaeologie*, 2 vols., Leipzig, 1910~~

KRETSCHMER, P., *Einleitung zur Geschichte der griechischen Sprache*, Göttingen, 1896

LAET, SIEGFRIED DE, *Archaeology and Its Problems*, London, 1957

LAMB, W., *Greek and Roman Bronzes*, London, 1929

LANDSTROM, B., *Ships of the Pharaohs*, London, 1970

LANG, A., *Custom and Myth*, London, 1844

LANGE, K., and HIRMER, M., *Egypt: Architecture, Sculpture, Painting in Three Thousand Years*, London, 1968

LANGTON, N. and B., *The Cat in Ancient Egypt*, Cambridge 1940

LAROCHE, E., *Catalogue des textes hittites*, Paris, 1971

LAUER, J.-P., *Saqqara, Royal Cemetery of Memphis, Excavations and Discoveries since 1850*, London, 1976

LAYARD, SIR AUSTEN HENRY, *Nineveh and Its Remains*, London, 1849
— *Early Adventures in Persia, Susiana and Babylonia*, 2 vols., London, 1887

LECA, A-P., *The Cult of the Immortal*, London, 1981

LEWIS, N., *Papyrus in Classical Antiquity*, Oxford, 1974

LICHTHEIM, M., *Ancient Egyptian Literature*, 3 vols., Berkeley, 1973–80

LINTON, RALPH, *The Tree of Culture*, New York, 1955

LITTMANN, ENNO, *Princeton University Archaeological Expeditions to Syria in 1904–5 and 1909*, Leyden, 1914

LLOYD, A.B., *Herodotus, Book II. Introd. and commentary*, 3 vols., Leiden, 1975

LLOYD, SETON, *Foundations in the Dust*, Oxford, 1947; revised, London, 1980
— *Early Anatolia*, London, 1956

— *The Archaeology of Mesopotamia*, London, 1978
LOISY, A., *Les mystères païens et le mystère chrétien*, Paris, 1930
LOWIE, R.H., *Primitive Society*, New York, 1929
LUCKENBILL, D.D., *Ancient Records of Assyria and Babylonia*, Chicago, 1927
LUKONIN, V.G., *Persia, II* (Archaeologia Mundi Series), Geneva, 1967
LURKER, M., *The Gods and Symbols of Ancient Egypt*, London, 1981
MACALISTER, R.A.S., *A Century of Excavation in Palestine*, The Religious Tract Society, London, 1925
MACAN, R.W., *Notes on Herodotus*, London, 1895
McLENNAN, J., *Studies in Ancient History*, London, 1886
MAGNUSSON, MAGNUS, *The Archaeology of the Bible Lands*, London, 1977
MAHAFFY, J.P., *History of Classical Greek Literature*, London, 1880
MALLAKH, K. al, and BRACKMAN, A.C., *The Gold of Tutankhamen*, New York, 1978
MALLOWAN, SIR MAX, *Mallowan's Memoirs*, London, 1977
MARSHALL, JOHN, *Mohenjo Daro and the Indus Civilisation*, (for Archaeological Survey of India), London, 1931
MARLOWE, JOHN, *Spoiling the Egyptians*, London, 1974
MATHESON, S.A., *Persia: An Archaeological Guide*, London, 1976
MATOUK, F.S., *Corpus du Scarabée Égyptien*, 2 vols., Beirut, 1972–6
MATTHIAE, PAOLO, *EBLA: An Empire Rediscovered*, Trnsl. Christopher Holme, London, 1977
MEEKS, DIMITRI, *Année lexicographique*, Paris, 1980
MEILLET, A., *Apercu d'une histoire de la langue grecque*, Paris, 1935
— *Introduction a l'étude comparative des langues indo-européennes*. Paris, 1937
MEKHITARIAN, A., *Egyptian Painting*, Geneva, 1978
MELLAART, J., *The Neolithic of the Near East*, London, 1975
— *The Calcholithic and Early Bronze Ages in the Near East and Anatolia*, Beirut, 1966
METZGER, H., *Anatolia II*, Geneva and London, 1969
MEYER, E., *Geschichte des Altertums*, Stuttgart, 1892–1902
— *Forschungen zur Alten Geschichte*, Halle, 1892–99
MICHALOWSKI, K., *The Art of Ancient Egypt*, London, 1969
MONTET, P., *Everyday Life in the Days of Ramesses the Great*, London, 1958
— *Le Lac Sacre de Tanis*, Paris, 1966
MOOREY, P.R.S., *Catalogue of Ancient Persian Bronzes in the Ashmolean Museum*, Oxford, 1971
MORENZ, S., *Egyptian Religion*, Trnsl. A. Keep, London, 1973
— and SCHUBERT, J., *Der Gott auf der Blume*, Leipzig, 1954
MORGAN, L.H., *Ancient Society*, New York, 1877
— *Systems of Consanguinity and Affinity of the Human Family*, New York, 1871
MUELLER, C., *Fragmenta Historicum Graecorum*, Paris, 1868–83
MURRAY, G., *Aeschylus*, Oxford, 1940

MURRAY, MARGARET, *My First Hundred Years*, London, 1963
MYRES, J.L., *Who Were the Greeks?* Berkeley, 1930
— *Herodotus*, Oxford, 1953
NAGEL, G., *Egypt*, London, 1978
NAUCK, T., *Tragicorum Graecorum Fragmenta*, Leipzig, 1889
NAUMANN, R., *Architektur Kleinasiens*, Tuebingen, 1955
NAVILLE, EDOUARD, *Textes relatifs au Mythe d'Horus recueillis dans le temple d'Efou*, Geneva, 1870
NEEDHAM, (NOËL)JOSEPH, *Science and Civilisation in China*, Vol. VI, Part II, 'Agriculture', by Francesca Bray, Cambridge, 1954–
NEUGEBAUER, O., *The Exact Sciences in Antiquity*, Copenhagen, 1957
— and PARKER, R.A., *The Calenders of Ancient Egypt*, Chicago, 1960
NILSSON, M.P., *Griechische Feste von religioeser Bedeutung mit Ausschluss der Attischen*, Leipzig, 1906
— *History of Greek Religion*, Oxford, 1925
— *Homer and Mycenae*, London, 1933
— *Minoan-Mycenean Religion*, London, 1927
— *Mycenean Origin of Greek Mythology*, London, 1932
NIMS, C.F., *Thebes of the Pharaohs*, London, 1965
NIZAN, P., *Les matérialistes de l'antiquité*, Paris, 1936
OAKLEY, K.P., *Framework for Dating Fossil Man*, London, 1964
— *Man the Toolmaker*, Chicago UP, 1963
OLMSTEAD, A.T., *History of the Persian Empire*, Chicago, 1948
ONCKEN, W., *Athens und Hellas*, Leipzig, 1865
OPPENHEIM, A. LEO, *Ancient Mesopotamia: Portrait of a Dead Civilization*, (Revised ed. Erica Reiner), Chicago, 1977
OTTO, E., *Egyptian Art and the Cults of Osiris and Amon*, London, 1968

P–Z

PALLIS, SVEN, *Early Exploration in Mesopotamia*, Copenhagen, 1954
— *The Antiquity of Iraq*, Copenhagen, 1956
PARKER, R.A., *The Calendars of Ancient Egypt*, Chicago, 1960
— and others, *The Edifice of Taharqa by the Sacred Lake of Karnak*, London, 1979
PAULY, A., *Realencyclopaedie der klassischen Altertumswissenschaft*, Stuttgart, 1842–66
PECK, W.H., and ROSS, J.G., *Drawings from Ancient Egypt*, London, 1978
PENDLEBURY, J.D.S., *The Archaeology of Crete*, London, 1939
PERRY, W.J., *Children of the Sun*, London, 1923
PETRIE, HILDA F., LADY, *Side Notes on the Bible from Flinders Petrie's Discoveries*, London, 1933

PETRIE, SIR W.M.F., *The Restoration of Judah and Israel: Plain Questions and Plain Answers* (Pamphlet), London, 1881
— *On the mechanical methods of Ancient Egyptians* (Repr. J. of Anthropological Inst.), London, 1883
— *The Arts of Ancient Egypt* (Lecture), London, 1884
— with LL. GRIFFITH and P.E. NEWBERRY, *Kahun, Gurob, and Hawara*, London, 1890
— *Ten Years' Digging in Egypt, 1881–1891*, Religious Tract Society, London, 1892
— and others, *A History of Egypt*, 6 Vols., London, 1894
— with A.H. SAYCE, LL. GRIFFITH, and C.J. SPURRELL, *Tell el Amarna*, London, 1894
— *Egyptian Decorative Art* (Lectures), London, 1895
— and D.G. HOGARTH, *Koptos*, London, 1896
— and QUIBELL, J.E., *Naqada and Ballas*, London, 1896
— *Religion and Conscience in Egypt* (Lectures), London, 1898
— *Syria and Egypt from the Tell el Amarna Letters*, London, 1898
— *Janus in Modern Life* (Essays), London, 1907
— and CURRELLY, C.T., *Researches in Sinai*, London, 1906
— *The Revolutions of Civilisation*, New York, 1909
— *The Growth of the Gospels as shown by structural criticism*, London, 1910
— *The Arts and Crafts of Ancient Egypt*, London, 1910
— *Egypt and Israel*, Christian Knowledge Society, London, 1911
— *Amulets, from Collection of University College*, London, 1914
— *Eastern Exploration, past and future* (Lectures), London, 1918
— *The Status of the Jews in Egypt*, London, 1922
— *Social Life in Ancient Egypt*, London, 1923
— *Ancient Egyptians* (Abstract), London, 1925
— *Religious Life in Ancient Egypt*, London, 1924
— *Seventy Years in Archaeology*, London, 1931
— *Objects in Daily Use*, Warminster, 1974
— *Shabtis*, Warminster, 1974
— *Scarabs and Cylinders with Names*, Warminster, 1974
— *Buttons and Design Scarabs*, Warminster, 1974
PHILIPPAKI, BARBARA, *The Attic Stamnos*, Oxford and New York, 1966
PIGGOTT, STUART, (Ed.) *The Dawn of Civilization*, London and New York, 1961
PIOTROVSKY, B.B., *Urartu* (abridged from Vanskoe Tsarstvo), London, 1967
PIRENNE, H., *History of Europe*, London, 1939
POPE, A.U., (Ed.) *A Survey of Persian Art from Prehistoric Times to the Present*, London, 1938
PORADA, E., *Ancient Iran: The Art of Pre-Islamic Times*, London, 1965
POSENER-KRIEGER, PAULE, *Les Archives du temple funéraire de Neferirkare-Kakai I et II*, Cairo 1976
PRITCHARD, J.B., *Ancient Near Eastern Texts*, Princeton UP, 1970

—— (Ed.), *The Ancient Near East*, Princeton UP, 1958

—— *The Ancient Near East in Pictures Relating to the Old Testament*, Princeton UP, 1974

RAWLINSON, G., *Memoir of Henry Creswicke Rawlinson*, London, 1898

RAWSON, PHILIP, *Ceramics*, Oxford, 1971

REDFORD, D.B., *History and Chronology of the Eighteenth Dynasty in Egypt*, Toronto, 1967

—— *A Study of the Biblical Story of Joseph*, Leiden, 1970

REINACH, S., *Orpheus: histoire générale des religions*, Paris, 1909

REYMOND, E.A.E., *The Mythical Origin of the Egyptian Temple*, Manchester, 1969

RIBBECK, O., *Anfänge und Entwickelung des Dionysoscultus in Attika*, Kiel, 1869

ROBERT, C., *Oidipus*, Berlin, 1915

ROBERTSON, D.S., *Greek and Roman Architecture*, Cambridge, 1929

ROBERTSON SMITH, W., *Religion of the Semites*, London, 1927

ROSE, H.J., *Primitive Culture in Greece*, London, 1925

ROSTOVTZEV, M., *Rome*, Oxford and New York, 1960

ROUSE, W.H.D., *Greek Votive Offerings*, Cambridge, 1902

SAGGS, H.W.F., *The Greatness that was Babylon*, London, 1962

SAUNERON, S., *The Priests of Ancient Egypt*, London, 1960; New York, 1969

SAVILL, SHEILA, and LOCKE, ELIZABETH, 'The Ancient Near and Middle East' and 'Classical Greece and Rome,' in *Pears Encyclopaedia of Myths and Legends*, London, 1976

SCHAFER, H., *Principles of Egyptian Art*, Trnsl. Oxford, 1974

SCHENKEL, WOLFGANG, *Die Bewaesserungsrevolution im alten Aegypten*, Mainz, 1978

SCHLIEMANN, HEINRICH (Henry), *Troy and its Remains*, London, 1878

SCHLIEMANN, HENRY, *Mycenae, A Narrative of Researches and Discoveries at Mycenae and Tiryns*, London, 1880

SCHMID, W., *Untersuchungen zum gefesselten Prometheus*, Stuttgart, 1929

SCHNEIDER, H.D., *Shabtis*, 3 vols., Leiden, 1977

SELIGMAN, G.C., *Pagan Tribes of the Nilotic Sudan*, London, 1932

SELTMAN, C.T., *Athens, its History and Coinage*, Cambridge, 1924

SHINNIE, P.L., *Ancient People and Places*, New York and London, 1967

—— *Meroe: A Civilization of the Sudan*, London, 1967

SHORE, A.F., *Portrait Painting from Roman Egypt*, London, 1962

SHORTER, A.W., *The Egyptian Gods*, London, 1981

SILBERMAN, NEIL A., *Digging for God and Country*, New York, 1982

SIMPSON, W.K., FAULKNER, R.O., and WENTE, E., *Literature of Ancient Egypt*, New Haven and London, 1972

SMITH, GEORGE ADAM, *The Historical Geography of the Holy Land*, (1894), 25th edition, London, 1931

SMITH, SIR GRAFTON E., *Tutenkhamen and the Discovery of his Tomb*, London, 1923

SMITH, W.S., *The Art and Architecture of Ancient Egypt*, London, 1982

SPENCER, A.J., *Death in Ancient Egypt*, London, 1982

STROMMENGER-NAGEL, EVA, *Habuba Kabira: Ein Stadt vor 5000 Jahren*, Main am Rhein, 1980

TAWNEY, R.H., *Religion and the Rise and Capitalism*, London, 1926

TAYLOUR, LORD WILLIAM, *Ancient Peoples and Places: The Mycenaeans*, London and New York, 1964

THOMPSON, GEORGE, *Aeschylus and Athens*, London, 1941

THOMPSON, R. CAMPBELL (Ed.), *The Devils and Evil Spirits of Babylonia*, 2 vols., London, 1903

— *Semitic Magic: Its Origins and Development*, London, 1908

— *A Pilgrim's Scrip*, London, 1915

TORCZYNER, HARRY, and others, *Lachish I: The Lachish Letters*, for Trustees of Wellcome Foundation, Oxford 1938

TOUTAIN, J., *The Economic Life of the Ancient World*, London, 1930

TRIGGER, B., *Nubia under the Pharaohs*, London, 1978

TURNER, E., *Greek Papyri, An Introduction*, Oxford, 1980

TYLOR, E.B., *Primitive Culture*, London, 1891

ULLENDORFF, E., *The Ethiopians*, Oxford and New York, 1965

VANDIER, J., *Manuel d'Archéologie Égyptienne*, 6 vols., Paris, 1952–78

— *Le papyrus Jumilhac*, Paris, 1961

— *Catalogue des Objets de Toilette Égyptiens au Musée du Louvre*, Paris, 1972

VAN GENNEP, A., *L'état actuel du probleme totémique*, Paris, 1920

VAN LOON, M.N., *Urartian Art*, Leiden, 1966

VELIKOVSKY, IMMANUEL, *Ramases II and His Time*, London, 1978

VERGOTE, J., *Joseph en Égypte*, Louvain, 1959

VERMEULE, EMILY, *Greece in the Bronze Age*, Chicago, 1964

VIEYRA, M., *Hittite Art*, London, 1955

WAINWRIGHT, G.A., *The Sky-Religion in Egypt*, Cambridge, 1936

WALLASCHEK, R., *Anfaenge der Tonkunst*, Leipzig, 1903

WARD, W.A., *Studies on Scrab Seals, Pre-12th Dynasty*, Warminster, 1978

WARNER, REX, (Ed.) *Xenophon, History of My Times*, (Hellenica), London, 1966

WARREN, CHARLES, *Underground Jerusalem*, London, 1876

WATERFIELD, G., *Layard of Nineveh*, London, 1963

WATSON, COL. SIR CHARLES M., *The Life of Maj-General Sir Charles Wilson*, London, 1909

WELLARD, JAMES, *By the Waters of Babylon*, London, 1972

WHEELER, MORTIMER, *Archaeology from the Earth*, Oxford and New York, 1954

— *Ancient Peoples and Places: Early India and Pakistan*, New York and London, 1959

WIDENGREN, G., *Les réligions de l'Iran*, Paris, 1965

WILLIAMS, WATKIN W., *The Life of General Sir Charles Warren*, Oxford, 1941

WILSON, COLIN, *The Occult*, London, 1981

WINSTONE, H.V.F., *Gertrude Bell*, London, 1978

WINTER, ADAM, *Die antike Glanztonkeramik*, Amsterdam, 1983

WOODHEAD, A.G., *Ancient Peoples and Places: The Greeks in the West*, London and New York, 1964

WOOLLEY, SIR (CHARLES) LEONARD, *Ur of the Chaldees*, London, 1921

— *Digging Up the Past*, New York, 1955; London, 1970

— *Spadework*, London, 1953

WUNDERLICH, HANS GEORG, Trnsl. RICHARD WINSTON, *The Secret of Crete*, New York, 1974; London, 1975

YADIN, YIGAEL, *The Art of Warfare in Biblical Lands*, trnsl. Pearlmann, London, 1963

ZAEHNER, R.C., *The Dawn and Twilight of Zoroastrianism*, London, 1961

ZENNER, F.E., *Dating the Past*, London, 1958

ZERVOS, CHRISTIAN, *L'Art de la Crête néolithique et minoenne*, Paris, 1956

— *L'Art des Cyclades*, Paris, 1957

Index